T. Z. LAVINE is currently Elton Professor of Philosophy at George Washington University. Professor Lavine received a Ph.D. from Harvard University and has received, among other awards, the Josiah Royce Fellow in Philosophy and a research fellowship in philosophy (Harvard). The author of numerous articles and books, Professor Lavine wrote and presented *From Socrates to Sartre* as a television series for the Maryland Center for Public Broadcasting, a series which is now included in the curriculum of the National University Consortium.

FROM SOCRATES TO SARTRE
The Philosophic Quest

T. Z. Lavine

BANTAM BOOKS
NEW YORK · TORONTO · LONDON · SYDNEY · AUCKLAND

FROM SOCRATES TO SARTRE
A Bantam Book / March 1984
7 printings through August 1989

Illustrations courtesy of The Bettman Archives and Culver Pictures.

ISBN 0-553-25161-9

Published simultaneously in the United States and Canada

**Bantam Books are published by Bantam Books, a division of Bantam
Doubleday Dell Publishing Group, Inc. Its trademark, consisting of the
words "Bantam Books" and the portrayal of a rooster, is Registered in U.S.
Patent and Trademark Office and in other countries. Marca Registrada.
Bantam Books, 1540 Broadway, New York, New York 10036.**

PRINTED IN THE UNITED STATES OF AMERICA

O   16   15   14   13   12

CONTENTS

The main branches of philosophy and the questions they raise
and try to solve. Why study philosophy? The attacks upon
philosophy. Try to imagine a world without philosophy. In this
book the works of six philosophers and their views of man, God,
nature, history, truth, ethics, and politics will be explored; and
the philosophic viewpoints dominating the contemporary scene
in philosophy will be examined.

PART ONE: PLATO

The historical situation: from the Golden Age of Athens under
Pericles to the defeat of democratic Athens by authoritarian
Sparta in the Peloponnesian War. The Rule of the Thirty;
Charmides and Critias. The Socratic philosophy. The trial and
death of Socrates (399 B.C.). Plato's life. Plato and counterrevolu-
tionary politics in Athens. The concept of the philosopher-king.

Plato as synthesizer of the conflicting philosophies of the Greek
world. The dialogue form. Plato's sources: Socratic method; Socratic
definition; the pre-Socratic philosophers: Heraclitus and Parmenides; the Sophists. Plato's metaphysical synthesis and its
expression in the Allegory of the Cave. Contemporary relevance
of the allegory.

reason. This was replaced by the supernaturalistic world view of
the Church, whose source is divine revelation and whose
fundamental beliefs must be accepted by faith, and are beyond
the power of human reason to explain or to prove. Platonists
versus Aristotelians. From the fourth to the fifteenth century the
domination by Christianity of the entire social and cultural world
of Europe. The survival of Plato and Aristotle in Christian
philosophy; the recovery of Aristotle in the twelfth century. The
emergence of the Renaissance, the regaining of classical learning
and art. The Discoveries and the rise of technology. The shift to
the view of truth as accessible to human reason. The rise of
astronomy: the transition from Ptolemy to Copernicus, Kepler
and Galileo; their challenge to existing beliefs. Galileo and the
Inquisition. The growth of mathematics, physics, chemistry,
physiology. The seventeenth century: The continued advance of
scientific methods, technologies, and discoveries: the rise of philosophic interest in the new scientific method. Descartes's historical situation. The life of Descartes. mathematician, physicist,
philosopher.

7 DOUBTING TO BELIEVE 91

Descartes's theory of knowledge. Rationalism versus empiricism.
Descartes's goal: to build a system of philosophy as certain and
imperishable as geometry by using the methods of mathematics:
self-evident truths and deduction. The first two Meditations: the
search for a self-evident first principle as foundation for philosophy.
Requirements this principle must meet. Skepticism as method of
discovering this absolutely certain belief. Deceptiveness of sense
perception; possible deceptiveness of mathematics by demon.
But I think, therefore I am (*Cogito ergo sum*): the one belief
self-evidently true. Meaning of thinking. Does the Cogito meet
the three requirements? Criticisms of Cogito proof. Influence of
Cogito: Subjectivism.

8 GOD EXISTS 100

From the proof of my existence to the proofs of the existence of
God. How to prove that God exists and that He is not a deceiver.
Three kinds of ideas: innate, invented, and from external world.
Cosmological proof of God's existence. Second proof: God exists
as the only possible cause of my existence as a thinking substance.
Third proof: ontological proof of God's existence. Criticism: "The
Cartesian circle."

can be no ideas. Use of the relation between impressions and ideas to attack any "suspicious" philosophic term: substance, self, God, causality (all Cartesian terms). For none of these can sense impressions be shown; therefore they have no meaning. "Commit it then to the flames." Ideas fall into groups. Association of ideas, by which one idea leads to another: the three laws of resemblance, contiguity, cause and effect.

make man free. The natural law of progress. The French
Revolution: paradoxes and reversals. The Enlightenment in
Germany. Kant: his theory of knowledge and his "answer" to
Hume. The Kantian turn in philosophy.

The life of Hegel. Hegel's philosophic sources. German Romanticism; Kant; the philosophy of science, natural rights, and
progress of the *philosophes*. Hegel synthesizes these into a powerful philosophy of conservatism, antiindividualistic nationalism.
Organicism and historicism. Philosophy is an organic totality
developing historically. This is the model for Hegel's theory of
reality, his metaphysics. Reality is the totality of truth, the
Absolute, Spirit or God. The Absolute is not separate from the
world but immanent in it. Hegel's absolute idealism. Dialectic:
The method by which reality can be grasped as rational. Hegel's
dialectic compared with Plato's.

The Phenomenology of Spirit a systematic survey of the human
spirit as it develops attitudes, religions, world views, philosophies.
Truth now to be seen not only as truth of substances, but truth of
the subject as well. Self-consciousness and its relation to objects:
mastery, negation, cancellation, death. Self-consciousness in relation to physical objects; to organic objects; to human objects. The
Struggle unto Death; Master-Slave; Stoicism; Skepticism; the
Unhappy Consciousness. The truth which religion presents sym-
bolically now to be transcended by philosophy. The end of the
Master-Slave relation.

Hegel's Philosophy of History is his dialectical method applied to
the whole of human history. History as a slaughter bench. But
Spirit, the Absolute, is embodied in human society. The Spirit of
a People. All history is the history of groups, nations. The dialectic of human history is the triadic movement in the development
of the concept of freedom from the Oriental World to the Graeco-
Roman World to the Christian-Germanic World. How is this
accomplished in the face of conflicting human desires? The Cunning of Reason accounts for the stability of societies and for social
change. Problems with Hegel's philosophy of history, raised also
against Marx.

PART FIVE: MARX

Present philosophic scene outside the Marxist world. The philosophical descendants of Hume and Hegel in polar opposition. Principles and themes of phenomenology; Husserl and focus on quest for certainty: Sartre and Heidegger: focus on issues and modes of conscious being in alien world. Linguistic philosophy. Logical positivism. Return to Hume. Theory of meaning. Verifiability principle of Vienna Circle. Attack upon metaphysics. Philosophy as an activity. Ludwig Wittgenstein: from logical positivism to analytic philosophy. First stage: logical positivism. *The Tractatus Logico—Philosophicus* and the picture theory of language; the meaninglessness of philosophic "problems" and their "answers." Second stage: analytic philosophy. *Philosophical Investigations* and the theory of language games. The appeal of analytic philosophy; philosophy as the activity of analyzing language games to dissolve philosophic problems. Criticism of Phenomenology and of logical positivism and of analytic philosophy. The death of philosophy? The search for a new philosophic vision. The promise of American philosophy, a synthesis of Hume and Hegel; the promise of history of philosophy; and of renewed research relating philosophy to the sciences and the arts—all of these having been buried under the avalanche of analytic philosophy.

PREFACE

This book came into being as the television program *From Socrates to Sartre*, produced by the College of the Air of the Maryland Center for Public Broadcasting in cooperation with Channel 44 (PBS) in Chicago, and offered as a three-credit college course in philosophy and the humanities. *From Socrates to Sartre* has been broadcast by these networks and has appeared on cable television; it is now included in the curriculum of the National University Consortium and is broadcast by satellite across the country to cooperating PBS stations; individual cassettes have been purchased by colleges and universities and private individuals.

I have tried to provide a sense of philosophy as product and producer of human civilization, and to present the historical, social, political, and intellectual situation to which each of these philosophies is a response; and to use biographical materials to reflect that aspect of philosophy which is humanly expressive of concrete personalities. I have also raised the question, especially for the modern period, What is the appeal of this philosophy? To whom, and why? Television as a medium demanded of me clarity, definition, simplicity of language, cogency, precise timing, contemporary references, avoidance of pedantry, and the maintenance of a high level of viewer interest. Philosophy, with its power, passion, seriousness, and irony lent itself readily to these requirements, while also demanding of me intellectual integrity as a philosopher.

I wish to thank especially Richard Smith, Director of the College of the Air of the Maryland Center for Public Broadcasting; and Dr. Frederick Breitenfeld, Jr., Executive Director, Maryland Center for Public Broadcasting; and Frances Pretty, Administrative Officer, National University Consortium for their support and assistance; and I wish to thank also the hardworking staff of the Maryland Center for Public Broadcasting who worked with me through the videotaping of thirty scripts. I wish to thank Susan Terry and Charles Bloch of Charles Bloch and Associates, western representatives for Bantam Books, for their staunch support; and also Toni Burbank and Jonathan Skipp, my consistently helpful editors at Bantam Books. And I wish here to express my thanks to the television viewers of this book for the hundreds of letters with which they have responded.

FROM SOCRATES TO SARTRE
The Philosophic Quest

INTRODUCTION
The Indestructible Questions

Do you sometimes ask, what is reality and what is mere surface appearance? Is this material thing, this rock, real? Is the world of physical things real, the world in which there are cows grazing silently in a green field under a bright blue summer sky? Are the city streets real, the shops and office buildings, the lines of cars and buses, the people crowding the sidewalks, the huge metal planes whizzing through gray cloudbanks overhead? Is the real only what is physical, material, tangible? Is reality only particles of matter in meaningless motion, ending in death, the death of the individual person, and in the vast death of the solar system? Or is all this physical reality only the surface, only what appears to the senses, only an illusion after all? Is reality to be found elsewhere—in the world of the mind, in eternal truths such as the Golden Rule, or in the wisdom and purpose of God?

And what about your own reality? Are you only a body, a material organism which avoids pain and seeks pleasure, a collection of atoms programmed to grow, to mature, and to self-destruct, a product of the genetic material you inherited from the past and a product of the environment in which you have lived? But if you refuse to regard yourself as a material body, then what kind of reality do you have? Does your reality consist in your being a mind or a soul? But what kind of reality is that and how can a mind or a soul inhabit a material body? As a ghost? *Metaphysics* is the branch of philosophy which asks these questions about reality: What is appearance and what is real? What kind of reality does the universe have—is it mind or matter or is it some kind of spiritual being? What kind of reality do you have as a human being? These are the questions that metaphysics asks.

Do you sometimes ask, what can we know? Is there any

1

truth that we can believe? Is a statement true only if it is
based on what your senses tell you, on what you can see or
touch? But is there any guarantee that what we observe by
our senses can establish truth about the world? Is truth
eternal and absolute, as some philosophies and all the great
religions say, or can truth be subject to change? The sciences,
which are largely based on observations by the senses, are
constantly changing, revising themselves, contradicting themselves, producing more and more numbers, charts, and com-
puter printouts, and more and more experimentation with
electrons and rats. Is science true? Or shall we turn for truth
to the great religions of the Judeo-Christian tradition? Or to the
great philosophies of the Western world? The defenders of
science sneer at both religion and philosophy in their claims
to truth, and insist that there is no other truth than what
science provides. As for the religions and the philosophies,
they not only are attacked and condemned by the defenders
of science but they also attack each other. Do you then ask,
what can we know, what is truth? These are the questions
that philosophy also asks. *Theory of knowledge* or *epistemology*
asks: What is mere opinion and what is truth? Does true
knowledge have its source in observation by the senses or in
human reason or in supernatural being? Is truth fixed, eternal,
absolute, or is truth changing and relative? Are there limits to
what we can know? These are the questions of the branch of
philosophy called theory of knowledge or epistemology.

Do you sometimes ask, why should I be moral? Do you
often notice that among the people you know the righteous
and good people seem to suffer all kinds of grief, that their
lives are lived in frustration and despair, and that often it is
the selfish and the cheats who are prosperous and happy?
Why not, then, live the playboy life, in which pleasure is the
highest good—the life of pleasurable indulgence in food and
drink and sex and drugs and sleep and all the titillations of
the body that can be produced? But if the life of pleasure
cannot be defended as ultimately good, then do you ask what
after all is ultimately good, worth living for, worth fighting
for? What, if anything, can be said at the present time to be
right or wrong? What standards are there to judge that an act
is wrong? Many people ask "Who is to say?" They are expressing a widespread public opinion that we have no justifiable
grounds for our moral judgments, and therefore that no one
can "say" that an action is wrong. Are all standards of what is

right or wrong, what constitutes a good personal life or a good society, merely relative to the individual person or to a particular social group, expressing nothing more than habit or prejudice, and serving individual or group interests and needs? These are the questions of the branch of philosophy called ethics. *Ethics* asks: Is there a highest good for human beings, an absolute good? What is the meaning of right and wrong in human action? What are our obligations? And why should we be moral?

Do you sometimes ask, what is the best kind of government? You could not avoid the question What is the best kind of government? when the United States waged war unsuccessfully to stop the communists of North Vietnam from taking over South Vietnam. Now that war is over and South Vietnam has become another communist nation. The question remains, is democracy the best form of government in the world today? Is communist totalitarianism the worst? What principles of jus tice or truth or freedom or equality do democracy and totalitarianism appeal to in order to justify their forms of government? Do principles of justice, truth, freedom, equality, have any firm, identifiable meaning or are they only high-sounding, inflammatory words which propagandists for democracy, dictatorships, and totalitarian governments use in order to manipulate and control us? Today governments of the Western world face serious problems which have been generated by nuclear weapons, communist aggressions, overpopulation, the exhaustion of natural resources like oil and coal, the pollution of air and water, and economic inflation. Our government is confronted by these problems as well as by the problems of maintaining health care, welfare, social security, public education, military defense, and a tax structure, and as a result the federal government has assumed an increasingly large role in our lives. A crucial question that we cannot help asking now is, how much control should government have over the lives of its citizens? What is the function of government—is it to protect our equal opportunity or is it to provide equal welfare for all? Political philosophy is the branch of philosophy which asks all these questions: What is the best form of government? What are the principles which justify government? Who should have power or control and how is this justified? What are the proper functions of government?

Do you sometimes ask, does human history have any meaning? Does the history of human beings in the world

have any purpose, does it show any pattern? Or are the
generations upon generations of human beings—with all their
activities, beliefs, and hopes—only a meaningless scurrying
about, an empty chatter, soon dust unto meaningless dust?
The hopes and struggles of individual men and women soon
come to nothing (one thinks of the political struggles of Hu-
bert Humphrey). The rise of great nations seems inevitably to
lead to their decline and fall (one thinks of the fall of the
Mayan civilization of Central America, or of the decline and
fall of ancient Rome). The dirty tricks of politics seem to
undermine the ideal of honesty in government (one thinks of
Watergate). Can you bear the torture of thinking about the
miseries and frustrations that are the repeated events of
personal history and of world history? Does history have any
significance that can justify its endless horrors and frustrations?
Do you ask these questions about history? These are also
philosophy's questions. These are the questions of the branch
of philosophy called *philosophy of history*.

Do you sometimes ask, how sound are the arguments with
which economists, politicians, theologians, philosophers,
journalists, attempt to convince you of their views? Are you
also concerned about the soundness of your own arguments?
What are the principles of valid reasoning? How can one
recognize reasoning which is not valid? What are the criteria
of correct or valid inference? Are there various types of errors
in reasoning which can be identified? These are the kinds of
questions which the branch of philosophy called *logic* asks.

You ask all of these questions sometimes, but are they not
always somewhere in the back of your mind, are they not
always simmering away slowly on a back burner? Someday
you will find that they are no longer simmering but have
suddenly burst into flame. These questions may be thought of
in yet another way—as figures who are standing offstage in
the darkness of the wings. But there are times when they
come to the front of the stage and shout and scream at you.
They will scream their importance on the center of the stage
when you have a personal crisis or when your whole society is
in crisis and a revolution seems about to break out. Sometimes they will come to the center of your stage and scream
at you when there is no objective crisis in your life or in the
society around you, but when you suddenly feel that you
have lost your bearings, that you don't know what you believe,
that you have no convictions, and that you have a sense of

vast inner emptiness, a sense of nothingness. These questions will then thunder loudly in that emptiness within you. But in no case will these questions go away. They never go away. Time will not banish them or get rid of them for you. They can't be ruled out of your thoughts, by you or anyone else, even though there are some scientists and philosophers who say that you don't need to worry about these questions, because they are not proper scientific questions; or other philosophers who say, these questions are meaningless, they distort the ordinary ways in which we use the English language; still others regard these questions as too dangerous, too unsettling, too destabilizing for most people to think about.

What is real? What can we know? What does it mean to be moral, to live a good life? What is the difference between right and wrong? What is a good government and what are its functions with respect to the citizens? Does human history have any meaning, pattern, purpose? These are the questions which the great philosophers of the Western world have asked for over twenty-five hundred years, since the days of ancient Athens in the sixth century B.C. To be a human being is to ask these questions. If we human beings are only material bodies, if we are only meaningless collections of atoms, it is nonetheless the case that we are the only known collections of atoms in the universe that can reflect upon the universe and ask such questions as, what is real and what does it mean to be moral?

Can you imagine a world in which nobody any longer asked the philosophic questions, nobody was philosophical? It would be a world in which nobody penetrated below the facts of everyday life to think about what is real, true, valuable, just, and meaningful in human life. It would be a world of mechanical men, women, and children moving among physical objects, a world in which we would have become hollow men going through meaningless motions and our speech would be empty chatter. Nothing would be questioned because it would have become pointless and hopeless to question anything anymore. But the great philosophers of the Western world are not hollow men, they are filled with enormous vitality and with the profound conviction that it is of fundamental importance to raise these questions and to answer them in the way they do.

We shall in this book be looking at six major philosophers of Western civilization: Plato, Descartes, Hume, Hegel, Marx, and Sartre. Most of them would be on anyone's list of the greatest thinkers of the Western world. Each of these philosophers gave over his whole life to probing into the indestructible questions of philosophy and to working out his own ways of responding to them. We turn first to Plato.

PART ONE
PLATO

**"Plato Conversing with a Student
at the Academy" by Puvis de Chavannes.**
(COURTESY OF THE BETTMANN ARCHIVES.)

1

VIRTUE IS KNOWLEDGE

> No one must have any private property
> whatsoever, except what is absolutely neces-
> sary. Secondly, no one must have any lodg-
> ing or storehouse at all which is not open to
> all comers . . . They must live in common,
> attending in messes as if they were in the
> field . . . They alone of all in the city dare
> not have any dealings with gold or silver or
> even touch them or come under the same
> roof with them.

Is this a description of an ascetic religious order? Or of a
communist group in training for a secret mission? Or is it a
science-fiction account of a society of the future preparing for
a space war? It is actually Plato's requirements for the ruling
class of his ideal Republic. (*Republic*, Book III, 415 E.)

Plato is the most celebrated, honored and revered of all the
philosophers of the Western world. He lived in Athens twenty-
four centuries ago, in the fourth century before Christ, and
throughout history since then the praise of Plato has been
expressed in figures of speech which compete with one another in their eloquence. He is said to be the greatest of the
philosophers which Western civilization has produced; he is
said to be the father of Western philosophy; the son of the
god Apollo; a sublime dramatist and poet with a vision of
beauty which enhances all human life; a mystic who, before
Christ and Saint Paul, beheld a transcendent realm of goodness,
love, and beauty; he is said to be the greatest of the moralists
and social philosophers of all time. The British philosopher
and mathematician Alfred North Whitehead said of him that

the history of Western philosophy is only a series of footnotes to Plato. And the American poet and philosopher Ralph Waldo Emerson said of him, "Plato is Philosophy, and Philosophy, Plato," and also, "Out of Plato come all things that are still written and debated among men of thought."

Historical Situation

Aside from the great achievement of his philosophy, Plato's life exhibits many tragic conflicts and deep frustrations, which arose from the larger tragedy which overcame Athens herself— her defeat in war and the subsequent decline of her great civilization. To understand Plato we must place him in his culture, in his time. He was born in Athens circa 427 B.C. at the end of what is conventionally called the Golden Age of Athens, or the Age of Pericles, who was its statesman-ruler.

The Golden Age of Athens, the Age of Pericles, which lasted from 445 to 431 B.C., has come to symbolize perfection in human civilized life. It may be said that the Western world has had a long-standing love affair with the Athens of the Golden Age. We feel closer to Athens, as our ideal and model, than to any other city in all of human history, except possibly Jerusalem. But we relate to Jerusalem not as an ideal city, but only in devotion to the great persons who lived there and to the sacred events that happened there. Why the long love affair with the ancient city of Athens? Athens is our ideal as the first democracy, and as a city devoted to human excellence in mind and body, to philosophy, the arts and science, and to the cultivation of the art of living; and we as a democratic nation empathize with her in her tragic defeat.

By the fifth century B.C. Athens had become a democracy, as the culmination of a long struggle between a small number of land-owning families of the aristocracy and great numbers of the poor. Pericles, elected annually as the first citizen of the state, skillfully maintained political rights for all citizens, for the aristocracy and for commoners, for rich and for poor (although not for women or slaves). Pericles extended and consolidated the empire of the Athenian city-state, while strengthening within Athens the new political doctrine of egalitarianism, equal rights for all citizens under the law. Most of the prominent and influential citizens of Athens were democratic or had become democratic in their political views.

In Athenian society, the poor were held to be as virtuous and as capable as the rich. Of the poor, the Greek dramatist Aeschylus wrote in one of his famous plays: "Justice shines in houses grimy with smoke." And the philosopher Protagoras said: "Anyone who is just and reverent is qualified to give advice on public affairs."

The Athenian state had a constitution and a supreme court, which incorporated a jury system of six thousand jurors, divided into panels, and formed the basis of Athenian democracy. All citizens were equal under the law, in basic education, and in political life through direct democratic debate and voting. There was freedom of speech and humane treatment of aliens and slaves. In the Age of Pericles there was full employment and great material prosperity through trade and domestic industry. The city government was viewed as a model of justice for the known world and Athenians had feelings of intense pride and loyalty for the city itself.

The years 445 to 431 B.C. were years of peace and internal improvements. Under Pericles Athens was made beautiful by vast building projects. Historians of comparative civilizations say no other city was ever so handsomely adorned by public buildings and works of art. Today the remains of temples and public buildings decorated by magnificent sculptures and statuary still stand. Supreme among these is the Parthenon, which was the chief temple of Athens, and dedicated to the goddess of wisdom, Athena, whose huge gold and ivory statue was carved under the direction of the sculptor Phidias. The Parthenon and the Propylaea, the great entrance hall, were among the many magnificent public buildings high on the rock cliff, called the Acropolis, overlooking the city. Pericles attracted to Athens the intellectually and artistically gifted from all parts of Greece. In literature there appeared the great Greek dramatists, Aeschylus, Sophocles, Euripedes; in architecture and sculpture there were Phidias and Mnesicles; in philosophy there were Parmenides, Zeno, Anaxagoras, the Sophists, and Socrates; in history there were the great historians Herodotus and Thucydides. There were brilliant achievements in all fields of culture, science, and medicine. The historian Thucydides writes that Pericles in a famous oration said of the Athenians: "We are lovers of the beautiful, yet simple in our tastes, and we cultivate the arts without loss of manliness."

Pericles's moderate policy in time ran into opposition by

extremists on both the aristocratic right and the democratic left. But a strong sense of loyalty to Athens unified the city politically when war with Sparta broke out in the spring of 431 B.C. At this time most of the communities of Greece were under the leadership of either the Athenian Empire (which was democratic, commercial, and industrial) or the Spartan Empire (which was authoritarian, militaristic, and agricultural). The Peloponnesian War as it developed became clearly a struggle between Athenian democracy and the authoritarianism of Sparta, which was ruled by a military elite with absolute power. In the second year of the war, an uncontrollable plague broke out in Athens which was overcrowded and rapidly becoming impoverished.

Democratic Athens finally surrendered to Sparta in 404 B.C., whereupon a revolution was staged by the aristocrats, who conducted a vicious reign of terror, the Rule of the Thirty. Among the leaders of this reign of terror were Charmides (Plato's uncle) and Critias (Plato's cousin). They represented the rich and noble families who had been virtually destroyed by the long years of war waged by democratic Athens. When democracy was restored and the Rule of the Thirty brought to an end, the philosopher Socrates was tried by an Athenian jury and was sentenced to death.

Plato's Life

What do we know of Plato's life during the war with Sparta? Plato was born three years after the war with Sparta began, a year after the death of Pericles, too late to experience in his own lifetime the peace and glory of the Age of Pericles. He was the son of one of the most aristocratic families in Athens. His father, Ariston, was descended from the last king of Athens. His mother, Perictione, was a descendant of Solon, the aristocratic reformer who wrote the constitution which established Athenian democracy. Both sides of his family were related to noble and aristocratic landowners of Athens, who increasingly opposed the flounderings and failures of the democratic government in its conduct of the war. Plato had grown up in an aristocratic family which had supported Pericles and the democratic government, but now felt itself betrayed by the bungling war policy of the democratic government. The resentment of such families increased as they saw their financial resources drained away during the long-drawn-out war with Sparta, a military autocracy which now appeared far more to their liking than democracy. Plato was no doubt brought up to think of democracy as a form of corruption in government. An armed counterrevolution appeared to the aristocracy to be the only solution to the weakness of Athens against the power of Sparta. Plato, too, must have believed that his relatives Charmides and Critias, who engineered the Rule of the Thirty and its brief reign of terror, would bring about the new order and that his teacher Socrates would provide its philosophy.

Trial and Death of Socrates

Plato was twenty-eight years old at the time of the trial of Socrates, perhaps the most famous trial in all of history. Plato had been studying with Socrates for eight years, although he had known Socrates as a friend of the family since his earliest childhood. In the dramatic dialogue called the *Apology* Plato presents Socrates's "apology" in his own defense and an account of the course of the trial which is believed to be substantially accurate. Plato himself was present at the trial and subsequently circulated his account of it in order to combat other accounts which were unfriendly to the cause of Socrates.

What were the charges which the Athenians brought against Socrates? He was charged with impiety, speaking against the gods, and also with corrupting the youth of Athens. In fact, however, the real charges were unmentionable since in an effort to put an end to the bitter hatreds developed within Athens during the war, the government had banned any public mention of specific war crimes. The specific war crimes of Socrates were that with the aid of his friends, Charmides and Critias, and of his favorite pupil, Alcibiades (a notorious traitor to Athens), Socrates had conspired to bring about a counterrevolution against the Athenian democracy during the war and was now, even after the end of the war and the defeat of Athens in 404, continuing to incite the aristocratic young men of Athens to revolt against the democracy.

It appears that the trial was intended to frighten Socrates away from Athens, so that he would not continue to weaken the morale of the exhausted democracy by his constant criticisms of democratic government in his philosophizing in public places. The Athenians had no desire to impose a death sentence upon him nor did they wish to make a martyr of him. As Plato himself brings out in the *Apology*, Socrates could have avoided death by leaving Athens before the trial began, as was customary at that time when acquittal in a trial appeared to be doubtful. Moreover, even if he had not left Athens before the trial, he would have been acquitted if he had shown any deference to the democratic feelings of the public and of the jury, or if at least he had not openly shown his contempt for them. He would have been acquitted, despite the contempt which his speech exhibited for the Athenian public and for democracy, if he had proposed, when requested, a moderate fine for himself. Finally, in the absence of any of these means by which he would have avoided the death sentence, he could easily have escaped after his sentence, since he was detained for a month before he had to drink the hemlock, and no one would have blamed him for escaping.

The Socratic Philosophy

But Socrates would not compromise with his view that he had been the benefactor of the Athenian public. To escape or to propose any penalty or fine, however trivial, would be to admit guilt. Moreover, when his friends begged him to allow them to arrange the escape, he argued that it would be legally and morally wrong to escape, since every citizen of a state has entered into a social contract to obey its laws. And he also argued that individuals who disobey the laws of their own society tear away at the foundation of group life.

Socrates took his stand upon the abstract principles of his philosophy. This was his "apology," his defense of himself. It was for the truth of this philosophy that he was willing to die. It was for the truth of this philosophy that he would not consent to be conciliatory to the judges or to the jury, or to suggest a milder punishment than death; thus he forced them to put him to death. But what was this philosophy for which he chose to die rather than to renounce it?

The main points which he himself brings out, as Plato recounts his speech at the trial, are these:

(1) The only true wisdom consists in knowing that you know nothing. He says this because the famous oracle at the shrine of Apollo at Delphi had said that no man living was wiser than Socrates. So, says Socrates to the jury, I wanted to test what the oracle had said in order to prove that it was false. And so first I went to the statesmen, he says in his speech, and I found that those whose reputation for wisdom was the very highest were in fact the most lacking in wisdom. And I knew that I was wiser than the statesmen, because at least I knew that I knew nothing. Then, he continues, I went to the poets to see if some of the poets were not wiser than I. But I soon found out that they create their poetry not by wisdom but by inspiration, "Like prophets who say many fine things but understand nothing of what they say." But the poets thought that they were the wisest of men in all other matters, too, because of their poetry. Then I went, he says, to the craftsmen, the artisans, and I found that they indeed did know many fine things that I did not know, like how to build ships or to make shoes, but like the poets, they believed themselves to be wise in matters of the greatest importance because of the skill that they have in their own craft, such as shoemaking. This tended to diminish the real knowledge that they did have. And so, says Socrates, I conclude after discovering that wisdom cannot be found among the statesmen, the poets, or the craftsmen, that what the oracle at Delphi meant was not that Socrates is wise but that he at least knows that he really knows nothing.

(2) Socrates's second philosophic point in his *Apology* is that the improvement or "tendance" of the soul, the care for wisdom and truth, is the highest good. This is why I go about, he says, persuading old and young alike not to be concerned with your bodies or your money, but first and foremost to care about the improvement of your soul. Not until you have pursued wisdom and truth ought you to think of money or fame or prestige or of the body. Virtue does not come from money, but from virtue comes money and every other good thing for mankind, public and private. This, says Socrates, is my teaching, and if this is the doctrine which corrupts the youth, I am a mischievous person. If anyone says that I teach anything else, he lies.

(3) Socrates's third point is to say to the Athenians that if you condemn me, you will sin against the gods who have given me to you. I am a gadfly, he says, whom the gods gave

to the state, which is like a great and noble horse, sluggish and slow in his motion because of his vast size, and needing to be stirred into life by my sting. That is why all day and in all places I am always alighting upon you to arouse and reproach you. You will not easily find another like me, he says, and therefore I would advise you to spare me.

(4) The fourth and most important point in Socrates's speech is the principle that virtue is knowledge. According to this principle, to know the good is to do the good. Evil, wrongdoing, or vice are due to the lack of knowledge or to ignorance, and to nothing else. If virtue is knowledge, and if to know the good is to do the good, then wrongdoing comes only from failure to know what is good. And so in a famous line Socrates says: "No one does evil voluntarily." Knowing the good, no man would voluntarily choose evil. But do we not often say: "I acted against my better judgment" or "I really knew better?" According to Socrates, this is absurd, because if you really did know better, if you really understood the right thing to do, you would have done it. If you really had had better judgment than you used, you would have acted on it, not against it. Socrates insists that when one does an evil act, it is always with the thought that it will bring one some good, some benefit. A thief knows that stealing is wrong but he steals the diamond ring believing that it will impress a desired female and will bring him sexual favors. So also people spend their lives striving for power, or prestige, or wealth, thinking that one of these is good and will make them happy. But they do not know what is good. They do not know that these are not good and will not bring them happiness. One needs to know human nature, the true nature of human beings, in order to know what is good for humans and what will bring happiness, and in order to know how to live and what to strive to achieve. And not to delve into this, never to know what is good for human beings is to live a life of striving to achieve but never finding happiness. Such a life Socrates calls unexamined. In one of his most famous lines Socrates declares that "The unexamined life is not worth living."

Ethics (Moral Philosophy)

Socrates's view of virtue, of what is right and what is good may be called a *rationalistic moral philosophy*. A rationalistic moral philosophy is a view which claims that reason, or rationality, is the exclusive or the dominant factor in moral conduct. It is, as Socrates himself says, the claim that to know the good is to do the good. Do you agree that to know the good is to do it? Most moderns do not agree. They would not agree that, even if I possess a true knowledge of human nature, of how to live, of what to strive for, of what will bring me happiness, there is any assurance that with this knowledge I will act upon it and do the good. Insofar as we moderns cannot agree with Socrates it is because we have learned too much about the many nonrational forces in human personality which combat reason—instincts, emotions, passions, impulses, drives—and to which reason appears always to be taking second place. It was the Roman poet Ovid who expressed this precisely: "We know and approve the better course, but follow the worse." As for Freud and for contemporary psychiatry, the unconscious is understood as a "seething cauldron" of powerful desires against which reason is weak if not helpless.

Death of Socrates: Interpretations

These are the main points of the Socratic philosophy that appear at the trial. The outcome of the trial is of course the sentencing of Socrates to drink the poison hemlock, and this he does in the presence of his sorrowing friends who had come in a final effort to persuade him to escape. It is Plato who is the first to offer the view of Socrates as a martyr, in the line with which he ends another of his dialogues, the *Phaedo*: "And that was the end of our friend—who was, we may say—of all those of his time whom we have known—the best and wisest, and the most righteous man." There are many who have come to think of the martyrdom of Socrates as the secular counterpart of the martyrdom of Christ. The analogy with Christ is that the best among us, the wisest, the noblest, the purest, the most righteous, we put to death. But this is only one of the many interpretations that have been made of Socrates's trial and death. By contrast with seeing Socrates as a martyr, there are those philosophers who see Socrates's trial and death as representing the hostility of the masses toward philosophy and philosophers. Another interpretation is made by political scientists who see Socrates's trial and death as expressing the power of the state over the individual and his freedom of inquiry. Still another interpretation is that of the sociologists who see Socrates's philosophy as a mask for his defense of aristocracy against Athenian democracy. Which of these interpretations do you find the most appropriate—is Socrates martyred for his purity? Is he hated for his intelligence? Is he destroyed in his free individuality by the oppressive power of the state? Or is he a masked defender of aristocracy who came into conflict with a democratic government?

Plato's Later Life

After the death of Socrates in 399 B.C., Plato left Athens with some of his close friends, not only out of sorrow for his teacher but also because he, too, might be in danger from the democratic government of Athens. The most important event in his travels was his visit to Syracuse, a wealthy and independent Greek city in the Mediterranean. There he met Dion, who was the brother-in-law of the king of Syracuse and who became completely devoted to Plato and his philosophy. There is a story that the king became enraged with Plato's influence upon Dion and ordered Plato sold into slavery. Plato, however, was ransomed by a friend and managed to return to Athens. On his return to Athens Plato purchased some property outside the city walls in a place known as the Grove of Academus. There Plato started his famous school, which has come to be called the Academy and where for the remaining forty years of his life he taught and wrote. The Academy was a school and an institute for philosophic and scientific research. His students were young men and women of the noble classes from all of Greece and Asia Minor who were intending to pursue a political career. The Academy was the direct forerunner of the medieval and modern university, and for nine hundred years it was the outstanding school in the world. After twenty years of teaching and study at the Academy, at the age of sixty, Plato returned to Syracuse at the request of Dion. The king had died and Dion saw a chance for Plato to educate the new young king, Dionysius II. "Now, if ever, is there a good chance that your own ideal can be realized, and true philosophy and power over a great dominion be united in the same person." Here, as we shall see, is the concept of the philosopher-king, the philosopher who becomes king or the king who learns philosophy—a Platonic political ideal which has exerted influence upon European kings and American presidents at certain moments in the history of the Western world. But Plato's second return to Syracuse in the year 367 in the attempt to apply his concept of the philosopher-king to the world of politics proved again to be a failure, as did a third attempt in 361, and he returned to Athens and to the Academy, where he continued teaching and writing until the age of eighty, when in 348 B.C., he died.

In the book called the *Republic* Plato had offered a blueprint for an ideal government of an ideal society. What was this philosopher's conception of the best kind of society and the best kind of government? This is the question which we have foreshadowed and to which we will next turn.

2

SHADOW AND SUBSTANCE

After Socrates was put to death Plato was more than ever convinced that a democratic state, a state ruled by the many, is doomed to disaster. The many, he believed, can never know what is good for the state: they lack the necessary level of intelligence and training; they are concerned only with their own immediate pleasure and gratification; and they are swayed by unstable, volatile emotions which render them susceptible to clever demagogues or to mob passions. He believed that a democratic government, run by the many, cannot produce good human beings, and, in turn, he believed that good people would find life impossible under such a state. (Plato's attacks upon democratically governed cities make us uncomfortable when they seem to describe some of the great cities of the United States.)

Having arrived at these conclusions, Plato withdrew from public life, although as a member of the aristocracy he was expected to play an important role in Athenian politics.

The Concept of the Philosopher-King

At first, he tells us in one of the few letters of his that remain, he looked into all the possible ways in which the decadence of public and private morality could be stopped. Initially, he thought that amending or revising the Athenian constitution might be the way to end the moral degeneration of the city. But soon he realized that the breakdown of public and private morals was widespread and not confined to the political problems of the city of Athens. He saw that the challenge was to philosophy to provide a true definition of justice, a philosophy of a just and good society, and a theory of the best form of government for such a society. And so he came to pin his hopes on the possibility of a society governed by a philosopher-king, who would have knowledge of true justice and the best form of government. Plato developed the theory that not until philosophers became kings, or kings philosophers, with the same person uniting within himself knowledge and power, would a society based upon justice be possible. Plato saw that his mission in life was to accomplish this goal: the development of a true philosophy and the education of potential philosopher-kings in the Academy.

Plato's Sources: Socrates

In constructing his philosophy Plato carried forward the philosophic work of Socrates. From the point of view of their respective personalities, this was a strange alliance: Plato the aristocrat, quiet, cold, and reserved, aloof from the democratic scene at Athens, a literary artist as well as a philosopher, using philosophy to serve the ideals of excellence of his social class; and Socrates, middle-class in origin, gregarious, a mixer with all types and classes in the city, short and stocky of build, pudgy and ugly of face (with bulging eyes and broad nostrils); but whose intellectual brilliance and wit were able nonetheless to win the love of any young man of Athens who happened to strike his homosexual fancy.

In the eyes of Athenians there was nothing remarkable about Socrates's homosexual relationships. Homosexuality was common among the middle and upper classes, with heterosexual marriage being commonly entered into only when a man wished to establish a family. As for Plato, we know only that, unlike Socrates, who was married late in life and had a family of three sons, Plato never married. On the internal evidence of his writing, his sexual feelings seem to have been directed solely to other men.

All of Plato's philosophical writing was done in the form of dialogues, conversations in which almost always the principal speaker is Socrates. These are the first philosophical dialogues of the Western world. So far as we know, Plato himself invented the dialogue as a literary form, apparently from his actual experience of listening to Socrates in his characteristic conversations. Socrates wrote nothing, but all the philosophy

Plato wrote is attributed to him, with the result that it is impossible to disentangle with complete certainty the Socratic from the Platonic element in the dialogues. Most scholars agree that aside from the very early dialogues in which Plato was seeking to present the true teaching of Socrates in order to defend him and to honor his memory, the dialogues represent Plato's own views. Plato wrote more than twenty dialogues, many of them of fine literary quality. Since they depict actual conversations, they are open-ended, flowing, informal, very different from the tight, systematic, rigorously deductive argumentation which we will find, for example, in Descartes. The persons who take part in the dialogues become three-dimensional as Plato sketches them—the pompous, blustering Thrasymachus in the *Republic*; the polite reasonableness of Adeimantus and Glaucon, Plato's two older brothers; the handsome and clever Alcibiades in the *Symposium*; and Socrates himself, master of the put-down, making fools of those who ventured to offer their opinions in response to his prodding, and making enemies of those he disagreed with in politics and philosophy.

Socratic Method

Most of the dialogues use the philosophic method which Socrates invented—the *Socratic Method*, sometimes called the *Method of Dialectic*, sometimes the *Elenchus*. It is a form of seeking ("boxing in") knowledge by question and answer. The question is put by Socrates, and is usually a general question: What is piety? What is courage? What is justice? The answer offered by the respondent takes the form of a definition: Courage is——. Socrates then proceeds to refute each definition by offering a counterexample designed to show that the definition which was offered is too narrow, too restricted, or is biased or uninformed. Plato uses Socratic Method superbly in Book I of the *Republic*. Socrates asks Cephalos, a wealthy and honorable old merchant, What is justice? Cephalos replies from the narrow point of view of the ethics of a businessman: Justice is speaking the truth and paying one's debts. But Socrates replies with a counterexample: Sometimes paying one's debts may be unjust, as when you owe a friend a weapon, but since he has subsequently become insane, would it not be unjust to return it to him? Cephalos agrees; his own definition is demolished. A new definition must be constructed to cover this type of case.

Socratic Definition

The Socratic Method uses the technique of the counterexample to mount a series of questions expanding the number of examples, cases, particulars, to be included in the definition. A definition must state what all the examples, cases, instances, particulars, have in common as examples of courage, justice, and so forth. Sometimes the definition arrived at shows the falsity of the original definition by completely reversing it. Sometimes, as at the end of Book I of the *Republic*, no definition is reached although many are rejected.

Under the influence of Socrates's emphasis upon the importance of universal and unchanging definitions, Plato's primary intention as a philosopher was to find definitions for the concepts of justice and of the state. These questions led him into more fundamental questions, such as: What is knowledge? What is the nature of reality? What is the nature of the physical world? What is human nature? What is the highest good for human beings? What is virtue, right conduct?

Plato's Sources: The Pre-Socratics

Like all philosophers who came after him, Plato constructed his philosophy in response to other philosophies. Plato built not only upon the thought of Socrates but also upon the theories of earlier philosophers, the so-called pre-Socratic philosophers.

The earliest philosophers of the Greek world—those of the sixth century B.C.—had wrestled with the problem of explaining physical nature by asking, what is the one basic material out of which the world is made? They all agreed that the many different kinds of things we see in the world are all transformations, changes of only one kind of thing. But they disagreed as to what is the one fundamental material out of which the many are formed: Is it water, or air, or fire?

In this way a second major philosophic problem took shape— the problem of change, of the transformations of the one into the many. Does the one change into many? Then how is it one? Are the many merely variations, transformations, or changes of the permanent, unchanging one? Then how are they many?

The two sides of this debate are represented by two major

pre-Socratic philosophers: *Heraclitus* and *Parmenides*. Heraclitus, who flourished at about 500 B.C., was a solitary, pessimistic member of the nobility of the city of Ephesus. Heraclitus argued that the fundamental character of reality is *change* itself. Everything in reality, said Heraclitus, is in process, in flux, is changing. "One cannot step twice into the same river," he wrote, since it is endlessly flowing, changing, moving with fresh waters.

By claiming that everything is change or flux, Heraclitus denied that anything can stay the same, be identical with what is has been or will be. Thus he denied any permanence or immutability in the world. He denied the unchanging one and affirmed the changing many.

In the fiercest opposition to Heraclitus stood Parmenides of Elea, in southern Italy, who flourished at about 465 B.C. and wrote his philosophy in the form of poetry. Parmenides argued that not change but *permanence* is the fundamental character of reality. Reality is one, single, permanent, and unchanging. How can a thing change into something else? How can it be and not be? Whatever is, must be what it is, identical with itself, unchanging. Parmenides therefore claimed that reality is a single, unchanging one, and he branded change as an illusion. He denied that anything can change, he denied any process or development in the world. He denied the many and affirmed the one. Change is mere appearance to the senses, Parmenides is saying; whereas truth is unchanging and is known by reason.

Plato's Sources: The Sophists

One response to this philosophic conflict between Heraclitus and Parmenides was that of the *Sophists*. The Sophists were philosophers from many different societies outside Greece who traveled about from city to city and in the fifth century B.C. came to Athens, where they made a reputation as teachers of rhetoric, the art of making persuasive public speeches. The art of rhetoric was immensely useful for achieving success in politics in democratic Athens, where debate in the public assembly was open to all citizens. The Sophists argued that since reason produced such conflicting claims as those of Heraclitus and Parmenides, one must doubt the power of reason to lead to truth. Thus the Sophists became the first exponents of skepticism, the philosophic position of doubting the possibility of any true knowledge. *Protagoras*, the best known of the Sophists, appears to have made the skeptical argument that since there is no way of determining the truth about reality, reality must be said to have whatever qualities are claimed for it. Thus the Sophists threw suspicion upon all preceding Greek attempts to discover the true nature of reality.

But, more important, the Sophists may be said to have turned Greek philosophy in a new direction—away from philosophizing about the physical universe and toward the study of human beings and their moral, social, and political life. The Sophists were intellectual sophisticates who had traveled about and knew many cultures and their differing customs, morals, laws, and governments. Much to the dismay of many Athenian citizens who believed that traditional Athenian morals, laws, and democracy expressed absolute truths, the Sophists were moral relativists and argued that all moral and political principles are relative to the group which believes them. None is absolutely true.

Moreover, the Sophists claimed that the laws of cities are not natural and unchangeable but are merely the product of custom or convention. Therefore, some of the more radical Sophists argued, one is not obliged to obey the law. One should obey the law only if it is to your advantage to do so. For example, in Book I of the *Republic*, *Thrasymachus* the Sophist argues that might makes right, that laws serve only to protect the interests of the powerful, the ruling party. Therefore, he concludes, only a fool obeys the law if it is against his own advantage.

Many people in our contemporary world are very close to the Sophists in their beliefs. Like the Sophists, they are skeptics, doubtful of any claims to knowledge, especially when authorities are in conflict and fight among themselves—for example, about how to teach children to read or how to stop economic inflation. Like the Sophists, many people today claim that the laws protect only the rich and powerful, that they are not based upon justice and need not be obeyed; they are moral relativists who deny that morality is valid other than for the group which believes in it.

Socrates and Plato found the skepticism and the moral relativism of the Sophists so hateful that there is a considerable doubt that the Sophists' views were fairly represented in

Plato's writing. The Sophists' claims were in head-on conflict with Socrates and Plato, who defended reason and argued that reason can provide true knowledge of reality and of moral principles, and that all human beings can be guided by this knowledge and act rationally upon it. Virtue, said Socrates, is knowledge. How could the Sophists' skepticism and moral relativism be answered? How could the dispute between Heraclitus and Parmenides about permanence and change be solved?

The way in which Plato solves these problems is to identify what is true in each of the conflicting philosophies and to marshall these truths into a single, unified, original philosophy of his own. Plato stands forth in the history of philosophy as one of the great synthesizers of the past conflicts of philosophers. From his synthesis of many points of view comes the rich variety, the depth and the scope, of Plato's philosophy.

The major line of Plato's synthesis is to show that Heraclitus and Parmenides were on the wrong track in supposing that one or the other, either flux or permanence, must be true of all of reality. Reality, says Plato, is not all of one piece, of one nature. Reality is not monistic, that is, characterized by a single quality, such as flux. Reality, Plato urges, must be seen to be twofold, or dualistic, in its nature. Plato offers a dualistic metaphysics.

Metaphysics is the name for that branch of philosophy which reflects upon fundamental reality and asks, what are its characteristics, what is the nature of reality? Plato's metaphysics claims that there are two kinds of reality—there is the reality of physical objects in space and time, which are objects of the senses and which are in flux, growing, decaying, changing, as Heraclitus's river. Heraclitus was right, but only about one kind of reality, physical or material, not about all reality. There is also another kind of reality, the reality of concepts, ideas, forms, or essences, which are objects of thought, like the idea of a triangle, and are not in space and time. The idea or essence of a triangle, which includes, for example, the property that its internal angles add up to 180 degrees, is universally true, unchanging, and immutable. There is, says Plato, a realm of eternally true and unchanging ideas such as this, which reason can know. This is the truth which Parmenides claimed, that reality is permanent and unchanging, but it is true only of one aspect of reality. There is Parmenides's world of universal and unchanging true ideas which are knowable by reason. And there is Heraclitus's world of flux and change, of things physical, which are perceived by the senses.

Allegory of the Cave

Plato illustrates his dualistic theory of reality by his famous Allegory of the Cave, at the beginning of Book VII of the *Republic*. Now then, says Socrates, as he introduces the allegory, imagine mankind as living in an underground cave which has a wide entrance open to the light. Deep inside are human beings facing the inside wall of the cave, with their necks and legs chained so that they cannot move. They have never seen the light of day or the sun outside the cave. Behind the prisoners a fire burns, and between the fire and the prisoners there is a raised way on which a low wall has been built, such as is used in puppet shows as a screen to conceal the people working the puppets. Along the raised way people walk carrying all sorts of things which they hold so that they project above the wall—statues of men, animals, trees. The prisoners, facing the inside wall, cannot see one another, or the wall behind them on which the objects are being carried—all they can see are the shadows these objects cast on the wall of the cave.

The prisoners live all their lives seeing only shadows of reality, and the voices they hear are only echoes from the wall. But the prisoners cling to the familiar shadows and to their passions and prejudices, and if they were freed and able to turn around and see the realities which produce the shadows, they would be blinded by the light of the fire. And they would become angry and would prefer to regain their shadow-world.

But if one of the prisoners were freed and turned around to see, in the light of the fire, the cave and his fellow prisoners and the roadway, and if he were then dragged up and out of the cave into the light of the sun, he would see the things of the world as they truly are and finally he would see the sun itself. What would this person think now of the life in the cave and what people there know of reality and of morality? And if he were to descend back into the cave, would he not have great difficulty in accustoming himself to the darkness, so that he could not compete with those who had never left the cave? Would he not be subject to their ridicule, scorn, even their physical attack?

Of the many allegories in the history of Western thought, the Allegory of the Cave is the one most often cited. But what is an allegory? An allegory is a kind of story in which what is talked about is being compared to something else which is similar, but what that something else is, is left unstated. An allegory is accordingly defined as an incomplete simile—the reader must supply what is similar to the events described. What, then, is the Allegory of the Cave to be compared with? The people in the cave are living out their lives in semidarkness, chained by their necks and legs, unable to turn around, never knowing that what they see before them on the wall of the cave are only shadows. They are in bondage, but unaware of it. They remain ignorant of themselves and reality. With whom may they be compared?

Each historical generation since Plato's time has been tantalized by the question, how does the Allegory of the Cave apply to our time, to our society? To what may the cave be compared in our lives? The question tantalizes us too: What is the relevance of the Allegory of the Cave to our present world? With what in our lives may it be compared? The following broad and general interpretations of the allegory have been made for generations and remain relevant and moving for many people in our own time: It is an allegory of sleep and waking, of our time as asleep in the dark of the cave and needing to awake to a clear vision of the world. It is an allegory of our time as needing to be born again, to emerge from the darkness of corruption into the light of truth and morality. It is an educational allegory of our time as needing to ascend through stages of education from the darkness of intellectual and moral confusion in its everyday beliefs, to the light of true knowledge and values. It is a religious allegory of Christian conversion from the cave of self-love and self-gratification to the love of God and devotion to His truth.

There are also interpretations of the allegory which are specifically relevant to our own society and to the present time.

(1) The Allegory of the Cave may be viewed as a devastating criticism of our *everyday lives* as being in bondage to superficialities, to shadow rather than to substance. Truth is

taken to be whatever is known by the senses. A good life is taken to be one in which we satisfy our desires. We are unaware that we are living with illusion, superficial knowledge, and false and conflicting ideals. Our lives are dominated by the shadow-play on the walls of our cave made by newspaper headlines, by radio broadcasts, by the endlessly moving shadows on the television screen, by the echoing voices of opinion makers.

(2) The Allegory of the Cave may be taken as an equally devastating criticism of much of the *science* of our time, with its emphasis upon that which is known by the senses. Science, too, is chained so that it can see only shadows. Its basis is in sensory observation, its conclusions are only in the form of correlations of observations. It does not venture into true causes or into long-range consequences. The empirical scientist is not so different from the winner on TV quiz shows who knows the dates of all the Humphrey Bogart films, or from the prisoners in the cave who excel in identifying the sequence of shadows on the wall. It is a criticism also of our scientific technology and industry, developing and producing to meet superficial needs, without regard for our true needs or for moral or environmental considerations.

(3) It is of course a *political* allegory. The life in the cave is the life of politics. Both the leaders and the public are ignorant and corrupt, without true knowledge of themselves or of the world, motivated by greed, power, and self-gratification. They are chained in bondage to ignorance and passions, to mob hysteria for or against fleeting issues, believing in current ideologies which are the illusions, the shadows of the moment on the walls of the cave.

(4) It is an allegory of the philosopher-king. The liberated one, having made the ascent to know the truth and the good, has a mission: to return to the cave, to bring enlightenment, to bring the good news, even though he may be killed for his services. Plato was thinking of Socrates; we think of Jesus.

For Plato, those who have completed the ascent out of the cave into the light of the sun are thereby alone fitted to govern, to be the philosopher-kings of society, to be its guardians. But here suddenly the Allegory of the Cave comes into conflict with contemporary views of ourselves, the world, and politics. Two questions are at issue: First, is there, as Plato believes, a single, absolutely true, immutable and eternal concept of justice, of virtue, of the ideal society, of the ideal human being? And are these concepts such that only a few persons of superior intelligence can be educated to know them? Second, would this knowledge justify an authoritarian government by this elite of intelligence and virtue who would rule with absolute, unchecked power? This would be in total opposition to modern democracy, which is government by the many through their elected representatives.

Plato answered *yes* to both questions. This was Plato's solution to the intellectual and moral decay of his time—an absolutist, authoritarian government by a small elite, educated to true knowledge and virtue, which are fixed in their essence for all time. After Plato's time, the history of Western philosophy struggles with these two questions. The modern world for the most part answers *no*.

(5) Finally, for us as for Plato, the Allegory of the Cave is an allegory of despair and hope. Like Plato, we live in a time of loss of meaning and commitment, of crumbling standards of truth and morality, of corruption in political life and decline in personal integrity. This is our despair. But there is a hope that we share with Plato's allegory, the hope of ascending to truth and values which are the best we can know as guides to the good life. For us, as for the prisoner freed from his chains, the first step is to recognize current illusions for what they are, the current flickering shadows on the wall of our cave.

3

THE DIVIDED LINE

What, then, is the true knowledge which is only to be found by the ascent from the cave to the light of the sun?

Theory of Knowledge

Plato offers his theory of knowledge from section 509 to the end of Book VI of the *Republic*. Socrates is represented as conversing at this point with Glaucon, one of Plato's brothers; and to illustrate his theory of knowledge, he gives directions for a seemingly simple diagram:

> Take a line divided into two unequal parts, one to represent the visible order, the other the intelligible, and divide each part again in the same proportion . . .

With these words Plato introduces his famous figure of the divided line, which is his effort to present his theory of knowledge diagramatically, as the cave presented it allegorically. A vertical line is divided into four segments, each of which from the lowest to the highest represents a level of knowledge. Each level of knowledge—imagining or conjecture, belief, understanding, reason—has its own objects and its own method for knowing them. The basic division, however, is between *knowledge*, whose objects are in the intelligible world, and *opinion*, whose objects are in the visible world. And now to examine the divided line and its levels of knowledge in some detail.

DIAGRAM: THE DIVIDED LINE

	THOUGHT	OBJECTS	
KNOWLEDGE	REASON (DIALECTIC)	HIGHER FORMS	**INTELLIGIBLE WORLD**
	UNDERSTAND-ING (SCIENCE, MATHEMATICS)	FORMS OF SCIENCE AND MATHEMATICS	
OPINION	BELIEF (PERCEPTION)	THINGS, OBJECTS	**VISIBLE WORLD**
	CONJECTURE (IMAGINING)	SHADOWS, IMAGES REFLECTIONS	

Imagining or Conjecture

Imagining represents the lowest rung on the ladder formed by the divided line of knowledge. Its objects yield the lowest degree of truth. It is the level of knowledge in which mental activity is at a minimum, as in the awareness of such objects as shadows, after-images, reflections in water or in mirrors or in smooth, shiny surfaces. Other examples of the level of imagining are optical illusions, dream-images, fantasies, soft borderline appearances at the point of waking or of falling asleep.

But Plato's references to shadows and to images and illusions as the objects of imagining are rich with many implications. Plato is saying many things at once here. He is saying that the awareness of images is the lowest level of knowledge, since images are only shadows of the actual objects known by perception, which is a higher level of knowledge. Plato seems to be alluding to artists, whose paintings or sculptures are, as Plato sees them, only images, shadows, copies of actual human beings and other real objects. A still-life painting of an apple is only an image of the actual apple. Painters, poets, sculptors, playwrights, whether of comedy or tragedy, are for Plato mere makers of images, fabricators of shadows and illusions, purveyors of make-believe; and Plato assigns them and their work to the lowliest level of the divided line of knowledge.

Why does Plato so degrade and devalue the artist? Plato is suspicious of all forms of communication which use images, such as painting, poetry, sculpture, drama, religious ritual. These art forms use images to provide fantasy rather than truth, and Plato feared that the passions of the public are easily stimulated, influenced and controlled by their persuasive imagery. (What would Plato think of our public relations industry, which is in the business of manufacturing images for its clients?) Plato also feared politicians as skillful image makers. He believed that the art of rhetoric which the Sophists taught was in its intent and effect the art of manipulating the public by false and clever images. For their own political purposes, Plato claimed, the Sophists taught a distorted image of the Athenian and any other constitution (as representing mere convention rather than truth), and thus they present only a shadow, a blurred image of the actual constitution. At the present time a good example of a mere shadow knowledge of our own constitution occurred in the responses to a recent questionnaire in which many people rejected as illegal a set of statements which turned out to be the Bill of Rights of the Constitution of the United States.

Belief

The next level on the ascent of the divided line of knowledge is that of belief, which is the perception of actual objects. Each higher level of knowledge enables us to make the level below it more intelligible. Initially we can see that the perception of objects makes the level of imagining intelligible as the knowing of mere shadows, images, distorted reflections, of the actual objects known on the second level. The level of belief is primarily the level of knowledge on which there occurs the recognition of things, of three-dimensional visible objects—apples, people, stars, dogs, cities. This is the level of knowledge at which the classification and organization of perceived objects begins. The actual things recognized are grouped together or classified insofar as they are similar, as apples are classified as McIntosh, Baldwin, Delicious, Rome, and Stayman.

But knowledge at the level of belief does not grasp the abstract concept of the object which is perceived, does not grasp the botanist's concept of the apple, which identifies the unchanging characteristics of each species of apple. Belief, which has its source in the perception by the senses of actual objects, is thus insecure. It is not based upon abstract truths or principles which are unchanging and which would give the farmer what the scientific botanist possesses: true knowledge on the basis of which he could rationally classify, predict, explain, and systematize what he knows.

The point that Plato is trying to make us see is that perception by the senses of objects in the visible world can never give us true knowledge and for two reasons:

(1) What can be known by the senses, he tells us, is only the world of flux, the world of Heraclitus, the world of particular things that are in the process of change. What we know at the level of belief is always subject to change, since we know only what we perceive in the visible world which is the world of continual change. Since the features that we perceive trees, horses, people, and cities to have are continually changing, we can never be sure of our knowledge of them. We only know how things seem to be, on the basis of our perception of them, not how they are. In fact, says Plato, we do not have knowledge at this level, but only opinion. It is, however, *true opinion,* since it does recognize actual objects, and does provide rough classifications and predictions. It is therefore to be distinguished from the level of imagining, which knows only images and shadows, and which can only be called *false opinion.*

(2) Plato is also trying to give us a second reason that sense-perception can never give us true knowledge. This second reason is that knowledge derived from the senses can never give us general, universal, unchanging, and abstract truths of the intelligible world. Rather, the senses can give us only particular, changing, and concrete observations of this house, that dog, that tree, of the visible world. Plato is thus maintaining that sense perception cannot give us certainty in knowledge or unchanging universal truths about reality. But certainty and universal truth about reality are precisely what true knowledge must provide. What then is true knowledge? How can true knowledge be reached? These questions are now pressing in upon us—Plato's answer comes in the third and fourth levels.

As he did with regard to the first level on the divided line of knowledge, Plato is saying many things at once about the second level, the level of belief. He is saying that this is the

level on which the commonsense mind, the mind of the
man-in-the-street operates. This is the type of mind that
never rises above the level of thinking or talking about concrete things—this city, that politician, this new scandal, the
latest gossip. The general, universal characteristics of cities
and their common problems, the universal characteristics of
politics, are never considered by this type of mind. Plato is of
course also saying that this is the mentality that is typical of
Athenian democracy. The average Athenian could supply, if
questioned, a roughly adequate description of the democratic
government of Athens—the concrete, particular government
which affects them personally. But such a person would be
unable to identify the principles on which the Athenian constitution rests, or the universal functions of government, or the
traits an ideal type of government should have.

What, then, is true knowledge? And how can true knowledge be reached? The pressure of these questions is now
intensifying for Socrates's friends Glaucon and Adeimantus, as
Plato describes the mounting tension of the ladder of
knowledge—and we, too, feel this tension as we climb the
ladder and look back at the world of everyday beliefs based
on unexamined commonsense experience, of how things seem.
Even farther down below us is the world of mere images,
shadows, dreams, and fantasies, but also the world of powerful yet deceptive illusions fabricated by artists, poets,
dramatists, mythmakers, and political demagogues.

With Plato we reject these lower levels of thinking, and
what they think about, and we reject the kind of life that is
lived by human beings on these levels of knowledge. And so
we ascend to the third level of the ladder of knowledge, the
level of rational understanding or intellect. The change is
from belief in the concrete, changing, particular objects of
perception, to the rational understanding or comprehension
of abstract, unchanging, universal concepts, which are the
objects known by intellect.

Whereas the traditional farmer, on the level of belief,
makes a rough classification of particular apples by perceiving
their actual different shapes, sizes, colors, and textures, the
scientific botanist has knowledge of the precise characteristics
of each species of apple, also of the principles of morphology
concerning the reproductive parts of the apple blossom, and
of the principles of genetics, that concern the genes of the
different species of apples and techniques for their improve-

ment. Whereas the farmer, on the level of belief, gains his beliefs about the change of the seasons by scanning the autumn sky and by observing the thickness of the furry coats on forest animals, the astronomer, on the level of intellect or rational understanding, distinguishes the seasons by a set of true concepts of the earth, sun, and the planets. And by precise and certain mathematical measurements of the motions of the earth in relation to the sun, the astronomer can calculate the changing of the seasons within seconds of time for any specific place on the planet.

Rational Understanding or Intellect

The change from the knowledge of the traditional, unscientific farmer to the scientific botanist or to the mathematical science of the astronomer—this is the change we have brought about by ascending from belief to rational understanding. And in making this ascent to the third level of the ladder of knowledge, we have come now to grasp the significance of the divided line. For on the third level, on which we have now arrived, we have crossed over the major division of the line of knowledge—we have entered the intelligible world, we have left the cave of everyday beliefs and the lowly level of artistic fantasy and have struggled upward into the light of the sun. We have left behind the concrete objects of the visible world, the everyday objects of the prisoners in the cave.

But what kind of objects are we ascending to in the light of the sun? What objects do we know by intellect when we cross over the line into the intelligible world? Plato's answer is that the objects which we know by intellect or rational understanding on the third level of knowledge are the true concepts to which we have already made reference in contrast to the objects of belief. We have already noted that whereas *the objects of perception* are concrete, *the objects of intellect* are abstract; whereas the objects of perception are particular things, the objects of intellect are general or universal concepts; and whereas the objects of perception are changeable, in process, in Heraclitian flux, the objects of intellect are unchanging, in Parmenedian eternal immutability.

Theory of Forms

Plato has a special name for such concepts: forms or ideas. But how do such concepts give us true knowledge? What is their relation to the concrete objects of perception? How many such concepts are there? How can we know them? How can we prove that they are eternally true? In asking these questions we have come face-to-face with Plato's famous theory of ideas or forms—his most creative and influential philosophical contribution and the central theme of his entire philosophy. Since we have crossed over into the intelligible world, whose objects are the forms, let us pause now before ascending to the highest levels of the divided line and examine the Platonic theory of forms.

For Plato, concepts such as the concept of a circle, a triangle, beauty, justice, as well as the concepts that make up our everyday vocabulary, such as house, yellow, man, have two crucial functions: The first of these functions is that they make it possible for us to know the actual world of things as well as the objects of mathematics, the sciences, and philosophy. Their second function is that they enable us to evaluate and criticize all these objects.

First, how do abstract concepts enable us to have knowledge of all objects, the objects both of the visible world, and of the intelligible world? Plato's point is that to think or to communicate at all requires the use of concepts. Concepts are the means by which the universe is made intelligible. The simplest statement—"there is a man"—uses the concept man; "there is an apple" uses the concept apple. Each concept, such as man or apple, refers to the qualities which a group of particular things—every Tom, Dick, and Harry, or every McIntosh and Baldwin—share. And it is only because we all know what qualities the concept man refers to that we are able to talk about a particular man, John Jones. But if there were not an objective, universal, and immutable set of qualities which the concept man designates, and if instead each person had a purely personal opinion as to the qualities which the concept man refers to, communication would be impossible. We would never know what anyone else meant when he or she used the word man—it could be what someone else would call a toad. (Here we can see that Plato's complex theory of forms is derived from Socrates's simple theory of universally true definitions.)

Now we can define an idea or form for Plato: Forms are the eternal and immutable, absolutely true definitions of concepts. The form triangle is the set of all those qualities which define the concept triangle. These are also the common qualities shared by the entire class of particular triangles, that is, by all the particular triangles that ever have been or will be constructed (for example, the quality that the sum of the internal angles of a triangle equals 180 degrees). The objective, universal, and immutable qualities which define our concepts such as justice, or man, are what Plato means by a form. He sometimes speaks of the forms as essences, meaning that they constitute the essence or essential qualities of particular things.)

We can now understand that the *forms or ideas* (both words are used in the translation of the Greek word *ideai*) are not *mere* ideas for Plato, they are not subjective, they are not merely mental entities confined to human minds. By "idea" we ordinarily mean any particular thing we think of, something within consciousness, or something private to my mind. But Plato's views of forms or ideas run completely counter to the bias of the person on the level of belief, who thinks that only what is visible and tangible is real. Plato's view is just the contrary of this. The forms are no mere ideas or mental entities for Plato. Of all the components that make up reality, the forms have the greatest claim to reality, are the most real. The forms are real, independently existing entities; they are eternal, immutable, intelligible objects in the intelligible world. They are the essential substance of any object, of whatever is real enough to be known on any level. Actual particular things of the visible world are *knowable* only insofar as we can name or identify them by a form, as a man or an apple, that is, as members of a class of things which share the same form, the same set of defining qualities. Particular things, such as men or apples, are *real* only to the extent that they measure up to, "copy," "partake of," or embody the eternal reality and truth of the form.

Plato's philosophy uses the metaphor of shadow and substance over and over again, as we have seen. Concrete, particular, changing objects are the shadow; the forms are the substance. Moreover, Plato specifies the shadow-substance relation of the things of the visible world to the forms of the intelligible world by referring to the concrete objects of the visible world as imperfect "copies" of the forms which they "partake" of.

We can see now how it is that the forms make true knowledge possible. As we have already discovered, *true knowledge* must meet two requirements: (1) *it must be immutable, unchanging, and unchangeable*; and (2) *it must be about what is real*. Knowledge based upon sense perception at the level of belief was, we found out, neither unchanging, because of its insecurity, nor about the real, since it was knowledge about the flux. By contrast, knowledge based upon the forms will be immutable and unchanging, since the forms are immutable. And it will be knowledge of the real, since the forms constitute true reality.

And now briefly to examine the second function of the forms, their evaluative and critical function. The pure and eternal forms establish the objective, universal, and immutable qualities which define our concepts. By the same token they establish standards or ideals by which to evaluate the world of things. In the world of flux, things are always in a state of change, they are coming into existence or passing away, and the qualities of a form—for example, apple—are very imperfectly copied in a concrete, worm-holed, rotting apple. Similarly, no actual lines that we can draw will meet the standard of the form equality: no two lines in the visible world are perfectly equal. Nothing in the visible world is ever perfect in its kind—only the pure, intelligible, immutable forms which establish the qualities defining the specific concepts man, justice, circle—are perfect. As we shall see, Plato will make his most striking use of the evaluative or normative function of the forms with regard to the ethical and political forms of goodness and justice. Whereas to most of us, as to the Sophists, the concept of justice is relative, in Plato's theory of forms the form of justice is, like all other forms, immutable and eternal. Would any contemporary political party or political philosophy accept this?

And now to return to the ladder of knowledge. The third level of knowledge is, as we have already seen, the level of rational understanding or intellect. Plato is here describing the kind of knowledge which characterizes mathematics and natural sciences. The objects of the mathematician's knowledge are forms, such as forms of triangles, circles, and other mathematical objects. These forms are known by the mathematician's rational understanding or intellect, and they are objective, universal, and immutable. These forms are unchanging and eternal. These forms do not vary with the changes of the visible world. They are not relative to the city in which triangles or circles are thought about, nor are they relative to the kind of personality which is thinking about them. Whatever city a Sophist might travel to or from, and whatever his personality or the personality of his client, π is a constant and the area of a circle is still and always πr^2.

But the mathematician's knowledge has deficiencies. It is still tied to the visible world by its use of diagrams in the proofs of geometry, the well-known figures like angles, triangles, circles, parallelograms. A second limitation of knowledge at this level is that it does not examine or prove its own assumptions and thus remains hypothetical, or conditioned, rather than being unconditioned—based upon first principles which are proven to be true. A third limitation is that the various mathematical forms are uncoordinated, their relation to one another or to other forms is unexamined. Like mathematics, natural sciences have as their objects the forms with which these sciences are concerned, e.g., the forms of air, water, animals, stars. And although the natural sciences, like mathematics, lie above the main division between knowledge and opinion, on the divided line of knowledge, and provide knowledge of the forms, both mathematics and science are limited in three respects: (1) they rest upon unexamined first principles; (2) they are tied to instances, particulars, examples, from the visible world; and (3) they are piecemeal, fragmentary, since they fail to show the coordination of the forms which are their objects.

Reason

We ascend now to reason, the fourth and highest level of knowledge. On this level the mind uses the method of dialectic, which in this context means the science which studies the forms. "We place dialectic," Plato says, "on top of our other studies like a coping-stone; . . . no other study could rightly be put above this." (*Republic*, 534c.) Dialectic is the crowning science of all sciences. Here the true philosopher has come into his own realm. He moves toward knowledge of the forms by the activity of his reason and through the use of dialectic as his method, the method of analyzing the essences or forms of all things in the universe, and seeing their relationship to one another.

In the dialogue called the *Symposium* Plato shows that the

philosopher moves toward the eternal forms out of the power of Eros, love, desire, which leads him from the love of a beautiful body to the love of all beautiful things, and then to the love of the beauty of the mind as greater than the beauty of the body. "Drawing towards and contemplating the vast sea of beauty, . . . at last the vision is revealed to him of a single science, which is the science of beauty everywhere." So in the *Republic* the philosopher uses dialectic to take up the unfinished task of the third level, and (1) establishes true first principles for mathematics and the sciences, (2) without employing diagrams or particular things from the visible world; (3) dialectic coordinates the forms and unifies fragmentary, isolated, unrelated sciences and mathematics into a single totality.

Dialectic identifies the entire range and variety of forms— from forms of artifacts such as beds and chairs; lowly things such as apples and dogs; relations such as equality and similarity; values such as beauty and goodness and justice. By the power of dialectic the philosopher not only identifies all these forms and establishes their truth, but also moves toward organizing the forms into a single structured order of truth and value. The forms tend to constitute a hierarchical structure, a pyramid, from the many least universal to the few most universal, from the most concrete to the most abstract; from the forms of inanimate physical things to the Idea of the Good.

How is this knowledge possible? How does the philosopher attain the knowledge which dialectic yields? The philosopher's ascent is made possible by the love of truth, which enables him finally to reach the highest reality, the supreme form, the Idea of the Good, the ultimate aim of the soul. The Idea of the Good is the end or fulfillment or purpose for which all things exist, and thus it alone gives intelligibility, truth, and goodness to all the other forms, which are dependent upon it, and it alone provides their coordination and unity. Seen in the light of the Idea of the Good, the plurality of the many forms becomes the unity of total reality.

Plato compares the Idea of the Good to the sun. As the light of the sun makes the concrete things of the world visible and is the source of their life, growth, and value so the Idea of the Good gives truth which makes the forms intelligible and is the source of their being and goodness. Plato says of the Idea of the Good that it is "The universal author of all things beautiful and right, parent of light and of the lord of light in this world, and the source of truth and reason in the other." And again he says, "The good is not essence but far exceeds essence in dignity and power."

In the Idea of the Good, Plato has given expression to a vision of an absolute source of truth and goodness. The Idea of the Good is the source of the intelligibility, truth, and value of all the other ideas or forms; the Idea of the Good is the source of the world's moral purpose. With the ascent to the Idea of the Good, to an absolute one of truth and goodness, Plato prepared the way for the Christian God. Like the God of Christianity, the Idea of the Good is the supreme value, it is the source of all other value. The Idea of the Good is Plato's conception of the absolute, the perfect principle of all reality, truth, and value. For two thousand years, when Christians thought of God they envisioned the divided line and the ascent out of the cave through the power of reason and the power of love to Plato's Idea of the Good.

4

THE TRIPARTITE SOUL

In the second book of the *Republic*, Plato describes Glaucon as saying to Socrates:

> The universal voice of mankind is always declaring that justice and virtue are honorable but full of grief and hardship; and that the pleasures of vice and injustice are easy to attain and are only condemned by law and opinion.

That the just and righteous suffer and the wicked prosper is the age-old complaint of the human race. In the Book of Job in the Bible, Job—whom the Lord Himself described as a "perfect and an upright man, one that feareth God and escheweth evil" (Job 1:8)—cries out to God in his suffering, "Thou knowest that I am not wicked." (Job 10:7.) Yet the sufferings of Job were terrible. "Wherefore," Job asks of God, "do the wicked live, become old, yea are mighty in power?" (Job 21:7.)

What will be Plato's answer to this challenge, made throughout the ages? We know that he will rise to the defense of justice, but what does he mean by justice and how good is his answer to the complaint that the life of the person who seeks to live by justice and virtue is rewarded by grief and hardship? His answer comes from his theory of forms, his central theory.

The Theory of Forms and Ethics. We have seen something of the personal problems of Plato the human being; we have seen the social and political situation in which Plato the philosopher developed his philosophy—the great war with Sparta and the bitter civil war within Athens between aristocracy and democracy. And we have seen also the philosophic

43

problems and scientific knowledge and problems which were the sources upon which he drew for his own views—the Socratic philosophy, the warring philosophies of Heraclitus and Parmenides, and the challenging, taunting skepticism and relativism of the Sophists. A generation older than Heraclitus, the mathematician-philosopher Pythagoras was the source of Plato's view of mathematics as the supreme example of true knowledge; the ideal life as the life of reason; harmony as the ideal for the human soul; and the theory of three types of human beings. (See below.) We have seen the shape which Plato gave to these various elements: his two-level view of reality, divided between the sensible world of things that change and the intelligible world of permanence. We have seen the divided line of knowledge of reality, the stages of knowledge through which the mind ascends from the two lower stages of opinion to the two higher stages of knowledge, in which what is known is the world of true reality, the world of unchanging and indestructible forms, the world in which everything that can be named, everything for which there is a concept, is represented by its eternal form.

The theory of forms refuted both the Sophists' skepticism about whether true knowledge is possible and their insistence that all standards of justice and morality are merely relative to time, place, social group, or even to the individual. In opposition to their skepticism about the possibility of knowledge, as we have seen, Plato pointed to the knowledge of the eternal forms—triangle, circle, angle—which is provided by geometry, a knowledge which is absolutely certain. In the same way, Plato argues, the perfect forms defining our concepts of natural objects such as man, animals, air, fire, and water are knowable by training in science and dialectic on the topmost rungs of the ladder of knowledge.

Moral Forms. Spartans, the Sophists argued, are committed to the standards of authoritarianism and militarism; Athenians, to the standards of democracy. In opposition of the Sophists' relativism, Plato argues that moral forms, such as courage and justice, are knowable with absolute certainty, exactly as the forms of arithmetic, geometry, or astronomy, as circles and planets are known, by sufficient education and training. Plato argues that the forms of courage and justice, like the forms of the triangle, or circle, are eternal and unchanging, and they are absolute standards by which actions, persons, and institutions in the visible world may be judged.

For example, the justice of ancient Sparta and Athens or the current justice of the Soviet Union, China, and the United States may be judged by the absolute, universal, and eternally true form of justice.

Cultural Relativism. Notice what is at stake here. The Sophists may again be seen to represent a position much more widely held in our own time than is the position held by Plato. The Sophists are very close to the contemporary viewpoint of cultural relativism. Cultural relativists argue that every society, every primitive tribe and advanced civilization, must be seen to be unique, one of a kind, each an organic totality having its own unique history and language, its own institutions of law, education, family, production and trade, religion. It follows, then, that no outside standards can be used to evaluate any society.

Ethical Relativism. As is frequently the case, the Sophists combined with their cultural relativism the position of ethical relativism, the view that moral concepts vary fundamentally with culture, history, or the individual person and that a universal or absolute ethics is impossible. Accordingly, no absolute standards for societies exist, and since none exists, none is available to evalute them. Then it also follows that no society can be evaluated or compared with any other with respect to meeting standards of liberty, physical health, mental health, education, the quality and extent of cruelty practiced, satisfaction of felt needs, distribution of wealth, democratic participation in decision making. For the Sophists and for present-day cultural and ethical relativists, there are no universal standards for any of these issues, and therefore no society can be judged better or worse than another for its performance on any of them. Athens is therefore no better than Sparta, but only different, the product of a different set of circumstances. Each culture evolved in its own way in its own region in its own time. This point of view is appealing for its tolerance of every kind of society. It is also appealing for not being "judgmental," for not "sitting in judgment" of other groups of persons, as some of its defenders like to say.

But there are obvious drawbacks to cultural and ethical relativism. The principal drawback was dramatically exposed, "writ large," as Plato would say, when the cultural and ethical relativists of the United States had to face the rise of Nazi Germany and the hideous cruelties of its work camps and extermination camps in which millions of human beings were tortured and murdered. But according to the relativist position, no judgment could be passed on the Nazis, no external, universal, or absolute standard could be applied to this unique culture, which had evolved in its own way with its own standards and values. But in opposition to cultural and ethical relativism, the voice of humanity cried out in judgment against the Nazis that this was a culture which had sunk to the depths of evil and had brought hell to earth. Two thousand years ago, Plato was attacking the Sophists for being cultural and ethical relativists, for failing to recognize that human beings share universal human standards, such as that of justice and human rights, and that they have a moral responsibility to judge, to speak out wherever the universal and absolute standards of justice are denied, violated, or distorted.

The Form of Justice. The case for Plato against the Sophists appears to be won by this argument, which shows the implications of the relativists' denial of the possibility of universal and objective ethical standards. But questions remain: What does Plato discover the form of justice to be? What is justice? Is the form of justice knowable with absolute certainty as is the form triangle? This of course is the dynamic center of the entire *Republic*. The problem of justice, of the truly just government, was present in Plato's consciousness, as we have seen, from his childhood. The long war with Sparta had raised the question of justice as between democratic Athens and authoritarian Sparta. And the last blow— the Athenian government's putting Socrates to death—could this be endured as justice? Long before he formulated it in the *Republic*, Plato was committed to rejecting democracy and to holding the view that not until philosophers became kings, or kings became philosophers, would a society based upon justice be possible.

Justice: *Republic,* Book One

But this leaves the question, what is the eternal and unchanging and absolutely true form or idea of justice? The philosopher-king must rule guided by the form of justice. Notice that Plato introduces the idea of justice in the very first book of the *Republic*. Some Plato scholars think that Plato may originally have written Book I of the *Republic* as a short, complete dialogue on the concept of justice and then later decided to use it as the introduction to the *Republic*, his second-longest dialogue, which gives an account of his quest for the form of justice.

In Book I Plato sets out to show what is wrong with various commonly held beliefs about justice, and especially to refute the Sophists' view of justice. Four views of justice are given. First presented is the view of Cephalus, the elderly, conventional, decent businessman, who when asked by Socrates, What is justice? replies from the perspective of the businessman reflecting upon justice in the daily transactions in the business world. Justice, says Cephalus, is speaking the truth and paying one's debts. Cephalus's statement represents a simple version of the creed of the businessman, to speak the truth about your merchandise to your customers and pay your debts to your suppliers of inventory. Socrates gleefully demolishes this definition by the familiar device of Socratic method, the counterexample, the example which the proffered definition does not fit. Would it be just for you to pay your debt to a madman if you owed him a weapon which he gave you at a time when he was sane? Would it be just, Socrates presses Cephalus, to tell the insane man where he could find his enemy in order to kill him with the weapon you repaid? Cephalus is shown to be far down the ladder of knowledge from a knowledge of the form justice. He is on the level of belief, of common sense, of the babble in the cave.

The second definition of the form justice is elicited by Socrates from Cephalus's son Polemarchus, who is one of the group of wealthy young men who gather about Socrates. Polemarchus offers the view that justice is "giving every man his due," being a friend to your friends and an enemy to your enemies. Socrates demolishes Polemarchus's definition of justice by pointing out that surely a just man would not favor a friend unless the friend were engaged in honorable action, nor would a just man do harm to anyone, even to an enemy.

And so the path is cleared for Thrasymachus, the Sophist, who is defiant of all conventional views of justice, such as being honorable in business or helping friends and hurting enemies. Thrasymachus flatly denies that the laws of the state or the morality of individual persons have anything to do with justice. What the strong wish is, he says, becomes law. As for the laws of any state, their justice is actually nothing but the interests of the ruler, the interests of the stronger. And as for the morality of the individual man, in abiding by the laws of his society he is merely conforming in blind and docile obedience to the laws that protect the powerful. Laws serve the strong, Thrasymachus argues; might makes right. Conforming to the laws is the morality of the weak, who do not recognize that the laws do not serve them, and are not in their own interest, but serve only the ruler. Here Thrasymachus is expressing a crude version of Karl Marx's theory of the false consciousness of the worker, the proletarian man. Neither Thrasymachus's docile man nor Marx's proletarian man sees that the laws of his society are exclusively in the interest of the ruling class—and that they are not only not in his own interest but in fact exploit him. Socrates next disposes of Thrasymachus's claim that "might makes right"—a form of ethical relativism which holds that the morally right is established by and is relative to the more powerful party in any situation. Socrates argues that Thrasymachus's position implies that the ruler is infallible in always achieving his own gratification. But if he makes a mistake and rules in a way that benefits his subjects, is he then just? Socrates also argues that if the ruler is a real craftsman in ruling, he will seek to benefit his subjects, not himself. Socrates also attempts to compare the ruler to the physician who seeks to benefit the human body primarily, although secondarily he takes a fee. So a ruler seeks to benefit his subjects first, himself second.

But Thrasymachus is not silenced. He is not satisfied that Socrates has succeeded in refuting his views. At the end of Book I Socrates is still trying to defend justice as what the wise ruler and the wise man practice, but what the form of justice is, how to define justice, still eludes him. However, with enormous skill in the literary art of the turnabout, the ironic reversal, Plato will show us later (beginning with Book IV) that it was Polemarchus who had the key to the form justice, that he spoke "better than he knew"; and that in some sense justice is, as he said, giving every man his due. But in what sense was the young Polemarchus right? How does Plato's theory of forms provide the definition of the concept of justice?

Plato's theory of forms is a view of all kinds of existences, physical, animalian, human, each kind with its own form or essence which defines and sets the standard for its nature. For Plato, any kind of being, a dog, a man, has virtue, is just or excellent insofar as it functions according to its nature, according to the standard set by its form. In order to know what is virtuous or just or excellent or right for man, we must therefore find out what is the form, idea, or essence of man.

The Tripartite Soul

With the guidance of Plato we discover that man does not have a simple essence or form, but that it is instead constituted by several elements in accordance with his various natural capacities or functions. The specific function which man has, which distinguishes him from other living things, is his power to use language and to reason. His other two elements are his bodily appetites, desires, needs; and a spirited element, expressed in emotional drives such as anger, aggression, ambition, pride, protectiveness, honor, loyalty, courage.

Of these three elements it is the capacity to use language and to reason which is of greatest importance in the essence of man and which therefore ranks supreme. The three elements of the form man fall into a natural hierarchy, a structure in which the rational element is the highest in power, in the capacity for truth, and in value. The bodily appetites are at the bottom level of the hierarchy, and the intermediate level is occupied by the spirited element. Here we have the outline of what is known as Plato's tripartite theory of the self or the soul or psyche or personality.

Justice in the Soul. Justice or virtue or excellence for a man, as for all other things, consists in functioning in accordance with his form or essence. Justice or virtue for a human being is thus functioning in accordance with an essence which Plato has discovered to consist of three distinct elements which form a hierarchical structure from the lowest (bodily appetites) to the highest (reason).

In Book IV, (443–44) Plato draws out this theory of the tripartite character of the human soul. Implicit in Plato's account of the three elements which together constitute the human soul is the insight that Plato has into psychological conflict. Here he has gone far beyond Socrates's doctrine that virtue is knowledge, that if we truly know the good we will act in accordance with it. What Plato sees instead is that although reason may know the good, the element of reason runs into conflict with the bodily desires. In the familiar scenario of the Hollywood Western, the cowboy in the saloon is pulled in one direction by his desires for the pretty waitress and for the alcoholic beverages she is luring him into drinking. But his reason pulls him in the opposite direction by telling him that he is getting into serious trouble.

Justice and Happiness. Since human beings have a tripartite soul, says Plato, the highest good for humans cannot be pleasure, since pleasure would be the goal of satisfying only the bodily appetites, which constitute only one of the three elements of the soul. The human being's highest good must be the sense of well-being or happiness which comes from functioning in accordance with his or her nature, from fulfilling the needs of all three elements which make up what it is to be a person. Only the fulfilling of all three needs, with reason governing the spirited element and the bodily appetites, can satisfy the complex nature of a human being. And when each element of the self functions in this way, in accordance with its appropriate role in the structured self, the life of such a person may be said to be just and he experiences this justice of the soul, this integration of his personality as well-being or happiness.

Morality, Plato is telling us, consists in knowing and maintaining the harmony and balance between the rational and the irrational elements of the soul. This balance or harmony in the soul is the justice of the soul, the soul's morality or virtue or excellence, and its product is happiness. But since this harmony or balance must be known in order to be achieved—it does not happen automatically—the Socratic doctrine that virtue consists in knowledge is in a limited degree true for Plato, in the sense that the harmony of the three elements, and the resultant well-being and happiness, come from knowledge, the knowledge of the complex form of human nature.

The Soul as Organism. Plato thought of the self or soul not merely as a hierarchical order or structure but as an organism. In a healthy living organism, the parts are in harmonious interdependence. Each part has a function which serves the whole organism, and the various parts are in a hierarchical order of importance to the life of the organism, with the heart and liver, for example, having essential functions which the appendix does not. The dysfunctions or malfunctions of any part of the organism have adverse effects upon the rest. So in the soul, the dysfunction of any of the three elements will drain away its sense of well-being. For Plato it is clear that neither a life devoted exclusively to bodily pleasures nor a life devoted ascetically to the denial of bodily pleasures would be functional.

Conflict Within the Soul. Moreover, Plato is very well aware of how much capacity there is in the human soul for inner conflict, for ill health and misery. Reason, the drive or need to reach the truth of the forms and the Idea of the Good, come into conflict with the bodily appetites, since human nature desires knowledge of the forms but also struggles against this knowledge. While the irrational appetites pull us toward their gratification, reason acts as an "inhibiting principle," as Plato tells us in paragraphs 434–436. The third and intermediate element, the high-spirited part of the self, consisting of such emotional drives as anger, ambition, courage, pride, aggression, serves as mediator of conflicts between the other two elements; it is capable of acting on behalf of either reason or the appetites.

The key to mental health and to morality and justice is the proper integration of these potentially conflicting parts of the self. The problems that reason has in mastering the appetites and the spirited element are illustrated unforgettably by Plato in another dialogue, the *Phaedrus*, in which he presents the figure of a man in a chariot, driving two horses. One horse (the spirited element) is good, needs no touch of the whip and spur, is guided simply by the charioteer's voice. The other horse (the bodily appetites) is bad, uncontrollable by the whip or spur, and keeps trying to plunge off the path and run away. The charioteer (reason) is pulling at the two horses, each rushing in different directions. Plato here portrays the three conflicting elements of personality and their potential for producing disorder, extreme conflict, and breakdown. And in another section of the *Republic*, Plato compares the element of reason to a man, the spirited element to a lion, and the bodily appetites to a many-headed dragon. The problem of achieving integration in the soul is this: how to persuade the lion to help the man to keep the dragon in check.

In the just, moral, or sane personality, reason rules, and when it is thus fulfilling its function as master of the other elements of the soul, reason exhibits its proper virtue, which is *wisdom*. In the same way, when the spirited element performs its aggressive, ambitious and heroic functions within the limits set by the structure of the soul, it exhibits its proper virtue, which is *courage*. One can be courageous in love, in war, and in athletic or business or intellectual competition. And finally, when the appetites perform their own functions appropriately, they exhibit their characteristic virtue, which is *temperance*, keeping bodily satisfactions within bounds or limits.

The Theory of the Three Types of Souls. Although all human beings are constituted of these three elements, humans vary according to which element is dominant in their personalities. Not all personalities are dominated by reason. Drawing upon Pythagoras's theory of three types of men, Plato develops the theory that there are three kinds of souls or personalities. Each is dominated by a different element, the fulfilment of which is its goal. There is the type of soul which is dominated by reason and whose desire is for truth and wisdom; there is the type of man who is dominated by the spirited element and who lives only for success and public acclaim; and there is the type of man whose personality is dominated by the bodily appetites, who lives only for money and material gain.

Freud's Tripartite Theory of Personality. The most famous tripartite theory of personality to appear after Plato is that of Sigmund Freud, whose famous id, ego, and superego constitute a tripartite structure of personality. As with Plato, Freud's tripartite theory stresses the necessity of harmonious interdependence of parts for the good of the whole, but also the potential for much conflict between the elements. The id is the seat of the sexual and aggressive instincts as well as of the self-preservative instincts; the superego is the seat of conscience, which places harsh restrictions upon the gratifications of the instincts; ego is the seat of intelligence, which mediates between the id's unrealistic demands for immediate gratification and the punitive superego's constraints upon them.

Plato's concept of the bodily appetites may be compared with Freud's concept of the id, which is, however, a very much more complex concept. Moreover, there are very basic differences between the two tripartite theories. Freud demotes aggression, a part of Plato's spirited element, to one of the drives or instincts. Plato had given aggression a more honorable status as a spirited element, thus revealing the importance of war in the Greek world and the honorable status which Athenians gave to warriors. Other big differences are that Freud breaks reason into two parts, ego and superego. He gave to ego reason's functions of perception and intelligence. He gave to superego reason's functions of moral judgments and knowledge of the good. Both changes entail the demotion of reason. The element of reason which Freud incorporates in the ego is demoted from providing knowledge of the eternal forms, to mere scientific understanding without knowledge of the forms. The element of reason which Freud incorporated in the superego is demoted from providing knowledge of the moral forms and of the Idea of the Good to the mere rationalizing of psychological instincts and defense mechanisms. Surely Freud knew Plato's tripartite theory—and knew it so well that on two occasions he used Plato's own figure of the unruly, uncontrollable horse. In relation to the id, the seat of sexual and aggressive desires according to Freud, the ego, the seat of reason, is like a man on horseback who has to hold in check the superior strength of the horse. And now we turn to Plato's political philosophy where, as he says, the form of justice is written in large letters. We turn from justice in the soul to justice in the state.

5

THE IDEAL STATE

Ethics: The Good Life

Why not live the playboy life, the life of gratifying the bodily appetites, the hedonistic life in which pleasure is pursued as the highest good, the life of pleasurable indulgences in food and drink and sex and drugs and sleep and all the titillations of the body that we can experience?

Plato answers this question over and over again in subtly different ways. His points are always: (1) Pleasure is not the highest good for humans. (2) If you pursue pleasure as the highest good, as your moral end, it will destroy you. Why is pleasure, the gratification of the bodily appetites, not the highest good for human beings? Because, says Plato, the highest good for anything, human or nonhuman, consists in fulfilling its own nature, in living up to its own form or essence. Moral ideals do not consist in going against my nature, but rather in fulfilling my nature, in realizing my capacities and powers as a human being.

And my nature as a human being does not consist solely in my bodily appetites, but also in the other two parts of the tripartite self—in my spirited element of ambitious and courageous, self-assertive and altruistic, drives and also in my powers of speech and reason. My highest good requires that I fulfill all three parts of myself, and not fulfill what only one part of me, my bodily appetites, requires. Moreover, my highest good will be in fulfilling the three elements of my own nature in accordance with their proper harmony or order. Their proper order is a hierarchy, with reason the highest, most worthy element, the bodily elements the lowest, and the spirited drives intermediate between them. "The just man," says Plato, "does not allow the several elements in his soul to usurp one another's functions." On the contrary, Plato continues in a famous line, "he sets his house in order," so that the bodily appetites do not take over the ruling position that reason should have. The just or moral person seeks by self-knowledge and self-mastery to satisfy in appropriate order all three elements of his nature.

The Harmony of the Soul. The three parts of the self, from the highest to the lowest together with the intermediate, form a harmony, like the highest and lowest and intermediate notes in a musical chord; a harmony, says Plato, "like the terms in the proportions of a musical scale." As in the case of the theory of three kinds of men, Plato is drawing upon the mathematician-philosopher Pythagoras here in making an analogy between the harmony of the soul and the harmony of mathematical proportions and the harmony of a musical chord. And the result of bringing the parts of the self into their proper harmony is that this person "is at peace with himself," because he has fulfilled his own nature. The good life is the harmoniously balanced life, the life which satisfies in proper order the needs of the three parts of the self. This is the Good Life, the life of virtue and excellence for a human being, and it offers no mere pleasures of the palate or of the sex organs—it offers human happiness, the sense of well-being of the whole person. The Good Life is not the life of the early Christian denial of the body and contempt of the flesh. The body must be satisfied and be healthy, strong, and beautiful. Nor is the Good Life the celebration of the Christian denial of the aggressive drives. Ambition, self-assertion, loyalty—these and other spirited energies must drive the self to activity and achievement, but must be directed and controlled by reason. Finally, the Good Life, as Plato describes it, is sometimes called the Life of Reason, but Plato does not mean that the Good Life is that of the narrow, overintellectualized person, lacking in strong drives and without a strong, healthy body. The Good Life is not the life of reason alone, but that of the dominance of reason over the spirited energies and the bodily appetites. And thus to the question Why not live the life of pleasure? Plato answers with his own formulation of the Greek ideal of the development of human beings who are excellent in mind, body, and character. It is a commonplace to say that for two and a half millennia the Western world has loved and idealized the ancient civilization of Athens. Perhaps, above all, we have been drawn to the Greek ideal of the good life and to Plato's version of the Good Life as the life of balanced fulfillment of our complex human nature, the life of healthy and energetic, courageous and honorable, intelligent and wise, happiness under the sun, the symbol of the Idea of the Good, the perfect principle of truth and beauty and goodness.

Plato's Ethics: Summary. This, then, is Plato's moral philosophy or ethics. Moral philosophy or ethics may be defined as the branch of philosophy which studies the nature of good and evil, right and wrong, duty and obligation. It asks questions such as, Is there a highest good, an absolute good for human beings or, as the Sophists argued, Are all goods relative to time and place, to history and to culture? Is the highest moral good the achieving of happiness or is it the performing of one's duty? Is the good knowable? Is the good rational, or is it merely the voice of the spirited and appetitive passions? What is the meaning of right and wrong actions? We have seen that Plato does indeed affirm a highest good for man, and that it is absolute, eternal, and immutable; and it is knowable and rational. For Plato's ethics what, then, is the highest good? For Plato, the highest good for human beings is the happiness or well-being which comes from the fulfillment of the three parts of the soul under the rule of reason. For Plato's ethics, what is virtue? Virtue, or the right conduct of life, is action which flows from knowledge, knowledge of the tripartite soul, the forms, and the Idea of the Good. Only the few have such knowledge and they should control the conduct of the other members of society. The heart of Plato's ethics is still Socrates's orginal view that virtue is knowledge.

Political Philosophy

Plato tells us that if we want to have a clearer picture of morality for the individual person, we must turn to the state, where, he says, it is "writ large" for us to see. Problems of the state form the topic to which the *Republic* is principally dedicated—the problems of political philosophy. Political philosophy is defined as the branch of philosophy which studies such problems as, What is the good society? What is justice? What is power and control and in whom ought they to be vested? What is the relation of subordination–superordination between the state and the individual? Does the state exist to serve the individual or does the individual exist to serve the state? Plato's political philosophy answers these questions by building upon his ethics, his moral philosophy. His moral philosophy has already established the form of justice in the human soul. The human individual is just or virtuous insofar as he or she lives in accordance with the harmonious structure of the three parts of the soul.

But what does justice in an individual person have to do with a city? Plato's answer is that human beings are naturally social animals, having a natural desire to live in communities. They depend upon society for their well-being and for their satisfaction in life. Cities and their governments are therefore just as natural as are human beings. Here Plato and the Greeks stand in sharp contrast to the Christian doctrine that the state is neither natural nor good, but is a necessary evil to control the greater evil which would result if human passions and violence ran rampant and unconstrained. And as we shall see, Plato's view of the state as natural and potentially good is also at odds with Karl Marx's view of the state as a dictatorship by the ruling class, exercised unjustly to exploit economically the other social classes and to prevent their development and freedom. But for Plato, the relatively small, closely knit city provides the natural setting for the life of man, the social animal. Whereas Christianity has traditionally stressed that the good life consists of the right relationship of the private, solitary individual to God, and has deemphasized the significance of social relationships, Plato and the Greeks believed that the good life is possible only in the good state. What, then, is the good state? What is justice in the state, which is the political organization or government of the city?

Justice in Man and in the State

A city, says Plato, is a man "writ large against the sky." The elements that make up a city correspond to the elements that constitute the individual human soul. And the justice or excellence or morality of the city is the same as it is for the individual. For Plato, unlike certain later political philosophers, there is not one morality for individuals and another for the state, which then would need pay no attention to the moral rules governing individuals. What, then, are the elements of the state that correspond to the elements of the tripartite soul? Like the tripartite individual human soul, every state of whatever type necessarily has three parts which are its three social classes—a producer class, a military class, and a governing or ruling class.

In the ideal city, the Republic which Socrates and his young disciples are designing, each of these three classes will perform a vital function on behalf of the organic totality which is the society. The producer class will provide themselves and the other two classes with the necessities of life—food, shelter, clothing, trade, and commerce. The producer class is made up of farmers, herdsmen, blacksmiths, fishermen, carpenters, shoemakers, weavers, laborers, merchants and retailers and bankers. The producer class corresponds to the appetitive element in the soul of the individual human being, as (see below) the guardians or rulers correspond to the element of reason; and as the auxiliary and military class, which aids and supplements the work of the guardians, corresponds to the spirited element.

Tripartite soul	Tripartite State
Reason	Guardians
Spirited element	Auxiliaries, Military
Bodily appetites	Producers

The members of the producer class will be drawn from that type of person in whom the bodily appetites are dominant and who lives for money. The members of the ruling class will be drawn from that type of man in whom reason is dominant and who lives only for truth. The auxiliary and military class will be drawn from that type of man in whom the spirited element is dominant and who lives for success in aggressive and courageous acts. Thus each class in the state is parallel to a part of the soul and its function. Also parallel to the hierarchical ordering of the parts of the tripartite soul is the hierarchical order of the three classes of the state. The ruling guardian class directs and controls the producer class. The military and auxiliary class, in close association with the guardians, is also under their direction and control. Strictly parallel to the justice or excellence of the soul, as the proper harmony, attunement, or order of its parts, is the justice of the state, in which each class performs its appropriate function harmoniously in a hierarchical structure under the rule of the most rational.

But why should the state be ruled by an elite group of the most rational? Plato's contempt for democracy and his reasons

for this contempt appear repeatedly throughout the *Republic*—
that the many lack the intelligence and knowledge needed for
governing; that they care only for money; that they are dominated by bodily appetites and by volatile and unpredictable
emotions; and that they are easily manipulated by demagogues.
All these characteristics of the masses make them unfit to
govern; yet democracy gives them the right to govern. Plato
expresses this thought most forcefully in the dialogue *Protagoras*, where he points out in everyday life, everyone, wise
and foolish, seeks out the advice of the wise specialist, the
expert, rather than the advice of the ignorant many. When
you are in ill health, says Plato, you go to the most competent
medical specialist you can find. You don't ask everyone you
meet on the street for advice, you don't take a vote among as
many people as possible to determine what your illness is or
what to do about it. Why is it, then, that with regard to the
problems of the body politic affecting the health of the state,
problems of the utmost political importance in domestic and
in foreign affairs, we consult the advice of the ignorant many?
Why is it, he asks,

> When we Athenians are met together in the assembly,
> and the matter in hand relates to building, the build-
> ers are summoned as advisers; when the question is
> one of ship-building, then the shipwrights . . . But
> when the question is an affair of state, then every-
> body is free to have a say—carpenter, tinker, cobbler,
> merchant, sea captain, rich and poor, high and low—
> anyone who likes gets up, and no one reproaches
> him, as in the former case, with not having learned
> . . . and yet giving advice.

Plato's point is that governing a society is a skill that
requires a specialized and intensive training not less but far
greater than the training of the shipbuilder, shoemaker, or
physician. What, then, is the training that is necessary for
those who would be capable of piloting effectively and wisely
the ship of state?

The Guardian Class: Selection and Education. Plato's answer to this is his theory of the selection and education of the
guardian or ruler class. How, first of all, are the members of
the guardian class to be selected? Membership in the ruling
class, the class of those individuals in whom reason is the

strongest element, is by natural level of intelligence. By nature, some human beings are equipped to be philosopher-rulers, some to be soldiers, some to be producers. Plato believed that heredity is the prime factor in intelligence and that for the most part, the children of the most intelligent will also be of the highest intelligence, and that the children of those who have the natural capacity only to be shoemakers will also have the natural capacity to be shoemakers. But since Plato was well aware of exceptions, Plato decided that the ranks of the guardian class, the elite class of the intelligent, must be open to the children of all classes and that through-out the Republic in the early years of child development all children must be kept under constant observation and testing in order to identify those children who are of sufficiently high intelligence to be trained for the guardian class.

The selection of the guardians, then, is from all classes by natural intellectual capacity. Women as well as men possess the natural capacity of intelligence to become members of the ruling class. Plato stands out in the history of Western philosophy as the first supporter (along with Socrates) of the intellectual equality of the sexes. Book V of the *Republic* has been hailed by the contemporary women's movement for its defense of the equality of the sexes. There is only one difference between men and women, Plato argues, and that is that males beget and women bear children. But this difference has no more to do with functioning in the political life of the city than the difference between being bald-headed or having hair. Women, like men, have the natural capacities which will fit some for the ruler class, some to be warriors and auxiliaries, some to be producers. Women in the Republic will therefore share in the life of all three classes.

How then shall the rulers be trained? Their training is by education and by service to the state. Education for those selected to be guardians begins with strictly censored music and literature for the mind and gymnastics for the strength and health of the body. They will then ascend on the divided line of knowledge to be trained in mathematics, astronomy, and other sciences, whose objects are in the intelligible world. Their mathematical education will not, however, be in "the spirit of merchants with a view to buying or selling," nor merely for the military uses of mathematics, but so that they may pass from knowing only the world of flux to knowledge of true being, from knowing the changing objects of the visible world to the eternal truths of the intelligible world.

By the age of thirty, those who have successfully come through a series of competitive examinations and proven themselves to have the intelligence, the strength and balance of character, and the bodily vigor and stamina will have completed their education on the third level of the divided line. Now for the last time, the group of candidates will again be weeded out, the ones remaining being eligible to advance to the study of dialectic, the highest level of knowledge, in which by reason alone the candidate for the guardian class will come to know the eternal truths which are the forms, each in itself, and all in their interrelationships and totality. Five years will be devoted to training in dialectic. Finally, he or she "attains at last the absolute good by intellectual vision, and therein reaches the limit of the intellectual world." At this point, when the candidates-in-training are thirty-five years old, they will be "sent down into the cave," says Plato, and compelled to hold any military or other post which the young are qualified to hold. The purpose of the return to the cave of political life from their years of study is to give them the experience of everyday politics, and to see how they handle various temptations. They will be required to spend fifteen years in this probationary period. At the age of fifty, those who have met this last test of intelligence and character will be admitted to the governing class, with the responsibility of governing themselves and all other classes, by the absolute truth which they have learned through their long education in knowledge and virtue. They will have become philosopher-kings.

What will their lives be like? It is a life so strenuously disciplined, so sternly self-denying, yet so totally dedicated to the truth and to the task, that no comparable training for rulership appears to exist in our present world or in the past, except in the case of a few religious orders. Both the guardian class and the military class are forbidden to possess any private property or any money. They must live, men and women, like soldiers in barracks, with common meals and sleeping quarters. Their food, clothing, and equipment will be provided by the producers. Their food must be simple and restricted to moderate quantities. They are to have no family life, in order to avoid any conflict between family loyalties and their loyalty to the state. While they are at the physical prime of life, their sexual gratification is restricted to officially

designated and infrequent occasions on which they are required to breed children to maintain the numbers of the
guardian class. These occasions Plato calls Sacred Marriages,
which are temporary unions for the sake of producing children.
These marriages are far too important to permit them to be
made on the basis of personal preference. Plato's plans for the
breeding of the rulers of the Republic are utopian beyond
anything foreseeable in our present society. He is thinking of
breeding humans as scientifically and with as much care as
his brother Glaucon breeds dogs or as we breed race horses
or prize cattle. Plato had none of the fears that many contemporary people express about using scientific knowledge of
genetics to produce humans of superior mental and physical
capacity. Since Plato's own theory of forms provided him with
an absolutely certain standard of human excellence in mind
and body and character, Plato planned the breeding of guardians who would possess these qualities. And so Socrates asks
Glaucon (*Republic* 459): "I see you keep sporting dogs at your
house . . . Do you breed from all indiscriminately? Are you
not careful to breed from the best as far as you can? . . . And
from those in their prime?" No less care will be devoted to
breeding the guardians of the Republic.

Who will mate with whom will be determined by the older
guardians and the best male guardians will be mated with the
best female guardians. But the participants in the Sacred
Marriages will not know that their mates have been selected
for them. To avoid their complaints, they will be told that the
mating is by lottery. This is a lie, but it is what Plato calls a
noble lie, a lie which is rationally justified for the good of the
state. The children who will be born from these matings will
be raised with exquisite care in a communal nursery. They
will not be permitted to form narrow exclusive attachments to
their natural parents, but will regard as their mothers and
fathers all the guardians who mated at the same Sacred
Marriage as their biological parents. Mentally defective or
physically deformed or defective infants born from these matings will be put away immediately to die in some unknown
place. Plato's bold treatment of genetic engineering and infan-
ticide for the defective figures prominently in the current
controversy on these issues.

The Life of the Producer Class. By contrast with the
severe discipline and asceticism under which the guardian
class lives, how easy the life of the producer class appears.

Except for governmental regulations imposed by the rulers, the lives of the producers follow the old familiar patterns of home and property, family and children, work and rest, recreation and the daily news. By nature the producers love money. The many, says Plato in a famous phrase, love "getting and spending"—as anyone can see who goes shopping on Saturdays, when after a week of working and getting the producer class in the United States does its spending, packing the stores downtown and swarming over the suburban shopping centers. Plato planned governmental regulation of "getting," the accumulation of wealth, in order to maintain economic moderation in the Republic. Plato is afraid that unless the accumulation of money is regulated, the cleverer producers will get richer and the rest poorer, and conflict would inevitably break out.

But the Republic makes the fewest demands for change upon the producer class. They alone of the three classes can keep gold and silver, live in nuclear-family units, work for the most part at their traditional occupations, are free in their sexual activities. Each member of the producer class will be educated by being taught a trade or profession—farming, banking, carpentry—according to his or her own capabilities and to the needs of the society, both of which will be determined by the guardians. Since they cannot grasp abstract concepts, education in the forms would be wasted on them. But they must be given another type of "education" as well, which calls into play governmental powers of propaganda and censorship.

In the plans for the Republic, Plato includes provision for governmental agencies of censorship and propaganda. The producer must be controlled by state propaganda cultivating loyalty, patriotism, work motivation, and social cohesion. The need for censorship of what must not exist in the Republic is as great, however, as the need for propaganda in order to bring into existence desired beliefs and attitudes. The task of the guardians is to safeguard all classes from the insidious attractions of the poets, dramatists, musicians, and painters. Fables, legends, stories about the gods, epic poems and tragedies, all require censorship. Plato is morally opposed to the poet Homer's portraying the gods as quarreling and vengeful and lying. He is also opposed to the portrayal of immorality by the dramatists, and to the slack and effeminate harmonies composed by musicians. "A young man," he says in Book II, "should not be allowed to hear at a play that he would be doing nothing surprising if he did the worst of wrongs" since the gods are said to do the same vicious things. Plato would surely see the frequency of television violence as having the same effect—communicating to the audience that there is nothing surprising about committing homicide, in fact, that it is quite commonplace, and so in a sense is acceptable. In the current debate over the influence of television violence on children, Plato would argue for censoring all violence, for adult viewing as well as for children, as destructive of the moral fiber of our republic. Plato offers two arguments for censoring violence: its frequent portrayal renders it commonplace, hence acceptable; its portrayal stimulates acts of violence.

Critics of Plato's *Republic* have accused it of being anti-democratic, which of course it is. Others have accused it of being communist, still others have called it fascist. Is Plato a totalitarian in his politics? Totalitarianism is a type of twentieth-century politics which cannot meaningfully be compared to the politics of the ancient Greek city-state. But there are certain resemblances. Like totalitarian governments, right-wing and left-wing, fascist and communist, Plato rejected individualism and democracy and argued for the subordination of the individual to the supremacy and power of the state. Like totalitarian governments, Plato denied individual rights, civil liberties, due process of the law; and he advocated government by an elite group, with state censorship, thought-control by propaganda, state control of the economy, the intrusion of the state into almost all areas of the private life. But Plato would have detested modern totalitarianism, just as he detested Thrasymachus's philosophy that might makes right. For Plato, there is only one justification for his regimented, absolutistic state—it is founded on true knowledge, on the eternally true essence of justice. Any other justification for government Plato would condemn as illegitimate—governments justified by power, race, wealth, aristocratic birth; glorification of a social class as in communism; or glorification of a particular leader as in fascism. Since Plato viewed the guardians of his ideal republic as having true knowledge of the essence of a good society and of a good human being, the state is entitled to absolute power in controlling the entire society and to complete responsibility for making its citizens virtuous. But isn't that what all absolutist governments and churches have always said—that their knowledge of the truth justifies their absolute control over everyone?

There are two challenges which must be made to Plato's Republic and to any other absolutist politics: (1) Are there, as Plato claims, absolutely true, eternal, and unchanging forms of justice, human nature, society, the good, in the same sense that it is absolutely true that a straight line is the shortest distance between two points? Has Plato proved this? Most moderns would disagree with him. (2) What is the guarantee that the rulers will not be corrupted by such absolute power? Who guards the guardians? What provisions are made in the Republic for checking on the policies and activities of the guardians and for removing them from office if necessary? All the Western democracies have such safeguards against the abuse of power, but no absolutist church or state and no totalitarian government has provided them. Plato, too, fails us here. Despite these and other problems, the *Republic* of Plato stands for all time as the original source of the rationalist tradition in Western civilization. Plato's Republic presents a philosophic vision of a realm of eternal truth, beauty, and goodness above the flux of changing opinion. It is Plato's vision that through the human love of truth and the power of human reason we may yet come to know the essence of all things and the Idea of Good itself, and with this knowledge design and construct an ideal society. This is the ancient and continuing promise of Plato's Republic.

SUGGESTIONS FOR FURTHER READING

PART ONE: PLATO

The Pre-Socratics:

Burnet, John. *Greek Philosophy: Thales to Plato*. London: Macmillan & Co., Ltd., 1956.

Cornford, F. M. *Before and After Socrates*. New York: Cambridge University Press, [1932] 1960.

Field, G. C. *Plato and His Contemporaries*. London: Methuen & Co., Ltd., 1948.

Kirk, G. S., and Raven, J. E. *The Pre-Socratic Philosophers*. Cambridge: Cambridge University Press, 1964.

Robinson, John Manley. *An Introduction to Early Greek Philosophy*. Boston: Houghton Mifflin Co., 1968.

Vlastos, Gregory ed. *The Philosophy of Socrates*. Garden City, New York: Doubleday-Anchor (Modern Studies in Philosophy), 1971.

Works of Plato:

The Great Dialogues of Plato, edited by E. H. Warmington and P. G. Rouse. New York: New American Library, 1963. Text adapted for television series. Paper.

The Collected Dialogues of Plato, edited by Edith Hamilton and Huntington Cairns. Princeton: Princeton University Press, 1961.

The Dialogues of Plato, translated with analysis and introductions by Benjamin Jowett. 4th ed., revised, 4 vols. Oxford: Oxford University Press, 1953.

Critical Studies:

Barker, Sir Ernest. *The Political Thought of Plato and Aristotle*. New York: Dover Publications, 1959.

Copleston, Frederick. *A History of Philosophy. Vol. 1, Greece and Rome*. (1944) Garden City, New York: Doubleday, 1962.

Demos, Raphael, *The Philosophy of Plato*. New York: Charles Scribner's Sons, 1939.

Gouldner, Alvin W. *Enter Plato: Classical Greece and the Origins of Social Theory*. New York: Basic Books, 1965.

Grube, G. M. A. *Plato's Thought*. Boston: Beacon Press, 1958.

Guthrie, W. K. C. *A History of Greek Philosophy. Vol. 4, Plato: The Man and His Dialogues, Earlier Period*. Cambridge: Cambridge University Press, 1975.

Nettleship, R. L. *Lectures on the Republic of Plato*. New York: St. Martin's Press, Inc., 1962.

Raven, J. E. *Plato's Thought in the Making*. Cambridge: Cambridge University Press, 1965.

Ross, Sir David. *Plato's Theory of Ideas*. London: Oxford at the Clarendon Press, 1951.

Shorey, Paul. *What Plato Said*. Chicago: University of Chicago Press, 1933.

Taylor, A. E. *Plato: The Man and His Work*. Cleveland: The World Publishing Company, [London, 1926] 1956.

Vlastos, Gregory, ed. *Plato: Metaphysics and Epistemology*. Garden City, New York: Doubleday-Anchor, 1971.

Vlastos, Gregory, ed. *Plato: Ethics, Politics and Philosophy of Art and Religion*. Garden City, New York: Doubleday-Anchor, 1971.

PART TWO
DESCARTES

6

HISTORICAL TRANSITION TO THE MODERN WORLD

Aristotle

A philosopher of comparative religions has spoken of the "Terror of History" in which all the achievements and aspirations of human beings are relentlessly and mercilessly wiped out and forgotten in the ongoing changes of history. We can feel the terror of history in the loss of the Greek civilization and its unique genius and zest for democracy, philosophy, the arts, mathematics, science, and the good life.

After Sparta's defeat of Athens at the end of the Peloponnesian War in 404 B.C., the Greek city-states became increasingly fragmented and fell into long years of conflict, until they were conquered by Philip of Macedon in 338 B.C. and subsequently absorbed by his son, Alexander, into the Macedonian Empire. Yet during these troubled years Athenian cultural and intellectual creativity continued: these were the years during which Plato wrote his dialogues and in which his great pupil Aristotle developed his own philosophic system.

Aristotle was born in 384 B.C. in the Macedonian town of Stagira, near the modern city of Salonika. He came of a long line of physicians to the kings of Macedonia. His own father, Nicomachus, was physician to King Amyntas, and the boy Aristotle grew up at the Macedonian court with Philip, the king's son. It is believed that in 367 B.C., at the age of eighteen, Aristotle came to Plato's Academy in Athens, where he studied and taught for twenty years, until the death of

Plato in 347. When Plato was replaced as head of the Academy by his nephew, Speusippus, a mathematician who appears to have been single-tracked in pursuing the mathematical aspect of Plato's teaching, Aristotle left the Academy and Athens. He appears to have been engaged in the study of politics and in biological research when in 342 he was summoned by Philip, now king of Macedon, to his court, where Aristotle became tutor to Philip's son, Alexander. Aristotle returned to Athens in 335 and founded his own school and research institute, the Lyceum, where for the next twelve years he directed research in the natural sciences and wrote most of his major works. When Alexander the Great died in 323, Aristotle fled for safety from the anti-Macedonian rage which swept Athens, fearful, as he said, "lest the Athenians should sin twice against philosophy." He died the following year, publicly acclaimed as the outstanding philosopher of the Greek world.

What was the relation of the philosophy of Aristotle to that of Plato, his teacher? Controversy has been continuous with regard to this question. There are, first of all, the partisans of Plato, who agree with the philosopher-mathematician Alfred North Whitehead that the whole of Western philosophy is only "a series of footnotes to Plato." From this viewpoint Aristotle's differences from Plato are underemphasized, and Aristotle is regarded as substantially derivative from Plato, for the most part amplifying, analyzing, and sometimes misinterpreting the truths of Plato.

Second, there are the partisans of Aristotle who see Aristotle as vastly surpassing Plato, especially in logic and in the theory of forms. From this viewpoint Plato's differences from Aristotle represent the early, inadequate stages of treating the problems of logic and the forms, problems for which Aristotle was able to provide eminently successful solutions.

But there are others who hold that the differences between Plato and Aristotle have nothing to do with the issue of intellectual superiority, but instead with fundamentally different visions of the world, visions so radically divergent that they may be thought to be rooted in different types of basic personality or temperament. From this viewpoint the differences between Plato and Aristotle represent two types of temperament and their respective intellectual outlooks upon the world. Everyone, it is said, is born either a Platonist or an Aristotelian.

To be a Platonist is to favor the abstract, perfect truths of mathematics and logic as a model to be followed by all fields of knowledge and by the ideals of moral and political life; it is to be more concerned with attaining perfectly certain, logically unified knowledge (the ladder of knowledge) and ideals (the life of reason) than with the practical question of how such knowledge and ideals can relate to the concrete changing actualities of existence. To be an Aristotelian is to favor the concrete, particular changing things of nature and human life (plants, animals, human beings, states of various types), taking biology as a model for understanding their genesis and developmental stages as well as the factors influencing their growth or decay; it is to be more concerned with gathering knowledge of actual things than with the logical unification of knowledge; more concerned with the ideals which are realizable by kinds of things within their particular circumstances than in ideals of excellence which are separate from and transcendent of the actualities of nature and human life.

These differences between Plato and Aristotle—philosophical and temperamental—are best exhibited by Aristotle's devastating criticism of Plato's theory of forms. For Plato, as we have seen, the immutable, eternal forms constitute reality and are transcendent of the sensible world of flux, of changing things which constitute mere appearance. Aristotle claims the very opposite: it is the concrete, individual things that are real—particular plants, animals, men, and states. Aristotle calls such particular things substances. Metaphysics, which is the study of the nature of reality, is for Aristotle the study of individual concrete substances. Aristotle attacks Plato's theory of forms with a barrage of arguments, the principal points of which are:

1. Plato's theory of forms claims to explain the nature of things but in fact the abstract forms are only useless copies of actual things, and fail to provide any explanation of the existence and changes of concrete things;

2. Plato's theory of forms sets up an unbridgeable gap, a dualism between the world of intelligible ideas and the world of sensible things; the theory makes it impossible to explain how sensible things and intelligible forms are related at all.

Does Aristotle then reject forms as mere illusions? Not at all. Aristotle appears to have been a committed follower of Plato's theory of forms during his twenty years at the Academy, and the Platonic influence remains strong. Aristotle's attack is not on the significance of eternal forms for knowledge, but upon the separation of the form or essence of a thing in another realm from the actual existent thing. Any thing, any individual particular substance, a frog or dog or man, is a unity, says Aristotle; it is not something that exists apart from its own essence. A thing, says Aristotle, is a unity of form and matter. The form of a thing is immanent in it, it is the universal and eternal form or essence which the thing shares with all other things of the same type or species, e.g., with all other frogs or dogs or men. Matter is the physical stuff of the particular substance, which is given shape by the substance's form. Matter and form are the inseparable aspects of every individual substance.

With his introduction of the inseparable principles of matter and form, Aristotle is able to overcome Plato's dualism of the intelligible and the sensible worlds. For Aristotle, intelligible form and sensible matter—the universal and the particular—are united in individual things. Every individual thing consists of formed matter. The form is the purpose or end which the matter serves: the oak tree is the purpose or end which the matter of the acorn serves.

In addition to the principles of matter and form, Aristotle introduces the principles of potentiality and actuality. The principles of potentiality and actuality enable Aristotle to account for developmental changes in substances, such as the stages of growth from acorn to young tree to giant oak: the acorn is the potentiality which is actualized by the oak tree. Aristotle acknowledges the close relationship of the two sets of principles: matter, he says, is the principle of potentiality; form is the principle of actuality. We can say, then, that the oak tree is the form toward which the matter of the acorn moves through its developmental stages from its potentiality to its actuality as an oak. Moreover, the oak tree is the actuality of the potentiality of the acorn, but the oak tree, in turn, may be the potentiality, or matter, of a house, which is its actualization. In the same way, organisms are the actualization of the potentiality of inorganic substances and are themselves the potentiality of the rational soul. For Aristotle, the universe consists of a hierarchy of existence, of individual substances of the various eternal types and species, related to each other as matter and form, potentiality and actuality.

Matter and form, potentiality and actuality, are constructed by Aristotle as explanatory principles of things and their changes. To these Aristotle adds his theory of the four causes. Four principles or types of causes determine the nature of any individual thing in the cosmos, whether it is a natural substance such as an oak tree or a man-made substance such as a house:

1. The material cause (the material of which the house is built)
2. The formal cause (the house to be built, the form to be actualized)
3. The efficient cause (the work and tools which produce the house as their effect)
4. The final cause (the purpose for which the house is built)

Many contemporary scholars see in Aristotle's four causes only two distinct types of causes: matter (the material cause) and form (the formal cause). Aristotle's efficient cause (work and tools) is viewed as one stage in the realization of the formal cause (the form, house, to be actualized). Aristotle's final or purposive cause is viewed as identical with the formal cause, as the purposive actualization of the house.

The enduring power of Aristotle's principles of causality is his view that anything at all is understood only when it is seen as determined by its material cause, the matter out of which the stages of the thing have developed, and the form or pattern into which it is taking shape. We have understood the newly hatched chicken, as Aristotle's research in his *History of Animals* shows us, only when we know its material cause and developmental stages in the egg and also the form of the mature hen into which it is growing. We can understand a human life, for example, Plato's life, only when we see how the later stages of his achievements as philosopher grew out of earlier "material" stages of his family lineage, his education, his relations to Socrates, Parmenides, Heraclitus, and the Sophists, his experience of democracy, oligarchy, and war. Knowledge of the things of the world requires that we discover their genesis (material cause) and their consequences (formal cause), which connect them, through strands of complex causal linkages, with all the rest of the world.

This view of the universe, in which everything is linked causally with everything else as material or formal cause, leads Aristotle to theology and to the concept of God. A universe which is characterized throughout by eternal change or motion requires an eternal first cause of motion which is itself unmoved. This is Aristotle's concept of God as the Unmoved Mover, as the eternal first cause of all change or motion in the universe. Here Aristotle provides an early philosophical formulation of the cosmological proof of God's existence, that God exists as the necessary first cause of the series of causal changes in the universe; this proof will later be employed by Saint Thomas and Descartes. In Aristotle's theology God is an eternal actuality which causes change, and a pure actuality, since if the First Mover were material, He would be subject, like all matter, to change. Aristotle's God is not the God of Judaism and Christianity; He is not the loving creator of the world and of man, nor is He an object of worship. Aristotle's God is only the first cause of motion in an eternal, uncreated universe. Yet Aristotle does identify God's pure actuality with thought or mind. What, then, are the objects of God's thought? God cannot have objects of His thought which involve change or sensation or any kind of inferiority to Himself. Therefore, the object of God's thought can only be Himself. God is Thought thinking Thought.

Aristotle's metaphysics is, as we have seen, teleological, in the sense that everything in the universe has its own form, or end, or purpose (*telos*) to fulfill. Aristotle's ethics, most completely formulated in his *Nicomachean Ethics*, follows from this teleological view of reality. The good, he says, is whatever the nature of a thing aims at as its formal cause. What is the good for man? It is what man by his nature seeks: happiness.

But people disagree about happiness: is it the life of pleasure, or wealth, or honor? Aristotle's answer is that we pursue these because we think that they will *bring* happiness; they are only means to happiness. Happiness as the highest good for man consists in the fulfillment of his function as a man, in the "activity of soul in accordance with virtue." What, then, is human virtue?

There are two kinds of virtues for man: moral and intellectual. Moral virtue, says Aristotle, consists in the rational control of the irrational desires and appetites of the soul. These virtues—courage, temperance, justice, self-respect, liberality—are developed by practice until they are established as habits. "We become just," Aristotle wisely says, "by doing just acts." Socrates was mistaken, Aristotle argues, in claiming that virtue is knowledge, that to know the good is to do the good; knowledge of the good can affect our conduct only if it is practiced so that it becomes habit. Moreover, each of the moral virtues is a rationally determined mean between the extremes of excess and deficiency. Courage is a mean between the vice of cowardice (excess fear) and the vice of rashness (deficient fear); self-respect is a mean between the vice of vanity (excess) and the vice of humility (deficiency). How does one determine the "golden mean"? Not by calculating a narrow, self-protective middle course. Determining the mean requires rational judgment based upon a consideration of all the facts in the particular situation. (Shall I buy shares in my relative's new business enterprise?) The determination which I make is neither subjective nor personal, but rational and objective, relative to the situation.

Happiness for human beings lies in activity in accordance with the moral virtues, but only when virtuous activity is sustained over a lifetime. "For," as Aristotle's *Nicomachean Ethics* tell us, "one swallow does not make a summer, nor does one day; and so too one day, or a short time, does not make a man blessed and happy." Moreover, Aristotle sagely remarks that "happiness . . . needs external goods as well" (as the practice of virtue). "It is . . . not easy to perform noble actions if one lacks the wherewithal . . . the help of . . . friends, wealth, and political power. And there are some external goods the absence of which spoils supreme happiness." For happiness one needs good fortune in one's physical appearance, one's family, children, friends, and type of political government. Aristotle's treatment of the moral virtues is clearly determined by his own Greek culture and traditions; but it also exhibits the sound, moderate common sense, the focus upon existing conditions and their potential consequences, and the respect for public opinion and the "wisdom of the ages" which we now associate with Aristotelianism.

In distinction from the moral virtues, the intellectual virtues consist in the contemplation of truth—the truths of science, art, philosophy, intuitive reason, and ethics. Since happiness lies in fulfilling our nature, the greatest happiness lies in fulfilling the best and noblest aspect of our nature: the activity of contemplating truth. The life of contemplation is man's ultimate good and his greatest happiness. Here in this account of the supremacy of the contemplative life, Aristotle is expressing the Platonistic values of the intellectual, while acknowledging that not all men have sufficient intellectual ability or leisure to engage in the contemplation of truth and to experience this highest quality of happiness. The ideal of the contemplative life was to become one of Aristotle's important influences upon the intellectual life of the Church, for which the contemplation of God is man's supreme happiness.

We turn, then, finally to a brief consideration of Aristotle's treatise *Politics*. Aristotle rejects the political theory expressed in Plato's *Republic* on the ground that it is too speculative, too utopian, too far removed from the actual world of city-states and their forms of government. Aristotle rejects the political absolutism of the *Republic*, even though the despots are philosopher-kings; for Aristotle, a good state is one in which the constitution is sovereign and the relation of ruler to ruled is that of free men who are morally equal. Moreover, Aristotle specifically rejects the *Republic*'s radical abolition of private property and the family for the guardian class. Aristotle's fundamental opposition to Plato's *Republic* is that it constructs an unattainable, speculative ideal with which it undertakes a criticism of existing states. In contrast, Aristotle looks to the ideals which are expressed in the laws, customs, and public opinion of the people of actual states; these are the materials which politics must respect, work with, and seek to improve. Aristotle builds no utopias.

But there are major areas of agreement between Plato and Aristotle on political theory. Like Plato, Aristotle views the state as having a moral end or purpose: the highest possible moral development and happiness of its citizens. Also, like Plato, Aristotle regards the state as having primacy over the family and over the individual. The state is a self-sufficient whole, whereas the family and the individual have no self-sufficiency but are only parts dependent upon the social life of the state. "He who is unable to live in society, or who has no need because he is sufficient for himself, must be either a beast or a god." It is only in the state that the virtues of the individual are developed and functional and that the good life, the life of happiness, can be lived. Aristotle also initially follows Plato's classification of types of government into three good and three bad states according to the number of rulers:

the good states—monarchy, aristocracy, polity; the bad states—
tyranny, oligarchy, democracy.

But Aristotle appears to have abandoned the Platonic search
for an ideal type of government. He turns instead to survey-
ing the constitutions of actual Greek states and to a new and
practical question: What type of government is best, most
workable, for most states? Aristotle's conclusion: the polity,
which is a mean between oligarchy and democracy. The
polity is the rule of those with property, as in oligarchy, but
the property qualification is low, so that the majority of the
citizens have a share in government, as in democracy. The
polity is in effect ruled by a large middle class; it will provide,
Aristotle believes, a stable, well-administered foundation for
the state, since this class is composed of "equals and similars"
of moderate means, who are most likely to follow rational
principles. "The best political community is formed by citizens of the middle class," holding the balance of power
against the very rich, who "can only rule despotically" and
the very poor, who "are too degraded" to rule.

The philosophy of Aristotle is regarded as the most complete synthesis of knowledge ever constructed. His philosophy differentiated for the first time the various fields of
knowledge: logic and mathematics; the sciences of physics,
biology, psychology; and the philosophic branches of metaphysics, ethics, politics, aesthetics. And Aristotle provided
the first classification of the sciences: (1) logic, the method of
study employed in all other sciences; (2) theoretical sciences,
concerned with pure, abstract knowledge: mathematics,
physics, biology, psychology, and metaphysics ("first philosophy"); (3) practical sciences, concerned with knowledge as a
means to conduct or action: ethics and politics; (4) productive
sciences, concerned with knowledge to be used in making
useful or beautiful things. The concepts by means of which
Aristotle achieved this massive unification of knowledge have
remained fundamental to the history of Western philosophy
and culture: substance, matter and form, potentiality and
actuality, the categories, the four causes. In the Middle Ages,
Saint Thomas referred to Aristotle simply as "the philosopher"
and the poet Dante called him "the master of those who
know."

The Medieval Synthesis:
Saints Augustine and Thomas

Although he was the lifelong friend of Philip of Macedon and tutor to Alexander the Great, Aristotle seems not to have had the vision to see that the Macedonian conquest of the entire Greek world and the East as far as India signified the end of the era of the Greek city-state in Western civilization and the end of the ideal of the good life as participation in the politics of the small city-state. A generation after the death of Aristotle the ideal which he shared with Plato, of man the political animal who can fulfill his potentiality for excellence only in the affairs of the city-state, has lost its relevance in a world empire of deracinated individuals.

Within two hundred years the Macedonians were defeated by Rome and later absorbed into the Roman Empire, which built upon its vast cultural inheritance from the Greeks, most notably in jurisprudence, philosophy, art, architecture, and literature. But then we see the decline and fall of the Roman Empire, which—having conquered Britain, all of Europe and the Middle East, and much of North Africa—in time became stagnant and paralyzed by the unmanageability of this immense, far-flung imperial territory. The empire was increasingly plagued by barbarian invasions, with the city of Rome itself invaded and plundered by the Visigoths in 410 A.D. By the fifth century, with the weakening of the empire, Christianity had become the official religion of the empire, and the church structure became the most powerful organization in Europe.

By this time Christian beliefs and values dominated the Roman Empire, and while some of the heritage of the classical Greek and Roman civilization was retained and used by the Church, many Greek and Roman writings and works of art were destroyed. The Church charged them with being pagan, un-Christian, and immoral. For over a thousand years, from the fourth to the fifteenth centuries, Christianity shaped the entire social and cultural world of Europe, its political and personal life, social institutions, economic relations, knowledge of the natural world, literature and the arts—all these were under Church direction and control. Philosophy, science, and art were all placed in the service of religion. This coherent integration of institutional, cultural, and personal life under Church direction and control has come to be called the medieval synthesis. The free, rational, independent philosophical speculation of the Greeks was brought to an end by Christianity and was not to be restored until the modern era in philosophy emerged in the seventeenth century, with Descartes as its first great representative.

The classical world view of Plato and Aristotle was of a natural cosmos, rational, ordered, moral, and purposeful, which is known solely by human reason. This was replaced by the supernaturalistic world view of the Church, whose source is divine revelation and whose fundamental beliefs, such as the Incarnation and the Trinity, are dogmas which must be accepted by faith, and are beyond the power of human reason to explain or to prove.

For the early Catholic world view the fundamental problem is that of the relation of the individual soul to a just and merciful, infinite, omnipotent, and perfect Father-God, who so loved the world that He sacrificed His only begotten son for the redemption of humanity. The world itself and human beings are the creation of God and fulfill His purposes. The crucial issue is personal salvation for the sinful, erring self in a corrupt and unjust society. The way to salvation is by purity of heart, repentance of sins, love of God and of one's neighbor as oneself. Essential to salvation is belief in Jesus Christ, through whose sacrifice and vicarious suffering the redemption of sinful mankind is purchased. Not science, philosophy, mathematics, the arts, are important; not the life of reason but the life of faith, devotion, prayer, good works, love and obedience to God and to His Church.

But in the terror of history, in which the achievements and aspirations of civilizations disappear, the great philosophies seem to survive through a kind of immortality. Plato and Aristotle survived. Ironically, the two greatest philosophers of Christianity, Saint Augustine and Saint Thomas Aquinas, produce their profound philosophies by fusing Christianity with precisely the pagan Greek philosophy which the Church had almost entirely destroyed: Saint Augustine with Plato, Saint Thomas with Aristotle.

Saint Augustine (354–430 A.D.) is now known as the Platonizer of Christianity, for his synthesizing of Christianity with the philosophy of Plato. By the second half of the fourth century, when Augustine was growing up in the Roman province of Numidia (now Algeria) in North Africa, intellectual darkness was rapidly descending over the Roman Empire. The empire was disintegrating, its vast institutional and cultural resources suffered from the empire's neglect and the Church's indifference or hostility to pagan culture. It is uncertain today how much, if any, of the writings of Plato himself or of Plato's followers was available for Augustine to study; by this time the books of pagan philosophers had been destroyed or lost. Yet in some form the influence of Plato reached Augustine. In Augustine's greatest work, *The City of God*, which he wrote to try to explain the sack and fall of Rome in 410 A.D., the voice of Plato can be heard. The Platonic distinction between the sensible and the intelligible worlds is expressed in Christian terms as the distinction between the earthly city of the flux of opinion, and the heavenly city of God's eternal truth.

The most important works of Aristotle, which had disappeared in the West after the first century, had survived in the Middle East. With the rise of the Islamic civilization, Aristotle's writings were translated by Arabs into Arabic and then translated by Jews into Hebrew and into Latin, and so were finally made available again to the West by the twelfth century. During the Middle Ages, the philosophers who undertook to construct a rationally defended philosophical system out of Christian beliefs with the aid of classical thought were called Schoolmen and their philosophic systems were called Scholastic philosophy or Scholasticism. *Scholasticism* is the name conventionally given to the philosophy of the medieval cathedral schools (later to become universities) which attempted to fuse Christian beliefs with the elements of the Greek philosophy of Plato or Aristotle, using the logical syllogism and debate. Scholasticism reached its highest stage of development in the philosophy of Thomas Aquinas.

Saint Thomas (1225–1274 A.D.) in the thirteenth century was able to build upon the recovery of Aristotle's complete philosophic works, and the enormous amount of information which Aristotle had gathered and ordered into separate sciences, and had unified by means of fundamental concepts into a great philosophic system of all the branches of knowledge. The synthesizing philosophy of Saint Thomas, set forth in the twenty-two volumes of his principal work, *Summa Theologiae*, is the most esteemed system within Catholic philosophy and one of the highest philosophical achievements of the Western world. The philosophy of the *Summa* was proclaimed the official philosophy of the Catholic Church by Pope Leo XIII, and its influence continues into the present. Thomism is a world view claiming absolute truth, based upon faith in divine revelation and upon supporting reason. The Thomistic philosophy included theology (proofs of the existence of God and of His nature); a metaphysical theory; a theory of evil; a theory of law (eternal, divine, natural, and human); a theory of knowledge; ethics; psychology; and politics.

Saint Thomas makes maximum use of Aristotle while avoiding conflict with Church dogma by sharply distinguishing between philosophy and theology. The dogmas of Catholic theology are not matters for the rational discussion and proofs of philosophy; as objects of theology, dogmas are revealed truths, matters of faith, and neither provable nor disprovable by reason. But there are some truths which are based upon faith, yet are also, like philosophy, provable by reason; such propositions constitute what Saint Thomas calls natural theology, which is to be distinguished from revealed theology. Natural theology can thus be said to belong to philosophy; it is the field of Christian philosophy, such as the philosophy of Saint Thomas himself.

Saint Thomas constructs a vast systematic philosophy, incorporating the scientific realm of human knowledge; above this, the rational principles of philosophy; above philosophy, the revealed truths of Christian theology. Aristotle's physics, biology, metaphysics, theology, ethics, psychology, and politics; the concepts of substance; form and matter; potentiality and actuality; the four causes; God as pure actuality; the cosmological proof of God; the teleological ethics; the classification of the virtues; natural law; the concept of the political animal—all of these are skillfully employed by Saint Thomas in support of his system of Christian philosophy. So, for example, he will agree with Aristotle that man is a natural being, a species of organism, a rational and political animal with his own natural end or purpose; but as a Christian philosopher, Saint Thomas affirms that man is also a spiritual being who serves a divine purpose, distinct from and higher than his natural end.

And from Plato and Aristotle, Saint Thomas takes their metaphysical conception of the universe as a great hierarchy of kinds of being, each with its own form, purpose, excellence, from the lowliest being to the summit of the Idea of the Good or the Unmoved Mover. But for Saint Thomas, God is the creator of this great chain of being, as well as its first cause and final purpose; God is ultimate truth and goodness, and the source of man's salvation. This Aristotelianized Christianity constitutes the structure of Saint Thomas's philosophical synthesis of the knowledge of the medieval world.

The Renaissance

But historical changes were at work. Saint Thomas's interpretation of Aristotle, so important an element in his formulation of Christian thought, was soon challenged by other scholars, now that Aristotle's writings were available for all to read. More and more, free discussion was demanded for all important problems, and the authoritative sovereignty of the two great medieval institutions, the Roman Catholic Church and the Holy Roman Empire, was beginning to be weakened. By the fifteenth century scholars and writers were turning away from the Aristotleanized Christianity of Scholasticism and toward the original texts of classical Greek civilization for new inspiration.

With the fall of Constantinople to the Turks in 1453 the vast world of art and learning of ancient Greek culture which had been preserved in the Eastern Empire was now made available to the Christian West. The courts of kings, the popes, the universities, artists and writers, were excited by the art and literature recovered from the past. Access to these classical treasures marked the end of the medieval synthesis and the emergence of the Renaissance, a period of the rebirth of classical learning and the emergence of a new mode of consciousness which extended into the sixteenth century.

With the recovery of classical languages, literature, art, history, and philosophic and scientific texts, there came a revival of the spirit of Greek humanism, in opposition to the prevailing Christian religiosity of the Middle Ages. Humanism may be defined as a cultural and intellectual viewpoint which affirms the dignity and worth of human beings, in respect of the power of human reason to know the truths of nature and the capacity of the human spirit to determine, express, and achieve what is good for human beings. Classical Greek humanism, which had been man-centered and nature-centered, now inspired many of the artists and intellectuals of the Renaissance to glorify man and celebrate the works of human genius, and to repudiate strenuously the prevailing

Christian themes of the worthlessness of man and the insignificance of nature in relation to the supernatural world.

The humanist concept of the dignity of man is central to the Renaissance mode of consciousness, which appeared first in Italy, later in northern Europe and England. A new emphasis upon individual achievement arises, stimulated by magnificent classical models of achievement. The new Renaissance mentality can be seen in the widespread belief in the superiority of the culture of the ancient world to that of the present. The principal concern expressed by the writers of the Renaissance is in the need to restore to man the capacities, strengths, and powers of the individual person which the medieval world had denied or ignored. It is in this sense that the Renaissance is sometimes credited with "the discovery of man." With the coming of the Renaissance there occurs an expression of a humanistic faith in man, in his power to direct his life and the life of his society toward freedom and justice, together with the sense that this power, which had been a possession of the individual in the ancient Greek world, had been lost in the world of medieval Christendom.

But some Renaissance humanists looked not only back to the glories of the classical past but ahead to the future, sensing that they were living in a rapidly changing world, in which the legitimacy of the existing feudal system, the Church, and the empire was increasingly challenged. The perception began to develop that the new Renaissance humanistic mentality was breaking through the hierarchical rigidities of the existing social order, and that a way would be opened to individual freedom, access to new knowledge, and a new mode of life.

The ferment of Reniassance humanism is best seen in the arts, in which human talents and achievements were celebrated and honored. Individual human beings were glorified in literature; and art turned away from the portrayal of suffering and death, toward the expression of the Greek joy in living. Nature became interesting in itself and not merely as symbolic of the supernatural. A visual revolution began to take place among artists, who increasingly turned away from painting and sculpting stereotypical Christian subjects and Christian symbolism to painting and sculpting things as they appear in nature to the eye of the artist. Artists discovered the human body again and began to study the physiology, the muscles and bones, of the human body in motion.

Michelangelo's "David" and Leonardo's "Last Supper" are examples of the highly developed Renaissance portraiture of the natural human body in action. Renaissance art reaffirmed the dignity and capacity for goodness of man as a rational and sentient being, rightfully claiming to know and to enjoy the world autonomously through literature, the visual arts, the sciences and philosophy.

The Renaissance was marked not only by the revival of classical learning and humanism but also by many other developments, each of which struck a blow at the weakening structure of the medieval world; the invention of the printing press, gunpowder, and the improvement of the compass for navigation all had formidable consequences. The fifteenth century was the time of the great discoveries: the discovery of the New World by Columbus and his successors, and the discovery of the all-water route to India and the Far East, around the Cape of Good Hope. In time, the discoveries of these new trade routes were to bring about the end of the medieval feudal regime and the emergence of a new social order. Moreover, the rise and rapid growth of the Protestant Reformation begun by Martin Luther struck a direct blow against the unity of the medieval Christian world.

The Rise of Modern Science

From a philosophic standpoint, the most significant development in the Renaissance and the discoveries is a revolutionary new view of truth. In opposition to the scholastic view that human truth is subordinate to a divine, supernatural, and transcendent reality which is forever inaccessible to human reason, the shift is to the new view that human reason has the power to know the truth of reality and that reality is neither divine nor transcendent. Especially did this new view influence astronomy, which was reborn in the fifteenth century.

All the best minds were attracted to astronomy by the sixteenth century, as so many minds are now attracted to the frontiers of space exploration. New and careful astronomical observations were made and discrepancies were found between these new observations and the prevailing astronomical theory developed by Ptolemy in the Egyptian city of Alexandria in the second century. Most of the ancient astronomers, including Aristotle, had held a geocentric view of the universe, the view that the earth was the center of the universe, around which the planets revolved. Ptolemy's contribution was to show that the astronomical data which had been observed could be explained by the hypothesis that the planets move around the earth in circles within one large circle. Ptolemy's geocentric theory was adequate for astronomical calculations and predictions and it had the additional benefit of being compatible with Church doctrine on the divine creation of the earth as the center of the universe. As a result the Ptolemaic theory prevailed for fourteen centuries.

But now in the sixteenth century, the Polish astronomer Nicholaus Copernicus (1473–1543), using observation and mathematics, the methods of empiricism and rationalism, overthrew the earth-centered Ptolemaic theory and offered the sun-centered, heliocentric, theory that the earth revolves on its own axis and around the sun, along with the other planets. This theory accounted for the new observations and greatly simplified the mathematical calculations of Ptolemaic theory. Ever since Copernicus overthrew the Ptolemaic theory in this revolutionary way, any drastic change in thought has been called a Copernican revolution. For us, it is difficult to imagine a similar challenge to our accustomed beliefs, to conceive of such a tremendous jolt to the imagination, such a reversal of what is taken to be immutable truth. It would be comparable for us to have the announcement of a communication from a society of superior conscious intelligence in outer space, a startling possibility which science fiction, Star Wars, and even some scientists have opened up for us.

The response of the Church to the Copernican revolution was extreme. Scientists supportive of the heliocentric theory were excommunicated from the Church and condemned to everlasting hell. If they refused to deny these new ideas, they were subject to imprisonment, torture, or even death. These punitive measures were accomplished either through the office of the Pope or through the courts of the reigning kings. Copernicus himself hesitated to publish his theory for fear of the Church's reaction, but his publication was unnoticed and it was only his followers in the next century who were caught up with by the Church authorities. In 1600 Bruno was burned at the stake in Rome as an atheist for accepting Copernican theory. In 1620 Vanini, who called himself a naturalist, was burned at the stake in Toulouse as an atheist. In 1621 Fontainier was burned in Paris as an atheist.

Among the scientists it was the Italian astronomer Galileo (1564–1642) who came under attack because he boldly undertook to prove the Copernican theory. Galileo developed a telescope capable of magnifying one thousand times, by which he observed the satellites of Jupiter, Saturn's rings, and the moon's surface. Unlike Copernicus, Galileo vigorously and actively tried to publicize the new heliocentric theory and met with formidable Church opposition which censured his views as contrary to Holy Scripture. But in 1632 he published his *Dialogue Concerning the Two Chief Systems of the World,* in which he showed his agreement with the Copernican rather than the Ptolemaic theory. For this, he was summoned before the Inquisition, the book was condemned, he was forced to deny the doctrine upon his knees, forced to recite the seven penitential psalms weekly for three years, and sentenced to life imprisonment, which he served in his own home in Florence until his death.

Descartes: Historical Situation

Meanwhile the scientific spirit moved on. New technology, new inventions, new observations, and new theory were appearing all over Europe. The telescope, microscope, and thermometer were invented. Among the new scientific developments were Boyle's theory of gases, laws of electricity and magnetism, laws of optics (constructed by Descartes and Snell), Harvey's theory of the circulation of the blood, Descartes's invention of analytical geometry. But what was the nature of the new science and its method? Two elements in scientific method were identified: (1) the empirical element, the use of sensory observation and experimentation; (2) the rational element, the use of mathematics and deductive reasoning, as by Copernicus and Galileo in explaining the motion of heavenly bodies. Almost immediately, conflicting theories of scientific method appeared, depending upon which element, the empirical or the rational, was claimed to be the more important. Francis Bacon in England looked at scientific method and claimed it for empiricism—a triumph of the method of observation and experimentation over reason, theories, and systems. Descartes, however, looked at scientific method and claimed it for rationalism—a triumph of mathematics, of

geometry, and of reasoning by axioms and deduction; it is
these which make science into knowledge which is certain.

The new age of the seventeenth century, in which all
beliefs were in transition and in which the new scientific
method and scientific discoveries were advancing so rapidly,
was one for which the medieval philosophy of scholasticism
no longer appeared to be adequate, and a new philosophy
appeared to be required. René Descartes is the first philosopher of the modern age and offers the first metaphysical
theory in response to the new scientific view of the universe
and in relationship to the counterclaims of the Church.

Life of Descartes

Descartes was born in 1596 at the start of the seventeenth
century, four years before Bruno was burned at the stake as a
Copernican. Descartes was the son of a lawyer in Brittany
and a member of one of the oldest and most respected
families in the region. Descartes was brought up with all the
amenities of noble and upper-class life. In his early years he
wore the green velvet dress and sword of French nobility.
From ten to eighteen years of age he attended La Flèche, a
famous Jesuit college. He became dissatisfied with his education there and unconvinced of any truth, weary of textbooks
based upon confused ideas and unconfirmed science, and
weary of the authoritative dogmas of the Church. When he
completed his studies at La Flèche, he stopped reading entirely and began to travel. In this response Descartes strikes a
very modern note—not unlike the despair of someone in our
time who longs for moral certainty and, finding none, stops
reading entirely and goes off to the Himalayas in search of a
guru. The longing for certainty was always paramount with
Descartes. Mathematics alone he regarded as certain—but
what relation did it have to other kinds of knowledge? And so
he began his travels.

In 1618 he joined the army of Prince Maurice of Nassau as
an unpaid volunteer. Army volunteer status at that time
represented a kind of undemanding war college for young
members of the nobility. Descartes was able to follow the
advancing army at his own leisure, while studying music and
mathematics. In 1619 Descartes transferred to the army of
the Duke of Bavaria, and was detained by the weather in

November in the small German town of Ulm, where he remained for a whole day shut up in his room in the company of a huge Bavarian stove. He had decided to review his situation, philosophical and personal. That night he had a vision in a dream and in his diary there is the following momentous entry: "10 Nov. 1619: I was filled with enthusiasm, discovered the foundations of a marvelous science, and at the same time my vocation was revealed to me." He took a vow that he would devote the rest of his life to establish this new science, and he promised to visit the shrine of Our Lady of Loreto to give thanks for the vision he was granted.

His vision was of a plan for a single, unified science in which philosophy and all the sciences would be interconnected in one systematic totality. All qualitative differences of things would be treated as quantitative differences, and mathematics would be the key to all problems of the universe. By contrast with Plato, who saw the unity of all sciences in the mystical Idea of the Good, for Descartes the unity of science was a rationalistic and mathematical unity based upon mathematical axioms. By contrast with medieval Aristotelianism, explaining change teleologically as the movement of matter toward the actualization of form, for Descartes all change is explained mechanically, as the movement of bodies according to the laws of physics.

The next nine years Descartes devoted to working out a method for unifying the sciences. Meanwhile he sold the estates in France which he had inherited from his father so as to have the funds to live "free from the obligation of making a living from my science." Leisure enabled him to sleep long hours. He usually stayed in bed until noon, and has come to be known as the philosopher who did his best work in bed. He recommends idleness to anyone who would wish to produce good intellectual work, and he values his leisure, which enables him to live "without cares or passions to trouble me."

Descartes remained always aloof from the moral and political conflicts of his day. Like some other philosophers of his time he did not become a professor at a university, since the universities were so censored by the Church that they had become stagnant, and hostile to the new science and to its supporters, like Descartes. Always a solitary man, he decided that he would make no social commitments and no marriage bonds, so as not to interfere with his vow to advance knowledge in accordance with his vision. He refused to be married, saying, "No beauty is comparable to the beauty of truth." But Descartes expressed a startlingly cynical view of marriage, saying: "When a husband weeps over a dead wife . . . in spite of this, in his innermost soul he feels a secret joy." And yet he had an illegitimate daughter whose death in early childhood appears to have saddened him greatly. At the age of thirty-two he settled in Holland where he lived for twenty years, enjoying the intellectual and religious toleration of the Dutch government.

In 1622 he finished his astronomical *Treatise on the World,* which applied his mathematical method and reaffirmed the Copernican hypotheses. As he was about to send the *Treatise* off for publication, he learned that Galileo had been condemned by the Inquisition of the Catholic Church and that Galileo's book had been publicly burned. Descartes immediately hurried to stop publication of his own book, saying, "It is imprudent to lose one's life when one can save one's self without dishonor." He attempted to have the word spread about that he held theology in highest esteem. Descartes scholars are divided on Descartes's real views about the Church and its teaching. Was his piety genuine or a pretense? He himself said, "I must find an expedience by which to speak the truth without startling anyone's imagination or shocking opinions commonly received." And he also said, "Now that I am to be not only a spectator of the world, but am to appear an actor on its stage, I wear a mask." Descartes's mask represents one way of dealing with persecution. But one thinks also of Socrates or the contemporary Russian dissenter Alexander Solzhenitsyn, who were outspoken in the face of persecution and willing to face death or exile.

Three years after Descartes's fright at Galileo's punishment, he published an application of his mathematical method to physics, prefacing it by the *Discourse on Method,* which remains a philosophic classic to this day. Ten years later in 1647 he published the *Meditations on First Philosophy;* twenty-two years later, in 1669, the *Meditations* were placed by the Inquisition on the index of books which Catholics were forbidden to read.

The last notable event in Descartes's life was his receiving a request from the intellectual Queen Christina of Sweden to come and help her understand his philosophy. He hesitated to go to what he called "the land of ice and bears"—but he complied. Five o'clock in the morning was the hour at which

Christina's mind was most active and was the time set for the instruction. Returning from court one November morning in 1650, he got a chill and died of pneumonia within a week. Thus perished the greatest philosopher of France at the height of his powers. What is the claim of Descartes to greatness as a philosopher? Etienne Gilson, a twentieth-century French philosopher, says of Descartes: "He lived by thought alone for thought alone . . . never was an existence more noble than his."

"Portrait of René Descartes" by Franz Hals.
(COURTESY OF THE BETTMANN ARCHIVES.)

7

DOUBTING TO BELIEVE

Historical Situation

A portrait of René Descartes, the father and originator of modern philosophy and France's greatest philosopher, hangs in the Louvre Museum in Paris. He looks out at you from heavy-lidded eyes, aloof and somewhat arrogant, and the smile is one of gentlemanly scorn and contempt. How did this seventeenth-century man shape the philosophy of the modern world in which we live?

Descartes appears to have felt only contempt for French society, for the court of Louis XIII, for the clergy of the French Church, for the professors in the universities and for the man in the street. His contempt was undisguised for what was taught in the universities, which he regarded as traditional, outmoded, stagnant, still clinging to medieval learning and submissive to Church authority.

Descartes is sharply critical of La Flèche, the Jesuit college which he himself attended and which had recently been established for the education of the sons of the French nobility. Of his eight years at La Flèche he says:

> From my childhood I lived in a world of books and
> . . . I was eager to learn from them. But . . . as soon
> as I had finished the course of studies . . . I found
> myself saddled with so many doubts and errors that I
> seemed to have gained nothing. Nevertheless, I had
> been in one of the most celebrated schools in all of
> Europe.

At college he had studied Greek, Latin, history, literature, science, mathematics, and philosophy. Of these, only mathematics, which had been well taught at La Flèche, and the modicum of science which was offered seemed to have any certainty or to provide true knowledge of the world. But Descartes goes even further in his criticism of education, to argue that our beliefs would be less contaminated by errors and on firmer ground if, from childhood, we had never been under the control of teachers and subjected to their confused ideas, but had been guided solely by our own reason.

Descartes had a special scorn for philosophy—philosophy was a term of contempt and derision for him. Rival philosophers contradict one another, he says, without there being certainty on either side. Philosophers are ignorant of mathematics and science; they base their logical argumentation upon authorities which are ancient and outmoded. The result has been, Descartes charges, that philosophy "has been studied for many centuries by the most outstanding minds without having produced anything which is not in dispute." With such statements Descartes, the father of modern philosophy, seems very modern indeed. He appears to resemble the revolutionary students of the 1960s who condemned the universities for their irrelevance to the problems of war, civil rights, and poverty. But Descartes is not asking for relevance, he is asking for truth, and for the overthrow of false beliefs in order that he may reach truth.

Truth is Descartes's passion: He says of himself:

> I have always had an extreme desire to learn how to distinguish the true from the false, in order to see clearly how I should act and to be able to travel with assurance through this life.

But is it possible for me to overthrow all the accumulation of my lifelong beliefs, however false or uncertain, and to use only my own reason as the basis for believing anything? This is what Descartes proposes and this is the way modern philosophy begins—with a revolutionary overthrow of all belief, and so with a complete break with the medieval world, including the authority of the Church-controlled Scholastic philosophy.

Modern philosophy may be said to begin with Descartes's *Meditations*, with the self in solitude, meditating, becoming conscious of the false and doubtful ideas one has accepted so far in life, and deciding that the time has come to overthrow

all of one's beliefs. In the first sentences of the *Meditations,*
Descartes says: "Everything must be thoroughly overthrown
for once in my life, if I ever want to establish anything solid
and permanent in the sciences." Descartes goes on to say:
"Today I have freed my mind from all cares. I am quite
alone. At last I shall have time to devote myself seriously and
freely to the destruction of all my former opinions." But can
I, by my own reason, establish solid and permanent truth?

Theory of Knowledge: Rationalism

Descartes's answer is that of Plato and all rationalism. Rationalism claims in support of reason that reason is universal in
all human beings; that reason is the most important element
in human nature; that reason is the only means to certainty in
knowledge; that reason is the only way to determine what is
morally right and good and what constitutes a good society.

But how can I, by using my own reason, establish solid and
permanent truth which past philosophers have failed to do?
Descartes's answer is again that of most rationalists: Let mathematics be your ideal, let mathematics be your model for the
use of reason. In his *Discourse on Method,* Descartes says:
"Of all who have sought for the truth in the sciences, it has
been the mathematicians alone who have been able to succeed in producing reasons which are evident and certain."
And it was the method of mathematics, using reason alone,
Descartes believes, which enabled the Polish astronomer Copernicus in the sixteenth century to revolutionize astronomy
with his new heliocentric theory of the universe, and enabled
the Italian astronomer Galileo in the seventeenth century to
provide the proof of the Copernican theory.

Mathematics is the method which Descartes the mathematician, himself the inventor of analytical geometry, wants
to use for philosophy. Mathematics, he thinks, can clear up
the confusions and uncertainties of philosophy. The method
of mathematics will gain the same clarity and certainty for
philosophy as for geometry, and as the scientists have gained
for physics and astronomy. By using the method of mathematics, philosophy could achieve absolute certainty and could
prove itself, as mathematics does, to my own reason, to all
human reason, and be acknowledged as universally true.
Philosophy could then reach final and certain truth which

would decisively end the disputes among the philosophers and the bitter controversy raging between the Church and the scientists. Philosophic certainty would also bring about an end to the fear of the Inquisition under which scientists lived, the fear of being sentenced to imprisonment or torture, the fear that Descartes himself had that he might suffer the same fate as Galileo.

The Method of Mathematics: Intuition and Deduction

But what is the method of mathematics? Descartes tells us in his *Rules for the Direction of the Mind*. Mathematics consists in the use of only two mental operations by which true knowledge can be achieved: intuition and deduction.

Intuition. By intuition he means our understanding of self-evident principles, such as the axioms of geometry (a straight line is the shortest distance between two points; or, things equal to the same thing are equal to each other) or such as an arithmetic equation $(3 + 2 = 5)$. These statements are self-evident in that they prove themselves to reason: To understand them is to know that they are absolutely true; no rational mind can doubt them.

Deduction. By deduction he means orderly, logical reasoning or inference from self-evident propositions, as all of geometry is reasoned in strict order by deduction from its self-evident axioms and postulates. "The chief secret of method," says Descartes, "is to arrange all facts into a deductive, logical system."

Descartes's goal as a philosopher is to build a system of philosophy based upon intuition and deduction which will remain as certain and as imperishable as geometry. No philosopher has ever made a bolder attempt to arrive at a philosophy of absolute truth. The entire series of the six meditations, day after day, is a single sustained effort to reconstruct philosophy, to find for philosophy the certainty of a mathematical proof. What Descartes is determined to find is a self-evident principle which will serve as the axiom or first principle for his mathematical philosophy, and which will serve as the foundation from which an absolutely certain philosophy can be deduced.

But what are the requirements which this foundational belief must meet? Descartes lays down three:

1. Its certainty must be such that it is impossible to doubt, it is self-evident to reason, it is clear (in itself) and distinct (from every other belief).
2. Its certainty must be ultimate and not dependent upon the certainty of any other belief.
3. It must be about something which exists (so that from it beliefs about the existence of other things may be deduced).

Theory of Knowledge: The Method of Doubt: Skepticism

But how will I find such a belief? Descartes asks. And he answers: By the method of doubt. The attitude of doubt was in the air in this transitional era of the seventeenth century, with old beliefs and philosophies losing their credibility and the new scientific theories under fire and not yet established on a firm philosophical foundation. Descartes, too, uses the method of doubt. But despite the solitary quiet of his *Meditations*, Descartes's doubting is revolutionary. He is going to overthrow all his beliefs, doubt everything. To achieve his bold quest for an absolutely certain philosophy, Descartes is willing, with equal boldness, to overthrow and destroy all he has ever believed, to cast doubt upon all his beliefs. *Skepticism* is the name for the philosophic position of doubt concerning the reliability of knowledge. Descartes's type of skepticism is called methodical, or methodological skepticism, defined as the use of doubt methodically in order to arrive at true knowledge.

Descartes uses methodological skepticism in order to overthrow his beliefs. Meditation I is entitled "Of the Things Which We May Doubt." But to doubt all of his beliefs by taking a complete inventory of them individually would be interminable. I will examine them, says Descartes, the lover of mathematical orderliness, by classes or groups to see if there is any one belief which defies doubt by meeting the three criteria: First, that the proposition be impossible to doubt; second, that it be an ultimate truth; and third, that it be about something that exists. And so, class by class, group by group, he goes through all his beliefs.

(1) First to be examined are the beliefs of sense perception.

These are the most readily believed of all, but they are often deceptive. What distant objects look like to the naked eye, for example, is now denied by the telescope (Galileo had invented the telescope in 1609). What minute objects look like to the naked eye is now denied by the microscope (which Kepler had designed in 1611). And what about optical illusions such as the pencil that looks bent in the water? And the hallucinations that affect the senses? Clearly, says Descartes, the senses are untrustworthy as a source of certainty. What has deceived me once may deceive me again. But surely, Descartes insists, I cannot doubt my senses telling me that "I am here, seated by the fire, attired in a dressing gown . . . and that these hands and this body are mine?" Yet have I not dreamed that I was sitting here? he asks. And may I not be dreaming now? (Descartes, who slept so much, must have had this dream often.) What I perceive by the senses may be the deceptions of a dream. (2) Descartes now goes to another class of his beliefs. What about beliefs in material things or the belief that a physical world exists? These must be doubted because they are based upon sense perception, which has been shown to be deceptive and therefore lacking in certainty. (3) Third, Descartes asks: What of beliefs from the natural sciences? These, too, must be doubted because they are based upon objects known by sense perception, which is now established to be untrustworthy.

(4) Fourth, Descartes moves on to mathematical beliefs. What about beliefs in mathematics? Why does he doubt these? He has always regarded mathematics as the very model of certainty, as completely certain in its propositions. Moreover, mathematical beliefs are not rendered doubtful by being derived from sense perception. "For whether I am awake or whether I am asleep" Descartes says, "two and three together will always make the number five and the square will never have more than four sides; and it does not seem possible that truths so apparent can ever be suspected of any falsity." These beliefs are known by reason, not by the senses. But is it impossible to doubt them? Mathematicians, he reflects, fall into error sometimes. Could they always be in error?

In an effort to push his methodological skepticism to its extreme, and for lack of a reason to doubt mathematics, Descartes invents one. Suppose, he says, there is an evil and powerful demon who deceives me in all the things I think I know best? In that case, I am always deceived, always in error, even in mathematics, even in the propositions I think are self-evident, such as $3 + 2 = 5$. This is the strongest possible doubt. Descartes himself says it is exaggerated, "hyperbolic." It seems contrived, not a genuine doubt. But he pushes his case. Can any belief withstand this doubt? Can any belief withstand my doubting all beliefs on the ground that I may be deceived by some malevolent demon in all my beliefs, even those I regard as absolutely certain?

Now Descartes enters with his famous triumphant reply: Even if I am deceived in all my beliefs, I must exist in order to be deceived. If I doubt all my beliefs, including those of mathematics, there is one belief that cannot be doubted: Every time I doubt, I must exist to doubt. In doubting the truth of every other belief, I cannot doubt the belief that I am doubting, therefore I exist. Even if all the beliefs I am conscious of are false, one belief remains true: At any moment that I am conscious of thinking, or of any mental act such as being conscious of doubting or willing, I exist as a thinking thing.

And so Descartes has found his absolutely certain, self-evident, and indubitable first principle. He formulates it in Latin as *cogito, ergo sum:* I think, therefore I am; in French, *je pense, donc je suis*. Thinking for Descartes includes any act of consciousness that we are immediately aware of. "By the word thought I understand all that of which we are conscious as operating in us." Thinking includes doubting, understanding, affirming, denying, willing, refusing, feeling. As conscious acts, all of these necessitate my existence. I think, therefore I am. I doubt that I think, I deny that I think, these only confirm that I must exist to deny or doubt.

How do I know this belief, cogito ergo sum? By immediately understanding as self-evident that to think (doubt or deny or will) I must exist and that my thinking without my existing is impossible. Cogito ergo sum is true each time I think it. Cogito ergo sum is true each time I deny it. But what is this I who thinks and therefore exists? The Cogito proves only that I exist as a thinking thing—and only when I am conscious of thinking. The Cogito proves only that I am a thinking thing, an existent substance, and that it is my nature to have thoughts, ideas, beliefs. But nothing has been proven by the Cogito about my body or its movements, my walking or eating. I cannot claim self-evident truth for: I move, therefore I am. My moving I can know only by sense perception, by observing myself to move. The Cogito proves only that whenever I am conscious of thinking, I exist as a thinking thing.

But does the Cogito fulfill the three requirements Descartes laid down for the first principle, the foundation of his philosophy? (1) Is it self-evident to reason, indubitable? Descartes answers: Yes, you can't escape the Cogito by doubting it. Every time I doubt it, I affirm it. (2) Is it independent of any more ultimate truth? Descartes answers: Yes, the Cogito is not inferred from the more ultimate truth: All who think, exist; I think, therefore I exist. On the contrary, I myself recognize as a self-evident truth that I exist whenever I think. (3) Does it refer to the existing world? Descartes answers: Yes, the Cogito refers to me, who exists as a thinking thing. *Sum*. I am. I exist.

And so Descartes claims that the Cogito checks out with his three requirements. Have later philosophers agreed? Does the Cogito proof withstand criticism as an absolutely certain foundation for philosophy? There have been hundreds of critical commentaries on the Cogito proof. Of these, the most frequent attack is one first made by Pierre Gassendi in letters to Descartes. Gassendi claimed that the Cogito does not meet the second requirement, that it is not ultimate but depends upon other truths. Two of these truths upon which the Cogito depends are: (1) That things or substances exist. (2) That thinking or any other action or state can exist only as the action or state of a substance. These two truths are necessary for the proof of the Cogito: Every time I am conscious of thinking, I, a thinking substance, exist; and thinking is an action which can exist only as the action or state of a substance. Descartes assumes these two statements as truths but does not prove them. In fact he borrows them from the very medieval philosophers whom he despises. His philosophy is no less based upon the existence of substances and their states, actions, or attributes than the philosophy of the medieval Scholastics.

And finally, what about the influence of the Cogito? Descartes grounds his entire philosophy on the absolute truth that when I am conscious of thinking, I know I exist. In Descartes's theory of knowledge, the one truth that is unshakable, safe and secure from any doubt, is that of my own existence as a conscious subject. Thus the Cartesian Cogito introduces *subjectivism* into modern philosophy.

Subjectivism

Subjectivism is the view that I can know with certainty only myself as conscious subject and my thoughts. It is the view that I can know with certainty only my own mind and its content. Subjectivism carries the implication that the knowledge of other minds and of material objects can be proved, if at all, only by inference from what I know with certainty, the existence of my own subjective consciousness and my thoughts or ideas. (Note the title of Meditation II: "Of the Nature of the Human Mind and That It Is Easier to Know Than the Body.") Therefore for subjectivism the knowledge of the existence of every thing other than my own mind becomes questionable, problematic: The existence of my body, the sun, other minds, God, the physical universe, these must be proved to exist and they can be proved to exist in only one way: by inference from my consciousness and its content, which are all that can be known with certainty.

But since my own mind and its thoughts are all I can know with certainty, and since the existence of anything else is therefore questionable, subjective consciousness and its contents are separated from the physical world of nature and from the social world of human beings. These are external to me, out there, separate from what I am certain of—my own consciousness and its thoughts. Can this chasm, this gulf ever be bridged? This problem and these questions begin with Descartes and plague all philosophy which comes after him.

8

GOD EXISTS

Theory of Knowledge

Descartes has begun his bold and grandiose attempt to build a rationalistic mathematical philosophy which no one could doubt. So far, in Meditations I and II, he has established a first principle, an axiom for his philosophy: *Cogito ergo sum:* Every time I think, I exist as a conscious being, a thinking substance. This he established as a self-evident truth, which no mind could doubt or deny.

But he is now afraid that he is stuck, trapped in the Cogito. The Cogito proof establishes that *I exist* as a mind with my own thoughts, and that this is all that I can *know* with certainty. This is the position of *subjectivism*. But Descartes fears that he may fall into the philosophical position of *solipsism*, the view that my mind with its thoughts it the *only* thing that exists, the only reality: and that other persons and the physical world are only ideas within my mind. Solipsism is dangerously close to being a philosophic expression of the form of insanity called schizophrenia. One striking feature of the schizophrenic personality is his withdrawal from the common world of reality into his own private world, in which his mind and his thoughts are all that exist for him, are the only reality. Has the Cogito proof that I exist as a thinking thing with my own thoughts become a trap, trapping Descartes in solipsism, the doctrine that my own mind with its own thoughts is all that is real? And trapping him also in the schizophrenic's withdrawal into a private, closed-in world as the only reality?

How can Descartes escape this strange solitude of solipsism and the private, cut-off world of schizophrenia? He can do this only by proving that something else exists besides his own mind and its thoughts. In that case, my mind would not be the sole reality. But how, with his demand for absolute mathematical certainty, can he prove that anything exists except his own mind and its ideas?

The Test of Truth. Descartes goes back to the Cogito: It at least is an absolutely true proposition. But what makes it true and certain? His answer is that a proposition is "true and certain" insofar as it is clear and distinct to the mind. A true and certain proposition is so clear in itself, and so different from any other idea, that the mind cannot help accepting it. This, then, is his criterion or test of certain truth—that in order to be certainly true, ideas must be self-evidently clear and distinct. But he has already run into a problem on this score with regard to mathematical propositions. Mathematical propositions he believes to be self-evidently clear and distinct, and thus as meeting the test of being "true and certain." But Descartes now sees that this very belief must be doubted, in accordance with the principle of methodological skepticism— doubting whatever can be doubted. How do I know that propositions which are clear and distinct are certainly true?

Once again, then, Descartes raises the possibility that in believing in the certainty of mathematics he is deceived by a malignant or evil god. It would be easy for him, says Descartes, if he wishes it, to cause me to fall into error, or to hold false beliefs, even when I believe myself to have the very best evidence. An evil, deceptive god could not deceive me with regard to the Cogito—I think, therefore I am—since even if I am deceived in believing it, I must exist as a thinking thing. But an evil god could deceive me with regard to any other belief. Then how, Descartes asks himself, can I know that anything else exists other than what the Cogito establishes, that I exist as a thinking substance? How can I know that there is any reality other than my mind? And so Descartes decides, near the beginning of his Third Meditation, "I must examine whether there is a God as soon as an opportunity occurs, and if I find there is one, I must also investigate whether He can be a deceiver, for as long as this is unknown, I do not see that I can ever be certain of anything."

Rationalistic Proofs of the Existence of God

Descartes therefore must prove that God exists and that He is no deceiver. But is it possible to prove that God exists? The great medieval Catholic theologians, such as Saint Anselm and Saint Thomas, tried to prove by rational deductive arguments that God exists. Reasoning from axioms which they believed to be self-evidently true, they attempted to deduce the existence of God. These are now called the Classical Rationalistic Proofs of the Existence of God, and they have been subjected to devastating criticism by modern philosophy.

But Descartes cannot at this point in his own philosophy make use of these famous medieval proofs of God's existence, because he now knows only that he himself exists. He cannot, therefore, argue, as Saint Thomas did, from the existence of the world, with its vast chain of causes and effects, to the existence of God as first cause. This type of argument, offered by Saint Thomas, is known as the Cosmological Argument or Proof of God's Existence, and it claims that since everything in the world has a cause there must be a first cause in the series of causes, and to this necessary first cause of all else, "everyone gives the name of God." Clearly, Descartes cannot argue that God exists as the necessary first cause of all other causes in the world, because Descartes has not yet proved that there is a world, and so is not entitled to use the world in an argument. Similarly, Descartes cannot use another of Saint Thomas's proofs of God's existence, the so-called argument from design, which also assumes that the world exists, and reasons that the harmony and orderliness and beauty of physical nature, by which humanity is provided with suitable temperature, light, air, food, water, shelter, and aesthetic delight, could not be accidental, but must have been planned or designed for the well-being of humans by an intelligent being. Standing on a mountaintop, or seated in a plane, overlooking a vista of mountains and valleys, who has not believed at that moment that this panorama is designed by God? God exists, reasons the argument from design, as the necessary designer, planner, and governor of the world. But Descartes cannot deduce from the beneficent and harmonious order of the world the existence of God as the master intelligence who designed such a world, because Descartes has not yet proved that the world exists.

How, then, will he make his move out of the Cogito, which establishes only the certainty that I myself exist, to prove that God exists? He can prove God's existence only by reasoning from the only proposition he has established as absolutely true—that I, Descartes, exist as a thinking thing, a conscious substance, having ideas.

Theory of Knowledge: Ideas. By "idea" Descartes means anything one is conscious of—feelings (of joy or pain or empathy); sense perceptions (of the sun, or of a tree, or of crowds of people on a city street); recollections or memories (of one's childhood, or of a recent war, or of a public scandal); thoughts of the intellect or reason (scientific, mathematical, or philosophical statements).

Once again, Descartes looks at his ideas and finds that he can identify three main features of ideas—where they come from, what kind of reality they have, and what they refer to. His first point is that when we ask what the source of our ideas is, where they come from, how do we happen to have them, we find that there are three kinds of ideas: there are those ideas which he claims are born with everyone, and which he calls *innate*, and appear to come from our own nature, and to be known by the light of our own reason, such as the ideas of substance or thing, cause, existence, time, space, the basic principles of mathematics and logic. Second, there are those ideas which appear to be invented by human imagination, and which he calls *factitious*, such as ideas of mermaids, unicorns, utopias, or future worlds. And third, there are those ideas which appear to come from outside us, which nature seems to suggest to us, and which come despite our will. These ideas he calls *adventitious*, for example, hearing a noise, seeing the sun, trees, or colors. Descartes has now shown the ways in which ideas differ with respect to their source or how we come to have them. *Innate ideas* are those that come from the nature of human reason itself and are natural to all human beings; *factitious ideas* come from human imaginative inventiveness; and *adventitious ideas* seem to be caused by things outside us in the world.

Now he proceeds to the second feature of ideas, the kind of reality they have. His point is that insofar as ideas are present in our minds, they exist actually in our minds and have what he calls *actual or formal reality*. And now Descartes makes his third and last point with regard to ideas. Here he is not concerned with where ideas come from or what kind of reality they have, but with what they are ideas of, what they are about, what objects do they represent? Ideas are ideas of something, of objects, ideas represent or refer to objects. This feature of ideas Descartes calls their *objective reality*. The objective reality of ideas consists in their referring to objects, their being about objects—as the idea of God refers to God, the idea of an oak tree refers to an oak tree, the idea of my army refers to an army.

The Idea of God. All of these ideas, he says, could possibly be factitious, my inventions, "made up" or caused by me, except for the Idea of God. Now Descartes is ready to begin talking about the Idea of God. But what is our Idea of God? God is an existent substance possessing all positive qualities in their most eminent degree, that is, in the fullest degree of reality, in their perfect form. And, Descartes adds, God is infinite perfect being. He has in Himself any infinite perfection for good that is not limited by some imperfection. The positive qualities of goodness, knowledge, power, duration, are possessed by God to this perfect degree. Descartes presents the Idea of God: "By the name God I understand a substance which is infinite, independent, all-knowing, all-powerful, and by which I myself and everything else that does exist, have been created." Descartes's argument will be that we can think this Idea of God only because a real God exists who is the cause of this idea. He is going to argue that what makes it possible for us to have this idea can only be God Himself, whose existence causes us to have it.

First Proof of God. How does Descartes prove this?

Ideas and Causes. First of all, he says, we have a clear and distinct Idea of God. But all ideas are the effects of causes. Then there must be some cause of our Idea of God. Furthermore, he says, we must remember three self-evident propositions about causes:

1. There must be as much reality in the cause as in its effect. "For pray," he asks, "whence can the effect derive its reality if not from its cause?"
2. Something cannot proceed from nothing.
3. What is more perfect cannot proceed from the less perfect.

Therefore nothing could cause my Idea of God as a perfect substance that is not as perfect as the idea. Although I could be the cause of my ideas of physical objects or animals or men—since there is nothing so great or perfect in these ideas that I could not have caused them—I could not, however, have caused the Idea of God because I am only a finite, imperfect being, whereas the Idea of God is of a perfect, and infinite, being. So something else, greater than me must have caused my Idea of God, something which is at least as great and perfect as the effect, my Idea of God. Therefore, the cause of my Idea of God, since it must be as great as the effect, can only be an infinite, perfect being, namely God Himself. Therefore, God exists as the only possible cause of my idea of Him.

This is Descartes's first proof of God. Having proved that God exists, we can now know that God cannot be a deceiver, since fraud and deception, says Descartes, have their origin in some defect, or imperfection, whereas God as perfect being has no defects or imperfections. God does not will evil or practice deception, since these are imperfections, the negation of perfect being.

Doctrine of Innate Ideas. Finally, Descartes claims that my Idea of God is innate in me, native to my mind. God is the cause of this idea in us. He has caused this idea to be innate in all human beings. God has imprinted it in us as the mark of Himself, the workman who has fashioned us. Many ideas are thus imprinted in us from birth; for example, the ideas of God, cause, substance, logic, and mathematics. They are not derived by generalization from experience, nor do they require empirical evidence. Innate ideas are clear and distinct, self-evident to the mind. We can know that they are absolutely certain truths since God has been proven to exist, and God would not deceive us in what is self-evident to the reason He has given us.

Criticisms of First Proof of God

There was a great flurry of objections by critics to this first proof of God presented by Descartes. The critics disagreed that God is the only possible cause of my Idea of Him. They argued that an individual person could cause the idea of an infinite being, since it is merely a negative idea, a negation of our limitations or finiteness. An infinite being is simply a being without my limitations. In defending himself against these critics, Descartes argued that the idea of the infinite is not merely the negation of the finite. Finitude, imperfection in knowledge or power of goodness, requires a standard of perfection. How would I know that I am imperfect, how would I know that something is lacking to me unless I had within me for comparison and as a standard the idea of a perfect being? Descartes is here identical with Plato in insisting that knowledge of the ideal, the standard, the pure form is necessary in order to judge the imperfections of the world and that this knowledge cannot come from the imperfect world. Descartes argues that the innate, God-given Idea of God is necessary for us to be able to judge our finiteness and imperfections.

Most moderns would also disagree with Descartes on several other points. They would argue that the Idea of God as he defines it is not universal and therefore cannot be innate in all human beings. God apparently has not imprinted this idea upon humans in the Oriental world; Buddhism, for example, has no idea of a supernatural God, such as Descartes claims is innate in all human beings. Neither do many African and American Indian tribes have such an idea. The Cartesian Idea of God is clearly the product, most moderns would say, of being socialized into cultures that are Judeo-Christian, as Descartes, Saint Thomas, and the scholastics were. Moreover, most moderns would challenge the claim that the concept of perfection is necessary for the concept of imperfection. Instead, they would say perfection, the idea of an infinite being, is the product of reasoning, extending and magnifying the qualities (e.g., knowledge, power) of a finite and imperfect being. And finally, moderns would argue against Descartes's rationalistic view of causality, in which the effect can be no greater than the cause, the more perfect cannot come from the less perfect, and something cannot come from nothing. Modern empiricism means by cause and effect only an invariant relation in space and time.

Second Proof of God. But Descartes offered two other proofs of God as well, since he feared that his first proof might be too complex for his readers, as indeed it turned out to be. And so we turn to his second proof. "I asked," he says, "whether I, who have the idea of an infinite and perfect being, can exist if this being does not exist?" Notice that this proof is, like the first proof, based on the Cogito, on my existence as a conscious being having ideas. What then are the possible causes of my existence? Descartes enumerates all the possibilities: Myself? My parents or some other source less perfect than God? Or God?

Descartes moves along in his argument by a process of elimination: (1) Not myself. I cannot have caused myself to exist because if I were the author of my own being and independent of everything else, nothing would be lacking to me, I would doubt nothing and desire nothing (so also says the twentieth-century philosopher Jean-Paul Sartre—to be without lack is what we all desire and can never have). If I could, says Descartes, I would have given myself all perfections, but I lack the power. Therefore I cannot be the cause of myself. (2) Not my parents or any other cause less perfect than God. My parents have caused me to exist, but one must then ask who caused them to exist, and then one falls into an infinite series of causes, going back further over the generations. (3) Therefore God exists as the only possible cause of my existence as a thinking thing.

Third Proof of God. Descartes's third proof of God is not presented until the Fifth Meditation. He still bases his argument on the Cogito, but he has already established the existence of God and the truth of all his clear and distinct ideas, since God does not deceive us. In the first proof, in the Third Meditation, he had asked what is the cause of my idea of a perfect being, God? In the second proof he had asked what is the cause of my existence as a conscious being having this Idea of God?

Here in the Fifth Meditation Descartes focuses upon his Idea of God as a clear and distinct idea. Having established that his clear and distinct ideas are true, he sees that this may be used for another proof of God. He says, all the properties I clearly and distinctly conceive God to have, truly belong to Him, just as the properties of a triangle that I clearly and distinctly perceive (for example, that the sum of its internal angles is 180 degrees) belong to the triangle. Descartes argues that just as the clear and distinct idea of a triangle includes that the sum of its angles is 180 degrees, so the clear and distinct idea of a perfect being includes the perfection of existence. To exist, he argues, belongs to the nature of God as a perfect being. If God lacked existence, He would be less than perfect. But God has no imperfections. The clear and distinct Idea of God is of a divine nature with all perfections, and necessarily with the perfection of existence.

Descartes is here offering what is called the ontological

proof of God, which argues from our Idea of God as a perfect being to the claim that His nature must therefore have the perfection of existence. This argument was developed by Saint Anselm in the eleventh century. In opposition to this ontological argument, Descartes's polite but hostile critic the empiricist Pierre Gassendi, who had been sent a copy of the *Meditations* for his comments, claimed that the Idea of God as a perfect being has nothing whatever to do with the actual existence of such a being. Years later, Kant and other philosophers offered the same criticism.

The Cartesian Circle. And now to mention what many regard as the most serious criticism of Descartes's *Meditations*. This is a criticism of what is commonly called the Cartesian Circle. ("Cartesian" is the adjective derived from Descartes's name.) We have seen that Descartes's strategy is to use the proof that a perfect, nondeceiving God exists in order to establish that I can trust my clear and distinct ideas and thus move beyond the Cogito to other certain truths. But is this not a vicious circle? Because in order to prove that God exists, Descartes had had to use the very clear and distinct ideas (i.e., substance, cause, the effect cannot be greater than the cause) that God's existence was supposed to guarantee. And so God guarantees my clear and distinct ideas: but my clear and distinct ideas are what guarantee the existence of God. Thus, to prove that my clear and distinct ideas are true, Descartes had to show that God exists and that He is not a deceiver. This he does, but in proving that God exists he relies on the truth of clear and distinct ideas that God's existence was supposed to guarantee. Few scholars believe that Descartes can avoid this vicious circle. In Descartes's own time his critic Arnauld perceived the Cartesian Circle immediately: God's existence is guaranteed by the clear and distinct ideas that His existence was supposed to guarantee, such ideas as the effect cannot be greater than the cause and the more perfect cannot come from the less perfect.

When we turn to Meditation IV, Descartes is finding it necessary to explain how we fall into error. Since he has proved the existence and truthfulness of God and the certainty of my clear and distinct ideas, then how is it possible for me to make errors, and false judgments. God is not responsible for my errors. Rather, says Descartes, error is the result of the imbalance between my understanding and my will. My understanding enables me to have clear and distinct ideas only about a very limited number of things. But my will ventures into claims about all manner of things. The way to keep from falling into error is to restrain the will from making judgments about what the understanding does not clearly and distinctly know. (Here we see again the prudence of Descartes.)

So far, Descartes's mathematical procedure has shown: (1) that what I can be most certain of is my own existence as a conscious being; (2) next, I can be certain of God's existence, and more certain of God's existence than of anything in the physical world. So far, he has proven only that he himself exists as a thinking thing and God exists. How can he show that the physical world exists? But the physical world is what the exciting new science was about—the new science of physics and astronomy, for which Galileo had been punished until his death. How can Descartes prove that the physical world exists, and that it is heliocentric, without being punished by the Church's Inquisition and dying as Galileo had died?

9

THE CLOCKWORK UNIVERSE

Day after day, hour after hour, the meditations of the solitary philosopher continued. Descartes began the First Meditation with the remark: "Today, then, since I have banished all care . . ." He began the Second Meditation with the words: "The meditation of yesterday plunged me into so many doubts . . ." And he began the Fourth Meditation with the words: "In these past days . . ." Are the six Meditations, then, the actual work of six days, like God's creation of the world? In fact, he had worked on the problems he dealt with in the *Meditations* for ten years, and the actual writing took perhaps two years. What then are we to make of Descartes's references to his six days of meditation? In part it is for literary effect, but it is also no doubt influenced by Descartes's student days at his Jesuit college, where for the six days of Holy Week all students were required to devote themselves without any communication with the outside world to studying the spiritual meditations of Saint Ignatius Loyola, the founder of the Jesuit religious order. But whereas Loyola's meditations tried to bring about commitment to Catholicism, Descartes's meditations tried to find a philosophy which any rational mind must accept.

The Reversal of Doubt

By the end of the Fourth Meditation, the doubt that had devastated all his beliefs has been riversed. The destruction has been replaced by a slow but rationally inescapable reconstruction of reality. We find Descartes composing the beginning of the Fifth Meditation, sitting at his writing table, eager to advance this tense, tightly reasoned, and dangerous philosophic argument, eager to push the argument through to its rational completion, with all the parts in their logical order. When finished, the *Meditations* will compel acceptance, he believes, from any rational mind.

Clear and Distinct Ideas: Meditations I–IV. By using his mathematical method he has reversed doubt by the end of the Fourth Meditation and replaced it with certainty. In order to accomplish the reversal of doubt, these are the clear and distinct, rationally self-evident ideas he has used, whether by proving them or by assuming them as axioms without proof: (1) I exist as a thinking thing (*Cogito ergo sum;* proof); (2) the test of truth is that what is clearly and distinctly perceived is true $(3 + 2 = 5)$; (3) only substances exist independently (as does my mind, a thinking substance); (4) qualities, states, or attributes can exist only as states or attributes of substances (thinking can exist only as a state of a thinking thing, a thinking substance); (5) something cannot come from nothing: (6) nothing can exist without a cause (a clock could not exist without a maker); (7) the cause must be as real and as powerful as the effect (the infinite universe could have had as its cause only an infinite substance, namely God); (8) the more perfect cannot come from the less perfect (so, according to Descartes, the ideas of a perfect God could not come from an imperfect human being); (9) God exists as a completely perfect being and is self-caused, not caused by or dependent upon anything other than Himself; proof; (10) since God is perfect and not a deceiver, clear and distinct ideas, including those of mathematics and logic, which appear to be absolutely true, can be known to be absolutely true; the possibility that I am deceived in believing them to be true has been eliminated by the proof that a perfect God exists.

Proof of the Existence of Physical Substance

Now that Descartes has proved that I exist as a thinking substance, and that God exists as a perfect substance, there remains only the last major proof—that physical substances exist independently of my mind, that physical things in a physical universe exist externally to me, a thinking thing. And so at the beginning of the Fifth Meditation, Descartes says, "My chief task is to rid myself of all those doubts with which I have been encumbered these past few days and to see if anything certain can be known about material things." Do material things exist, Descartes asks? Can I know this with certainty, and know what the properties of physical things are? My knowledge of physical things has usually come to me through my senses. I refer my feelings to my own body as their source. And I perceive other human bodies and physical things by my senses of sight, hearing, touch, taste, and smell.

Although I once believed my senses to be telling me the truth about physical things, I came to see reasons for doubting the senses, says Descartes. On the basis of what I know now, what should I believe of all that the senses tell me? All my life my senses told me that I have a head, hands, feet, and all the other parts of the body, and that contact with other bodies sometimes gave me pleasure and sometimes pain. I noted that physical objects have size and shape and that they move; also that they are hard or soft, warm or cold, to my touch. I have also felt hunger and thirst and other appetites, and I have felt joy and sadness. I observed by my senses light, color, sounds, tastes, and smells, and these enabled me to see the sky, the earth, and the sea. It was therefore natural for me to believe that these ideas were due to objects outside me and that these objects were similar to the ideas which they caused in me.

Later, however, says Descartes, various experiences gradually ruined all my faith in the senses. I found that judgments based upon the external senses (such as sight) were erroneous; huge statues seen from a distance look tiny, and square towers appear round. Internal senses are also deceptive: I have heard that people with amputated limbs sometimes feel sensations in them. (Notice that Descartes's examples of the untrustworthiness of the senses are weak and strained—Descartes the rationalist is trying to refute empiricism, which claims that the senses are our best source of knowledge.)

What shall I now believe, he asks? Are my ideas which are based upon the senses caused by objects outside me which are similar to them? Here we see Descartes moving toward the final reversal of doubt, toward reconstruction after the skeptical destruction. I now know as certainties, he says, that I exist as a thinking thing and that God exists as a perfect being. I also know that nothing exists without a cause. What then is the cause of my idea of bodies, my own body, others' bodies, the physical world? Here Descartes is repeating the argument he used in his first proof of the existence of God: He began from the Cogito, from my existence as a thinking thing, with an idea of God, and asked what could be the cause of my idea? Now Descartes asks what could be the cause of my idea of a physical body? His procedure is again a process of elimination.

Could I myself be the cause of my idea of physical bodies? But I cannot be the cause. The size and shape of my body, the town, the people, the sun, the fields—all these ideas of bodies were passively received by me. They do not depend upon my willing them. In fact, these ideas of bodies often occur contrary to my will. When I am in a small boat far out at sea, I cannot control the gathering storm clouds. But there is another argument against my being their cause: I could not be the cause since I am a thinking substance. Inasmuch as the effect must be like the cause, the cause of the idea of physical substance must be itself a physical substance. He now asks whether God could be the cause of this idea. But then He would be deceiving me in allowing me to have a strong inclination to believe that the cause of these ideas is in physical things. Therefore we must conclude that physical things, material bodies exist as the causes of our ideas of them. And so physical substance, the last of the three components of reality—self (thinking substance), God, nature (physical substance)—has been proved to exist.

"But this does not mean," says Descartes, the rationalist, hastily, "that material bodies exist exactly as our senses show them to be." It is only my clear and distinct idea of physical things that can tell me what their true nature is. But what is a physical substance? Do I have a clear and distinct idea of it? This is the right moment, as he knew, in which to pick up from the Second Meditation his analysis of the piece of wax. This was Descartes's first consideration of material substance in the *Meditations*. He had brought it in immediately after his successful proof of the Cogito, of my own existence as a thinking substance. "I am a thinking thing . . . I am not that assemblage of limbs which is called a human body." But, he continues, in the Second Meditation, let me indulge my mind, which cannot help thinking that it knows bodies perceived by the senses better than it knows my existence as a thinking thing, which is known to me by reason. Let me indulge my mind in thinking about body, so that later, at the right moment, the reins may be drawn in and the mind submitted to control. (The time for tightening the reins on our thinking that we know body by the senses comes in the Sixth Meditation.)

The Piece of Wax. Let us speak, he goes on, not of bodies in general, because such talk is confusing, but of a particular body, the bodies we touch and see. Let us take this piece of wax. Not too long ago it was in the beehive. It has not yet lost the sweetness of the honey. It still has something of the scent of the flowers from which the bees made it. Its color, shape, and size are observable to sight. It is hard and cold to the touch. If you strike it, it will give off an audible sound. In these few lines Descartes has accounted for all of the senses as they respond to the wax. But now he brings a flame to the wax. Gone immediately is the taste of honey, the smell of the flowers, the color; the shape is changed, the size increases, it liquifies, becomes hot where it had been cold. If you strike it, there is no sound.

Is it the same piece of wax? Everyone would say yes. But all its properties perceived by the senses are now changed. What property remains, in virtue of which it is the same piece of wax? The real properties of anything, Descartes argues, are those that remain constant throughout change. The property that remains in the wax is that it is something that is extended and changeable. The properties of being extended in space and capable of change are the only true characteristics of the wax or of any material body. And these properties are known by reason, by the intellect, by my rational reflection about physical things—and not by the senses. (Here we see Descartes the rationalist arguing that reason is the only method for reaching true and certain knowledge of myself, of God, of physical nature.)

Thus Descartes has concluded that nothing belongs to physical things but extension in space, length, breadth, and depth, in various sizes and shapes, and in motion. Physical objects, then, have only the properties or qualities of spatial extension, the qualities of size and shape and the capacity of motion, and these are the only qualities or properties which physical things truly have, the only objective qualities which physical nature has. What, then, does Descartes have to say about other qualities, those that did not remain when the wax melted, the qualities of color, touch, taste, smell, sound? Do these qualities *not* belong to physical things? Did they not belong to the piece of wax before it melted? Are the golden color and the sweet smell of the wax objective qualities? Do they exist as the qualities of physical substances or not?

What is Descartes prepared to say about the color and sounds and smells and tastes of the piece of wax, of the physical world? Descartes is prepared to say only what the physicist Galileo had said—that the only objective, real qualities of physical objects are the qualities of being extended in space with some size and shape, and being capable of motion. These are the qualities which reason knows by a clear and distinct idea to constitute the true nature of physical things. Moreover, these are the qualities which a physical body must have in order to be a physical thing—the piece of wax could lose its softness, its smell of honey, its sweetness of taste, and still be a physical thing. Why? Because it still has spatial extension, it still has length, breadth, and depth. In other words, physical things need not have colors or tastes or odors in order to exist, but in order to be physical things at all, they *must* have size and shape.

What, then, is the case against colors, tastes, sounds, as objective, real qualities that belong to physical substances? (1) Colors, tastes, sounds, and smells are not necessary qualities of physical things, such as the piece of wax, whereas having spatial extension, having some size and shape is necessary for the piece of wax to exist at all as a physical thing. Colors, tastes, sounds, are not qualities which are necessary to the existence of a physical thing. (2) We have a clear and distinct idea of spatial extension as the necessary, essential quality of the piece of wax, but we have no clear and distinct idea of the color of the wax as belonging essentially or necessarily to the piece of wax. In fact, as Descartes says in the Sixth Meditation, what we apprehend by the senses (colors, tastes, and sounds) are not qualities of physical objects at all, but rather they are qualities which exist only in us. They are caused by external objects which stimulate our sense organs. The stimulation of the eyes, ears, nose, throat, and skin has the effect of our seeing colors, hearing sounds, and experiencing odors, tastes, and tactile sensations like hot and cold, hard and soft, rough and smooth. These qualities are not in physical objects, they are not real attributes of the physical world—they are merely in us, the result of the impact of physical objects upon our bodily sense organs.

We have already seen that Descartes himself classified such ideas as adventitious ideas, ideas which come to us from things outside us in the world. By contrast, the idea of spatial extension as the essential, necessary quality of physical things Descartes has classified as an innate idea, an idea which is born with every human being, and is known by our reason, not by our bodily sensations. The qualities of color, sound, taste, which Descartes calls adventitious and says are in us and not in the physical object, were named *secondary qualities* by the empiricists of Great Britain before the seventeenth century ended—and this is what they have been called ever since. The name of *primary qualities* was given to those qualities which Descartes identified as known by reason, as the qualities necessary to a physical thing—size, shape, and the capacity of motion. For Descartes, primary qualities of physical things are known by reason, by a clear and distinct idea; the empiricists will argue that both primary and secondary qualities are known only by the senses. Descartes's friend Mersenne had collected a sixth set of "objections" to the *Meditations* from his own circle of philosophers and mathematicians in Paris. Descartes replied with a strong defense of his theory of physical substance:

> I observed that nothing at all belonged to the . . . essence of body except that it was a thing with length and breadth and depth, admitting of various shapes and various motions . . . which no power could make to exist apart from it; and on the other hand that colour, odours; savours and the rest of such things were merely sensations existing in my thought, and differing no less from bodies than pain differs from the shape and motion of the instrument which inflicts it.

Descartes's theory of physical substance was of great advantage to the new physical sciences. By denying the objective reality of secondary qualities and insisting that the only qualities of physical objects are the spatial qualities of size, shape, and the capacity of motion, Descartes limited the properties of matter to those which scientists could measure, quantify, and explain by mathematics. Not only did Descartes show that the physical world exists—but that the physical world has exactly those qualities which the new science says it has—it is nothing but particles with size and shape moving according to the laws of mechanics. By claiming that the physical world is knowable by the absolutely true laws of geometry and mechanics, Descartes laid the foundations for contemporary mathematical physics.

But if physical bodies are nothing but spatially extended things, if they are only sizes and shapes in space, analyzed by geometry, the science of space, they are only static geometric figures. How can Descartes account for the motion of physical things? What is the source of motion? The clear and distinct idea of spatial extension does not include the idea of motion. Whence motion? From God Himself, says Descartes. God causes motion to exist in the world. He is the first cause of motion in the physical universe and he provided a fixed and constant amount of motion or energy. But after creating the world and setting it in motion according to the laws of geometry and mechanics, God does not interfere with the mechanical clockwork of the universe.

God's noninvolvement with the world in the philosophy of Descartes was very upsetting to the French mathematician and philosopher Pascal, born a generation later than Descartes, and a devout and profoundly religious Catholic. Pascal writes:

> I cannot forgive Descartes. He would have liked, in the whole of his philosophy, to be able to bypass God. But he could not help making Him give a shove to set the world in motion, after that he has nothing further to do with God.

Mechanism: The Clockwork Universe

Descartes's theory of the physical universe is called *mechanism*. Mechanism is the theory that all of nature can be explained by the mechanical motion of material substances. In Descartes's mechanistic view of the world, the world is infinite in extension, with bodies of all shapes and sizes continually moving and changing. All motion of bodies is due to mechanical impact, like the mechanical workings in a clock. The infinite universe is through and through mechanical, from the vast celestial clockwork of the motion of the planets, which Galileo described, to all inorganic physical things— these too move mechanically on impact. This is what the physical universe is for Descartes: a mechanical clockwork system of bodies in motion according to the laws of physics. The physical world consists of bodies of various geometrical sizes and shapes, colorless, soundless, without smell, taste, or texture. They move on impact with one another in purposeless, mechanical motion in a clockwork universe.

Descartes's Theory of Animals as Mechanical Clockworks. For Descartes all living bodies, all living organisms are also mechanical clockworks, extended in space, moving on impact with other bodies. Descartes is famous for his view that animals are automata, mechanically responsive to the stimulus of other bodies. Descartes would at the present time be called a behaviorist with regard to animals. He denied that animals have reason, intelligence, mind, or any inner mental states. Such feelings as they have arise only from the mechanical motions of their bodies. Descartes reduced animals to being nothing but matter in motion. Descartes claimed that if machines were constructed to look like animals, we could not tell them apart.

The fact that animals cannot use language to express themselves, says Descartes, "does not show merely that the brutes have less reason than men, but that they have none at all, since it is clear that very little is required in order to be able to talk." And although it is true that animals are sometimes very skillful (as for example, beavers are skillful in building dams) this "shows rather that they have no reason at all, it is nature which acts in them according to the disposition of their organs, just as a clock, which is only composed of wheels and weights, is able to tell the hours and measure the time more correctly than we can do with all our wisdom."

In opposition to Descartes's theory of animals stands the Darwinian theory of evolution, showing the evolution from a common origin of all living species. Whereas Descartes sees rationality as completely separating humans from animals by an unbridgeable gulf, Darwinian theory shows no sharp divisions or separations, but a continuous gradation of capacities and functions, from the lowest living organisms to those of the human species. The medieval scholastic philosophers and Catholic theologians had also argued that there is a continuity of all living species and that animals do indeed have souls, but of a lesser nature than the souls of humans. But for Descartes whatever is not rational, thinking substance is nothing but a mechanism, nothing but matter in motion.

Recent scientific experiments have focused upon the intelligence of various animal species, and have shown that one of Descartes's automata, the porpoise, is a creature of high intelligence, capable of communicating with humans. There is also a profound opposition to Descartes's view of animals from many people who love and honor animals for their moral qualities of innocence and lack of hypocrisy, while condemning humans for their hypocrisy and lack of innocence.

As for human beings, Descartes believes that we are thinking things, rational, moral, and spiritual beings; as such, we are not extended in space and cannot be a mere clockwork as animals are for him. But human bodies are extended in space and they are a clockwork as mechanical as the bodies of animals. Any human activity that does not depend upon thinking is to Descartes as mechanical as animal behavior: the beating of the heart, digestion, respiration, circulation of the blood. And Descartes seems to be looking ahead to our present world of automation and thinking machines in his account of the mechanical aspect of the human body: "This will not seem strange to those who know how many different automata or moving machines can be made by the industry of man." Is Descartes looking into a future of mechanical men whom we will not be able to tell apart from human beings—as he says we could not tell apart mechanical animals from real ones? Under the influence of Descartes, the view that the bodies of both animals and humans are only mechanical clockworks explained by the science of physics gathered momentum. There appeared during the first half of the twentieth century the Unity of Science movement, with the claim that explanation of all phenomena can be provided by the science of mathematical physics alone—an explanation of everything inorganic, organic, and human. But was this not the vision which came to Descartes on the night of November 10, 1619—the vision of a marvelous mathematical unification of all the sciences?

Descartes's Theory of Physical and Mental Substances

But Descartes's philosophy contains more than a mechanical clockwork physical universe of substances moving according to the laws of physics and the principles of geometry.

There is also a perfect being, God, who provided the original motion for the clockwork. And there are also finite, imperfect selves like us, finite thinking beings. Reality includes self, God, and matter. All are substances (since everything is either a substance or an attribute). But what is a substance? He defines it as a thing which so exists that it needs no other thing in order to exist. Only God can be substance in this strict sense. All other substances require God to exist. Both physical and thinking substances are created by God. They represent completely different kinds of substances.

Thinking Substance. Mind, *thinking substance,* occupies no space; is not in motion; is not part of any clockwork; has the capacity for reasoning, remembering, denying; has free will and is morally responsible for its action.

Physical Substance. Matter by contrast is spatially extended; is in mechanical motion; is infinitely divisible; is totally determined by the impact of other bodies; without the capacity for reasoning; without free will or any moral qualities. Each kind of substance is independent of the other. For each kind of substance there is a distinct and appropriate discipline which studies it. Matter is studied by physics, the new science of Copernicus and Galileo. Mind is studied by Church theology and by philosophy.

Has Descartes cut the pie of reality in half, giving the mental half to the Church and the physical half to science as a strategy on behalf of science, to pacify the Church and allay its suspicions that the new science is going to undermine all the teachings of the Church? Or is Descartes's claim that there are two kinds of reality, physical and mental, a true description of what reality is? Or was the strategy also a truth?

10

BODY AND SOUL

It was the influential twentieth-century French philosopher
Alain who made the best known of all the comments on the
famous Frans Hals portrait of Descartes: "This is a terrible
man to have as your teacher. He looks at you as if to say:
Here is another one who will never get things straight, who is
always going to be off the track."

Metaphysical Dualism

We have seen Descartes's hard, cold mathematical reasoning combined with his passionate personal quest for certainty
arrive at a chain of rational, absolutely certain proofs. Step by
step he established first that I exist, then that God exists,
next that all of my clear and distinct ideas are true since God
guarantees them, then that the physical world exists, and
finally, that the reality of the physical and human worlds
correspond to my clear and distinct ideas of them. Thus my
rational, clear, and distinct ideas are the key to all of reality.
And mathematics is the key to reason. Cartesian rationalism
is as bold a claim for human reason as has ever been made. It
is the claim that the structure of the world corresponds to the
structure of our rational ideas.

But let us look at this reality, at this world which Descartes
constructed and which he claims to be a true picture of the
world in which we live. The most striking feature of the
Cartesian metaphysics, of reality as Descartes's philosophy
describes it, is that it erects a split, a division, a duality, a
dichotomy, between two different kinds of reality: between
mental, spiritual, thinking substance (such as myself and God)

and physical, spatial, extended substance (such as my body, the planets, mountains, trees, and dogs). These two kinds of substances constitute two different and separate worlds. They represent two different and separate realities between which there is a gap which can never be closed. Descartes has presented the classic case of *metaphysical dualism*, of a dualism within reality. *Dualism* is the name for any theory which claims that there are two ultimate and irreducible components in the subject to be explained. *Metaphysical dualism* is the term applied to a metaphysical theory which claims that there are two ultimate and irreducible kinds of reality. Cartesian metaphysical dualism is called psychophysical dualism to indicate that the duality consists on the one hand of the mental, psychological, conscious kind of reality and, on the other hand, of the physical, material, spatial, extended kind of reality.

Cartesian psychophysical dualism may be defined as the doctrine that reality consists of two kinds of substances, mental and physical, and that the one kind of substance can never be shown to be a form of, or be reduced to, the other. So for psychophysical dualism, mind can never be shown to be derived from, or a form of, or a function of, or reducible to, matter. Cartesian psychophysical dualism formulates its doctrine in terms of substances, since Descartes, as we have seen, accepts as a clear and distinct idea that attributes such as mental or physical cannot exist except as belonging to substances. You remember that he used this clear and distinct idea to show that my being conscious of the attribute of thinking proved that I exist as a substance in which thinking is going on. Also, you remember, this is how he showed that my clear and distinct idea of the attribute of extension proved that substances with the attribute of extension exist as the cause of my ideas. Now we can understand why Cartesian psychophysical dualism is regarded as the sharpest and clearest formulation of metaphysical dualism. It is because Descartes has made one attribute, one property or quality, the principal attribute of each kind of substance. He established the principal property of each kind of substance by this question: What is my clear and distinct idea of this thing, what is my clear and distinct idea of its essential, necessary quality or attribute?

For mental, spiritual substance the principal attribute is thinking; it is therefore a thinking kind of substance, substance which is conscious (which means, for Descartes, it thinks, doubts, understands, affirms, denies, wills, refuses, imagines, and feels). But this attribute of thinking is the very attribute which is distinctly lacking in the piece of wax, in spatially extended bodies, and in the motion of bodies from one space or place to another. It is lacking in earthly clockwork mechanisms and in the celestial clockwork of the planets, in the clockwork bodies of animals and humans—there is no consciousness in any of these.

Physical substance is defined, on the other hand, by its principal attribute of being extended in space. It is measurable by geometry, which is the science of spatial measurement. Its motion is mechanical, the result of impact, as the cogs in a machine impact upon the cogs in other wheels, or as one billiard ball impacts upon another. But being physically extended is the very attribute or property which is lacking to mental substances. Minds, thinking things, consciousness are not extended in space, they are not measurable, they are not in motion, they do not move on impact, they do not function like clockworks. Was it by mechanical clockwork that Descartes resolved for once in his life to doubt everything, to overthrow all his beliefs, to attempt to use methodological skepticism in order to reach an absolutely certain belief? That was no clockwork, that was nothing mechanical—that was the masterful triumph of a free spirit, a thinking thing, a mental substance.

Thinking substance, mental, spiritual reality, by definition lacks any spatial extension, occupies no space, is not measurable or quantifiable, is not in motion. (Where, for example, is thinking? In my head?) Physical substance, spatially extended, mathematically measurable, lacks any mental, spiritual, or conscious attribute. Physical things have no consciousness and cannot think. And so we are confronted by the dual, two-fold substances and their attributes of Descartes's world: on the one hand, spatially extended mechanical substances which have no consciousness, no mind; on the other hand, mental, conscious, spiritual, thinking substances which have no body, no spatial extension. Descartes's psychophysical dualism is well expressed by an old English couplet:

> What is mind? No matter.
> What is matter? Never mind.

There is no way in which the absolute differences between these two kinds of reality can ever be bridged, abolished, or overcome. For this reason Cartesian dualism is the most extreme example of psychophysical dualism in the history of philosophy.

The Problem of Free Will and Determinism

But we may see how extreme Cartesian psychophysical dualism is by looking at it in terms of another problem, a problem which has tormented philosophy ever since Saint Augustine: the problem of free will and determinism. Since, as Descartes says, nothing comes from nothing, and everything that exists has a cause, determinism developed historically as the view that everything that exists is the necessary and inevitable result of its antecedent causes and could not be otherwise than it is. Modern determinism from the time of Descartes is dictated by scientific, causal laws, and is the view that everything happens necessarily in accordance with some one or more scientific causal laws. Determinism characterizes the Newtonian universe of spatially extended substances in motion: Physical bodies move as the necessary result of pressure or impact on them of other bodies. This is the way the planets move, their motion being determined by the necessary, mechanical laws of astronomy; this is the way the machinery of a clockwork moves, by the necessary causal impact of one cogged wheel upon another, with the movement of the second wheel being the necessary and inevitable effect of the first wheel.

In total opposition to the necessary, dependent, bound, inevitable, and mechanical determinism of the physical universe, which Descartes, Copernicus, and Galileo had described, there stands the free will of spiritual, thinking, mental substance. The doctrine of free will is the denial that determinism applies to the actions of human beings. Free will is the doctrine that claims that human actions, unlike the mechanical motion of the planets or of clockwork machinery, are not determined by antecedent causes. Human beings as conscious, thinking substances are free in their actions and moral choices, not causally determined. So if I pass through a picket line; if I make a contribution to a church or to a political party; if I am insulting to another human being; if I am physically cruel to an animal; if I am a criminal or a saint—the doctrine of free will claims that these acts are done out of my own free will, that I am a free agent in doing them, and in all my other deliberate actions as well. Therefore, since my will is free, since antecedent causes do not necessitate my actions, I am responsible for my actions. But the doctrine of determinism claims that I am not responsible, that my actions are the inevitable and necessary result of a host of antecedent causes. This issue, between free will and determinism, is especially controversial today in the field of criminal psychiatry, in which the question arises, is the criminal's act the necessary result of antecedent causes, so that he could not help doing what he did—or was he free to do otherwise and therefore responsible? These questions have important consequences for treatment of criminals. Did his biological heritage determine his action, or an unloving family, or the capitalistic system? Is society to be blamed for this act or is the criminal responsible for his own action? For Descartes it is of course the case that human beings, as thinking, conscious, mental, spiritual, moral substances, are free in their thinking, affirming, denying, and willing. As he specifically says, the freedom of the human will is infinite, unlimited. Human beings have infinite freedom in the power to make moral decisions and are accordingly responsible for them. Thus Descartes's dualism of thinking and spatially extended substances establishes the opposition between thinking substances as having free will and physical substances as being subject to causal determinism.

The Mind-Body Problem

But the full impact of Cartesian dualism is yet to be mentioned: It is the impact of Cartesian dualism upon me, the individual human being. It is not only the world which consists of two irreducible, divergent, distinct, opposing substances and their attributes, but it is the individual human being, who now may be seen to be split in two by Cartesian psychophysical dualism: Am I not a thinking thing, a mind, a consciousness with free will? But am I not also a body, spatially extended, measurable, quantifiable, an organic mechanism, a clockwork which is causally determined?

But now I see that according to Descartes my mind and body are utterly, absolutely distinct. As in the universe itself, with its two kinds of substances, mental and physical, there is in me the same absolute, unbridgeable gulf between mind which occupies no space and body which cannot think. There is in me the same lack of unity, the same division and duality. I myself consist of two separate substances. Moreover, the two substances which make up the human being are not of equal significance, for did not Descartes show that I am a thinking thing, that I am a substance whose nature it is to think, and that my principal attribute is thinking?

I am, then, a mental substance, a thinking thing. What, then, is the relation of my body as extended substance to myself as thinking thing? Descartes himself tries to tell us in Meditation VI: "Since on the one hand I have a clear and distinct idea of myself insofar as I am only a thinking thing and not an extended being, and since on the other hand I have a distinct idea of body insofar as it is only an extended substance which does not think, it is certain that this I (that is to say, my soul, by virtue of which I am what I am) is entirely and truly distinct from my body and that it can exist without it." My mind, according to Descartes, is not only entirely different in its attributes from my body, but it is totally independent of my body, and may exist without it; and as Descartes has shown I know my own mind better than I know any physical thing, including my own body.

Then how shall I understand my relationship as a thinking thing to my own body? My body does not belong to my nature. Perhaps it is the case that the soul uses the body to house itself? Or is it that the soul not only uses the body as its habitat but also directs some of the movements of the body, and so is like a pilot on a ship, directing it, as Descartes himself suggests. Descartes's sharp correspondent Antoine Arnaud, a young theologian who was the first to point to the Cartesian Circle, pounced upon this problem immediately. He wrote to him that since Descartes has clearly and distinctly perceived himself to be a thinking thing, this leads to the conclusion that man is "entirely spirit, while his body is merely the vehicle of spirit; whence follows the definition of man as a spirit which makes use of a body." In the twentieth century the British philosopher Gilbert Ryle similarly attacked Descartes's mind-body dualism for representing mind as a "ghost" in a machine.

Descartes has led us into this extreme dualism of mind and body, of an immaterial soul and a material body, according to which they are so completely different that there can be no interaction between my own mind and body. But this runs counter to the evidence of everyday life, in which my mind and body are constantly interacting. My body influences my mind when my body has to cope with a huge Thanksgiving dinner, or with a large intake of beer or hard liquor, or even a small amount of a narcotic. My mind in all of these cases will soon register that it has been affected; it becomes dull, my ideas are no longer clear and distinct, the distinction between dream and reality begins to blur. But how is this possible on the basis of Descartes's dualism? And, conversely, the evidence of everyday life shows that my mind influences my body, that the causal relation can also be from the mind to the body. For example, I decide to salute the flag or to wave good-bye or to shake hands or to whistle for my dog or to run for a bus—and I salute, I wave, I shake hands, I whistle, I run. But according to Descartes's dualism, these could not happen. These actions which my mind has caused in my body are impossible, for how could my mind, which occupies no space, and is not physical, make my body move? Motion is an attribute only of physical things and can be caused only by billiard-ball or clockwork impact upon other physical things.

Why has Descartes led us into this impasse in which his extreme dualistic separation of mind and body denies what anyone can plainly see, that mind and body do interact, that they are not such different kinds of reality that mind cannot produce at will a handshake and that body cannot produce a feeling of pleasant dullness in the mind. The answer to why Descartes has led us down this blind alley is that he was seeking, as we know, a compromise between the powerful new science, with its mechanical, deterministic laws of motion of physical bodies in space, and the powerful old Church, with its dogmas of a perfect, infinite spiritual being who created man, a finite and imperfect spiritual being, and who also created an earthly habitat for him. For the Church, truth about reality came from divine revelation, not from science. It seemed to Descartes that his dualism provided a compromise to ease the bitter enmity between the new science and the Church. He believed he achieved this compromise by the dualism of completely distinct substances. This dualism provides that physical substance, its motion according to causal laws, its determinism, its predictability, would be the exclusive province which science controls. And immune from science, from the laws of physics, and from determinism is mental substance. Mental substance is not spatially extended, not causally determined, not quantifiable, not predictable—but conscious, thinking, remembering, and feeling; able to know the true ideas which are innate and divinely imprinted within it; capable of spontaneity; with free will; responsible and moral. This kind of substance would be under the exclusive jurisdiction of the Church, with no interference from science. Thus the Cartesian theory of dual distinct substances appeared to Descartes to effect a compromise and reconciliation between the Church and the scientists: to each its own jurisdiction—to the scientists, matter and its mechanical laws of motion; to the theologians, mental substance, the souls of human beings. This has been called the Cartesian compromise.

But Descartes himself was unhappy with his psychophysical dualism. He was perfectly well aware of the interaction between mind and body and he tried to show that interaction *was* possible on his strictly dualistic theory. He argued, in what is the weakest contribution of his entire philosophy, that interaction between the soul and the body is possible because the soul is primarily located in the pineal gland in the brain, and there it performs its mental functions and also receives sensations from the body. The pineal gland is therefore the transfer point between soul and body. Through it the soul can move the muscles and nerves of the body, and the motions of the body can in turn influence the mind. Unfortunately, there is no evidence that the pineal gland has such functions. Moreover the pineal gland theory cannot explain how an unextended immaterial soul can have an effect on a part of the brain, or how the physical pineal gland can have any effect upon the immaterial soul.

A last point on Descartes's psychophysical dualism may be mentioned. Descartes's attempt to show that there was indeed the possibility of interaction between soul and body, mind and matter, had destructive consequences for the Cartesian dualism and the compromise upon which he had placed so much emphasis. For if the immaterial, spiritual soul *can* bring about through the pineal gland changes in its body, and by means of the body changes on other bodies, this would destroy the new science and its mechanical motion, by introducing a spiritual element into causality. I myself as a thinking thing become then an alien cause in a mechanistic causal world. On the other hand if through the pineal gland my body can bring about changes in my mind, then my mind is affected by the laws of motion of the body and becomes part of the mechanical clockwork of the body. So interaction would destroy the mechanistic laws of science and the independence of the mind as immaterial substance. Thus the Cartesian compromise failed for two reasons. First, insofar as Descartes presents mind and body as distinct substances (mind under the Church jurisdiction, matter under scientific jurisdiction), their complete distinction runs counter to the facts of interaction between mind and body. Second, Descartes attempts to show interaction between mind and body rather than their being separate and distinct. This also fails because the pineal gland does not explain interaction. More important, interaction would destroy either the mechanism of science or the independence and freedom of the mind.

Although the Cartesian compromise failed, the influence of Descartes remains alive and a potent force; for over three hundred years, since the *Meditations* appeared in 1641, Cartesianism has dominated the intellectual world. To be a philosopher at all you must deal with him. You can agree, or disagree, or find another path—but you must deal with Descartes's skepticism, his rationalism, his mathematical model of truth, his Cogito proof, his subjectivism, his metaphysical dualism of mental and physical substances, and his treatment of the mind-body problem. The mind-body problem has perhaps been the area of Descartes's greatest influence. The difficulties of his dualism of mental and physical substance led to solutions in the form of theories of psychophysical parallelism, psychophysical interactionism, behaviorism, and phenomenology. Descartes's incisive formulation of psychophysical dualism is the point of reference for the perennial discussion by modern philosophers of how to understand the relation between nonmaterial consciousness and the material processes of the brain.

Writing one hundred years later, the Scottish philosopher David Hume dealt with Descartes by violently opposing him. Hume opposed Descartes's rationalism with a more powerful empiricism. He opposed Descartes's skepticism with a more powerful skepticism. He rejected the Cogito proof and Descartes's proofs of God as nonsense. He rejected Descartes's metaphysical dualism and its claim that there are two kinds of substances by denying that we can ever have any proof that mental or physical substances exist. He opposed Descartes's causal mechanism by destroying Descartes's idea of cause and effect. We may say that Hume dealt with Descartes by destroying him. In turning to David Hume we are about to encounter the excitement of the most destructive force in the history of Western philosophy.

SUGGESTIONS FOR FURTHER READING
PART TWO: DESCARTES

Works of Descartes:

Descartes: Discourse on Method and Meditations, translated by L. J. LaFleur. Indianapolis: Bobbs-Merrill, 1960. Text adapted for television series.

Descartes: Selections, edited by Ralph Eaton. New York: Charles Scribner's Sons, 1927.

The Philosophical Works of Descartes, 2 vols. Translated by E.S. Haldane and G.R.T. Ross. Cambridge: Cambridge University Press, 1911–12; 1931. Volume II contains criticisms ("Objections") to the *Meditations* by theologians and philosophers and Descartes's replies to them.

Critical Studies:

Balz, Albert A. *Descartes and the Modern Mind*. New Haven: Yale University Press, 1952.

Beck, L. J. *The Method of Descartes: A Study of the Regulae*. Oxford: Clarendon Press, 1952.

Beck, L. J. *The Metaphysics of Descartes: a Study of the Meditations*. Oxford: Clarendon Press, 1965.

Doney, Willis, ed. *Descartes: A Collection of Critical Essays*. Garden City, New York: Doubleday-Anchor, 1967.

Frankfurt, Harry G. *Demons, Dreamers and Madmen: The Defense of Reason in Descartes's Meditations*. Indianapolis: Bobbs-Merrill, 1970.

Gibson, A. Boyce. *The Philosophy of Descartes*. New York: Russell and Russell, 1932.

Haldane, Elizabeth S. *Descartes: His Life and Times*. New York: E. P. Dutton, 1905.

Keeling, S. V. *Descartes*. London: Ernest Benn, 1934.

Kenny, Anthony. *Descartes: A Study of His Philosophy*. New York: Random House, 1968.

Maritain, Jacques. *The Dream of Descartes*. New York: Philosophical Library, 1944.

Smith, Norman Kemp. *Studies in Cartesian Philosophy*. London: Macmillan, 1902.

Smith, Norman Kemp. *New Studies in the Philosophy of Descartes*. London: Macmillan, 1952.

PART THREE
HUME

11

HOW DO YOU KNOW?

Do you believe that we are living in a time of progress in
scientific knowledge—in nuclear physics, space exploration,
communication by satellite, electronic technology, genetic
research, agricultural research, the control of disease? Do
you believe that this vast accumulation of knowledge is continually improving in certainty and spinning off more and better
technologies for the benefit of human life? If you do, you
share the mentality of the eighteenth century—a mentality
that believes in the truth and progress of science and its
benefits to the progress of humanity. Against this type of
mentality and its cardinal belief in the truth and progress of
science, British empiricism, and especially the empiricism of
David Hume, mounts a devastating attack.

Historical Situation: The Enlightenment

A *Treatise of Human Nature* is Hume's first and most
significant philosophic work. The time is 1740, almost exactly
one hundred years since Descartes wrote the *Meditations* in
1641, and the world has profoundly changed. During the
period of one hundred twenty-five years from Descartes's
death in 1650 to the death of Hume in 1776, the philosophic
life of Europe was at the highest point of intensity and
self-confidence, of vitality and optimism, it has ever known.
This period, from 1650 to 1770, is known as the Age of
Enlightenment. The philosophic outlook and the mood of the
Age of Enlightenment swept across Europe and America. In
America, the Founders of the Republic—Jefferson, Madison,
Adams, Hamilton, for example—were committed to the phi-

losophy of the Enlightenment. The Age of Enlightenment perceived itself as a time in which human reason was shedding its great light upon nature and humanity, banishing the darkness of the Middle Ages with its scholastic philosophy, religious dogmatism, and political absolutism.

What was the source of this great, surging self-confidence, vitality, and optimism? So great and widespread was the optimism of the Age of Enlightenment that it could only have come from many different sources. Some of its self-confidence had been building from the time of the Renaissance and its celebration of human reason. Other sources of the sense of change and growth came from the great new rush of trade; new mining and agricultural methods; the beginning of the use of coal in place of wood; the development of steel and textile manufacture; the rise of new urban centers. The new upper middle class, who were in the vanguard of all these developments, soon began to outstrip in wealth and power and status the old landed aristocracy. For people living at this time, the experience of these various developments must have contributed to the conviction that a great change had come over the world, that human reason had now been liberated and was generating knowledge with a potentiality for human happiness beyond what had ever been imagined.

Newton's Principles: The Scientific Model. A major source of enlightenment, self-confidence, and optimism came from the rapid growth, vitality, and progress of the new sciences. The greatest achievement was that of the British physicist Sir Isaac Newton, in his *Mathematical Principles of Natural Philosophy* in 1687. Newton's *Principles* was without doubt the centerpiece and the most esteemed of all the scientific achievements of the Age of Enlightenment. It was so tremendous a work of synthesizing the scattered fragments of existing knowledge in astronomy and physics under a few simple principles that it stands forth as one of the greatest scientific achievements of any age.

Descartes, Kepler, and Galileo had shown the power of human reason to penetrate the laws of nature. But their discoveries had been limited to specific areas only, for example, to planetary motions. A question still remained: Could mathematical physics explain the whole of the physical universe and not only isolated parts? Newton proved that it could. His law of gravity established a law for the whole of nature. The same law of gravity holds for the planets and their satellites, the

earth and its satellite, for the moon's tidal effects on the
oceans, and for all terrestrial objects.

The entire physical universe, according to Newton, is
mechanical, a world machine. Everything about the machine,
from the motion of the planets to the falling of an apple from
a tree, can be explained by the mechanical laws of motion.
The physical universe is thus a system of causes and their
necessary effects, completely deterministic in all its operations.
Everything that happens in the physical universe is the necessary and inevitable result of antecedent causes; nothing can
be other than what it is; everything is what it is by causal
necessity. No material body can be free from this necessary
causal determinism.

Newton soon became the Enlightenment's symbol of the
man of science, he was the very symbol of the power of
scientific reason to discover the rational laws which govern
the physical universe. Poets sang the praise of Newton. Among
them was the famous British poet Alexander Pope, who wrote:

> Nature and nature's laws lay hid in night;
> God said, Let Newton be, and all was light.

The Rational Order of Nature, Physical and Human. Under the influence of Newton, the eighteenth-century Enlightenment philosophers turned away from the model for philosophy which Descartes had provided, the model of a philosophy constructed like geometry, as a system of deductive
reasoning from self-evident axioms. Influenced by Newton's
discoveries of the universal orderly and harmonious laws of
physics, the eighteenth-century philosophers moved on to a
new model for philosophy—the search for order, harmony,
and lawfulness in all of nature, physical and human. If physical nature is a harmonious order, governed by necessary laws
of nature which reason can discover, why is this not also true
of human nature as well? Is not the human sphere also part of
nature, and is it not also governed by harmonious, orderly
natural laws?

In England, the philosopher John Locke argues as early as
1664 that there is a law of nature governing human beings
and that it is knowable by human reason. The law of nature
for human beings, John Locke argues, was that all human
beings are rational, all are equal, in possessing the same
natural rights of life, liberty, and property, and the same
obligations not to infringe upon the rights of others. John

Locke's words are memorable: "And reason . . . teaches all mankind who will but consult it, that being all equal and independent, no one ought to harm another in his life, health, liberty or possessions."

With these words John Locke justified the English Revolution of 1688, often called the Bloodless Revolution, which finally ended the absolutism of the British monarchy and placed power in the people and their representatives in Parliament. Locke's words affirming a law of nature and natural rights for all human beings were soon used to justify the American Revolution of 1776 and the French Revolution of 1789. And they entered loud and clear into the Declaration of Independence of the United States in the language of Thomas Jefferson: "We hold these truths to be self-evident, that all men are created equal, that they are endowed by their Creator with certain unalienable rights, that among these are life, liberty and the pursuit of happiness . . ."

For the Age of Enlightenment human reason reigned as king. It had shown that the universe is orderly, lawful, and harmonious, as demonstrated by the scientific laws of astronomy, physics, chemistry, and physiology. Reason had also found a place for human beings in this rational harmony of the universe, through Locke's law of nature and natural rights. But within the age of reason and optimism, another viewpoint was developing which was destined to undermine and destroy the self-confident rationalism of the Age of Enlightenment.

Newton's Principles: Rationalism or Empiricism. This other viewpoint was, of course, *empiricism*, which regards observation by the senses as the only reliable source of knowledge. Empiricism arose in the early years of the seventeenth century, under the same pressure as rationalism, to offer a theory of the method used by the new sciences, the most important intellectual development of the modern world. What kind of method did Newton use in establishing his law of gravity? Both rationalists and empiricists claim Newton for their side. Rationalism, as we have already seen, is the claim that *reason* is the most important source and test of truth. The rationalists agreed with Descartes that in all areas in which knowledge is sought we must begin with clear and distinct, self-evident and true, axioms, from which we deduce other truths, constructing a deductive logical system of truths. Rationalism points out that this is what is true of the new developing sciences, the use of rational principles and deduction in order to construct an absolutely certain system of knowledge. According to the rationalists, this is how Newton constructed the deductive system of mechanics. Reasoning from basic concepts such as mass, energy, and the laws of motion, he deduced an explanation of the whole physical universe.

But empiricism looks at the work of Newton and points out that Newton's method was by no means like Descartes's. Newton's method was just the opposite. According to the empiricists, Newton began with observation of facts, with the data of sensory experience aided by new scientific instruments. Only on the basis of the order which he discovered by observation of the data of experience was Newton able to construct a logical system out of the laws he discovered.

The Rise of British Empiricism

Who were the empiricists? The great names of classical empiricism are all British. The high point of the flourishing of empiricism is in England, Scotland, and Ireland in the seventeenth and eighteenth centuries. The classical British empiricists and their principal works in theory of knowledge are: John Locke (1632–1704), *Essay Concerning Human Understanding* (1690); George Berkeley (1685–1753), *A Treatise Concerning the Principles of Human Knowledge* (1710); and David Hume (1711–76), *A Treatise of Human Nature* (1738–40), revised as *Enquiry Concerning the Human Understanding* (1751). Foreshadowed by Francis Bacon (1561–1626), the development of the logic of British empiricism was the work of these three philosophers. The fundamental principle of empiricism is that sense perception (including direct observation by the senses, indirect observation by the use of instrumentation, and experimentation) is the only reliable method for gaining knowledge and for testing all claims to knowledge.

Empiricist Anti-Cartesianism. From the very early days of empiricism in the work of John Locke, empiricism shows itself to be a deliberate and defiant rejection of philosophic rationalism, and especially of Descartes. All the empiricists rejected what they came to call Cartesianism—the rationalistic building of great deductive systems of philosophy purporting to have grasped by the powers of reason alone the nature of total reality—man, nature, and God—and to have achieved complete mathematical certainty in this knowledge by the use of logical deduction from self-evident axioms. In sharpest rejection of this, the empiricists are suspicious of metaphysical systems constructed by reason.

Empiricism constructs no great metaphysical systems of philosophy, it offers no speculations or world views for humans to live by. It remains only a theory of knowledge, a theory of what we can know. Empiricists claim that we can know reliably only what comes to us by sensory experience, by observation and experiment, and by testing through experience. Empiricism is thus basing knowledge upon the senses, upon the flux of the sensible world, which the two great rationalists, Plato and Descartes, rejected as an inferior way of knowing. From this basis in sensory experience as the source and test of knowledge, empiricism as a theory of human knowledge becomes a powerful "engine of destruction," as it has been called, a wrecking ball which is soon swung against all the structures built by reason in philosophy and theology and demolishes them for providing no knowledge at all.

The Empiricist Wrecking Ball: (1) How Do You Know?

How was this done? Beginning with Locke, empiricism as a theory of knowledge raises two questions about our knowledge: First, for any proposition in any field whatsoever that purports to tell us about the world, the empiricists raise the seemingly simple, seemingly innocuous question: *How do you know?* To this little question, there is only one kind of acceptable answer for an empiricist—an answer that can point to the sensory observations that are the source of the knowledge. To the empiricists, if you cannot answer the question How do you know? by showing that your knowledge rests upon sensory experience, observation of data, or experimentation with data, you have no knowledge, your claims to knowledge are worthless, bankrupt.

But can Descartes's metaphysical dualism of mind and matter meet the question How do you know? by showing that it is based upon sensory observation? Can Plato's theory of the forms pass the empiricist's test question How do you know? They cannot. The source of these metaphysical theories is in rational reflection, not in sense perception. Do you hold any philosophic beliefs about the world, or any religious beliefs about a divine being, or any political beliefs about how society ought to be governed? If so, is there any way in which you can successfully answer the empiricist's question How do you know? What sense perceptions or observations of data or scientific experiments can you point to as the sole source of your philosophic world view, your conception of a divine being, or your political philosophy? Since you can point to none, your philosophic ideas are subject to demolition by the empiricists' wrecking ball.

The Empiricist Wrecking Ball: (2) What Are the Limits of Knowledge?

The second question which the empiricists raise is a more fundamental one. Like the first question, it was designed as an attack upon Cartesianism and upon all rationalism, whether in theology, metaphysics, theory of knowledge, ethics, or politics. This second question is: What kind of instrument is the human mind? What are its limits? What is it equipped to know? This second question is also intended to devastate, reject, rebuke, and demolish Descartes and all builders of rational, theoretical structures. Before you undertake to construct a great philosophic system, say the empiricists, why don't you ask the basic question: Is the mind equipped for such metaphysical excursions into the heart of reality? Are there perhaps limits as to what the mind can know, limits set by the origins of its ideas, limits as to the certainty it can achieve?

These two questions—How do you know? and What are the limits of knowledge?—dominate the powerful development of British empiricism from Locke to Berkeley to Hume. This development gathered momentum as the devastating, relentless questions became more sharply understood by the empiricists themselves.

John Locke

John Locke, as the earliest in the line of British empiricism, is the most conservative and the least destructive in pursuing the hard questions of the empiricist program. Yet he states clearly and prophetically the role which empiricism will have in the subsequent development of philosophy. There are, he says, "Master-builders whose mighty designs in advancing the sciences will leave lasting monuments to the admiration of posterity." But, he adds, "It is ambition enough to be employed as an under-laborer in clearing the ground a little, and removing some of the rubbish that lies in the way of knowledge." In these prophetic words Locke is looking into the future horizon of philosophy. It will indeed be the case that the two empiricist questions How do you know? and What are the limits upon knowledge? will cast so much doubt upon the construction of great systems of philosophy that there will come a time when there will be no more master builders in philosophy. There are no master builders in philosophy today.

The role of philosopher is also as Locke prophesied: to be an underlaborer, clearing the ground, removing rubbish. What is the rubbish the philosopher removes? Rationalistic rubbish, of course, such rubbish as Plato and Saint Thomas and Descartes wrote. But what is the under-laborer clearing the ground for, since nothing is to be built, and there are no master builders? The empiricist has no answer to this question except that it is desirable to recognize rubbish and to clear it out.

Attack upon Theory of Innate Ideas. The first rubbish which John Locke decided to clear away was, as you would expect, a piece of rubbish created by Descartes himself: Descartes's theory of innate ideas. The theory of innate ideas asserts that clear and distinct, self-evident ideas are innate in the sense that they are "born with us," as Descartes said, they are imprinted upon the soul. Examples of innate ideas are the ideas of substance, cause, God, and the principles of logic.

Locke's line of attack is clear. It is by way of the question How do you know that these ideas are innate in all human beings? What data of experience, what sensory observations, what empirical evidence can you offer in support of this claim? Can you show by pointing to the data that all humans, from infancy on, possess these ideas? Surely there are many who do not possess the ideas of God or of logic, from infancy on, or ever. Do you argue instead, as Descartes did, that by innate ideas you mean ideas that a person sees to be true once he is sufficiently educated to understand them? But the fact that people can learn to understand such ideas does not mean that such ideas have to be born with them, or be innate in them, but only that human beings are rational and are capable of learning.

Therefore, said Locke, the theory of innate ideas is worthless rubbish. The mind is not a closet which is filled at birth with such innate ideas. The mind is an empty closet. Changing the metaphor, Locke argues that the mind is a blank tablet, blank white paper, on which experience writes, and this writing by experience is all the mind can know.

Locke's Theory of Knowledge. From Locke's empiricist viewpoint, all our ideas have only one source and that is experience. What then is Locke's theory of knowledge? His aim is to show that the origin of our knowledge is in sensory experience, through the mind's receiving impressions made upon it by external objects. The only other source of knowledge is our reflection about our sensory experience, such as in reasoning, doubting, and believing. Locke takes over Descartes's view of an idea as meaning anything my mind is conscious of, thinks about, any objects of the mind.

Locke also takes over the subjectivism of Descartes, the view that what I know best is my own mind and its ideas. Thus there enters into empiricism the problem inherent in subjectivism which we found in Descartes: the chasm or gap between my own mind with its ideas and the physical objects and human beings to which my ideas refer, and which are external to me, in the physical and social world. How can I know them since I am confined to knowing with certainty only my own ideas? How can I have true knowledge of objects as they are independently of my mind in the world?

Descartes had patched up an answer to this problem by his theory that my clear and distinct rational ideas are true since they are guaranteed by God. (God is, however, guaranteed by my clear and distinct ideas. This was the Cartesian circle.) Therefore, Descartes argued, I can know that physical substances exist and that they have as their essential qualities the same qualities as my clear and distinct ideas of them, the qualities of being spatially extended and capable of motion. On the other hand, my ideas of sensory qualities, such as colors, sounds, textures, and tastes are not in the physical objects but in me, the result of the impact of physical objects upon my sense organs. The essential, necessary qualities are mathematically measurable, like length, height, and distance, and are useful to the mathematical science of mechanics.

Locke takes over Descartes's idea of physical substance, constructs the distinction between primary and secondary qualities and runs into excruciatingly painful problems. As an empiricist, Locke can only know what originates in sense perception. He cannot claim to know anything by clear and distinct, rational ideas or by the help of God. How, then, does he know that physical substance exists? Has he ever had experience of a physical substance? How does he know that our ideas of primary qualities belong, as he claims, to physical objects? How does he know that secondary qualities are "nothing in the objects themselves" but are "sensations in us [produced] by their primary qualities?" And so the wrecking ball of empiricism takes aim at John Locke himself and his theory that physical substances exist and have primary qualities which produce secondary qualities in us.

George Berkeley

It is George Berkeley, the Anglican Bishop of Cloyne in Ireland, the second in line of British empiricists, who conducts the attack upon Locke. How could Locke, an empiricist, indulge in the now outmoded concept of material substance? Locke had failed to follow through on the basic empiricist principle, which is that we can know only what comes to us in sensory experience. And so Berkeley pushes ahead with the argument of empiricism and demolishes Locke's acceptance of the belief held by Descartes and Newton that physical substances exist.

Berkeley's Theory of Knowledge. We can never have sensory experiences of material substances, says Berkeley. We can experience only sensory qualities. What is my actual experience of substance? It is only the experience of qualities. I perceive a tree as a certain size and shape, I perceive the diameter of its trunk, the length of its branches, the brown color of its trunk and branches, and the green color of its leaves; I touch its rough textures and smell its woody aroma— but I can never perceive its substance itself. All that I have perceived of the tree are its qualities. I have no perception of a substance.

The existence of physical substances, Berkeley concludes, is only in their being perceived. Physical substances cannot be known to have any other existence than in the qualities we perceive. Thus Berkeley's empiricism is more radical than Locke's in that Berkeley destroys the belief in the existence of physical substance to which Locke was still clinging. What follows from Berkeley's argument is that the material world exists only in our perceptions.

For Berkeleian empiricism matter, physical substance, the physical universe do not exist. Bishop Berkeley left intact, however, two major structures of thought. He believed that mental substances exist, in the form of finite minds and also in the form of God as infinite mind. Berkeley also believed that the laws of nature which the new sciences had discovered were reliable in their orderliness and regularity. He could not, of course, say that the laws of nature were laws of physical bodies, since physical bodies for him do not exist. The laws of nature for Berkeley are only the regularities of our own perceptions or ideas. But like Descartes, Berkeley called upon God to solve problems in his philosophy. Berkeley assured us that with the help of God our perceptions are reliable and orderly and that we can therefore trust in the uniformity of experience and in the dependability of scientific laws.

Enter the Scotsman David Hume, the last and most rigorously persistent and destructive of the classical British empiricists. As a bishop of the Church of England Berkeley had spared from the wrecking ball of empiricism mental substances, God's mind, and human minds. But Hume gleefully asks the empiricist's little question How do you know? How does Berkeley know that mental substance exists? Under this attack we will see collapse the idea that there are mental substances. But there is a second structure which Berkeley left standing, and that is the solid reliability and uniformity of scientific laws of nature. Will Hume let this last structure stand?

The Age of Enlightenment, of reason, of optimism springs from the passionate conviction that human reason had at last discovered many of the true laws of nature, and that these laws of nature were absolute and necessary causal laws. And we have seen that the great burst of optimism was based upon twin beliefs: upon the belief that the future would see the continued discovery of scientific laws which would generate technology for the benefit of humanity; and also upon the belief that growth in the understanding of man's natural law and natural rights would bring about a world of democracy and peace. Is this not what you believe in your better, happier moments? It is what the Age of Enlightenment was passionately committed to, and nowhere was this commitment greater than in the United States of America at the time of the founding of the Republic.

But Hume demolished this vision of progress of the Age of Reason. He shattered the pride of the Age of Enlightenment in the necessary causal laws of Newtonian mechanics and of the other new sciences by denying that there are any necessary causal laws at all. How Hume managed to swing the wrecking ball of empiricism at this great structure we will now proceed to see.

**An engraved portrait of David Hume based
on the painting by Allan Ramsay, 1754.**
(COURTESY OF THE BETTMANN ARCHIVES.)

12

"A WELL-MEANIN' CRITTER"

When he was an adolescent, David Hume's mother said of him: "Davey is a well-meanin' critter, but uncommon weak-minded." His mother was a poor judge of her son. Her son Davey was to become David Hume, the sharpest intellect in the history of British philosophy—not what you would call weak-minded. And as for being a "well-meanin' critter"—her son Davey was far from being well-meaning. He was the most mercilessly destructive of all the British empiricists and he took delight in demolishing the claims of philosophy, shocking the defenders of religion and undermining the validity of scientific laws and the Enlightenment belief in progress.

Hume's Life

His life in its outward details is uneventful. Hume was born in Edinburgh in Scotland in 1711. He grew up in genteel poverty at the Hume family estate called Ninewells in the Scottish Lowlands, a few miles from the English border. Ninewells is described by a recent biographer of Hume as "the pleasantest place imaginable," situated on a bluff overlooking the rushing waters of the White-Adder River in a magnificent landscape of distant mountains, a small village of thatched-roof cottages nearby, and sheep and cattle grazing on the slopes of surrounding hills.

Hume attended the University of Edinburgh for three or four years, leaving before he was sixteen years old without taking a degree. At first he tried to do what his family wished him to do, and he began to study to become a lawyer. But he tells us in his autobiography that while his family thought he was reading law books, he was secretly devouring philosophy.

Hume's Breakthrough: "A New Scene of Thought". After three years during which he was working out his philosophical views, while at the same time struggling to keep up with his study of law, he reports that "there opened up to me a new Scene of Thought" which was so exciting that it made him want to give up everything else and devote himself entirely to it. The law now appeared "nauseous" to him. As a result, he promptly abandoned the study of law and gave up the financial security it could have given him. For six months he worked on the new "Scene of Thought" which had opened up to him, with a sense of discovery and breakthrough, and feelings of great power. What had he seen? What was the new Scene of Thought which led him to feel that he was the master, conqueror, and destroyer of all past philosophy? We can reconstruct the source of his excitement from his memoranda, his correspondence, and his autobiography. He had discovered the works of Francis Hutcheson, a Scottish moral philosopher at the University of Glasgow, who had argued that moral principles are not based upon the Bible, as Christianity says, nor are they based upon reason, as Plato and Socrates had said. Our moral beliefs, said Hutcheson, rest only on our feelings, our sentiments of approval or disapproval.

The breakthrough which Hume the empiricist had was this: Why not extend this view, that moral beliefs are neither divine nor rational but only express our feelings, to all our beliefs? What if all our scientific knowledge is not knowledge at all, and has no certainty, has no way of being shown to be certain, but is only based upon our feelings that what the senses give us is true? Then all the achievements of the great new sciences of astronomy, physics, chemistry, and physiology—all these marvels of the Age of Enlightenment—bite the dust. They are nothing but sentiments, feelings that what we perceive over and over again in orderly fashion is true.

Hume's exciting new philosophic outlook combined the empiricism of Locke and Berkeley, who argued that knowledge comes only from sense perception, with the moral philosophy of Francis Hutcheson, who argued that morality comes only from sentiment or feeling. Putting these two conceptions together, Hume began to move toward the shocking thought that our best knowledge, our scientific laws, are nothing but sense perceptions which our feelings lead us to believe. Therefore it is doubtful that we have any knowledge; we have only sense perceptions and feelings. Here in these thoughts of the young Hume was a radical, extreme skepticism, an extreme form of doubting the possibility that certainty in knowledge is attainable. Descartes's methodological skepticism looks conservative by comparison. Descartes had planned, by the method of skepticism, to find a foundation for knowledge that would establish its certainty. Hume seemed to be planning to destroy any foundation for knowledge that would establish its certainty.

Is it any wonder that after the first flush of excitement, the first gratification of feeling that he was the young David Hume slaying the Goliath of all science, philosophy, and theology—that he panicked, that he was overcome by anxiety, that the bottom of everything dropped out for him? In the fall of 1729 he had a severe nervous breakdown, which lasted for the next five years, manifested in physical symptoms and in feelings of depression and weakness. "My disease," he wrote in one of his letters, "was a cruel encumbrance to me." His physician told him he had the "disease of the learned," depression, lowness of spirits, the "vapors," as it was called at the time; the feeling of being in the "abyss" or "the pits," as it is called at present. Hume struggled to read and to continue to write, using up great stacks of paper, but he complained that he was "not able to follow out any train of thought" or to write the polished prose that he demanded of himself. "I had no hopes," he complained, "of delivering my opinions with such elegance and neatness as to draw to me the attention of the world."

After five years of this, he decided to give up philosophy. But in a few months he decided that action might be a cure and he left home and went to France, to La Flèche, one hundred fifty miles southeast of Paris, the location of Descartes's old Jesuit college (a fact which Hume pointedly ignored). There Hume holed up in a small apartment on a country estate, and made use of the college library. At the end of three years of intensive writing, his first book, the *Treatise of Human Nature*, was almost completed in 1737. He returned to London, edited the manuscript, and arranged for the *Treatise* to be published. He had expected the *Treatise* to be hailed immediately as a philosophic masterpiece, but he was bitterly disappointed. The reviews of the book were unfavorable. Few people seemed to have read it; fewer seemed to have understood it. Hume said of the book that "it fell deadborn from the press."

Hume next tried to get a professorship at the University of Edinburgh, but was turned down on religious grounds, because of his skepticism and his atheistic, mocking contempt for religious belief. Some years later the University of Glasgow turned him down for the same reasons. Hume was never to become a university professor. He supported himself first as a tutor and later as secretary to various wealthy and influential persons, including the British Ambassador to France, finally reaching the position of Under-Secretary of State.

As a mature man Hume was described in this way: "His face was broad and fat, his mouth wide, and without any other expression than that of imbecility. His eyes vacant and spiritless and the corpulence of his whole person was far better fitted to communicate the idea of a turtle-eating alderman than of a refined philosopher. His speech in English was rendered ridiculous by the broadest Scotch accent, and his French was, if possible, still more laughable, so that wisdom never before disguised herself in so uncouth a garb." Edward Gibbon, the eminent historian, also lampooned Hume as "the fattest pig in the sty." Despite these unflattering descriptions, Hume became a celebrity, a well-established literary figure as an historian and philosopher.

By the time Hume went back to France in 1763 as secretary to the British Ambassador, he was a huge success, feted in Paris as Britain's most brilliant, witty, exciting man of letters. He had fulfilled what he said was his "ruling passion—the love of literary fame." He had at last accomplished what in the depths of his early depression and nervous breakdown he thought he would never be able to do—"draw to himself the attention of the world." In his lifetime, his fame came more from his writing a history of Great Britain than from his philosophy. Why had he switched in 1752 from philosophy to history? Was it that, having demolished philosophy, he thought there was nothing more to say? Or was it that the worldwide fame he always craved seemed more likely at that time to come from history, from writing an account of England's history than from further analysis of the philosophy of empiricism?

Theory of Knowledge:

1. The Foundation of All Knowledge. We must now take a closer look at Hume's philosophy and the way in which his wrecking ball will work. In the introduction to the *Treatise of Human Nature* he says his purpose is to study the science of man and to explain the principles of human nature. Like Newton, he is going to reduce the science of man, as Newton reduced mechanics, to a few simple principles. But why is he going to do this? It is because all other sciences are based upon the science of man. Therefore to study the science of man, the science of human nature, is really to study the foundation of all human knowledge. What Hume intends to do is to ask, with regard to all our knowledge: (1) How do you know? What is the origin of this knowledge? (2) What are the limits of human knowledge? These are the questions which empiricism raises, and Hume will push them consistently and relentlessly. And he already knows what he will show: that we have no knowledge, but only beliefs which we feel are true.

2. Attack on the Doctrine of Two Kinds of Knowledge. Why did Hume, in hot pursuit of philosophers and theologians with these empiricist questions, begin his *Treatise* with the search for the foundations of human knowledge? His purpose in asking what are the foundations of all knowledge is to show that there is only one foundation, consisting of one kind of knowledge, knowledge by sense perception. His purpose is to destroy the age-old philosophic belief that there are two kinds of knowledge. (1) One kind is the lower-level ordinary knowledge of the sensible world, the world of flux which Plato called true opinion and which Descartes called the confused ideas of the senses. (2) For both Plato and Descartes there is a superior level of knowledge which has reason as its source and which provides certainty. Plato presents the divided line of knowledge, and the imagery of ascent on the ladder of knowledge from the visible world to the superior type of truth which is gained by the knowledge of the eternal forms of the intelligible world. Descartes called this superior type of knowledge rational truth, the truth of clear and distinct ideas.

Both Plato and Descartes argued from the assumption that there are these two types of knowledge: that above ordinary knowledge by sense perception there is a kind of knowledge whose source is in reason, and that this knowledge enables us to know the truth about reality, and so to have a metaphysics, a theory about the nature of reality. Plato's metaphysics is centered upon his theory of forms; Descartes's metaphysics is centered upon his theory of mental and physical substances.

Enter Hume. He denies that there are two kinds of knowledge. The notion that there is a superior kind of knowledge that philosophers can reach by reason, knowledge of the nature of reality, metaphysical knowledge—this notion, he says, is completely false, a total illusion. Philosophers who foist this notion upon a gullible public are guilty of fraud and deceit. Metaphysics such as that of Plato or Saint Thomas or Descartes is the product, says Hume, of "rash arrogance," "lofty pretensions," and of "superstitious credulity" on the part of those who believe them.

We can never know the nature of ultimate reality, Hume argues. Those philosophers who claim to know the nature of ultimate reality are either knaves or fools—fools because they do not understand that this is a kind of knowledge that humans can never have, since we are limited to sense perception in what we can know. They are knaves insofar as knowing the limits of our knowledge, they persuade us to follow them in their false philosophy.

The fact is, says Hume, that we shall never know what are the causes of the sense perceptions that we have. We shall never know what are the true qualities of things in the world or why they are as they are. Reason can never discover the nature, the purpose, or the plan of the world. Hume says:

> These ultimate springs and principles are totally shut up from human curiosity and inquiry.

Human understanding is limited—and the things that metaphysics seeks to know, we can never know. Metaphysics must be shown to be pretentious nonsense, along with the doctrine on which it rests—that there are two kinds of knowledge, ordinary knowledge by sense perception and superior metaphysical knowledge by reason.

3. Sense Perception: Impressions and Ideas. What, then, does Hume offer as his theory of sense perception, which according to him is the only source of knowledge that we have, and to which all that human beings can ever know is limited? The contents of consciousness in general he calls *perceptions*. (Descartes had called them ideas.) He divides perceptions into *impressions* and *ideas*.

Impressions are our immediate sensations, passions, and emotions, the immediate data of seeing, touching, hearing, desiring, loving, hating. *Ideas* are copies or faint images of impressions, such as we have in thinking about or recalling any of our immediate impressions. Hume goes on to say that the difference between impressions and ideas is in the greater force and liveliness of impressions. Impressions enter our consciousness with more "force and violence." By contrast, ideas are only images of our impressions, which occur in our thinking, reasoning, and remembering. For example, if you look at the room you are in, you have an impression of it, sensations of its size, its chairs, tables, rug, and other furnishings, the color of its walls, its windows, the ticking of the clock. Hume looks at his own room and he says,

> When I shut my eyes and think of my chamber the ideas I form are exact representations of the impressions I felt; nor is there any circumstance of the one which is not in the other . . . ideas and impressions appear always to correspond to each other.

Hume quickly sees, however, that he has been "carried away too far" by the principle that ideas and impressions always correspond to each other, since the rule does not seem to hold for complex ideas. For this reason Hume (Section I) now makes a distinction between simple and complex impressions and the simple and complex ideas which are images of them. My perception of red is a simple impression, and my recollection of this red color is a simple idea. "The rule here holds without exception," Hume says, ". . . that every simple idea has a simple impression which resembles it; and every simple impression, a correspondent idea." What if I stand on the steps of the Lincoln Memorial in Washington at night and perceive the brightly illuminated Capitol building in the distance? This is an impression, too, but a very complex one, consisting of many sensations of darkness and lights, blackness and yellow globes of lamps, white marble grayish in shadows, stretching out into the vast wings of the building, and above all, the great dome, brilliantly white against the black sky. It is a complex impression and my

recollection of it is a complex idea. Hume admits that it is
probably not the case that my complex idea corresponds in all
its details to the original complex impression. Also, he asks,
what if I imagine a city? Hume himself gives the example. "I
can imagine to myself such a city as the new Jerusalem,
whose pavement is gold and walls are rubies, though I never
saw any such." Is this not a case of a complex idea without a
corresponding impression? But this complex idea of the new
Jerusalem can be broken down into the simple idea (e.g.,
gold, walls, rubies) out of which the imagination has fabricated it. And we can show, says Hume, that every one of its
simple ideas has a simple impression which it resembles.

Hume is making an important empiricist argument here—
that we cannot know anything which we have not had a prior
impression of in sensory experience. Even in our religious
fantasies of a new Jerusalem or in our scientific fantasies of a
new world in outer space, we cannot imagine anything which
we have not had an impression of in sensory experience.
Finally, on the matter of complex ideas, while they may not
correspond to all the details of an immediate impression, the
rule does hold, says Hume, for all our simple impressions,
that every simple idea has a simple impression which precedes it and every simple impression has a correspondent
idea.

4. The Empiricist Principle. The fundamental principle
that Hume sees that he has established is this: "All our
simple ideas in their first appearance are derived from simple
impressions which are correspondent to them and which they
exactly represent." How is Hume going to use this seemingly
innocent account of experience as consisting of impressions
and ideas? How is he going to use his claim that every idea
has a corresponding impression from which it arises? He will
use it dramatically and devastatingly to analyze and demolish
a number of ideas. It is his most powerful wrecking ball. All
he needs to do is to ask, from what impression does this idea
come? If from no immediate impression, the idea is meaningless. As Hume says in his *Enquiry Concerning the Human
Understanding:*

> When we entertain, therefore, any suspicion that a
> philosophical term is employed without any meaning
> or idea (as is but too frequent), we need but enquire,

from what impression is that supposed idea derived? And if it be impossible to assign any, this will serve to confirm our suspicion.

Hume turns to the idea of substance, used by Saint Thomas, by the Scholastic philosophers of the Middle Ages, and by Descartes, and asks, from what impressions does the idea of substance arise? Hume's point is that an idea is nothing but the impressions from which it is derived and to which it corresponds. With regard to the idea of substance, when we ask, from what impressions does it arise, the answer cannot claim to be from an impression of substance, but only from impressions of qualities we experience, such qualities as size, shape, color. Then the idea of substance is nothing but these qualities which we experience. We cannot, therefore, say that substances exist. We can know that something exists only if we have an impression of it, only if we have sensory experience of it. And so Hume destroys the claim that substances exist by showing that we have no impressions of physical substances.

Hume accuses philosophers of using empty, meaningless words like physical substance, mental substance, mind, self, as if they actually refer to things which have independent existence. On analysis, says Hume, we find that there are no impressions of any of them (substance, mind, self), but only of particular qualities which we experience. And so these words, substance, mind, self, have no meaning, since they come from no impression.

And so Hume is able to demolish all such ideas as these by using his rule that all ideas arise from impressions to which they correspond. His rule is simple and powerful: Where there is no impression, there is no adequate idea. Where there is no impression, the idea is meaningless. Thus Hume's empiricist rule is not only a test of the worth of our ideas as knowledge (where there is no impression, the idea is worthless) but is also a test of the meaning of our ideas (where there is no impression, the idea is meaningless).

5. The Association of Ideas. Hume has presented a view of our experience as made up of atomic elements, of distinct and separable impressions and ideas, each an atom constituting our experience. This atomistic view of experience began with Locke and the empiricists and as the theory of associationism, dominated the beginning of psychology in the eighteenth and nineteenth centuries. The task for the psychologist was to discover how the atoms of experience, the sensations or impressions, are connected. What are the laws by which these atomic sensations or impressions are connected? How do they become "associated" into the complex ideas of everyday experience and science?

Theoretically, we could associate any simple idea with any other simple idea. And the imagination associates ideas as it pleases, producing, says Hume, "winged horses, fiery dragons, and monstrous giants." But in the ordinary course of conversation or in scientific analysis we find that our ideas do not follow one another by chance, helter-skelter, or at our will. We find, instead, the same simple ideas leading regularly into the same complex ones. And so, Hume argues, there must be "some bond of union among them, some associating quality, by which one idea naturally introduces another."

There must then be some universal principles in our thinking which operate in us, not with necessity, but nevertheless as a force or impulse to associate ideas in certain ways. Hume describes this impulse as "a gentle force, which commonly prevails." The association of our ideas is based upon three qualities of our ideas, which tend to lead the mind from one idea to another, to connect or associate one idea with another. These three qualities are the basis of *the three laws of the association of ideas*.

The first law is that ideas are associated or connected by the *resemblance* between ideas. So, our minds easily run from one idea to another that resembles it. Hume gives as an example that "a picture easily leads our thought to the original." We could say that a picture of Abraham Lincoln leads our thought to our ideas of him. The second law by which we associate or connect one idea with another is by *contiguity*, one idea being close to, or adjacent to, another in space or time. Our minds tend to associate one idea with another that is physically or temporally adjoining it, contiguous with it. Hume gives as an example that mentioning one apartment in a building "naturally leads us to think about the others." The third law of the association of ideas is by *cause and effect*. Our minds seem impelled to associate a cause with the effect it brings about. For example, Hume says, "If we think of a wound, we can scarcely keep ourselves from reflecting on the pain which follows it." The idea of the wound leads us by this law of the association of ideas to the idea of the effect of the wound, the resultant pain.

These three laws, by which our thinking is naturally impelled from one idea to another which resembles it, or which is next to it, or is its effect—these three laws characterize all our mental operations, including all our reasoning, and specifically they characterize our scientific ideas. Of the three laws of association of ideas, the association or connection of ideas by cause and effect, says Hume, is the most powerful connection between our ideas.

Hume's "Breakthrough" Carried Out

Is this just an innocuous set of laws, merely a scholar's pedantic and "picky" distinctions? You know Hume better than to believe that he is wasting time on harmless academic niceties. The laws of association of ideas are part of his wrecking-ball strategy and he is now going to use the law of association of ideas by cause and effect to destroy the claim that we can have scientific knowledge that certain causes necessarily produce certain effects. Watch where his strategy has brought you so far.

Hume has said that our atomic ideas, which correspond to our impressions, are connected or associated by three laws of association, which are a gentle force leading us to associate one idea with another. These three laws pertain to all our thinking, thus also to our scientific thinking. He has also taken you on to another step in his strategy. Of the three laws of association the one that gives the most forceful impulse to connect one idea with another is by *cause and effect*. Now for the next step. Hume claims that anything we can say about objects, about matters of fact, beyond talking about our immediate impressions of what we see and touch, must be based upon the cause-effect relationship. All our reasoning about matters of fact, says Hume, is causal reasoning. And our most important reasoning about matters of fact is scientific reasoning, with its causal laws of nature.

But what has Hume made you agree to? Has he not made you agree that scientific knowledge is nothing but ideas which we associate by the laws of association of ideas? Is scientific knowledge, then, nothing but ideas that the laws of human psychology associate together as cause and effect? Are the causal laws of astronomy, the laws of mechanics and of gravity and of the movement of gases—are these laws merely expressions of our psychology of associating ideas by cause and effect? Hume has led you to this outcome. But if this is so, then we have no scientific knowledge whatsoever. We have in place of scientific knowledge only feelings of compulsion, of a gentle force that makes us feel that our ideas are connected by cause and effect. Here in this astonishing conclusion we see the outcome of Hume's early breakthrough: his notion of combining empiricism with Hutcheson's view of morality as coming only from sentiment or feeling. This had led Hume to the startling thought that what is true of morality is also true of science: that our scientific laws have their source only in feelings. Hume has now carried out his breakthrough: Scientific laws are based upon nothing but sense impressions connected by the psychological laws of association and the feelings of compulsion they exert.

Physics, he is now saying, is nothing but our own psychology and is worthless as knowledge, as are all the other laws of nature discovered since Copernicus. The scientific laws which were the pride and hope of the Enlightenment are smashed by Hume's empiricist wrecking ball. They become nothing but psychological associations of ideas. Hume's most original contribution to philosophy and his greatest influence is his analysis of the cause-effect relationship. It is his major work of destruction. We turn next to this.

13

WILL THE SUN RISE TOMORROW?

What causes the moon to orbit the earth, the low and high tides, the changes of the seasons, the changing positions of the planets in the sky? What causes material bodies to fall, gases to expand, or the blood to circulate through the body? These causal questions had been asked and answered by Copernicus, Kepler, Galileo, Boyle, Harvey, and Newton.

What causes cancer, the degenerative process of physical aging, schizophrenia? What causes the degradation of American cities, economic inflation, or the outbreak of wars? These are causal questions which plague us in our time. Do you agree with Hume that all our thinking about matters of fact is causal and that whenever we are concerned about matters of fact we think about what causes a given effect—for example, unemployment—or we think about what effect will result from a newly introduced cause—for example, a store selling pornographic materials which is opening in your area?

Hume's Analysis of Causality

Hume claims that the relation of cause and effect is the crucial concept in all our thinking about factual matters. But if the causal relationship plays so dominant a role in everyday life, science, philosophy, theology, and morals, then surely, says Hume, we must ask some questions about it to try to understand it, rather than assume we already know what it means. First of all he asks the typically Humean question: From what impression does the idea of cause come?

We already know what Hume is up to. He is using the devastating empiricist principle he has already established. Hume's principle—where there is no impression, there is no idea, i.e., the idea is worthless as knowledge; or, where there is no impression, the idea is meaningless, is nonsense, is a fraud—this principle is, as we have seen, his most powerful empiricist wrecking ball. Applying his empiricist principle, Hume now asks the powerful, seemingly harmless question: From what impression, if any, does the idea of cause arise? Hume's first point is that the idea of causation must arise in the mind from the way in which objects are related to each other. And so Hume asks What are the sensory impressions of relations between objects from which the idea of cause arises? What are these relations?

Causality: (1) Contiguity; (2) Temporal Priority; (3) Necessary Connection

The popular, everyday idea of causality, says Hume, arises from our impressions of two kinds of relations between objects.

(1) First is the *relation of contiguity* or contact. We ordinarily consider that for something to be the cause of something else, it must touch it, be spatially connected to it, as when we see one billiard ball roll toward another, and make contact with it. When the second billiard ball moves we are likely to say that the first ball caused it to move.

(2) Another relation between objects which is essential to our everyday idea of causality is that *the effect should immediately follow the cause*, in other words, that the cause should be prior in time to the effect. We consider billiard ball 1 the cause of the motion of billiard ball 2 when we have two impressions of the relations between them—that billiard ball 1 is spatially contiguous with, in spatial contact with, billiard ball 2 and that its motion is temporally prior to the motion of ball 2. These two relations taken together, the cause being spatially contiguous with the effect and temporally prior to it, Hume calls their *conjunction*.

(3) But a third kind of relationship must also be present in our everyday idea of cause and effect. The third relationship, says Hume, is *necessary connection*, and he adds, "that relation is of much greater importance than any of the other two . . ."

The Analysis of Necessary Connection

By necessary connection is meant the relation between cause and effect in which the cause necessarily produces the effect, for example, the impact of billiard ball 1 on billiard ball 2 is the cause which necessarily produces the effect of the motion of billiard ball 2. But from what impression, Hume persists, do we derive the idea of necessary connection between cause and effect? This is no easy matter, says Hume, and he uses a hunting expression to convey how difficult it is to get at an answer to it. He says he has "to beat about all the neighboring fields" in order to flush out of hiding the answer he is hunting for.

Two questions turn up from this beating about in neighboring fields. First, he asks, why do we believe in the causal principle itself, that everything that occurs has some cause that necessarily produces it? This principle, that everything must have a cause, that nothing is uncaused, that something cannot come from nothing was regarded by Descartes, and by the scholastic philosophers before him and the rationalistic philosophers after him, as a self-evident truth that proves itself directly to reason.

Hume wastes no time in destroying the rationalists' defense of the causal principle that everything has some cause that necessarily produced it. The rationalists have not shown, he says, that the causal principle is absolutely certain, self-evident to reason, and needs no further proof, as is the case with propositions like $2 + 2 = 4$. Moreover, although rationalists claim that the causal principle is self-evident and requires no further proof, they have gone on to offer proof by arguing from the proposition: Nothing comes from nothing. This, however, is circular reasoning, since this proposition is asserting what the causal principle itself asserts, that nothing is uncaused. Hume concludes that there is no rational proof whatsoever of the causal principle. He says flatly: "Every demonstration which has been produced for the necessity of a cause is fallacious." If we believe in the causal principle, he says, it is only through habit or custom that we do so, there is no rational basis for it.

(2) But now Hume moves on to a second question on which he is going to concentrate his energies. Why do we think that a particular cause must necessarily have a particular effect? We cannot know this by reason. We cannot make a rational

analysis of the essence of fire which will show that the fire of a lighted match in contact with my finger produces the necessary effect of burning the skin of my finger. As we will see, he argues that reason can tell us nothing about factual matters like fire. He restricts reason to the areas of mathematics and logic. In this way he makes nonsense of the efforts of Plato to offer rational analyses of the forms, and of the efforts of Descartes to offer rational analyses of physical and mental substances.

But suppose, he says, we look for the sensory impression of necessary connection between a particular cause and effect, for example, between a burning match in my hand and the sensation of heat as the flame begins to reach my fingers. But I can find no sensory impression of necessary connection. I see a flame—and I feel a burning sensation. The flame is spatially contiguous and temporally prior to the sensation of heat in my fingers. These are the first two relations that are required for the everyday idea of causality. But the third, the impression of necessary connection, I do not have. Nor can I have it, since it is already clear that all that I can have impressions of are separate, spatially contiguous, temporally sequential sensations. But if neither reason nor sensory impressions give us the right to say so, why do we say that a particular cause necessarily has a particular effect?

Hume finally comes up with the answer. We have the idea of a necessary connection between a particular cause and effect after we experience their conjunction repeatedly. He calls this *constant conjunction*. If repeatedly we have sensory impressions of fire as spatially contiguous to my fingers and temporally prior to my fingers' having a sensation of burning, "without any further ceremony," says Hume, "we call the one cause and the other effect."

But Hume is not satisfied. Impressions of the constant conjunction, spatially and temporally, of the flaming match and the burning sensation in the fingers still do not provide an impression of necessary connection. Repeated instances of the flaming match burning my fingers do not give us an impression of necessary connection between the flame and the burning sensation. The necessary connection between the two is not something that can be observed. I have a sensory impression of the fire—I can see the flame. I have a sensory impression of a burning sensation—I feel the painful burning. But where can I observe necessary connection? Where can one have an impression of necessary connection between the two, that the effect of burning must occur, that it is the necessary result of the fire as cause?

But if the idea of necessary connection has no corresponding impression, then on Hume's empiricist principle: no impression, no idea—the idea of a necessary connection between causes and effects is worthless as knowledge and is meaningless, a fraud, nonsense.

The Psychological Laws of Association of Ideas

But Hume hangs on, because the causal relation is so important. He asks, where, then, does the idea come from, this crucial and powerful idea, since it does not come from a sensory impression? What then is its source? Since it does not come from sensory impressions, it must be subjective, it must come from the mind, and specifically from the psychological laws of association of ideas. The idea of necessary connection between causes and effects is not in the objects we observe, but only in the mind, he concludes. For after we have observed the constant conjunction of fire and the sensation of burning in our fingers, we feel a necessity of the mind to *associate* fire with burning. After we have experienced A followed by B repeatedly, by the association of ideas we come to *expect* B to occur after A occurs; we have formed a *habit* of anticipating that B will occur after A; but even more, we feel *compelled*, we have a feeling of compulsion or propulsion to expect B.

It is this compulsion or necessity of the mind, by the law of association of ideas, to associate A with B, the flame with the burning sensation, that is the internal and psychological source of our idea of necessary causal connection. Thus the *idea of necessary connection* between particular causes and effects is derived not from rational self-evidence and not from any empirical sense impression, but only *from the psychological association of our ideas*.

We have now followed the main lines of Hume's very detailed analysis of causality. As an extreme, radical empiricist he has demolished the claims of science to have discovered necessary causal laws of nature such as the laws of mechanics, gravity, and the circulation of the blood. Hume has shown that causal necessity is not an objective relationship between things which scientists can observe, but is only a subjective compulsion to relate things by the psychological laws of association. Causal necessity has no source in sense impressions but only in the laws of our own psychology. There are no necessary connections between objects, between the bite of a rabid animal and the onset of rabies in the bitten human. There is only the psychological necessity of our associating ideas with one another. As Hume himself says: "Objects have no discoverable connection together, nor is it from any other principle but custom . . . that we draw any inference from one . . . to the other."

Scientific Causal Laws and the Denial of Necessary Connection

Do you think that scientific laws establish necessary causal connections? Do you think that every time an electric spark passes through a mixture of two parts hydrogen and one part oxygen that the necessary result will be that the gases will disappear and that water will form? But Hume says all you can know is what you have observed. How do you know that the next time you pass the electric spark through the mixture of gases water will form? Aren't you assuming that the electric spark in the mixture of gases is the necessary cause of the formation of water? But Hume has tried to show you that you have no reason to talk of necessary connections.

Hume's point is that the idea of necessary connection between cause and effect is something that experience can never give us. Each impression is a separate experience. What impression will follow another, what will happen when the spark touches the mixture of gases, this we can learn only by experience. But experience cannot guarantee that this effect is necessary. It cannot even guarantee that it will ever happen again, even though it has happened repeatedly in the past. But when we have impressions of the constant conjunction of the mixture ignited by the spark and the water forming, we come to feel compelled to expect that this will happen in the future, and we mistakenly think that there is a necessary causal connection between the two.

Accordingly, Hume now redefines the idea of the cause-effect relation. A cause is an object in constant spatial and temporal conjunction with another such that the experience of the one compels the mind to expect the other. This is all that we can mean by the cause-effect relationship.

What impact does Hume's empiricist demolition of necessary causal laws have upon the sciences? For no scientific law is it possible to claim that it establishes a necessary connection between X and Y, between the gravitational pull of the moon and the rise and fall of the tides, between the injection of penicillin and the killing of bacterial organisms that have invaded the body. In the Humean theory of causality these are only observed constant conjunctions, together with our psychological compulsion to relate the one with the other.

But could we not try to save the idea of necessary connection for scientific laws by relying upon the idea of the uniformity of nature? Can we not know that the constant conjunctions which have been observed in the past will continue to hold in the future because nature is uniform? If nature is uniform and the same regularities are constantly repeated, then can we not know that the future will be like the past, that the same constant conjunctions will always be observable?

But Hume will not let you save the idea of necessary connection by calling upon the principle of the uniformity of nature. Immediately he asks How do you know that nature is uniform? This you cannot prove by reason or by experience of sensory impressions. And thus the outcome of Hume's driving, consistent empiricism, which requires that the basis for our knowledge be solely in sensory impressions, leads to the conclusion that we have no knowledge. We cannot know that any scientific law will be true in the future, no matter how often it has been confirmed in the past. The whole edifice of scientific laws collapses under the wrecking ball of Hume's empiricism.

Two Kinds of Propositions

(1) Matters of Fact

Perhaps at this point you will try to think of some way out of Hume's attack upon the validity of scientific causal knowledge. You may remember from Descartes the importance of mathematics as the very model of absolute, self-evident truth. Has Hume forgotten mathematics as a source for truth? Not at all. One of his greatest influences on twentieth-century thought is his view of mathematics and logic, the two types of reasoning which for Descartes were the models of certainty in our knowledge and were the models for the new sciences. For Hume there are only two kinds of propositions and they are mutually exclusive. We have been talking about one kind, namely, propositions of matters of fact. This, as we have seen, consists only in our impressions and ideas. There is no necessity that any particular impression will follow any other impression. The contrary of what usually occurs in observed constant conjunction is possible. How do you know, Hume asks, that the sun will rise tomorrow? No necessary causal law guarantees it. It is just as intelligible and without any logical contradiction to say "The sun will not rise tomorrow." There is no more logical necessity for the one than for the other. We can never know that a fact must be so, that a fact is necessary.

(2) Relations of Ideas

But there is another kind of proposition which Hume sets up in opposition to propositions of matters of fact. This other kind of proposition he calls "propositions of the relations of ideas." Logic and mathematics, specifically arithmetic, geometry, and algebra, give us knowledge of the relations of ideas. This is the domain of certainty. The propositions of mathematics are either self-evidently or intuitively certain, or they can be demonstrated by deductive reasoning to have complete certainty. The truths of mathematics assert relationships between ideas, between abstract symbols. They are formal abstract truths. They tell us nothing about matters of fact, and on the other hand, matters of fact cannot refute them. The truth $2 + 2 = 4$ is a formal truth. It is true independent of any experience we might have. Furthermore, one cannot, without contradiction, deny a proposition which states a mathematical relation between ideas. Can you deny, without being illogical, that $2 + 2 = 4$? But Hume says you can deny that the sun will rise tomorrow without being illogical.

Has Hume been trapped into admitting that we do have some knowledge, namely mathematics, which can give us absolute certainty? But—there is a catch. Mathematical propositions must pay a price for yielding absolute truth. The price is that mathematics is not truth about anything which exists, about any matters of fact. Mathematics is only empty, abstract, formal truth, which tells you nothing about existence. No proposition which states a relation between ideas (the propositions of arithmetic, geometry, algebra, or logic) can establish any truth about existence. Thus there is a trade-off. Statements about formal relations of ideas, like $2 + 2 = 4$, give us knowledge which has certainty, but on the other hand it is merely formal truth, empty, abstract, it gives no information about existence. Statements about matters of fact, on the other hand, give us information about facts, about existence, but they provide no certainty, not even a basis for probability.

And now we have seen that Hume, in conceding that mathematics gives us absolutely certain knowledge is by no means agreeing with the view of absolutely certain knowledge held by rationalists like Descartes. Descartes tried to show that the Cogito was both a self-evident truth and also a statement about a matter of fact, namely my own existence. But this is impossible on the basis of Hume's distinction between two fundamentally different kinds of statements, relations of ideas which have certainty but no factual content, and matters of fact which have empirical content but no certainty. From Hume's point of view, Descartes was either totally confused or a total fraud.

Hume's distinction between two kinds of statements or propositions has been maintained by most twentieth-century empiricists. His propositions stating *relations of ideas* are now called *analytic propositions*. His propositions stating *matters of fact* are now called *synthetic propositions*. Like Hume, most contemporary empiricists maintain that no synthetic proposition can have certainty. Certainty is the exclusive property of analytic propositions, propositions about formal relations of ideas.

The Limits of Knowledge

One of the goals which Hume set out to achieve was to discover the limits of human knowledge. The limits of human knowledge which Hume the empiricist has fixed are now becoming clear. As far as our knowledge of the world of facts is concerned, we are limited to our atomistic impressions and their corresponding ideas. These impressions and ideas appear repeatedly in our experience. We have no way of knowing what causes them. We have no knowledge that an external world exists, that physical substances exist, that a God exists. These deceptive and meaningless ideas are the work of the imagination—we have no sensory impressions of any of them. Our knowledge is limited to our sensory impressions and their images as ideas. We can, however, reason mathematically and logically about the relations which hold with certainty between formal ideas. And so metaphysics, which is concerned with the ultimate nature of reality, is impossible; it attempts to transcend the limits of our understanding, to know that which we cannot know, that of which there are no possible impressions. The idea of physical substance is worthless as knowledge and meaningless as an idea. This is also the case for the idea of mental substance, and specifically for Descartes's claim that I am a thinking substance. There is no sensory impression to which the idea of thinking substance corresponds: The idea is worthless as knowledge and meaningless as an idea.

Not only is metaphysics impossible, science is also impossible. The causal laws of science have been reduced by Hume to the psychological laws of association of ideas. There is no necessary connection between causes and effects; there is not even justification for the probability of their connection. Science cannot provide objective causal explanations of events or predict the future, since there is no justification for the assumption that regularities observed in the past will continue in the future. But not only are metaphysics and science impossible, so too is the commonsense knowledge of everyday life, with its accounts of the necessary causal connections between fire and the burning of a finger held to it, between smoking cigarettes and lung cancer, between the planting of seeds and the growth of plants. These necessary connections of common sense are reduced to psychological associations of ideas; there is no justification for their providing explanations or predictions of events. Is it any wonder that at the end of Book I of the *Treatise*, when Hume looks at what his wrecking ball has demolished, he describes himself as badly shaken? He writes:

> The intense view of these manifold contradictions and imperfections in human reason has so wrought upon me and heated my brain that I am ready to reject all belief and reasoning and can look upon no opinion even as more probable than another. Where am I, or what? From what causes do I derive my existence and to what condition shall I return? . . .

I am confounded with all these questions and begin to fancy myself in the most deplorable condition imaginable, invironed in the deepest darkness and utterly deprived of the use of every member and faculty.

Was this outpouring of anguish genuine? Or was it a literary device to call attention to the undeniable brilliance and audacity with which his empiricism has destroyed the foundations of knowledge?

14

REASON: "SLAVE OF THE PASSIONS"

By the summer of 1776 David Hume knew that he was dying; he had been for some time suffering from the same disease which had killed his mother. Yet he appeared calm and serene, still the witty and urbane conversationalist to all visitors who came to the handsome house which in 1770, at the peak of his fame, he had built in a new section of Edinburgh, on a street which was soon called, in his honor, St. David's Street.

Among the visitors he received was James Boswell, who later became famous as a diarist and as the biographer of Samuel Johnson (1709–84), the most distinguished literary figure of his time. Boswell, with a weakness for alcohol and women, was a timid man, fearful of damnation in hell, subject to periodic attacks of deep depression, and inclined toward religious piety. Boswell had for a long time been repelled and fascinated by Hume's bold and jaunty attacks upon religious belief and churchgoers. It appears that Boswell, like Samuel Johnson, was morbidly afraid of death. Boswell could not resist the temptation to go to see Hume, the God denier, on his deathbed, to ask him if he had repented of his blasphemy, if he had changed his mind, perhaps, about denying the immortality of the soul. "Don't you believe," the nervous Boswell asked Hume, "that there is life after death, that your soul will live on after you are dead?" In complete ease, with the good humor and irony that had made Hume a celebrity, he replied: "Yes, it is possible that the soul is immortal. It's also possible that if I toss this piece of coal into the flames of that fire, it will not burn. Possible, but there is no basis for believing it—not by reason, and not by sense perception, not by our experience." You can imagine Hume chuckling as Boswell backed out of the room, startled, ashamed, his neurotic fear of death stimulated by seeing Hume inexorably wasted by disease. Hume threw out a few more remarks which Boswell, with his genius for total recall, wrote down when he returned home. Hume said, "That the soul is immortal and that people should exist forever is a most unreasonable fancy. The trash of every age must then be preserved and new universes must be created to contain such infinite numbers."

Hume's Rejection of the Idea of the Soul and the Self

But how could Boswell think that Hume would abandon his own completed philosophy which had finally brought him the fame and wealth he had always craved? How could Hume be expected to believe that the soul was immortal when he had triumphantly demolished the idea of any substance whatsoever, mental or physical? Since the soul is held to be a mental substance, the Humean question mounts an immediate attack: "From what impression is the idea of the soul derived?" But since we have no sensory impression of the soul, the idea of the soul is worthless, incapable of passing the empiricist test of being an image of a prior sense impression. Therefore it makes no sense whatever to inquire whether the soul is immortal—the soul is a meaningless idea.

But suppose you are willing to forego the question of the immortality of the soul. What about your existence as a self, as permanent, identical, continuously the same throughout your life? Did not Descartes establish the Cogito—I think, therefore I am a thinking thing—as the rock upon which he built his entire philosophy? Hume answers this challenge by swiftly demolishing Descartes's Cogito proof and its idea of the self. Not only did Descartes fail to base his idea of the self as a thinking thing upon a sensory impression—he could not have done so. For as Hume points out, the idea of a self which is permanent, identical, continuously the same must be derived from an impression that is permanent, identical, continuously the same. But, Hume adds, "There is no impression constant and invariable . . ." Hume appeals again to his theory of impressions: All impressions are separate, distinct, and transient. "Pain and pleasure, grief and joy, passions and sensations, succeed each other and never all exist at the same time. It cannot, therefore, be from any of these impressions, or from any other, that the idea of self is derived; and consequently there is no such idea . . ."

Hume's Theory of the Self. What then is Hume's own theory of the self? Doggedly applying his empiricist principle, he says:

> When I enter most intimately into what I call myself, I always stumble on some particular perception or other, of heat or cold, light or shade, love or hatred, pain or pleasure. I never catch *myself* . . .

But there are some philosophers who claim they do, says Hume sarcastically, "and who imagine that we are every moment intimately conscious of what we call our SELF." But setting them aside, Hume says, "the rest of mankind . . . are nothing but a bundle or collection of different perceptions, which succeed each other with an inconceivable rapidity, and are in a perpetual flux and movement." This is Hume's famous "bundle of perceptions" theory of the self. On empiricist principles we cannot claim to have any knowledge of the self as a unity, as permanent and continuous, but only as a series of perceptions. Strictly speaking, Hume cannot claim that the flux of our perceptions have even the unity of a *bundle*. Hume is here getting close to the view of self as a stream of consciousness which appears in writers like James Joyce in his novel *Ulysses*, or Marcel Proust in *Remembrance of Things Past*, in which the stream and flow of fragmentary perceptions make up the self. Hume himself says, "The mind is a kind of theater, where perceptions successively make their appearance, pass and re-pass, glide away and mingle in an infinite variety of postures and situations." There is no continuity, no permanence, no identity, in these appearances in the theater of the mind. But suddenly Hume catches himself and says that, strictly speaking, there is not even a theater that we can know anything about through a sense impression.

Why then do you have the meaningless and unintelligible idea that you are a single self, with the same personal identity throughout your lifetime? You are misled, says Hume, into belief in the self by memory, which by the association of your past separate ideas connects one idea with the others, and leads you to form the fictional idea that these impressions that you recall are united in some sense in a permanent self. But this fiction must be demolished by the clarity of philosophy, which shows that there is no impression from which this fictional idea could possibly be derived.

How can Hume's wrecking ball demolish your idea of yourself as continuously the same? How can he deny that you have been a single self throughout your life? That you have personal identity? Do you not, after all, have memories of your very early childhood? Can you not recall events from kindergarten, early playmates, the family, the neighborhood, growing up, relatives, school, crucial events like the birth of a brother, Christmases and vacations, your first date, your first job? Could you not write your own autobiography in which all these events were gathered together and put in chronological order, so that you can say to Hume: "This is my life, David Hume. I am a continuous, identical person. I am a single self."

But Hume has an answer for you. An idea of the self, if it is to be intelligible and meaningful, must be derived from an impression. But your self, the subject of your autobiography, and which you claim is a single, continuous self, is not derived from any one impression. Rather, Hume replies, you are referring all those impressions to a self which is imagined to exist and to underly them or contain them. But where is the impression of such an underlying self? Where is the impression of the single, selfsame continuous self to which all these impressions occurred or in which they took place? Hume knows that you will have to admit that you have no such impression.

Hume's Philosophy of Religion

There remains for us to consider Hume's views on religion and on ethics. First, as for Hume's writings on religion, they have three principle targets: (1) The rationalistic proofs of the existence of God which the medieval theologians had developed, and which we found Descartes using after he had established the Cogito; (2) Deism, the rational theology which was currently attracting most of the philosophers and theologians of Hume's day—in London, Edinburgh, Paris, and in the new colonies which were to become the United States of America; and (3) the traditional religious belief in miracles.

Religion: (1) Hume's Attack Upon the Rationalistic Proofs of God

As for the classical proofs of God's existence by reason, Hume rejected them all. Reason, as we have seen, cannot prove anything about existence, about matters of fact. It can offer only logical, and mathematical, proofs, it can tell us only about relations of ideas. The existence of God is not a self-evident idea, nor a logically demonstrable truth. One can deny that God exists without contradicting oneself. Hume accordingly attacks all three of Descartes's proofs of God. Descartes's first two proofs of God's existence were causal proofs. They tried to prove that God exists as the only possible cause of my idea of Him and of my existence as a thinking substance. But we have no sensory impression of God as cause, nor do we have any impression of thinking substance as effect. Moreover, in both of these causal proofs of God's existence, Descartes relied upon the clear and distinct idea that a cause must have as much reality as its effect. This idea, which to Descartes was clear and distinct and such that no rational mind could doubt it, to Hume is totally meaningless, it can provide neither a rational nor empirical basis for causality.

As for Descartes's third proof of the existence of God, which he presented in the Fifth Meditation, it used the ontological proof which Saint Anselm offered in the eleventh century. It argued from our innate idea of God as having all perfections, and therefore necessarily having the perfection of existence, to the inference that God necessarily exists. Hume destroys this proof by first of all reminding us that the empiricist philosopher John Locke has already shown that there are no innate ideas, that we have only those ideas which come to us from our experience of impressions. Saint Anselm's ontological proof of the existence of God claims that the idea of God is self-evident to reason: God has all perfections, he is all-knowing, all-powerful, and good, and therefore he could not be lacking in the perfection of existence. Hume replies to this with his empirical test of ideas: If there is no impression in experience, the idea is worthless, meaningless. But we can have no sensory impressions of a supernatural being, and thus the idea of God cannot pass the empirical test.

Hume mercilessly attacks those who have tried to prove that God exists by using this ontological proof. How do you know God has these attributes? Where is the sense impression of each of these attributes? Here are his own biting words: "Our ideas reach no farther than our experience. We have no experience of divine attributes. I need not conclude my syllogism. You can draw the inference yourself." And so the classical ontological argument which seeks to prove by reason that God exists from our innate and self-evident idea of Him is destroyed.

Religion: (2) Hume's Attack Upon Deism

One classical proof of God which Descartes did not use is called the argument from design. This ancient attempt to prove by reason that God exists was used by Saint Augustine in the fourth century, and by Saint Thomas in the thirteenth century, and it bases itself upon the wonderful order, harmony, and beauty that is found throughout nature. Order cannot come into being by chance but only by the plan of a designer. From these premises it is argued that God exists as the necessary intelligence which planned and designed this entire enormous harmonious order of nature for the benefit of humanity.

This was the proof of God that Hume considered most important to demolish, since it was the most widely accepted proof of God's existence in the Age of Enlightenment. Never before in the history of the Western world had educated human beings had so clear a picture of the magnificent orderliness of the physical universe as was evidenced by the Newtonian world machine and by the rapid progress in scientific discoveries and technological inventions. The celestial clockwork of the planets, the clockwork of the circulation of the blood in the human body, the clockwork motion of all bodies on earth, are the workings of the laws of nature, providing the harmonious order of the universe. Science was just beginning to see the dimensions of this vast harmony. What better evidence of the orderliness, regularity, benevolence to mankind, of the entire design of the universe could there be than the laws of science? And no other evidence, in the mind of the Age of Enlightenment, was needed to prove that a master intelligence, a master designer, of this universal machine necessarily exists and that this benevolent all-knowing and all-powerful designer is God.

This was the form that the Newtonian age gave to the argument from design, to the rational proof that God exists as the only possible source of the harmonious design and arrangement of all the parts of the universe. The argument from design became the central belief of a new Christian doctrine called Deism, a religious view which proudly based itself upon reason alone, rejecting revelation and all appeals to faith, to prophecies, and to miracles as irrational and absurd for the modern age of science. Deism demanded that the concept of God be made consistent with reason and with science. The necessary laws of nature and the necessary order which they bring about is enough proof, indeed it is the best proof that God exists, said the Deists.

Hume's lifelong delight was the demolishing of the argument from design which was the heart of the religious doctrine of Deism. In his book *Dialogues Concerning Natural Religion* he used the form of a Platonic dialogue with which to mount his most powerful attack upon Deism. Three characters play the roles of an extremely orthodox, pious believer in Christianity; a Deist who argues for a natural, rational, scientifically relevant religion; and a skeptic who undermines both of them. The voice of Hume speaks through Philo the skeptic, who pokes fun especially at the Deist who claims to have a rational, natural religion. Our sense impressions, says Philo the skeptic, are the basis of all our scientific knowledge, and they give us no evidence for the claim that the universe is perfectly orderly and harmonious, nor do they guarantee that such order as it does exhibit will continue.

Moreover, Hume's analysis of causality showed that the causal order within the universe is nothing but a constant conjunction of our impressions. The Enlightenment notion that the scientific laws of nature are absolute, fixed, necessary, and eternally true must be abandoned on Hume's theory of causality. It follows that the idea of the harmony and complete orderliness of nature is derived from no sense impression and is a meaningless idea.

As for the claim that a conscious mind, a supreme designer, namely God, designed the world and planned it purposefully for the benefit of mankind—upon what constant conjunction of impressions is this based? Since we have no impressions of

God as the designer of the world, we cannot even claim that there was a single designer at the beginning of the world. A great number of people join in building a ship, or in framing a constitution for a state; why not suppose that several gods put together the world? On the other hand, why is it necessary to suppose that the world is a machine put together or planned by a conscious intelligence? Why not by natural processes of motion and growth? "The world," said Philo, "plainly resembles more an animal or a vegetable, than it does a watch or a knitting-loom."

Moreover, says Hume, look hard at the world and see whether it is the work of an all-powerful and all-competent architect. If an architect showed you "a house or palace where there was not one apartment convenient or agreeable, where the windows, doors, fires, passages, stairs and the whole economy of the building were the source of noise, confusion, fatigue, darkness and extremes of heat and cold, you would certainly blame the contrivance . . . You would assert . . . that if the architect had had skill and good intentions, he might have . . . remedied all or most of these inconveniences."

And in the human world, adds Hume, do you find evidence that it was well-designed by a benevolent and loving designer? How then can you explain the misery, pain, and evil in human life?

> Look 'round this universe . . . inspect a little more narrowly these living creatures . . . how hostile and destructive to each other . . . how contemptible or odious to the spectator . . . a blind nature, pouring forth from her lap without discernment or parental care, her maimed and abortive children.

These arguments in the *Dialogues Concerning Natural Religion* were Hume's most powerful attack upon the religion of Deism of the Age of Enlightenment. He raised, finally, as was typical of him, the question Why then do people accept this mistaken belief in the existence of God on the basis of the argument from design? For two reasons, says Hume. They learned these beliefs in early childhood, and by the process of socialization they continue to hold them. But how can it be explained that these beliefs are passed on to children? What is the origin of religious beliefs? Hume's reply is that the origin of belief in God is fear: fear of death accompanied by the desire for immortality, fear of the many forms of human misfortune. The roots of religion are in human feelings.

Religion: (3) Hume's Attack Upon Belief in Miracles

Hume is also famous for his essay "Of Miracles," which he wrote in 1748, in which his target is not the rational, scientific religion of Deism, which denied the truth of miracles and prophecies, but the traditional Christian religion, which accepts their truths.

Do you believe in miracles? Do you believe in the Old Testament miracle that the Red Sea parted to let the Israelites escape from bondage? Do you believe in the New Testament miracle that Jesus died and was resurrected? Hume has a few words to say to you. What, he asks, is a miracle? A miracle is a violation of the laws of nature by a divine, supernatural being. But the laws of nature, says Hume, state the constant conjunction of impressions in human experience. The weight of human experience outweighs any one single experience which claims that a miracle or a violation of the laws of nature has occurred—outweighs it so far, in fact, that it "amounts to an entire annihilation" of the belief in the miracle. To claim a miracle has occurred is to stand in opposition to all human experience, to all scientific knowledge, to all of the orderly and constant conjunction of human impressions. No single experience can carry more weight than the constant conjunction of human experiences. And according to the constant conjunction of human impressions, men who have died remain dead. "It is a miracle," says Hume, "that a dead man should come to life, because that has never been observed in any age or country."

When a miracle is alleged to have occurred, says Hume, error in some form will have infiltrated the claim. The wise man will decide that the testimony of the witness should be evaluated. The witness may be sincere but under a delusion; or the witness may be deliberately lying. But, Hume concludes, no human testimony can have enough force against the bulk of human experience of the laws of nature to prove that a violation of these laws has occurred, that is, to prove a miracle. And finally, says Hume, no miracle can be an adequate foundation for religion. Insofar, then, as Christianity rests upon belief in the miraculous resurrection of Christ, it offends human intelligence.

One American philosopher, J. H. Randall, Jr., comments on Hume's essay "Of Miracles" that Hume so demolished the religious accounts of miracles that ever since Hume, the defenders of Christianity have been busy trying to explain not that miracles are true, but how this illusionary notion that there are miracles could have ever crept into Christianity at all.

Hume's Ethics

Last we turn to Hume's ethics or moral philosophy, the branch of philosophy which is concerned with the meaning of good and evil, of right and wrong action. Hume's ethics is a deliberate attack upon all rationalistic ethics, such as Socrates and Plato represented. Both Socrates and Plato hold to the fundamentally rationalistic view in ethics, that reason has primacy in moral conduct, that reason is the most important determinant in moral life. This rationalistic ethics is the position which Hume rejects and sets out to attack. In deliberate opposition to Plato's metaphor of reason as the charioteer who is master of the horse, Hume turns the metaphor around and says in one of his most famous statements:

> Reason is, and ought only to be, the slave of the passions, and can never pretend to any other office than to serve and obey them.

What can he mean by this? That it is an attack upon Plato is clear, but how can Hume defend this turnaround, in which the horses, the lion, and the dragon are the masters of the man, of reason? How can he argue that reason ought to "serve and obey" the passions?

Hume's point is that we have two kinds of knowledge, knowledge of relations of ideas as in the formal, abstract statements of mathematics and logic; and knowledge of matters of fact which is derived from sense impressions. But, Hume argues, these two kinds of knowledge—knowledge of formal abstractions and descriptions of factual constant conjunctions—cannot motivate my moral conduct as Plato thought, nor can they fight against the passions. What does move us to act is our desires, feelings, sentiments, the prospect of what will give us pleasure or pain. Knowledge of mathematics and causal relations are useless to motivate us to act. They are useful only to help us get what we are motivated toward by desire. A used-car dealer's knowledge of mathematics and of the trade-in value of cars will not motivate him to virtue. It will only be of service to him in his sentiments of honesty or dishonesty, whichever dominates. This is what Hume means by saying reason is the slave of the passions and should serve and obey them. Reason provides the means, the instruments or devices, for gaining what the passions desire. Moreover Hume insists that reason cannot criticize my motives, it cannot find fault with the passions and feelings which move me to act, no matter what they are. Hume makes this point in a striking and terrifying way: "It is not contrary to reason to prefer the destruction of the whole world to the scratching of my finger." Reason does not require me to choose one or the other. Reason can bring to bear only formal relations of ideas or constant conjunction of fact—and both are irrelevant to what motivates my choice: my passions.

But if reason cannot govern our moral action, contrary to Socrates and Plato and rationalistic ethics, and if reason cannot criticize the motives for action which arise from desire, then how is ethics possible? How is it possible to determine the meaning of good and evil, of right and wrong? How is it possible to make moral judgments about my own or another person's acts or character? Since moral judgments are not based on mathematics or matter of fact, on what are they based?

Hume's answer is that they are based upon certain sentiments or feelings which can be discovered to be in constant conjunction with certain actions. Let us not ask what people ought to regard as good, he says, but instead what in empirical fact they do approve. Let us see whether there is any constant conjunction between moral approval and the kinds of actions which are approved. And he concludes that morality is based upon a universal sentiment of benevolence or fellow feeling. We approve of traits such as being just, truthful, humane, altruistic, cooperative—all these traits please our sentiment of benevolence and are useful to us or to others. By contrast, we feel disapproval universally of traits contrary to the sentiment of benevolence: unjust, lying, deceitful, murderous, or viciously antisocial traits.

Hume gives as an example a man being congratulated on the fine character of his future son-in-law, as a man of honor, of humanity, fair and kind in his treatment of others, quick to learn, sound in his knowledge, witty, cheerful, courageous. All these traits approved of in the prospective son-in-law are considered virtuous, Hume points out, because they exhibit the sentiment of benevolence and are useful to society at large and to the persons making the moral judgments. Thus moral judgments, according to Hume, are based on nothing but our feelings and sentiments of what is agreeable and useful to us and to others.

But you may well ask: Hume's empiricist ethics tells us what people actually do approve of as good, but how does this tell us what we wish to know—what is really good? Only a normative ethics such as Plato's, which defends standards or ideals for conduct, can tell us what is worthy of being approved of. Hume has once more been the destroyer. In ethics he has taken aim at the rationalists who claim to give us rational moral rules to live by, a normative ethics. Hume has left us with an ethics which is nothing but the expression of our feelings of benevolence, fellow feeling, pleasure, and utility.

The Outcome of Humean Skepticism

How does Hume manage to live with so much destruction, the wreckage of so many enduring traditional beliefs? How much skepticism with regard to our knowledge can we live with? Hume prods us on into skeptical doubt as to the reliability of our scientific knowledge and to the destruction of normative ethics and religion as meaningless and misleading nonsense. He urges:

When we run over to libraries persuaded of these principles, what havoc must we make? . . . Take in hand any volume of divinity or school of metaphysics . . . and let us ask: *Does it contain any abstract reasoning concerning quantity or number?* No. *Does it contain any experimental reasoning concerning matter of fact and existence?* No. Commit it then to the flames: For it can contain nothing but sophistry and illusion.

What then have we left? What have Hume's empiricist principles left for us? In the world of fact we are limited to our impressions and our ideas. We do not know what causes them to appear and reappear. We have no knowledge that an external world exists. We have no knowledge that we have personal identity as a continuous self through our lifetime. We have no knowledge of ultimate reality or of God. The idea of both physical and mental substance is meaningless. The scientific laws of nature are nothing but constant conjunctions of our own impressions and psychological compulsion. Religious beliefs are worthless pretensions to knowledge. The traditional rules of reason for moral guidance are without any motivating power. There is no logical, rational, or objective foundation of any kind for our knowledge. Science, religion, and ethics are reduced to human psychology, to the laws of association of ideas or to sentiments and fears. What then is left?

Hume's answer is to offer a mitigated, modified skepticism. When reason fails, nature takes over. The guiding principle in human life is other than reason. Like animals, humans are creatures of instinct. Our animal instinct predisposes us to have trust in the senses and to rely on such limited knowledge as we have. Total skepticism is impossible—"No one can persevere in it even for a few hours." Philosophical reasoning such as his own cannot, says Hume, destroy our instinctual beliefs in an external world, that fire burns, that the sun will rise tomorrow. Through animal instinct we have animal faith in the world of the senses, and thus we are able to function in the world. Animal faith, not philosophy, governs our lives.

By introducing the psychological factor of animal faith, Hume has mitigated, modified, lessened, his extreme skepticism with regard to all our knowledge. But he has done this, not by showing us some objective foundation for our knowledge but by showing us once again that our commonsense knowledge, like science, religion, and ethics, is based only upon human psychology. Through animal faith our ordinary life continues; we do not walk out of the top window of the Washington Monument. But in the intellectual world, animal faith does not lessen the destructiveness of Hume's philosophy to our claims to knowledge.

But is Hume consistent in denying the existence of the self and the validity of scientific laws? Are atomic sensations adequate to account for human experience? Is the mind merely passive in perception? These criticisms we will see raised against Hume. But "refuting" Hume will be a task for all theory of knowlege that follows him; subsequent philosophers, and especially Immanuel Kant, will attempt to "answer" Hume's skepticism and to find a foundation for knowledge. Hume remains a strong influence, as we will see, upon contemporary British "analytic" philosophy.

SUGGESTIONS FOR FURTHER READING

PART THREE: HUME

Works of Hume:

Berlin, Isaiah, ed. *The Age of Enlightenment*. New York: New American Library, 1956. Text adapted for television series.

Philosophical Works. Edited by T. H. Green and T. H. Grose. 4 vols. London, 1875. Reprinted, 1912.

A Treatise of Human Nature. Edited by L. A. Selby-Bigge. Oxford: Clarendon Press, 1965.

An Enquiry Concerning Human Understanding. New York: Liberal Arts Press, 1955.

Hume's Moral and Political Philosophy. New York: Hafner Publishing Co., 1948.

Dialogues Concerning Natural Religion. New York: Liberal Arts Press, 1962.

Critical Studies:

On the Age of Enlightenment:

Cassirer, Ernst. *The Philosophy of the Enlightenment*. Translated by Fritz Koelln and James Pettegrove. Princeton: Princeton University Press, 1951. Paperback, Boston: Beacon Press, 1966.

Cobban, A. *In Search of Humanity: The Role of Enlightenment in Modern History*. New York: George Braziller, 1960.

Gay, Peter. *The Enlightenment: An Interpretation*. 2 vols. New York: Alfred A. Knopf, 1966–69.

Randall, J. H. *The Career of Philosophy: From the Middle Ages to the Enlightenment*. New York: Columbia University Press, 1962.

Todd, William B., ed. *Hume and the Enlightenment: Essays Presented to Ernest Campbell Mossner*. Austin, Texas: University of Texas, 1974.

Willey, Basil. *The Eighteenth Century Background*. New York: Columbia University Press, 1940.

On Hume:

Ayer, A. J. *Hume*. New York: Hill and Wang, 1980.

Basson, A. *David Hume*. Hammondsworth: Penguin Books, 1958.

Cavendish, A. P. *David Hume*. New York: Dover, 1968.

Church, R. W. *Hume's Theory of the Understanding*. London: Allen and Unwin, 1935.

Chappell, V. C., ed. *Hume, A Collection of Critical Essays*. Notre Dame: University of Notre Dame Press, 1968.

Hendel, Chas. W. *Studies in the Philosophy of David Hume*. Princeton: Princeton University Press, 1925. Reprinted New York: Liberal Arts Press, 1963.

Laird, J. *Hume's Philosophy of Human Nature*. London: Methuen and Co., 1932.

Morris, C. R. *Locke, Berkeley, Hume*. Fairlawn, New Jersey: Oxford University Press, 1931.

Mossner, Ernest Campbell. *The Life of David Hume*. Austin: University of Texas Press, 1954. 2nd ed. Oxford: Oxford University Press, 1980.

Noxon, James H. *Hume's Philosophical Development: A Study of His Methods*. Oxford: Clarendon Press, 1973.

Price, H. H. *Hume's Theory of the External World*. Oxford: Oxford University Press, 1940.

Sesonske, A., and Fleming, N., eds. *Human Understanding: Studies in the Philosophy of David Hume*. Belmont, California: Wadsworth, 1965.

Smith, Norman Kemp. *The Philosophy of David Hume*. London: Macmillan, 1941.

Taylor, A. E. *David Hume and the Miraculous*. Cambridge: Cambridge University Press, 1927.

Zabeeh, Farhang. *Hume, Precursor of Modern Empiricism*. The Hague: Nijhoff, 1973.

PART FOUR
HEGEL

15

A REVOLUTION IN THOUGHT

When during the French Revolution the steel blade of the guillotine began to descend, cutting off the head of the queen, Marie Antoinette, and the heads of hundreds of men and women of the aristocracy, priests, nuns, the managerial staffs of the great feudal estates, anyone suspected of being an enemy of the people, and finally, leaders of the revolution themselves—it is a certainty that by the time this violence was happening, the Age of Enlightenment was dead. The French Revolution had been the third great revolution inspired by the philosophy of the Age of Enlightenment. It was in France that the philosophic ideas of the Age of Enlightenment were most fully and radically developed in all their glorious and shattering significance.

Historical Situation:
The Enlightenment in France

Who developed these philosophic ideas which inspired the French Revolution? Strangely, no one who would ever appear on a list of the world's greatest philosophers, such as Plato, Descartes, Hume, or Hegel. The significance of the philosophy of the Age of Enlightenment was spelled out in France during the middle years of the eighteenth century by a group who came to be called the *philosophes*, by which the Frence meant that they were not professional academic philosophers such as might teach at the Sorbonne in Paris, but rather that they were intellectual types, opinion makers, political activists in the sciences or the arts, journalists, café philosophers. These were the people who popularized and disseminated the ideas of enlightenment to large and varied audiences throughout France.

The Philosophes

Best known among the *philosophes* is Voltaire (1694–1778), poet, dramatist, historian, essayist, famous for his satire *Candide*. There was also Diderot (1713–84), essayist, dramatist, philosopher, novelist, the greatest genius of the French Enlightenment, editor (with D'Alembert) of the famous *Encyclopedia* which slyly propagandized for revolution; there were La Mettrie (1709–51), Helvétius (1715–71), and Holbach (1723–89), philosophers, essayists, reformers, all ardent proponents of philosophical materialism and the new sciences; and there were the mathematician-philosophers D'Alembert and Condorcet.

By now in the middle of the eighteenth century Descartes and Newton were only bygone symbols of the rapidly advancing Age of Science which was revealing the order, harmony, and lawfulness of all of nature, physical and human. A truce had ended the battle between the Church and the new sciences. The *philosophes* did not fight the battle of rationalism versus empiricism, the battle of Descartes versus Hume. Rather than debating the differences between rationalism and empiricism, the *philosophes* were eclectic and capitalized on both of them. They used the advantages of each side for their own philosophical and political purposes, which were to reform or bring down the dominance over France of the Catholic Church and the absolute monarchy, and to establish a new social and political order, based upon the Enlightenment philosophy of the truths of science and of the natural rights of mankind.

The Fettering of Reason. Why have these truths of physical nature and human nature, of science and natural rights, been so long in becoming known to us? It is because reason has been in chains, say the *philosophes;* reason has been fettered throughout history by the greed and the lust for power of certain identifiable historical groups. Reason is only now breaking free from the chains placed upon it by the institutionalized power of the Kings of France and of the

Church of Rome. The French intellectuals charged these two institutions with monopolizing literacy and education, which are the means to enlightenment, and with conspiring to keep the great mass of people illiterate, ignorant, and thus powerless and impoverished.

Indoctrination with False Beliefs. Moreover, the *philosophes* charged King and Church with indoctrinating the public with false beliefs (*préjugés*: presumptions, prejudices) which serve to protect the interests of these ruling institutions—false beliefs such as the inferiority of the ordinary people, in intelligence and morality, to royalty and the clergy.

But now that reason is breaking its chains, these ideas can be shown to be false, (1) by appeal to the empiricists' question How do you know? or (2) by appeal to the new truths of physical nature established by science or (3) by appeal to the new truths of human nature established by reason, the truths of natural rights, equality under the law, and universal rationality. And so the belief in the inferiority of the commoners to aristocracy or to the clergy is shown to be false by the principle that all men are equal; the belief that the lower classes are not fit to govern is falsified by the principle that all men are rational; the medieval belief in the inevitability of suffering from disease and poverty is challenged by the question How do you know?; the belief that the earth is the center of the universe is falsified by Newtonian science. It was clear to the *philosophes* that throughout history powerful groups such as the Church and the State in France used philosophic and religious ideas to promote their own interests. Here the French *philosophes* had come close to hitting upon the concept of ideology which Karl Marx was soon to develop. In its simplest form, ideology for Marx signifies the set of seemingly true but deceptive ideas by which one social class dominates the thinking of another, in order to exploit them, as the capitalist class dominates the thinking of the workers.

The Truths of Physical Nature and Human Nature Will Make Men Free. The *philosophes* proclaimed that now for the first time in history human beings through the power of their reason are grasping truth, the expanding truth of science and natural rights, and these truths will make men free. The new man of the Age of Science is now equipped by reason with a theory which he can put into practice. The institutions which are based upon false ideas, superstitions, prejudices, which are contrary to the truths of physical nature or human nature, must be reformed or eliminated. The human world must be reconstructed with institutions which will serve the natural law of progress. *"Ecrasez l'infame"* was Voltaire's cry against the Church of Rome ("Crush the infamous one"). The rule of the absolutist king must also be destroyed and replaced by a republic. Since human beings are oppressed, victimized, exploited, by these evil institutions, the absolutist Church and State must be brought to an end, along with the false beliefs which defend and protect them. "Let us destroy," says the *philosophe* La Mettrie, "the belief in God, the soul, immortality and all Church dogma."

Never before had human beings been so confident in their knowledge of physical nature, human nature, morality, and politics. They believed they could rebuild the social and political world on a foundation of universal truth. They believed they were, or would be soon, in command of all the knowledge necessary to improve the world. (This boldly optimistic, future-oriented Enlightenment philosophy has since the Founders been the philosophic outlook of the United States. But today we are less confident that we have the knowledge to solve the problems of energy; the ecological problems of air, water, and land; economic inflation; unemployment and poverty; the decay of our cities; racial problems; the world population explosion; or the spread of communism in Europe, Africa, Asia, and Latin America. Have we lost our Enlightenment heritage of optimism?)

The Natural Law of Progress. The most moving and dramatic appeal of the French Enlightenment was the call for the natural rights of liberty, equality, and property. The *philosophes* spoke for the universal brotherhood and sisterhood of humankind, and they called for an end to class conflict or conflict based upon race or sex or nationality. They looked ahead to the bright future for all humanity, which was guaranteed by a necessary natural law of progress: the natural law of human reason is to discover scientific truths about nature and turn this expanding knowledge into practice in the form of technology for the benefit of humanity; and to discover truths about human nature and to turn these truths into practice in the form of reforming or overturning all social institutions.

In this heady, exhilarating concept that human beings now have truth by which they can change the world, the French *philosophes* foreshadowed the political vision of Karl Marx in the nineteenth century (as they also foreshadowed Marx's concept of ideology)—that we now have the theory (or philosophy) which is sufficient to determine practice, to change the shape of the human world. Already in the thought of the *philosophes* philosophy is no longer regarded as merely passive reflection on eternal truth or even on problems of the present, but as a force, a power, which can transform the world.

The Reign of Terror

By 1793 the French Revolution had moved into the phase called the Reign of Terror. As the revolution had intensified, it passed into the control of the radical party of the extreme left, the Jacobins, and a revolutionary mob soon ruled. Rather than the truths of reason, the voice of the people became the sole source of truth. The enemy to be destroyed was not false beliefs, but any individual persons or political groups who seemed to oppose the will of the people. This was the Reign of Terror, in which the Revolution devoured its own leaders, one of the bloodiest scenes of horror and violence in European history.

To the *philosophes*, most of whom had died by this time, the Reign of Terror would have appeared as the heart of darkness, as indeed it did to the Marquis de Condorcet, the last of the *philosophes*, who was one of the heroes of the American Revolution. Along with our own Tom Paine, Condorcet wrote the first draft of the constitution of the new French republic, after the initial violent phase of the Revolution had taken place. But the draft was rejected, and when Condorcet criticized the revisions that were made, he was denounced for conspiring against the republic and condemned to the guillotine. While in hiding, Condorcet still clung to the intoxicating idea of progress and to the ideals of freedom, equality, universal education, universal peace. He wrote a philosophy of history, in which he presented the history of the human race as moving ahead, despite obstacles, through stages of progress into a glorious future of the perfecting of universal humanity, in intelligence, health, and happiness and in the abolition of all inequalities. He speaks for the whole Age of Enlightenment with these glowing words:

> The day will come when the sun will shine on free
> men only, who will regard Reason alone as their

master; and when tyrants and slaves, priests and their treacherous tools will exist only in the pages of history and in the scenes of the theater.

And he concludes with this moving thought:

This picture of the human race . . . advancing with firm and sure steps toward the attainment of truth, virtue and happiness . . . presents to the philosopher a spectacle which will console him for the errors, the crimes, the injustices with which the earth is still polluted and whose victim he often is.

And victim he was. He was tipped off that his hideout was going to be raided, and he escaped to the outskirts of Paris, where he was soon caught hiding in a tavern. Fortunately for him he died, either from a heart attack or by taking a capsule of poison, before he could be dragged off to the guillotine to be beheaded.

The French Revolution: Paradoxes and Reversals

The French Revolution, which has become the supreme example of revolution in the modern world, is now seen to be riddled with paradoxes and to give out conflicting messages. Its guiding philosophy is the Enlightenment philosophy of reason, of the rational order and harmony of nature and human nature—but its unintended outcome is a reversal, the opposite of reason, the Reign of Terror and its irrational passions and mob violence. Its political goals are those of overthrowing the regime of Lous XVI and replacing it with a republic—but the revolution ends with another reversal, the unintended consequence of the rise of Napoleon to power as the emperor of France, whose iron rule was a far more efficient absolutism than that of the executed king. Moreover, the French Revolution stands forth as a glorious spectacle of the human struggle for freedom, but also it stands forth as the very opposite, as a spectacle of the shameful human capacity for being swept up into self-righteous mob frenzy and murder. None of these paradoxes will be lost on the German philosopher Hegel, who will build reversals, ironies, and paradoxes into the very structure of his philosophy.

The Enlightenment in Germany (Aufklärung)

We shift the scene now to Germany, where the next major philosophical development takes place. In Germany the Enlightenment was a quiet backwater which scarcely felt the distant stormy seas of the English and French Enlightenment. What then was the German Enlightenment, the *Aufklärung*? Unlike England and France, Germany did not have an Enlightenment revolution in which the rising middle class struck for autonomy and power against a king. Germany had not taken part in the new commercial and industrial developments that had transformed the social, economic, and political structures of England and France and had culminated in their revolutions of 1688 and 1789. Germany had no financially strong upper middle class, with the economic power to strike for independence in their life, liberty, and property from the ruling powers. No flourishing economic interests demanded a voice in the government as in England and in France.

Germany had remained feudal, agricultural, and rural while England and France had become industrialized and urban. Political beliefs remained feudal and absolutist. Moreover, Germany had no national unity—it was a collection of dukedoms, baronial estates, imperial cities, principalities, and small states.

In the cultural life of Germany the Lutheran Protestant Church, which had arisen in Germany and had initiated the Protestant Reformation, remained strong in its influence, especially in the north; metaphysics was taken seriously in the intellectual world; science and technology had not developed sufficiently to have social or philosophical importance. The new science of Newton, as it became known during the eighteenth century, was seen as of limited significance, incapable of explaining anything more than material and mechanical matters and by no means the sole method for arriving at knowledge. Nor were the German philosophers greatly impressed by the radical empiricism of Hume. Most German philosophers of the eighteenth century regarded Hume as dissolving all rational truths and scientific laws and leaving only animal faith in their place. This philosophic outcome was totally unacceptable to them. Germany was to find another path in philosophy.

Immanuel Kant

Out of this provincial German cultural and intellectual background came the towering genius Immanuel Kant (1724–1804), who provided for the first time a philosophical answer to Hume's skepticism. But Kant's answer to Hume accomplished something else as well. It brought about one of the great *turns* in philosophy, a switch to a new way of looking at the entire enterprise of philosophy. Kant's most influential work is the *Critique of Pure Reason* and was published in 1781, eight years before the French Revolution.

Kant recognized the force of Hume's empiricist arguments. But Kant saw that the logical outcome of Hume's radical empiricism, claiming as it does that the basis of all knowledge lies in experience, leads to the conclusion that there isn't any knowledge. There is only association of ideas through habit, psychological expectancy, and compulsion. Finally, in Hume's empiricist view, there is nothing but animal faith to rely upon for assurance that the regularities of experience and science will continue, that the sun will rise tomorrow, or that water will begin to freeze at 32 degrees Fahrenheit.

Kant's Theory of Knowledge

(1) **The Sensory Component.** Kant urged that the cure for this disaster into which Hume led philosophy lies in not taking the first step—the step of radical empiricism, which claims that knowledge is solely from sensory experience. In opposition to this radical empiricism, which seeks to derive all knowledge solely from sense perception, Kant introduces a new conception of knowledge. Knowledge does indeed have as a source the Humean element of impressions, the sensory element in relation to which the mind is passive, merely receiving impressions which it copies as images in thought.

(2) **The Pure Concepts of the Understanding: The Rational Component.** But, Kant continues, here is another element in our knowledge which is not derived from sensory experience. Nor is this other element derived from independent reality. This second element comes from the mind itself. The human mind is not a blank tablet or an empty cupboard as the empiricists Locke and Hume claimed. It is equipped with its own pure concepts by means of which it organizes the flux of

sensory impressions into substances, qualities, and quantities, and into causes and effects. In opposition to Hume, the mind, says Kant, is not empty, but furnished with twelve pure concepts or categories.

Kant: The Pure Concepts of the Understanding

Quantity	Quality	Relation	Modality
unity	affirmation	substance–accidents	possibility
plurality	negation	cause–effect	actuality
totality	limitation	causal reciprocity	necessity

Secondly, the mind is not passive, as Hume and other empiricists also claim. The mind does not merely receive, as on a screen or in a theater, as Hume said, a stream of sense impressions; it is not a blank sheet of paper on which nature writes. Rather, mind is itself active. Mind actively interprets the world rather than passively receiving and recording in memory what comes to it from the external world through the senses. It is the categories of our own minds that organize the sensory flux and give it meaning as substances, with qualities, and quantities, or related as causes and effects, or in reciprocal causation.

(3) **The Pure Concepts (Categories) As A Priori.** These pure concepts (categories) of the understanding Kant considers to be *a priori*. By this he means (1) that *they are logically prior to experience;* they are presupposed by all experience; and (2) that *they are independent of experience;* experience can never change them. They give us the kind of experience and knowledge that we have because they are our ways of understanding anything. Moreover, Kant shows, the pure concepts of the mind are (3) *universal:* they form the structure of any mind, of any consciousness. A further aspect of these concepts is (4) they are *necessary: they are a necessary condition of experience*; without them, there is no knowledge, there is not even any experience. They furnish the necessary element which Hume said that knowledge lacked. It is mind that supplies the necessary concepts which organize and unify the flux of sensation. Without the *a priori* concept of substance to organize the flux of sense impressions, you could not experience a thing. Without the *a priori* concept of cause, which is a constituent of all minds, and organizes sense

impressions into causes and effects, you would never experience causality, but only a sequence of atomistic sense impressions.

Kant's Answer to Hume

Hume's theory of knowledge, which reduces our experiences and knowledge to nothing but sense impressions, is false, Kant charges, since it cannot account for the fact that we do experience things and causal relations (not merely sense impressions), or for the fact that we do have scientific knowledge of things (not mere psychological expectations or animal faith). How is experience of objects possible? How is science possible? This, says Kant, is the question Hume avoided in his relentless driving of empiricism as far as it would go, single-tracked in his insistence that scientific knowledge consists in nothing but sense impressions. Something, then, is wrong with Hume's sense-impression theory of knowledge. What is wrong with Hume's theory is that he fails to see that knowledge consists not only of sense perceptions, the empirical element, but also of the a priori concepts by which we understand things, the rational element in knowledge. These *a priori* concepts organize sense impressions and make experience of objects and scientific knowledge possible. Hume had attacked the causal laws of science by denying that we have any sense impression of necessary connection between causes and effects. Kant's answer to Hume on this score is that there is and always will be a necessary connection between causes and effects because the mind itself imposes the concept of necessary connection between causes and effects. Cause and effect is an *a priori*, universal, and necessary concept of the human mind.

Notice that Kant's pure concepts of the understanding are not the same as Descartes's innate ideas, for example, that everything has a cause, or that God exists. Descartes says that our innate ideas correspond to the structures of independent reality, and that they are imprinted in us by God so that we can know the true nature of reality. But Kant does not claim that the categories or pure concepts of the understanding correspond to independent reality. They are only forms of our consciousness, he says. They are only the way in which we understand things. They do not tell us anything about what things are like in themselves, independently of our way of understanding them by our concepts.

Nor are Kant's pure concepts the same as Plato's ideas, since Plato's ideas are themselves what is real, they are the ultimate structures of reality which the world of the flux copies. But for Kant the categories are not structures of reality, they are only structures of our consciousness, our minds. They are significant only epistemologically, that is, in relation to our knowing; they have no significance metaphysically, or ontologically, that is, in relation to reality. And so we can know that the laws of nature will continue to hold true, because the universal and necessary concepts of our own minds structure them.

Appearances (Phenomena) and Things-in-Themselves

But there is a price to be paid for this certainty that the concepts or categories of the understanding provide—that the causal laws of science state necessary connections and not mere association of ideas, as Hume claimed in his skepticism; and a price must be paid for the certainty that the laws of nature will be true in the future. The price we must pay for the certainty that the categories provide is that we are able to know only appearances (phenomena), only things as they appear to us by means of these pure concepts. Things-in-themselves, things as they are independent of our concepts, we can never know.

The Kantian Turn in Philosophy

The new turn in philosophy which Kant introduced opposes Hume's reduction of knowledge to sense impressions. Knowledge is a complex, composite affair—this is Kant's major argument against Hume. Knowledge consists not only of the sensory element in which the mind is passive but also of a rational element, the twelve pure, rational concepts of the understanding with which the mind actively synthesizes, unifies, organizes the sensory flow into things with qualities, into causes with effects. With these two components of knowledge, Kant has found roles for both the empiricist and rationalist elements in his new theory of knowledge. He emerges as one of the great synthesizers in the history of philosophy, a synthesizer of rationalism and empiricism, the two great conflicting philosophies of the seventeenth and eighteenth centuries.

But notice that a strange thing has happened to Kant on the way to answering Hume. Kant has saved the scientific laws of nature, and most especially Newtonian physics, from the destructive skepticism of Hume, by showing that the necessary connections of Newton's causal laws have their foundation in the necessary causal concept of the human mind. But what has Kant done? In order to save the truth of the sciences, Kant has had to make the laws of science dependent upon the mind and its concepts: He has had to say that the order which Newtonian laws establish is not in nature but comes from the universal and necessary concepts of the human mind.

Kant has had to say that the independently real external world of nature does not give us its laws, either through sense impressions, as Hume and the empiricists said, or through corresponding with our clear and distinct rational ideas, as Descartes and the rationalists had said. Nature does not give the human mind its laws, Kant has discovered. It is the other way around. The mind gives its own laws to nature— its own laws in the form of its own necessary concepts which organize all sensory materials. These are the concepts which form, organize, and structure all our experience, all our knowledge of nature. In Kant's famous words, "Mind is the law-giver to nature." Thus the laws of nature are dependent upon the concepts of the human mind. With the philosophy of Kant, the world order has become mind-dependent, as the American philosopher C. I. Lewis has said.

Here we have the most startling and influential significance of the new turn which Kant gave to philosophy. It is the turn away from the external world of independent nature to the inner world of the activity and powers of the mind as the key to what we experience and what we know. The new turn in philosophy has this significance: After Kant, and under his influence, whatever is experienced or known will be shown in part to be due to the mind itself, to the concepts by which the mind understands things.

Are you familiar with the psychotherapist's maxim that we live in a world of our own making? That if your world is cold and cruel, that is the way your own mind has made the world appear? And that if you learn how to change your thinking, your concepts and attitudes, the world will appear differently to you, no longer cold and cruel? And when a historian speaks of the world of Thomas Jefferson, or when an anthropologist speaks of the world of the Zuni Indians, they are saying that Jefferson's own mind made the world appear to him as it did, that the Zuni's own beliefs and values make the world appear to them as it does.

All this began with the Kantian turn in philosophy, in which the object is always in some degree the creation of the subject. This Kantian turn opened wholly new horizons for philosophy, for the sciences and the humanities. Hegel and Marx in the nineteenth century and Sartre in the twentieth century are all committed to this new viewpoint, in which what counts is the way our minds interpret or understand things, not the way things are in themselves. We move on now to Hegel, the greatest genius of German philosophy after Kant, and one of the greatest of the master builders in Western philosophy.

16

THE REAL IS THE RATIONAL

Do you think of yourself as having a particular kind of philosophy because you are an American, or an American Indian, or of Hungarian or Chinese or Latin American ethnic origin, or because you are a woman, or because you are a black? Does belonging to a particular social group affect the philosophy one has? Do different social groups give rise to different philosophical outlooks on the world, different ways of perceiving reality? If this is your viewpoint, you agree with Hegel, Marx, and Sartre, who all take this position, following the Kantian turn in philosophy with its claim that whatever is experienced or known is in part due to our own minds, to our way of thinking.

In the modern world, it has often been observed that France, England, and Germany—these three great national groupings—have each of them developed its own characteristic philosophy, its own way of viewing the world. The characteristic philosophy which arose in France, and which remains in many ways the typical philosophy of France, is the *Continental rationalism* of which the French philosopher *Descartes* is the supreme example. The British also developed their own characteristic way of philosophizing, the philosophy usually called *British empiricism*, of which *Hume* is the outstanding example. Similarly, there developed in Germany, beginning with Kant and the Romantics, a type of philosophy which is regarded as characteristically German, and for that reason is usually called *German idealism*, and *Hegel* is its preeminent example.

**"Hegel in His Study," based on a
lithograph by L. Stebbers, 1828.**
(COURTESY OF THE BETTMANN ARCHIVES.)

Hegel's Life

Georg Wilhelm Friedrich Hegel (1770–1831) was born in the same year as Beethoven and the English Romantic poet Wordsworth. Hegel was the oldest of three children in a middle-class family in the town of Stuttgart in southern Germany. The family's roots had been in Austria, but they, like other Protestants in the sixteenth century, fled from persecution by Catholics in Austria to the safety of Lutheran Protestant territories in Germany. Hegel's father was a minor civil servant; all that appears to be known about his mother is contained in a reference to her high intelligence and her unusual learning for a woman of that time and place. Uneventfully he went through the schooling conventional for his social class, and after he was graduated from the Stuttgart Gymnasium in October 1788 he entered the famous theological seminary, nearby at the University of Tübingen, to study theology for the Protestant ministry. Tübingen Evangelical-Theological Seminary is located in the buildings of an old Augustinian monastery on a cliff overlooking the River Neckar, surrounded by hills and with the snow-topped craggy peaks of the Alps in the distance. At Tübingen in the academic year 1790–91 Hegel shared the dormitory on the top floor of the old seminary tower with his friend Hölderlin, who was to become one of Germany's major poets, and with Schelling, who quickly became famous, earlier than Hegel, as a German idealist philosopher.

After Tübingen there followed long, hard years of struggle to earn a living and to develop as a philosopher. Hegel's first university position as a philosopher was at the University of Jena, from 1801 to 1807, where he began as an unsalaried lecturer, being paid a fee by the students who attended. From 1802 on, Hegel had repeatedly announced a forthcoming book, year after year. Having delayed so long, he angered his publisher and ended up having to finish the manuscript in October 1806, while the army of Napoleon was attacking the town of Jena. Is it part of a legend that the last pages are said to have been written on the night of October 12 to 13, the night of the final battle of Jena, in which the French under the invincible Napoleon defeated the Prussian army and conquered Prussia, the most powerful territory in Germany? On October 13, 1806, the city of Jena was captured and Napoleon entered the walled city. Hegel wrote about the event to a friend and benefactor with these words of hero worship of Napoleon:

> I saw the Emperor—that world-soul—riding out to reconnoiter the city; it is truly a wonderful sensation to see such an individual, concentrated here on a single point, astride a single horse, yet reaching across the world and ruling it . . .

A week later, on October 20, his house was plundered by the soldiers of the invading French army. There was no winter semester for Hegel and no longer a teaching position at the University of Jena. The book, however, had been finished. The book was *The Phenomenology of Spirit*. It is now regarded as exemplifying the writing of the young Hegel, and usually is contrasted with his *Philosophy of Right* (published in 1821), which is regarded as exemplifying the mature or the late Hegel. The book is one of the great works of genius that Western civilization has produced—but it is difficult, conceptually and stylistically, and in some parts almost impossible to penetrate. (A few critics have protested that it is deliberately obscure.)

Hegel's Philosophic Sources

Hegel had thought deeply about what his approach would be. But what was available to the young Hegel, what philosophical viewpoints were present in his historical time, the first years of the nineteenth century, and in his place, the university life of Prussian Germany? There were, first of all, French rationalism and British empiricism, and beyond these, and synthesizing them, was the formidable philosophy of the German philosopher Kant, which had been the capstone of the Enlightenment philosophy. But there was also a newer philosophy which had appeared in Germany, and this was the viewpoint called Romanticism.

German Romanticism

What was German Romanticism? It was a revolutionary movement, in the realm of literature, philosophy, and the visual arts, rather than in the realm of politics. It was a wholly new way of looking at the world which arose with a great burst of creative energy on the part of German artists and intellectuals who rejected the Enlightenment as a philosophy confined to and dominated by reason—by mathematics, logic, mathematically formulated scientific laws, and by abstract natural rights. They were disillusioned with the promises of progress and the perfectibility of the human race made by the age of optimism.

1. The Inward Path. What then did Romanticism have to offer in place of the philosophy of the Enlightenment? It was fortified by the Kantian turn in philosophy and this opened up for the German Romantics the "inward path" to truth, the new horizon for philosophy in which the path to truth is through the world within, since it imposes its thought upon what is found in the outside world. It was in the inner world of the self that truth and the meaning of the human condition was to be found, not the external world of the physical sciences. Like French existentialism of the twentieth century, German Romanticism of the early nineteenth century used literature—novels, poems, dramas, essays, short stories—to express the inner world of human feelings and to offer powerful protest against philosophies which ignore them.

2. The Quest for the Totality of Experience. Science is far from exhausting the complexities of human existence, they argued. The real world contains much more than science can disclose. It is the totality of experience, its joys and sorrows, growth and change, paradoxes and fulfillments, that Romantics longed for and that they demanded philosophy to seek to understand. To understand the world we must go to experience as it is lived, not merely to the empiricist's sense perceptions or to the rationalist's clear and distinct ideas. We must explore the dark, hidden areas of the mind and the realms of feeling and imagination; we must discover the inner workings of the human spirit and the way it relates to nature, society, history, and God. The ideal for the philosopher is not to be confined to the narrow territory of science but to be always in pursuit of the fullness of meaning, always in quest of the elusive blue flower, the symbol created by the poet Novalis for the yearning love of beauty beyond the finite.

3. The Primacy of Will. To the Romantics what is of supreme reality and value in human nature is not reason but the will of the human individual. The will strives for self-fulfillment, and can find this only in the striving for infinity;

the will seeks to possess the totality of experience, of nature, history, and culture ascending from human finitude to the divinely infinite. It strives endlessly, as did Goethe's Faust, to experience, to enjoy the concrete fullness of totality. It was the Romantic yearning for every experience, for infinity, that led Faust to sell his soul to the devil.

4. Nature As Spirit. The Romantics protested that the real is spiritual, not material as the Enlightenment had claimed. In the literature of Romanticism nature is spiritualized. Nature is no gigantic, mechanical clockwork, operating by Newtonian laws, but is instead a living spirit, a vast will, and a wiser teacher than a scientific treatise. In communion with nature is wisdom to be found—this is the message of the English Romantic poet Wordsworth.

> One impulse from a vernal wood
> May teach you more of man
> Of moral evil and of good
> Than all the sages can

Behind natural phenomena, the Romantic poet intuits an all-encompassing great will, a spiritual power. God is not the engineer-designer of the world machine, as the Enlightenment Deists claim. God is the indwelling soul of the universe.

5. Romantic Polarity. Finally, the Romantics celebrated two-sidedness, polarity, ironic reversals (as in the French Revolution and its outcome) which, they said, characterized human thought and feeling, and the entire realm of human history. The Romantic ideal is to experience both sides of every polarity, and never to become rigid or static, never to become confined, the prisoner of any one mode of thought or way of life, but always to be in pursuit of the infinite. "Insofar as I am static, I am enslaved," proclaimed Goethe's Faust.

The Formation of Hegel's Metaphysics

When Hegel entered the Tübingen Evangelical-Theological Seminary, where he studied philosophy and theology for five years, these intoxicating ideas of Romanticism were in the air. Which of the three kinds of philosophical viewpoints and methods would Hegel use—Romanticism, the philosophy of spirit, will, and endless polarity; or the rationalism and empiricism of science, progress, and natural rights of the French *philosophes;* or the Kantian philosophy? He would fuse elements from all of them.

Like the Romantics, whose influence pervades his thought despite his frequent attacks on it, Hegel is looking for a philosophy that will reach to infinity, encompass all human experience, incorporate all knowledge: science, history, religion, politics, art, literature, architecture. How to bring these vast reaches of the human spirit into systematic, logical unification in a theory? He will do this with his concept of *absolute mind* or spirit. And how to incorporate within it the unending creative destruction, conflicts, reversals, unintended consequences, reconciliations, renewed conflict, which appear to be the enduring traits of all these aspects of reality? He will do this by his theory of *dialectic*.

But such a totalizing philosophy, seeking to comprehend total reality, is a metaphysics, a study of the nature of total reality. Here Hegel runs into a problem. Is metaphysics any longer possible? The empiricists, beginning with John Locke, had taken a hard line with regard to metaphysics. To the empiricists, metaphysics makes grandiose claims about the whole of reality as being one or many, material or mental, permanent or in flux. These large statements, Locke said, can't answer the empiricist's question: How do you know? Based upon what observation or data is your claim? Locke also raised the more fundamental question: Is the human mind equipped for such metaphysical excursions into total reality, or are there limits as to what the mind can know? And Locke offered this advice to philosophers: Don't try to be a master builder of a great metaphysical system. It is enough to be an underlaborer, removing the rubbish of past metaphysics. Hume carried on the empiricist's attack upon metaphysics. Metaphysics is worthless as knowledge and even meaningless, according to Hume. The statements made by metaphysics fail to pass the empiricist's test of knowledge and meaning—to show from what sense impressions these statements are derived. Hume's second argument against metaphysics raised again the point that metaphysics attempts to go beyond the limits of human understanding, which is confined to sense impression. Therefore metaphysics is impossible. Commit it to the flames, says Hume, for it contains only illusion. But then Western philosophy moves on to Kant, who fights back against Hume's skepticism and defends the certainty of science by pointing to the a priori categories of the mind as the necessary and universal conditions of scientific knowledge. As we have seen, however, a high price was paid for the certainty that Kant provided for scientific knowledge. The price was that we cannot know things as they really are in themselves. We know only things as they *appear* to us through the universal and necessary categories of the human understanding. We cannot know things-in-themselves, things as they are in reality, independent of the categories by which we have to understand them. Metaphysics, however, is precisely the attempt to know things as they are in themselves, it is precisely the study of independent reality. Since Kant claims that we cannot know things-in-themselves, he argues that metaphysics is impossible, that the nature of reality, which metaphysics seeks to know, is unknowable to us.

The empiricists and Kant declared that metaphysics is impossible. What route, if any, to a metaphysics of total human experience is open, then, to Hegel in this situation? The Kantian turn in philosophy had given primacy to mind, had made mind the law-giver to nature, such that whatever we know is in part due to our own concepts. But Kant had placed severe limitations on these concepts. To construct through these concepts a metaphysics which seeks knowledge of total reality is impossible.

But for Hegel metaphysics is possible. Hegel accepted from Kant the primacy of the mind's concepts in determining what we know. But he had three objections to Kant's restrictions on the pure concepts. He refused any limitation on the number of concepts. Second, he refused to limit them to use in sensory experience. And third, Hegel refused to limit the knowledge gained by the categories to the status of mere appearance. He argued that the categories do pertain to reality. It is reality itself which these concepts tell us about.

We can now see what Hegel wants to do—he wants to build upon Kant and upon the Kantian turn in philosophy, upon the primacy which Kant gave to the pure rational concepts. Hegel wants to keep this primacy which concepts have over sense impressions. But he also wants to build upon the Romantics, and to be able to be expansive, unlimited, like the Romantics and to incorporate their new, modern sense of the varieties of psychological, religious, historical, cultural, and creative experience, and of many new kinds of knowledge. He wants therefore to be unlimited in using rational concepts to understand this vast variety of experience and knowledge. He wishes also to bring into his philosophy Romantic opposition, conflict, irony, contradiction, paradox, and to express the new sense, after the French Revolution, of the turnabouts of historical change. To achieve these goals and also to incorporate the truth embedded in rationalism and empiricism, Hegel has to construct a new theory of reality as the heart of his metaphysics.

What is this new theory of reality which Hegel constructs? Hegel has found a way to bring the vast reaches of the human spirit into unification in a theory. The totality of concepts used in the vast stretches of all knowledge, all the arts and sciences, religion, political thought, history—they are unified in the absolute mind or absolute spirit, or God, which is ultimate reality. Reality is thus a vast and complex totality of rational concepts and this totality constitutes absolute mind or absolute spirit or God. The real, says Hegel, is the rational, and the rational is the real. This totality of thought is absolute, and characterizes absolute spirit, in contrast to finite minds such as ours; it is objective mind in contrast to the subjectivity of human minds.

Hegel's Metaphysics: Absolute Idealism

Here we have identified Hegel's theory of reality, the metaphysical theory of absolute idealism. As we have already seen, idealism is the name of the type of metaphysical theory which claims that reality has the characteristics of mind or thought, that reality is rational, logical, or spiritual. Absolute idealism is a subtype of idealism.

1. **Reality as Totality of Conceptual Truth.** Absolute idealism is the claim that reality is rational, conceptual totality, that reality is an absolute mind, or the mind of God, an integrated and total structure of conceptual truths.

2. **Reality as Absolute Mind.** For Hegel reality is absolute mind, consisting of the totality of conceptual truth, which reveals itself in all areas of human experience and knowledge, from logic to physics to biology, from history and politics to art, religion, and philosophy.

3. **"The Real is the Rational and the Rational Is the Real".** Reality is this vast structure of rational concepts. Like Plato, Hegel claims that the rational, the concept, the idea—

this is what is real. In Hegel's own famous words: "The real is the rational and the rational is the real." Hegel fills out in rich and concrete detail this vision of the absolute, of absolute spirit, of a God who is total reality and truth, who reveals Himself to our finite minds in every area of human knowledge. You may want to respond to Hegel by agreeing that empiricism is shallow, and that Hegel's absolute idealism offers what the human spirit craves to understand: the meaning of human experience, and the totality of truth to be found in the arts, sciences, history, religion, politics. You may also find yourself agreeing with Hegel about the nature of reality, because when you want to understand the reality that you have to confront in your job, in your family, in the political tensions that greet you with the daily news, you find that you have to think about these things, you have to penetrate them to find what they mean, you have to understand the psychological or social or political concepts that are involved. You don't solve these problems of your life by getting a batch of Humean sense impressions.

4. The Rational Is the Existent Object "More Deeply Understood." Hegel is right, you may say, the real is the rational. But what about existent, the factual objects of the world, the vast realms of physical and organic nature, and human societies? Have all these forms of existence no reality for Hegel? Is only the rational, the conceptual real? Hegel's answer in his own words is that the reality of the rational concepts "is not *another* object than the existence, it is the same object more deeply understood." Absolute idealism claims to penetrate existence to find the rational, conceptual truth, which is its core or kernel.

Here you can see an important distinction between Plato's theory of concepts or ideas and Hegel's theory of concepts. For Plato the eternal and immutable ideas exist separately and independently in their own intelligible realm of being, as distinct from the merely sensible realm of things in flux. However, the separation of the eternal forms from the sensible world of things created a difficulty for Plato's philosophy which was noted even by Plato himself: How can the relation of the immutable forms of the intelligible world to the changing things of the sensible world be explained? For Hegel, on the other hand, the rational concepts have no separate, independent existence apart from the concrete world of things, but constitute their rational core. Hegel thus avoids Plato's problem but creates one for himself. If the real is exclusively the rational concept, then are not the concrete observable objects of nature irrational and unreal? But if they have no reality, how can penetrating them to their rational core be explained?

5. Reality Is Knowable by Its Intelligible, Rational Structures. You can see how strongly Hegel denies the claim of Hume and Kant that reality is unknowable. Hegel is as confident a rationalist as Plato had been. To Hegel, "Whatever is, is rational." By that he means that everything has an intelligible structure or core, which human reason, with the power and flexibility of its concepts, can grasp. Every aspect of human experience is knowable through its underlying rational structure.

6. Absolute Mind as Unity-in-Diversity. Absolute mind is a unified totality of all rational truth, covering all areas of experience and knowledge—yet organizing all this diversity into a coherent unity. The absolute, or absolute mind, is, says Hegel, a unity-in-diversity, a single identity incorporating all these differences, it is a one that includes the many.

7. The Task of Metaphysics: To Show the Diversity of Components of Reality, Their Limits and Interconnections in a Unified Totality. Absolute mind, Hegel says, is the one single reality which reveals itself to us in the concepts of all the areas of human experience. Different aspects of this reality are revealed in different areas of human experience. This single reality manifests itself to us in ordinary experience, in logic and natural science, in psychology, politics and history, in painting, poetry, and architecture, and in religion and philosophy. We understand physics and art and psychology by means of the concepts used in each of these fields. Each of these areas of reality yields a true view of reality, but each yields only a partial, limited, and incomplete view. Physics, for example, reveals one important aspect of reality, but it is only one aspect, it is not the whole of reality. (Here the voice of the Romantics is speaking.) The task of metaphysics, of a theory of all reality, is to identify all of the dimensions or aspects of reality, all of the ways in which reality, in its great variety and complexity, is grasped by our concepts and to show the limits of each dimension of reality and how they are interconnected.

This is the meaning of reality for Hegel—that reality is the whole truth, grasped by our rational concepts. Reality is the absolute truth, it is the totality and synthesis of all partial and limited truth. Reality, properly understood, is the totality of truth of absolute mind. This breathtaking vision of absolute, total reality is linked to the method by which it is known. This is the famous method of dialectic to which we now turn.

Hegel's Theory of Dialectic

Dialectic is one of the oldest of philosophic concepts. Its earliest appearance is in very ancient Greek thought more than five hundred years before Socrates. This is the "four elements" theory, that reality is composed of earth and air, in constant opposition, as are also fire and water. Later, close to the time of Socrates, Heraclitus wrote that all is strife, everything turns into its opposite. Socrates himself meant by dialectic the use of argument in order to make the opponent contradict himself in the course of the famous Socratic method, with the result that Socrates would then resolve the contradiction and be able to move to a true definition of the concept. In the *Republic* Plato meant by dialectic, as we have seen, the highest level of knowledge, a stage in which opposition or contradiction has been overcome. The stage of knowledge which Plato calls dialectic is one on which each of the forms is known in its own immutable truth, and all forms are known in their relationship to each other and to the Idea of the Good. Hegel is the master of dialectic. He incorporates Heraclitus, Socrates, and Plato in his theory of dialectic and offers the most completely developed, ambitious, and powerful theory of dialectic that has ever been formulated.

What does Hegel mean by dialectic? Dialectic, he says, is the synthesis of opposites. Every concept, as we think about it, begins to show us its limitations, and passes over into its opposite, into the very negation of itself. As a result, dialectic in the Heraclitean sense of opposition, conflict, polarity, or contradiction characterizes all human thought.

As an example of each concept passing over into its opposite we may turn to Heraclitus in ancient Greek philosophy and his claim that everything is changing. Heraclitus's concept, once it is reflected upon, begins to show its own limitations and it passes over into its very opposite in Parmenides's claim that nothing changes, that reality is eternally what it is. We

THE REAL IS THE RATIONAL

saw then the dialectical opposition, conflict, contradiction, or polarity between Heraclitus and Parmenides.

Hegel labels the first concept, that of Heraclitus, the *thesis;* he calls the second concept, that of Parmenides which arises to oppose it, the *antithesis.* But then Hegel points out, not unlike Socrates, that this conflict, this opposition, in which thesis and antithesis struggle against each other, can be overcome. There emerges finally, when we think through this conflict, the thought of a new concept which will resolve the conflict, unify the opposing concepts, retain what is true and valuable in each of them. This third concept Hegel calls the *synthesis.* Plato's philosophy provided the synthesis for the thesis of Heraclitus and the antithesis of Parmenides. Plato retained Heraclitus's concept of change, but confined it to the sensible world. Plato retained from Parmenides the concept of the unchanging, but confined it to the intelligible world. And Plato unifed or synthesized thesis and antithesis by going beyond them in his own philosophy, which was more complete, more true than either of the previous concepts.

Here we have the basic diagram of Hegel's theory of dialectic. Dialectic is a process which consists of three stages, or moments: for this reason, Hegel's theory of dialectic is called *triadic.* The process of dialectic moves from a first stage or moment (the thesis) to a second stage or moment which negates, opposes, or contradicts the first (the antithesis); and this opposition is overcome by a third stage in which a new concept (the synthesis) emerges as a higher truth which transcends them. *Synthesis* has these three functions:

1. It *cancels* the conflict between thesis and antithesis.
2. It *preserves* or retains the element of truth within the thesis and antithesis.
3. It *transcends* the opposition and raises up or *sublimates* the conflict into a higher truth.

This triadic process of dialectic, says Hegel, is not restricted to the history of philosophy. Far from it. For Hegel, dialectic as the triadic process of the synthesis of opposites is the rhythm of all reality. The rational conceptual truths which underlie all the areas of human experience and knowledge are not static, but in dialectical movement from thesis to opposing antithesis to reconciling synthesis. Absolute mind, which is the totality of these concepts, is thus itself a process, revealing its truths to us dialectically, unfolding them stage by stage, from thesis to antithesis to synthesis, to our finite minds. We, in turn, grasp these unfolding truths in our developing knowledge. The whole of what is known at any historical period is what absolute mind has dialectically revealed or manifested at that point.

If we compare Hegel's theory of dialectic with that of Plato, we find some striking differences. (1) Whereas for Plato dialectic as the highest level of knowledge has as its goal the removal of contradictions, for Hegel contradiction can never be overcome. The generating of contradiction, of opposites and their synthesis, is in Hegel's view the very nature of rational thought and thus of reality itself.

(2) For Plato, dialectic yields the immutable, static truth of the forms; for Hegel, dialectic yields the dynamically changing truths of the concepts. Hegel offers us a vision of dialectical reason, moving dynamically through tension, opposition, conflict, polarity, contradiction, toward resolution in a synthesis. Hegel's view of dialectical reason is distinct from Plato's reason, which grasps the pure forms in their identity and their interrelatedness; from Descartes's mathematical model of reason, which intuits self-evident axioms and deduces necessary conclusions from them; from the Enlightenment's theory of two kinds of reason, the scientific, analytical, and organizing reason of Newton and the "natural light," intuitive reason of Locke.

(3) For Plato, dialectic yields forms or ideas which are rational and timeless, derived not from the visible but from the intelligible world, and represent a transcendent realm of truth. But for Hegel, conceptual truth is immanent in existent things, in the changing processes of the world, and is time-bound. Then does it not follow that absolute mind, consisting of conceptual truth, is not a transcendent realm of truth but is merely tied to, immanent in, the changing processes of the world and to time? How then can Hegel refer to absolute mind as God, or as absolute, or as a totality? Has not Hegel reduced absolute mind to the partial, incomplete, evolving thought of merely finite mind? How can this partial, changing finite truth be called God? Hegel remains ambiguous on this point, perhaps deliberately.

Despite these significant differences between Plato and Hegel on the theory of dialectic, there are important agreements. (1) Both regard dialectic as the highest level of knowledge in that it seeks to grasp reality in the form of underlying rational conceptual truths. Both regard dialectic as a superior, more profound approach to reality than sense perception or than the method of "understanding" with which science operates. (2) Like Plato, Hegel uses the method of dialectic to construct a great totalizing philosophy in which rational concepts organize and synthesize all aspects of reality into a single, interconnected, meaningful whole.

Dialectic is both an essential character of reality itself, and the method for understanding reality. It is both the rhythmic movement of all human thought and history, and the method for understanding them. We will now turn to the dialectical fate of the human spirit in its pilgrimage through history.

17

MASTER AND SLAVE

The Phenomenology of Spirit

You are alive now, in the last years of the twentieth century. But are you in touch with the world in which you live? Do you despair of having any inkling of what it all means? Hegel has some words of wisdom for you; you can get a commanding grasp of the world in which you live by understanding its roots in the past, and the forces of change and development now working within it.

Hegel develops this theme in his masterpiece, *The Phenomenology of Spirit*, which tries to understand the human spirit of the present time by looking back at its development, at its roots in the past. *The Phenomenology of Spirit* presents a biography, not of a particular person, but of the spirit of humanity over the long centuries as it develops, grows, matures in its striving, valuing, and philosophizing.

Hegel will place before you all the types of world views, religious faiths, philosophic visions, that human beings have held and he will present the truths they claim to have discovered. Hegel will also ask what kind of persons hold these views of the world, and under what circumstances, but Hegel will also indicate how each philosophy in the history of the human spirit, when it is reflected upon and lived with, reveals its own limitations, shows itself to be only a partial truth, one-sided, distorted, inadequate. As a result, each philosophy is unstable, tipsy, and passes over dialectically into an opposite viewpoint which presents the other side of the issue, basing itself upon what the first philosophy left out. But in time this opposing viewpoint will also be seen to be limited, partial, and one-sided in its negation of the first philosophy, and a new viewpoint will emerge which will synthesize the two opposing philosophies into a more complete truth. But the new, synthesizing viewpoint will in time reveal its own limitations, and an opposing viewpoint will arise to assert its deficiencies and so on, until an all-embracing, all-inclusive vision of total reality is reached.

1. The History of Philosophy

Hegel begins his celebrated preface to *The Phenomenology of Spirit* by talking about the history of philosophy, as a crucial part of the biography of human spirit. He says that in the history of philosophy opposing philosophic systems compete and struggle with each other, each claiming to have found the exclusive, one and only truth, each denying any truth to the opponent. We have been observing the bitter enmities of conflicting philosophies, beginning with the conflict between the philosophies of Heraclitus and Parmenides. We have seen Plato against the Sophists, Descartes against the empiricists and the Catholic Scholastics, and Hume against Descartes, Kant against Hume.

Hegel points out that the followers of a particular philosopher tend to believe that they have received the one true philosophy from him, and as a result they brand every other philosophy as false and try to ruin its reputation. These zealous people exhibit the notion that philosophic truth is capable of reaching a fixed, rigid, static, finished, and final form; they believe that one particular philosophy can achieve this final truth; and that such a philosophy must be defended against any opposing views. These philosophers, Hegel says, do not comprehend that the disagreement between philosophies, when adequately understood, exhibits not conflict but the growth and development of truth. Differing philosophic systems should be seen not as at war with one another but as "elements of an organic unity."

Hegel is referring to his view that philosophy, like all of reality, is organic in character, a functional interdependence of parts, as is the case with a living, growing organism. To present this organicist and developmental view of philosophy, Hegel slips into one of his most famous metaphors: he says that the history of philosophy may be compared to a living, growing, fruitful tree, and that different philosophies are like the stages of growth of the bud, the blossom, and the fruit.

Each philosophy may in this way be seen as having significance as a stage in the growth of philosophy, as bud or blossom or fruit. The bud and the blossom disappear to make way for the fruit; we don't think of them as false, but as part of an organic process. So also no philosophy is false. Each is a necessary part of the organic growth and unity of all of philosophy. In Hegel's famous words:

> The bud disappears when the blossom breaks through, and we might say that the former is refuted by the latter; in the same way, when the fruit comes, the blossom may be explained to be a false form of the plant's existence, for the fruit appears as its true nature in place of the blossom . . . But the ceaseless activity of their own inherent nature makes them at the same time moments of an organic unity, where they not merely do not contradict one another, but where one is as necessary as the other; and this equal necessity of all moments constitutes . . . thereby the life of the whole. But contradiction as between philosophic systems is not wont to be conceived in this way.

Hegel's point is of course that this is exactly how conflicting philosophies should be understood. Each one displaces the other, but they do not falsify each other. Each is a necessary stage in the development of the whole truth, of the dialectical manifestation or revelation of absolute spirit to the growth of finite, human spirit.

2. Organicism

How does it happen that Hegel views philosophy through this metaphor of biological growth and developmental change? We saw no mention of it in Descartes or in Hume. The answer is that when Hume wrote his treatise the scientific world was still limited to Newtonian physics. But that was in 1738. It is now 1806 and some important changes have taken place in the intellectual life of Europe in the intervening years. In the field of science the biological sciences are beginning to develop. Hegel has been influenced by their fundamental concepts of the organism as a hierarchical, interdependent unity of parts, in which each of the parts (like the heart, the liver, and the lungs in the human organism) plays a necessary role in maintaining the life of the whole. The parts do not, however, exist or function as independent atoms. On the contrary, each is a dependent part of an organism, and functions to serve the organism as a whole. Hegel is thus an early exponent of the *doctrine of organicism*, which claims that an organism, as a developing unity of hierarchical and interdependent parts serving the life of the whole, is the model for understanding the human personality, societies and their institutions, philosophy and history. From the time of Hegel on, the rest of nineteenth-century philosophic thought will be influenced by this newly dominating concept of the unity and functional totality of the organism, and will apply it to understanding the development of human thought, human society, and the growth of human institutions.

Another even more influential source of the notion of organicism, arose primarily from Romantic philosophers and artists in deliberate opposition to the atomistic, mechanistic, and rationalistic views of man and nature held by the Enlightenment. Kant viewed the *a priori* concepts and other structures of consciousness as an organic unity; Goethe viewed nature as an organic totality; the Romantic poets, Schlegel, Wordsworth, and Coleridge, all viewed true art as achieving organic unity out of multiplicity; social philosophers such as Rousseau, Herder, and Burke viewed society, not as an Enlightenment aggregate of atomic individuals, but as an organic unity.

3. Historicism

In this same biological metaphor Hegel also introduces another concept which held no significance for Descartes or for Hume: This is a new concept of the importance of history, which along with the model of the organism becomes a dominant way of viewing every aspect of experience and knowledge for much of the nineteenth and twentieth centuries.

The view of the significance of history which appears in Hegel's metaphor is called *historicism*: historicism is the claim that the understanding of any aspect of human life must be concerned primarily with its history, its evolution, its genesis, or its roots, rather than with empirical observation of it as it is now. Historicism is the view that adequate knowledge of any human phenomenon must be historical.

And is this not what Hegel has said in his bud-blossom-fruit metaphor about philosophy? Hegel has said that to understand any specific philosophy, do not look at it by itself, in isolation, torn out of its historical setting. Look at it as part of the historical development of philosophy, and you will then see why it was necessary for this philosopher to take the line that he did, and why it will be necessary for the philosopher who follows him to differ from him in the way that he does, since he has found his predecessor's deficiencies, the limitations, weaknesses, omissions of his argument.

What does this mean for philosophy? It means that Hegel has brought into the world a new way of viewing philosophy, the historicist way of viewing philosophy. Philosophy cannot be understoood as Plato or Descartes or Hume understood it, as a zero-sum game, in which there is only one winner, only one true philosophy. Philosophy must be understood as the evolving, changing historical development which it is, with all its conflicts playing their necessary parts in the developmental process. The meaning of philosophy, then, can only be found in its own historical development: The history of philosophy is philosophy.

4. Truth As Subject As Well As Substance

And now in the preface to *The Phenomenology of Spirit* Hegel moves on to present what is being contributed by his own philosophy.

> It is not difficult to see that our epoch is a birthtime, and a period of transition. The spirit of man has broken with the old order of things hitherto prevailing, and with the old ways of thinking . . .

We get from these words of Hegel his sense of *threshold*—that he and his time are about to step on the threshold of a door opening into a new world. Hegel gives us the sense of change, growth, progress, of a ripening process that is now ready to burst forth. This is exactly how he describes it, as the changes that lead through a ripening process to childbirth:

> But it is here as in the case of the birth of a child; after a long period of nutrition in silence, the continuity of the gradual growth in size, of quantitative

change, is suddenly cut short by the first breath drawn—there is a break in the process, a qualitative change—and the child is born.

This is one of many famous passages in the writings of Hegel that Karl Marx will employ for his own purposes; he will regard this passage as fittingly describing the bursting forth of communism from the capitalist world.

But how does Hegel describe his own contribution to philosophy? Hegel believes that the time is now ripe for him to offer a philosophy which talks not only of objects, of substances and their properties, as the scholastics and Descartes had done, but which recognizes that the subject, the human consciousness, in part creates the object that is known. Here Hegel is basing himself upon Kant; this was the point of the Kantian turn in philosophy. The truth, says Hegel, is not only truth of substances, but it is the truth contributed by the knowing subject. The time has passed, says Hegel, for us to talk about the truth of independent physical or mental substances without recognizing that any truth is truth only as it is created and understood by a subject living in his own time. Truth is living, growing, and changing, it is the truth of the human spirit as it has dialectically developed over the centuries through all the philosophies in the history of the human spirit.

The new task of philosophy, and his own task, is now clear: It is to bring together all the changing attitudes, religious beliefs, and philosophies in the long history of the human subject in its quest for truth, and to unify them into a single, organic totality, into a single unity-in-diversity, a single dialectical system, which will constitute a "systematic science."

The Development of Self-Consciousness

1. **Mastery of Physical and Living Objects.** So much for the preface. As for the rest of *The Phenomenology of Spirit* we shall have time only to cover briefly part of the history of the development of human self-consciousness, the stages along the way of human self-knowledge. At an early stage of human development the self is conscious of objects. The human self relates to objects, says Hegel, through desire. The self desires objects for its own gratification, in order to satisfy its bodily needs. But it also finds gratification in mastering,

overcoming objects in some way, in making them serve the desires of the self—for example, by devouring them, as we crunch an apple, or "put away" a meal, or "polish off" a steak; or by destroying them, as we crumple, tear, shred, smash, and discard paper, boxes, cans, bottles; or by taming, mastering, and dominating them as we do with animal objects, such as sheep, horses, dogs, or snakes. In all these ways we gratify ourselves through mastery of objects. We devour them, incorporate them, appropriate them. We overcome, master, and annul their existence by destroying them; we cancel them out.

We are beings, says Hegel, who take mastery as our goal, and our personal histories and the history of the whole human race show this. Hegel sees such mastering actions as examples of the principle of negation, the power of the negative, or as he sometimes calls it, the principle of death. It is the principle of negation, at work in all human thought, which produces an opposing, negating antithesis to every thesis and produces also a synthesis which negates every negating antithesis: the same principle of negation is at work in the human subject, producing the subject's relation to all objects through the will to mastery. He is saying that the principle of negation and death is at work in the self's characteristic relation to objects, in its desire to negate them, to overcome them in some way, to destroy them, to incorporate them, to cancel them out of existence.

2. "The Struggle unto Death." But the negative, death-dealing attitude which human self-consciousness takes toward objects runs into trouble when the object is not a sirloin steak but another human being. The desire of the self with regard to objects which are other human beings remains the same: We desire to master them. The principle of negation is ever at work within the self, which desires to negate the other person he sees before him, to cancel, annul, overcome, destroy, and kill the other. But the other self has the same attitude, and seeks to kill the first self. Each self seeks to assert its own selfhood by killing the other.

The two selves now enter directly into what Hegel calls the trial by death, or the "struggle unto death," in which each party risks his life, puts it on the line, in the struggle to kill the other party. The great satisfaction of the self is not simply to overcome the object, but to have the object know and acknowledge that it has been overcome, defeated, and negated by me. What the self really desires, says Hegel, is not so much the mastery of physical objects or animals but the greater satisfaction of mastering another self and to have that self recognize my mastery. I derive consummate satisfaction from this, the overcoming of an object which is capable of knowing that I have mastered it.

But there is a hitch. I need to have the other self exist in order to be conscious of my own selfhood. I require, in order to become conscious of my being a self, that another self recognize me as a self, look at me as a self. Hegel's point is that we cannot become aware of ourselves, become conscious of being a self, except as another self serves as the mirror for us. Notice that Hegel is in complete opposition to Descartes, whose Cogito argument established the existence of the self in solitary reflection. Hegel argues that I cannot know myself in isolation. I know that I am a self because I see you looking at me, responding to me, as a self. It is clear, then, that consciousness of my own existence requires the existence of another self.

Then, if I kill the other self, in the struggle unto death, I will lose on two counts. If the other is dead, I cannot gain the satisfaction he would give me by being alive and recognizing that I am the victor, and have mastered him; and second, if he is dead, I have no other self to recognize me as a self, no other self to be the mirror in which I see that I am a self and recognized as such.

3. The Master-Slave Relation. When these limitations of the outlook of the life and death struggle are seen, this outlook is left behind and spirit moves on to a new and more adequate viewpoint. In this new viewpoint, the victor learns not to kill the other, but to keep him alive and make a slave of him. This new stage in self-consciousness is the master-slave (or lord and bondsman) relationship. Hegel regards the master-slave relationship as having an historical role, as well, occurring commonly in primitive societies, nd occurring also during wars, in which in the course of battle one self overpowers and enslaves another.

But the master-slave relationship is filled with contradictions and limitations which are the seeds of its own destruction. The slave is enmeshed in matter. He is reduced to being a thing; and he is made to work upon material things for the benefit of the master. Strangely, however, within the relationship which seems so clearly to benefit the master, there are elements which work to favor the slave over the master. First, the master is dependent on the slave's recognition of him as master, and this is precarious since there are no masters unless others recognize them as such. How long will the slave continue to acknowledge the other as his master? Second, the slave has as his mirror another self who is an independent person, while the master, on the other hand, has as his mirror only a dependent slave-self to relate to; this is the master's only reflection of himself.

The third, and most important, element is this: although it appears that the master has the advantage in having the slave labor on material things for the master's benefit, the long-run advantage of this is in fact for the slave. For in laboring, in shaping and making things, the slave will find himself in what he makes. He will have objectified himself in his work, he will come to recognize that the object which he has crafted, which he has transformed from raw materials into this usable object—corn into bread, cotton into clothing—is his own product, the work of his hands, and that he is the independent self who crafted it. And thus in labor, which carries out the will of the master, the slave nevertheless discovers that he is not a thing, not a slave. He discovers his own independent existence as a consciousness with a mind and will and power of his own.

As we will see, for Karl Marx the master-slave chapter in Hegel's *The Phenomenology of Spirit* is the most significant section in all of the eight hundred pages of that book. Marx calls this section of the *Phenomenology,* "the true birthplace and secret of the Hegelian philosophy." Marx says that Hegel has grasped truly the meaning of labor: that man's nature is the result of his labor. Hegel has seen, according to Marx, that the slave lives by the work he performs and he becomes independent through this work, whereas the master remains dependent on the slave's labor. In his massive work *Capital* Marx states the philosophic point to be found in Hegel's master-slave relation. Marx says, "As man works on nature outside himself and changes it, he changes at the same time his own nature." This is what Hegel's slave has succeeded in doing: transforming his own nature from a degraded being into an independent self. For Marx, the urban proletariat, the industrial laborer or worker is to be compared to Hegel's slave and the capitalist to his master. For Marx, the relationship of capitalist-worker is the modern form of the master-slave relationship.

4. Stoicism. Because of all these contradictions, paradoxes, limitations, contained within the master-slave relation, it is left behind and the human spirit moves on in its development to a new viewpoint which Hegel calls stoicism. Stoicism is of course the name of an actual Greek and Roman philosophy. Connected with stoicism are the names of many honored philosophers, especially that of the Roman slave-philosopher Epictetus (50–130 A.D.) and that of the Roman Emperor Marcus Aurelius (121–180 A.D.). What does Hegel mean by the stoic consciousness, this next development in the growth of human self-consciousness? What do you mean when you say you are trying to be stoical about some of the troubles you have?

The stoic philosophy, as Hegel views it, asserts that in my thoughts I can be independent and free, whether I am an emperor or a slave. Moreover, a stoic believes that through my rational understanding of the laws governing the universe and human life, and my acceptance of these natural laws as necessary and unavoidable, I can become strong and self-sufficient, untroubled by misfortune. To live according to nature is the highest good; reason then governs me as it does the cosmos and I can be indifferent to pain or disappointments, I can be calm, imperturbable, and serene.

People become stoics, says Hegel, under two conditions: when they live in a time in which there is widespread fear of becoming enslaved or dominated in some way, and when there is a high regard for the powers of intellect to know the truth. It is then that stoicism makes its appeal as a philosophy with its claim of interior freedom—that I have a refuge, a place of safety in my own mind—and its understanding of universal and necessary truths. No one can enslave my mind and its thoughts. Here in my mind I am independent and free, calm and serene, detached from the world.

But Hegel shows the limitations of stoicism which bring about its negation and its downfall. Stoicism, he says, has still not overcome, gone beyond, the master-slave attitude. The stoic still has the fears of a slave, even though he is master of his own thoughts. And the stoic is a slave to the necessary laws governing nature and human life: He bows down before their power over him like a slave. Also, like the slave, the stoic lives in isolation, cut off from the rich, full content of

existence; and because of this the stoic's philosophy consists
of only vague generalizations about reason and truth and
freedom. And finally, says Hegel, the stoic has no actual
freedom to enjoy life in the real world, but only retreats to an
abstract idea of himself as being free.

5. **Skepticism.** The dialectic of the human spirit now passes
beyond stoicism to skepticism. The stoic rejects the world to
the point of withdrawing from it into the quiet refuge of his
own rational mind. The skeptic goes beyond the stoic—he
rejects the world completely by doubting it. Skepticism, Hegel
shrewdly observes, uses doubt as a negative and destroying
force. This is the skeptic's form of mastery. Skeptical doubt,
says Hegel, actually functions to negate and dissolve all the
beliefs of ordinary experience and all the laws of science.

What are the limitations of skepticism? Skepticism is limited in that it is torn apart by an inner contradiction. Among
the things which skepticism attacks and doubts is the very
existence of the self. On the one hand, skepticism destroys
the self, it dissolves the self, as Hume did, into mere flux, a
shifting, changing bundle of sensations. But on the other
hand, says Hegel, there is another self which the skeptic does
not recognize—the self that is powerfully subjecting everything to its doubting.

Skepticism is thus split between two selves. The one self is
like the master, secure and powerful, dominating every claim,
and doubting, denying, negating, dissolving everything including consciousness itself. The other self is like the slave,
which is mastered, subjugated, dissolved by doubt, and shown
by the master-self to be only a bundle of passing perceptions.
This is Hegel's answer to skepticism, including that of Hume.
Skepticism is a confused viewpoint. It does not recognize that
it is operating with a split self, a masterful self which doubts,
and a slave self which it destroys. Since skepticism contains
this glaring contradiction, which, however, it is unaware of, it
passes over into another world view.

6. **The "Unhappy Consciousness."** This new world view
Hegel calls the "unhappy consciousness" and he identifies it as
the religious consciousness of medieval Christianity. The medieval Christian unhappy consciousness is indeed aware of itself
as divided, as a split self in which there is endless conflict
between a true self, which longs for God but cannot reach
him, and a false self, which clings to the world and to worldly
pleasures. The religious consciousness is unhappy because it

knows itself to be a divided self. Within it there is raging the old conflict between the master and the slave, with the true self attempting to be master and to dominate, subjugate, deny, and negate the unworthy, false self.

The religious world view recognizes its internal conflict and also recognizes the truth, that what the true self longs for is God or absolute spirit. Nevertheless, says Hegel, the religious world view has its own limitations. Although it knows the truth, it is only a figurative truth that it offers, of pictures and symbols of the truth—e.g., the Holy Trinity of God the Father, God as incarnate in the Son, and as the Holy Spirit. A second limitation is that it has not overcome the master-slave relation, for to the religious consciousness God is master and humans are His slaves.

7. **Reason.** Hegel ends this section of *The Phenomenology of Spirit* by saying that the religious consciousness must now pass over into the realm of reason and philosophy. The profound truth which the religious world view expressed in pictures and symbols must now be grasped by the rational concepts of philosophy. The self must learn that the true absolute is not a personal God but is absolute mind, the totality of truth, which manifests itself dialectically in finite minds in human history. The self must also learn that a free human being should be a slave to no one, not even to God.

Mastery is indeed the goal which human beings desire, but there is only one worthy form of mastery for a free human being: it is to master the totality of truth which God reveals to us in our time in history. But this is also God's goal for us—not to be slaves but freely to receive and master His unfolding truth in history. But then the human spirit will have nothing left to master and the master-slave relationship will be overcome at last. The finite human spirit will then become conscious of its union with the absolute, and despite its limitations in time and place, it will recognize itself as participating in the ongoing movement of absolute spirit as it reveals itself in human history.

What then is the truth that the absolute reveals through the ages of history? What is the rational truth of the totality of human history? To learn this we turn to Hegel's famous philosophy of history.

18
THE CUNNING OF REASON

Does history have any meaning? Does the history of human beings in the world have any purpose? Can any pattern, any significance be found in history? Or are the generations upon generations of human beings, with all their activities, their beliefs and hopes, a meaningless scurrying about, an empty chatter, the life of Plato's cave, soon dust unto meaningless dust?

Where can we find an answer to this kind of question? Not from what Hegel, in *Reason and History*, calls Original History, the firsthand reports of people who were present at important historical events, such as Thucydides provided in his *History of the Peloponnesian War*, an eyewitness's account of the damaging effects of the war on politics and people in Athens. And not from what Hegel calls Reflective History: accounts of universal history by professional historians; nor from the history of one specific country; nor from history designed to instruct the present with "lessons" drawn from the past; nor from specialized histories, e.g., of religion or art; and surely not from methodological studies of history.

Philosophical History

To answer the question Does history have any meaning? we need to look at the whole sweep of history, at world history. And we need to be concerned, not with the accumulation of facts regarding what actually happened here or there, but with penetrating the mass of historical facts to see if there is any underlying order, any rational core or pattern, or if any underlying meaningful process is taking place. Such an approach to history Hegel calls Philosophical History. Philosophical History is clearly the approach to history of Hegel's own philosophy of Absolute Idealism and its basic principle that the real is the rational, and can be discovered only by penetrating the surface of existence to its rational and dialectically developing conceptual core. This principle of Absolute Idealism must, in Hegel's view, be applied to history (and to every other area of knowledge) if we are to grasp its truth. This is what Hegel means by Philosophical History: the search for the underlying rational truth of history. The rational concepts which are the core of history do not challenge the existence of the facts of history, nor do they constitute a separate set of objects (as do Plato's forms) superior to the facts; instead, these rational concepts which underlie the facts of history are only the facts themselves "more deeply understood."

The Meaning of World History. From this absolute idealist conception of Philosophical History, Hegel developed a vastly influential philosophy of world history. Hegel's philosophy of history ranks with the Christian philosophy of history developed by Saint Augustine; the Enlightenment philosophy of history, most explicitly formulated by Condorcet; the historical materialism of Karl Marx. These have been the four most influential philosophies of history of all time. What, then, does Hegel discern as the underlying truth of history? World history has this as its meaning, Hegel tells us: It is the scene in which the truth of the Absolute unfolds itself, reveals itself to the consciousness of humanity. Philosophically understood, history is the rational structure of the truth of the Absolute, unfolding, becoming manifest, being revealed in time to finite spirit. And as this rational structure reveals itself dialectically in time it exhibits God's plan for the world. In this way Hegel argues that history has an underlying rational structure and that it is teleological, that it has a purpose; history is a purposeful movement toward God's goal for humanity. And so history is rational, purposeful, and good. In Hegel's words, reason, which is the unfolding, developing truth of the Absolute, rules the world.

You are thinking: How can Hegel make such seemingly preposterous claims? How can he say that history is rational and purposeful and good in the face of the evils that he knew of in his own lifetime—the injustices which the French lower classes endured and which led them to revolt; the hideous cruelties of the Reign of Terror which followed; the deprivations of the German serfs working out their lives on the feudal estates; the sufferings of the German people in the War of Liberation against Napoleon; the raging epidemics of disease which swept through Europe (an epidemic of cholera was to bring Hegel himself to an early death)? And how can he say that history is a rational structure of God's truth unfolding in time? Where is the evidence of rationality in the bloody centuries of human history? Does Hegel not hear the cries of human pain throughout history? What good purpose could possibly be achieved out of so much suffering and despair?

History and the Problem of Evil: The Slaughter-Bench. Hegel does not deny the evils which humans have experienced in history. Hegel is no Pollyanna about the past, no Dr. Pangloss, no hypocritical optimist. Hegel himself is the originator of the concept of the "terror of history," which expresses the fearful agonizing realization of the misery, destruction, death, and obliteration that have befallen even the noblest human hopes and achievements in the past and that wait in store for our own dreams and struggles as well. Hegel says:

> Without rhetorical exaggeration, a simply truthful compilation [transl.?] of the miseries that have overwhelmed the noblest of nations and politics, and the finest exemplars of private virtue—forms a picture of most fearful aspect, and excites emotions of the profoundest and most hopeless sadness, counterbalanced by no consolatory result. We endure in beholding it a mental torture . . .

This is Hegel on the evils of history, acknowledging that history is the scene of such ruination of the noblest nations and the best human beings that it is a mental torture to think about it. But there is more that Hegel has to offer on the terror of history. It is his horrifying image that history is a slaughter-bench, a place where victims are tied down to be killed as a human sacrifice. In his own words:

> History is the slaughter-bench at which the happiness of peoples, the wisdom of states, and the virtue of individuals have been victimized.

Philosophy of History As Theodicy

But then the question arises, for what purpose, if any, have these enormous human sacrifices been offered? How can the goodness of God and God's plan for the history of the world be justified in the face of overwhelming human suffering? Hegel claims that his philosophy of history is a *theodicy*, a theory which undertakes to justify God, to vindicate God against the charge that He has permitted evil to overrun the world.

How then does Hegel justify God in the face of the evils of history? How does his philosophy of history serve as a theodicy seeking to absolve God from being charged with the evil in the world? He points out, first, that the slaughter-bench view of history sees only the surface, rather than what underlies the surface appearance and lies latent and potential in history. What is latent in history is Spirit, the Absolute; and the essence of Spirit, Hegel says, is freedom. The whole sweep of world history is the process in which Spirit manifests to finite human beings the meaning of their own freedom. History may thus be said to be the progress of humanity in the consciousness of its own freedom.

Reason and Desire

But how is this accomplished? How does the Absolute, working in and through human history, bring human beings to consciousness of their freedom as spiritual beings? Hegel's answer in his own words is that "two elements enter into history." The first is reason, the rational concept of freedom which the Absolute, the totality of rational truth, is seeking to unfold, reveal, externalize, manifest, and express to finite spirit. The second is human passion. The Absolute has therefore primarily only one human element to work with in bringing about in finite minds a consciousness of their freedom: This element is human desire and passion. The desires of human beings, their passions, their private personal aims, their drive to gain satisfaction of their selfish wants—these are the most effective springs of human action, says Hegel. Passion, not rationality, is what motivates human beings. Human beings are driven to action by their own private, subjective wills to satisfy their natural instincts, needs, inclinations, and interests.

But let us not put down human desires, says Hegel. Desires are much "closer to the core of human nature" than are laws and morality which try to restrain them. Moreover, desires are expressions of the human will and they may work for good. Yet even a selfless goal has to involve me, elicit my desire to promote it; I must be "into it." If I am to become committed to any goal, it must in some way be my goal, I must find in it my own satisfaction. And this seems to be true. Are you, for example, engaged in a protest movement against the contamination of a river by industrial wastes, or against the using up of the wilderness land for more suburbs and shopping centers? If so, these actions elicit your personal passions, you find in them your satisfaction. Hegel's point is that my motivation toward any goal, whether it is consciously for my own benefit or for the benefit of others, has its source in my desires. Nothing is ever accomplished unless individuals desire it and find their satisfaction in bringing it about. And Hegel adds, "Nothing great in the world has ever been accomplished without passion."

The Cunning of Reason

This is the complex web of human desire which the Absolute must work with to bring about its goal for human history. Human desire, with its vast variety of motivations, from my selfish interests to my satisfaction in feeding the hungry whom I will never see, in remote villages of Africa or Asia—this complex web of desire serves as the means by which the Absolute accomplishes its end, its goal in history. The Absolute may be said to use human wills as a means to bring about the goal of its divine will. How is this done? By cunning, says Hegel, by the masterful shrewdness, cleverness, subtlety of the Absolute in bringing the rational truth of freedom to human minds. Reason, in the form of Absolute, which is the totality of rational conceptual truth, governs the world, and it does so through what Hegel calls the Cunning of Reason. The Cunning of Reason is the power of the Absolute to use the immense force of human passion as means to its end of human freedom. To accomplish this goal, the Cunning of Reason utilizes (1) the great nation-states which appear successively in history and (2) the great historical individuals who bring about profound changes in history.

Let us turn first to Hegel's view of the nation-state. The

Absolute Spirit does not manifest itself in the individual human spirit, such as you or me. The Absolute unfolds and manifests itself in the spirit of an entire people. Here we have come upon one of Hegel's major contributions to the philosophy of history and to the development after him of the social sciences.

The Spirit of a People *(Volksgeist).* By the Spirit of a People Hegel means something very close to what today we call culture, in part because Hegel has taught us to think in this way. Hegel defines the Spirit of a People as consisting in the historical and living unity of the culture of a specific people, "its culture generally," as he says—it's language, religion, art, music, poetry, architecture, morality, philosophy, science, and law. The Spirit of a People is embodied in all these elements of the culture of a people; it pervades them all and unifies them into an organic totality. The "spirit" or character or style of the people, indwelling in all the parts of the cultural totality, expresses itself through them, leaving its own mark on every aspect of culture. Nothing in a specific human culture can be understood in isolation; its religion, music, language, politics, and art are all expressions of the one Spirit of the People and exhibit as a result the same style and character. (Here Hegel's theory of organicism is at work, his view that nothing in the human sphere can be understood in isolation but only as a dependent part of an organic totality which it reflects and serves.) Thus in ancient Athens the unique spirit of the Athenian people, expressive of cheerful, youthful freshness, freedom, intellectual vitality, harmony with nature, and "beautiful individuality" can be seen in its characteristic style of art, religion, politics, and philosophy.

The Nation-State: The True Individual of History. But now Hegel moves on to show that the Spirit of the People is incorporated, embodied, in the life of the nation-state. The state, says Hegel, is an organic totality which includes the government and other institutions of a nation as well as the whole of its culture. And Hegel makes this startling pronouncement: it is the State, the totality of the national culture and its government, which is the true Individual of History. In Hegel's own words, "the Individuals of World-History are nations." For the purposes of the Cunning of Reason, the important individuals who will bring humanity to consciousness of its freedom are not individuals such as you and me, but the great nation-states.

The Cunning of Reason uses the great nation-states, which incorporate institutions and culture, as the true individuals of history and as the vehicles of freedom. It is to these great individuals, the nation-states, rather than to particular existing human individuals, that the consciousness of freedom is manifested. But how is this done? Through the Cunning of Reason at work in history, the spirit of the people in each successive leading nation-state embodies one stage in the Absolute's manifestation of freedom, one stage in man's developing truth of freedom. And so each nation-state has a specific and limited role to play in the unfolding of the consciousness of freedom in the great theatre of history. This is the way in which the Cunning of Reason uses nation-states to achieve God's purpose in history.

Human Individuals: (1) The Role of Desire. What, then, you are asking, about the actual human individual? Human individuals have no independence from the nation-state; they are dependent parts of the state, like the cells of an organism. Here again we see Hegel's organicism; you as an individual are part of a larger organism, the nation-state. You are part of its life, you share in and are formed by its culture, and you exist as the parts of an organism exist, serving and served by the whole, which has more importance than any of its parts. But, you will reply, I serve my own purposes, I do what I desire to do, within the law.

(2) The Individual As System-Determined and System-Determining. I do not intend by my actions to serve the nation-state. But that, says Hegel, is just the point. Individual human beings are motivated by their own desires. But the Cunning of Reason uses individual human desires as means to its own end, which is to sustain and support the nation-state so that it can play its role in developing the consciousness of freedom. And so while you are going about, pursuing your own desires, buying the foods and clothes and electronics that you like, building the career you have chosen, what you do is channeled into the ongoing manufacturing, marketing, financial, and educational functions of your nation, and so helps to sustain the nation, although you did not intend this or even understand it when you did these things. Your actions flowing from your own desires have unintended consequences in the industrial, financial, and educational functions of your society which you do not recognize. In this way, the Cunning of Reason uses the desires of human individuals to sustain the ongoing functions of the nation. Moreover, when you pursue your own desires you not only sustain or *determine* the continued existence of these various functions of your society, but your desires themselves are sustained or *determined by* the society. Your choice of clothes or a career is determined by the various options which your culture has developed and made available for you to desire and to choose. These Hegelian insights have been borrowed and built upon by various twentieth-century social scientists who regard a society as an organic totality or system, and see human actions, as Hegel did, as system-determined and system-determining. Thus your desire for a certain type of blue jeans or sport jacket is determined by the advertised fashions of the social system and also determines the continued operation of certain manufacturing, merchandising, and financial functions of the social system.

(3) **The Individual As Culture Carrier.** But what about my beliefs, you may ask, my attitudes, values, my religious convictions? Have I no independence even here from the culture of the nation-state? None, says Hegel. Your thoughts, your values, beliefs, attitudes, are derived from the cultural totality of which you are a dependent part. You are a carrier of the culture, of the spirit of the people. You are also a carrier of the changing spirit of the times within your own culture. Do you not feel that a different spirit pervades this nation now from what existed a decade ago—or from the intensities of political and personal change which swept through the late 1960s? And have you not been touched by this new spirit? In Hegel's own words: "All the worth which the human being possesses, all spiritual reality, he has only through the state."

But there is more. In Hegel's view, not even the greatest philosophers can escape from being the products of their own culture and of their own time. Philosophers, too, are culture carriers within a nation-state embodying the spirit of a people, and they derive their thoughts from the culture and the times. In a passage from *The Philosophy of Right* which has become famous, Hegel says:

> . . . every individual is a child of its time [and] it is
> as silly to suppose that any philosophy goes beyond its

contemporary world as that an individual can jump
beyond his time, can leap over [the great statue of]
Rhodes.

Philosphy, says Hegel, cannot transcend its own time, it
cannot predict the future, it cannot provide a blueprint for an
ideal society, as Plato tried in the *Republic*. Philosophy is
only "its own time reflected in thought." From Hegel's per-
spectives of organicism and historicism, the philosopher, like
other human individuals, is a carrier of his culture and of his
time. Since he cannot transcend them, his inescapable task as
a philosopher is to reflect and to penetrate to their conceptual
truth and their dialetical changes.

World-Historical Individuals. As we have seen, the Cunning
of Reason uses the desires of ordinary individuals to maintain
the ongoing functions of the great nation-states, each of which
embodies a stage in humanity's consciousness of freedom.
But the Cunning of Reason also uses the great heroes of
history and their desires in order to bring about major
historical changes, so that the consciousness of freedom will
progress. Hegel calls these heroic figures World-Historical
Individuals, since they are the great individual agents of
change in history. Who are these figures? They include Alexander the Great, Julius Caesar, and Napoleon. All of these
are political heroes who were motivated by their own desires
and passions for power and greatness in their own times. But,
says Hegel, the Cunning of Reason uses these World-Historical
Individuals for its own ends, to bring about a new stage in
history toward the further development of the consciousness
of freedom. So, for example, Napoleon was motivated by his
personal passion for political power. But in gaining power
over many other nations, Napoloen was actually serving the
Cunning of Reason in bringing to these nations the new
freedoms of the Enlightenment which France had obtained.
As a result many of these countries liberalized their laws,
freed their serfs, and improved and extended education in a
great leap forward of their consciousness of freedom.

Like Napoleon, World-Historical Individuals in pursuit of
their personal desires had no clear idea of the larger goals of
the Absolute which they were unwittingly and unconsciously
serving. They were, says Hegel, all of them, "practical, political men," who "had insight into the requirement of the

time—*what was ripe for development.*" This they made their own, their "single" "master" passion. To this extent they are the "clear-sighted ones" of their epoch. But these "great men have formed purposes to satisfy themselves, not others." Yet others follow them because the great men bring to consciousness what in other human beings is unconscious; the same thought as to what is the "next step" is part of their inmost soul, they feel unconsciously that the leader is on the right track. Hegel is talking here about the psychology of leadership and saying that the successful leader gets a strong following because he is doing what the followers themselves unconsciously want and approve. But the greatness of the leader is limited; the leader is only the formulator and activator of what is already ripe for development. He has no knowledge of the next stage of history, which he is serving to bring about.

In the same bitter tone in which he talked of history as a slaughter-bench, Hegel says that the Cunning of Reason uses World-Historical Individuals primarily as change-agents, as innovators, and therefore they must destroy many existing peoples and institutions that stand in their way. So Alexander, Caesar, and Napoleon devastated many peoples, their cultures and their governments, in order that a new stage of freedom be brought into existence. But although this may be viewed as morally wrong, especially by the victims, the World-Historical Individual is justified by his serving a "higher ground" than the morality of individuals—the goals of the Cunning of Reason. And so Hegel says, "So mighty a form [as the World-Historical Individual] must trample down many an innocent flower and crush to pieces many an object in its path."

But this destructive mastery with which the World-Historical Individual deals with people who stand in his way is in turn how the Cunning of Reason deals with the World-Historical Individual himself. The whole nature of the World Historical Individuals was nothing but their master-passion. Once they have served the purposes for which the Cunning of Reason used them as means, they fall off, says Hegel, "like empty hulls from the kernel of corn." They die early, like Alexander the Great. They are murdered, like Caesar. They are transported into exile, like Napoleon at St. Helena.

And this destructive mastery is also turned upon the nation-states. Once they have been used in history to develop a stage in the consciousness of freedom, the Cunning of Reason moves on to another nation-state to embody the next stage of development of freedom, leaving the original nation-state to stagnate and lose its historical importance. In any specific historical period, only one nation-state is the vehicle of freedom. "This people," Hegel says, "is the dominant people in world-history for this epoch—*and it is only once that it can make its hour strike.*"

But none of these disasters or tragedies is really evil in Hegel's theodicy. Each disaster has its role to play in bringing about the greater good which the Absolute has in store. Evils are the instrumentalities used by God to increase good. Human failures are thus the successes of the Absolute. And thus God is vindicated against the charge that He has permitted these evils to exist in the world.

History As Progress in the Consciousness of Freedom

Finally we come to the actual account which Hegel gives of World-History as progress in the consciousness of freedom. The progress through World-History of the consciousness of freedom takes the form of the great triadic dialectic of history which the Cunning of Reason brings about by using the nation-states as the great social structures of history; the passions of their private individual members, which sustain them; and the passions of the great World-Historical Individuals, which bring about historical change.

The great dialectical triad of history is from the Oriental World in which there is consciousness only that One is Free; to the antithesis of this in the Greek and Roman World, in which the human spirit has by this time learned that Some are Free; and finally, to a synthesis in the Modern Christian-Germanic World in which at last the human spirit has learned that All are Free and the consciousness of freedom has at last become complete.

In the Oriental World, of which the supreme example is China, the individual human being is scarcely differentiated from matter; he has no spiritual individuality, he exists without being differentiated from others in the caste structure of society, in which religion, custom, and law are not yet separated. Most importantly, in the Oriental World only one individual is free, the Oriental Despot. Having played this role in the begining of the development of the consciousness of freedom, the nation of China is left to live out its life in slow stagnation, and Spirit moves on through the intermediary stages of India and Persia to the rise of Ancient Greece. The consciousness of a new development of freedom is reached in the awareness of Athens that Some are Free, namely the citizens. The nation-state of Rome carries on the Athenian consciousness that Some are Free, but also sustains the incompleteness of this consciousness of freedom, which is shown by the denial in Athens and Rome of freedom to slaves and to conquered peoples. And finally, through the intermediary stages of feudalism and the Enlightenment, Spirit moves on to the development of the complete consciousness of freedom in the Modern Christian-Germanic World. The Christian-Germanic state preserves from the thesis, the Oriental World, the importance of having a head of state, a monarch; it preserves from the antithesis, the Greek and Roman worlds, the importance of a constitution granting to all the freedoms which the Greek and Roman world had, and which the Enlightenment had developed in England and in France. But it remained for Germany, not yet unified as a nation-state, to have the role of embodying the most complete consciousness of freedom, because it lifted up the thesis of the Oriental monarch as free, with the antithesis of Enlightenment constitutional freedom of all, into a new synthesis, fusing with them the Lutheran Christian sense of the spiritual freedom of all human souls. It is in the constitutional monarchy of the (Protestant) Christian-Germanic people that progress in the consciousness of freedom reaches a dialectical synthesis and fulfillment. And so the Germanic peoples emerge as the pinnacle of the consciousness of freedom and as the pinnacle of World-History.

Hegel's Philosophy of History: Evaluation

Is Hegel's philosphy of history a whitewash over all the evils of history? Is he not saying that everything, including all the told and untold human sufferings of evil, is for the best? Is Hegel's philosophy of history, as some critics have said, only a glorification of the German people and Lutheran Protestantism?

It is impossible to deny that Hegel's philosophy of history as the manifestation or unfolding of the Absolute justifies everything that has occurred in history as the work of the Absolute. Moreover, Hegel's dialectical method permits him to justify evils as necessary stages in the antithesis to a higher good in the synthesis. Hegel himself formulates this principle in his pronouncement that "The history of the world is the justice of the world." Then is there no other meaning of justice than that whatever exists is just? And is he not also saying that might makes right: that whatever are the forces that triumph in history, they are justified? But does Hegel's dialectical method have validity? Does it rest on anything but the persuasiveness of Hegel's intuitive judgments? What evidence supports his claim that necessary dialectical laws operate in history and that he has correctly identified their stages? Hegel can offer no satisfactory answers to these questions.

Finally, note how far this philosphy of history is from the Enlightenment's optimistic view of history as simple, direct progress in science, technology, and the natural rights of individuals. For Hegel, history rests with the group, not with the individual. History is concerned with the spirit of a people, with their whole culture, not with science and technology. History, for Hegel, does not move directly, straightforwardly toward progress, but dialectically, in a roundabout way. History is not clear and conscious to reason, but is filled with unconscious desires and with unintended consequences.

History, for Hegel, does not bring progress to individual human beings in the form of the growth of science and technology, or in the form of the growth and spread of natural rights and democracy. The Enlightenment had had a vast optimism that these great developments of science, technology, and democracy were taking place, that history was finally moving toward the betterment of human life on earth. But all of this Hegel flatly denies. History is not "a theatre of happiness," he says. It is a movement toward freedom, but for nations, not for individuals; and it moves not through good alone but necessarily through evil. And it moves not through our conscious intentions, but through using our personal desires for consequences which we do not know. Individual persons are only very small pawns in the game of history.

But the greatest difference between Hegel's philosophy of history and that of the French Enlightenment raises political questions: What of the political rights of the individual? What does my freedom really mean for Hegel? How powerful is the state over me? How much am I subordinated to it? To the formidable politics of Hegel we will next turn.

19

THE OWL OF MINERVA

Were the protestors against the United States in its Vietnam War policy justified in their opposition? Do you believe that you can be justified in taking a stand against your nation and its institutions? What do you think justifies such opposition? Appeal to universal moral principles? Appeal to universal legal principles? Appeal to religious beliefs against killing? Appeal to your own private conscience? Appeal to God Himself?

Hegel's Moral Philosophy

The philosophy of Hegel will shock you by cutting off any appeals to universal moral, legal, or religious principles, or to a transcendent God or to your private conscience in justification of your opposition to your nation. In the philosophy of Hegel, there is no moral authority above the state. There are no moral or legal or religious principles that transcend the state. Beyond the state, there is no higher court of appeal. Does this claim—which is central to Hegel's philosophy—run counter to all your beliefs? Then it is time for us to take a look at Hegel's moral and political philosophy.

1. Organicism

Hegel's approach to moral philosophy has its source in his organicism, his view that nothing can function in isolation, but rather only as a sustained and sustaining part of the organic totality to which it belongs. We have seen that Hegel introduced the concept of the Spirit of the People, which is embodied in the totality of the culture of a specific people, with its own characteristic style of language, laws, morality, music, poetry, architecture, religion, and philosophy.

However, the Spirit of the People is embodied not only in the culture but also in a people's social, economic, and political institutions, and all of these are incorporated in the ongoing life of the Nation-State. This great organic totality, the Nation-State, is the source of culture, institutional life, and morality. The ethical life for the individual member of society is provided by the Nation-State itself, by the Spirit of the People as it is embodied in the culture and in the legal, political, economic, religious, and educational institutions of the society. Ethical life, the moral life, is life lived in a community, in an organized society.

2. The Nation-State As Source of Ethics

You can live the moral life, says Hegel, only by acting in accordance with the moral principles expressed by your own society in its own institutions. In your moral life, as well as in your beliefs, your personal goals, your philosophy, you are a culture carrier, a receptacle for the moral values which are embodied in the culture, in the political and economic way of life, and in the religious and educational institutions of your society. The moral values that are embodied in your Nation-State provide the only morality you have, your only moral ideals, your only moral obligations. The moral life has its source only in the Nation-State and can be fulfilled only in the Nation-State.

3. Ethics is Social Ethics

Hegel is saying that, despite much lofty talk about universal or religious ethics, all ethics is social ethics, the ethics of a particular society, that the moral life is the life lived in accordance with the moral standards of your society. In Hegel's own words, in *Reason in History*: "Everything that man is, he owes to the state; only in it can he find his essence. All value that a man has, all spiritual reality, he has only through the state." And again in *Reason in History* Hegel says: "No individual can step beyond it; he can separate himself certainly from other particular individuals but not from the Spirit of the People." You cannot separate yourself from the beliefs and values of your own society in your own time.

(a) **Social Immorality.** But do you not find yourself rejecting Hegel's social ethics? Ethics which has no other ground than the values of a particular society goes against the grain. Are you not thinking that the Spirit of a People may go wrong, may become immoral, even demonically evil, as in periods of witch hunts, such as in Salem in the seventeenth century and in Congress in Washington in the 1950s? And surely a government can go wrong, as the Watergate episode of the United States Government shows. How, then, can Hegel claim that our culture and our government are, as he says, the very substance of ethics? Hegel has an answer: It is that our very criticism of Watergate as a moral and legal scandal is based upon the moral and legal ideals of our own United States culture.

Hegel has never argued, he will tell you, that actual cultures or governments are perfect; rather, his point is that our ideals are those that our nation has produced, and these are the ideals to which we appeal when we criticize our government. For example, we criticize the government for denying voting rights to blacks, on the grounds that the government was not living up to its own Constitution and the Fifteenth Amendment, which states that the rights of citizens to vote shall not be denied or abridged on account of race, color, or previous condition of servitude. Another example: We criticize the courts for jailing or imposing fines upon a protest group, on the grounds that this is a violation of the Bill of Rights in our own Constitution, which guarantees freedom of assembly. These democratic ideals to which we appeal have shaped the legal, political, and educational institutions of our society and in so doing have shaped our lives. For we have internalized these ideals and moral beliefs of our society, we have made them part of our inner lives as our own ideals.

(b) **Private Conscience.** But you may want to register another protest against Hegel's social ethics. You may want to argue that the best safeguard against a corrupt contemporary world is to rely on your own private conscience for moral guidance, and in this way to be autonomous, independent in your moral decisions and actions. But Hegel will view this suggestion of yours with extreme suspicion. Your private conscience is by no means infallible, Hegel will say, in fact it may deliver erroneous or contradictory moral judgments. And this is because a purely private conscience can have no objective standard on which to base itself. Moreover, for this reason, the private consciences of different individuals run the risk of conflicting with one another, without means of resolving conflicts.

(c) **Universal Moral Principles.** You may grant the point, and instead of arguing that private conscience can be the source of morality, you may propose universal rational moral principles, such as: Act always as you would have everyone else act toward you. This rational moral principle is close to the fundamental principle of the moral philosophy of Kant and it is clearly a version of the golden rule: Do unto others as you would have others do unto you. But Hegel denies that such universal principles can be an adequate basis for guiding our moral action—such universal principles are so empty and hollow that they cannot direct you to any specific action or prohibit you from committing any action. Hegel has sharp, biting words for such universal principles: They are empty, formal, vacuous, contentless.

(d) **God.** And if as a last protest you say to Hegel, I will turn to God as my moral source instead of to my culture, Hegel is ready with two answers for you. First, how can you be sure that the voice you hear is God's and not your own or that of your society? And second, Hegel has a trump card to play; the Nation-State is a manifestation or revelation of God. The true significance of God is not as the personal God of religion, but as the Absolute, the totality of truth as it unfolds and is revealed in the spirit of different peoples and their nation-states. From Hegel's viewpoint, there is something sacred, something divine about the Nation-State. For in incorporating the totality of culture and all political, economic and social institutions, the Nation-State embodies the Absolute. The Nation-State represents one stage in the progress of God's rational truth as it moves through World-History. In Hegel's words, the Nation-State is the "divine idea as it exists on earth." Hegel is trying here to express something similar to the Old Testament utterance that God will deliver His judgment to the nations. For Hegel, God manifests one stage of His truth to each of the key nations of history and each in its historical turn becomes a carrier of His divine truth.

4. Participation in Larger Life and Truth of the Nation

We are now able to probe more deeply into Hegel's theory that ethics is social ethics, the ethics of the community, the ethics of the Nation-State. The Nation-State embodies one stage of the truth of the Absolute in its culture and institutions. For the individual, to live as a contributing member of the Nation-State is to participate in the life of the Absolute which the culture expresses, it is to participate in a larger life than that of merely personal, private, individual desires and concerns. The moral center of your life as an individual becomes, then, not yourself as an isolated atom, but this larger life of the spirit of the whole people, the spirit of the unfolding Absolute.

In participating in the life of our nation and its culture, we live beyond ourselves in the larger life of developing truth. And we live this larger spiritual life by taking part in the public life and the political process of our time, in which all the standards, deep-lying values, moral and political beliefs and aspirations of the culture come to the surface, are debated, are thought through, and undergo dialectical development. By participating in the ongoing public life of politics, religion, art, education, and work, you enter into the truth for your time, into the truth of the Absolute as it is manifested in your nation.

5. The Moral Ideals of the Individual and the Nation-State Are Identical

The moral ideals which are expressed in this ongoing public life are the ideals by which the Nation-State defines its moral identity. You yourself, as an individual, find your own moral identity, your moral selfhood in this larger life in the Spirit of the People, in the truth of the nation. This is what Hegel's moral philosophy means by its insistence that ethics is social ethics.

6. The Need for Unification

In total opposition to the Enlightenment and its idealizing of the atomic individual as rational, automonous, independent, and free by virtue of his inalienable rights, Hegel has perceived that greater than the need of the human being for independence, and to be separate, and autonomous, is the need for unification with others, and to participate in a larger purpose than one's own, to become part of the social whole. You cannot help feeling the power of what Hegel is saying here. He is touching a sore and sensitive spot with us; our sense of living in isolation, of living in a world which has become fragmented and atomized, and our sense that there is no larger totality to which we belong. At the time that he was writing, Hegel was speaking to the needs of the German people for wholeness, their need to form into a unified and strong nation. But Hegel speaks also to our present need for wholeness, our need to sense that we are part of a larger, meaningful totality.

7. Stages of Internalization of the Ethical Substance of Society

How then do I acquire the moral ideals of my culture, enter into its ongoing spiritual life and gain a sense of belonging? Hegel's answer is that you acquire the beliefs of your culture by the process of internalizing them, by making them a part of yourself, by incorporating them, by appropriating them to yourself. You incorporate the ethical substance, the morality, of your culture, says Hegel, as you develop as a person from early childhood into maturity. This development, this growth process in your personal history takes a dialectical form in which there are three stages, three important moments which constitute the ethical life of society. These three stages are first, the family; second, as antithesis to the family, civil society; and third, the synthesis of these two, which lies in the developed state.

(a) **The Family.** The family, says Hegel, is the first way in which the self enters into the moral life of the nation. The family is the initial social group which one experiences. In the family there is a sense of unity; a unity of feeling, a bond of love unites the family members. The members of the family do not relate to each other, says Hegel, as persons with individual rights as against the other members of the family, but as members of a deeply felt unity. When, however, it happens that family members relate to each other through insisting upon their individual rights, the right of children against their parents, or husbands and wives against each other, rather than through their unity of feeling, the family is in process of dissolution and decay, says Hegel. (The contemporary American family?)

(b) **Civil Society.** Hegel next points out that the child outgrows the family and passes over into a new stage of the moral life of the nation, which is that of civil society. In the family unity, the members existed simply in-themselves, says

Hegel, that is, as unself-conscious parts of the felt unity of love of the family, rather than existing for-themselves as self-conscious individual personalities. Hegel has here distinguished between two kinds of existence, existence which is *in-itself*, and which is unself-conscious existence and, on the other hand, existence *for-itself*, in which one exists as a self-conscious personality. (Sartre will take over this distinction from Hegel.)

In the transition to the new stage of life, the young adult becomes a self-conscious individual personality, with his or her own will, aspirations, life plans, and social connections. In these ways the person becomes individuated, separated from the family and enters civil society. By civil society Hegel means the economic aspect of modern capitalistic society, the society from the standpoint of the ways in which human individuals relate to each other in terms of satisfying their individual economic needs and interests. Hegel had studied very carefully the works of Adam Smith and of other British economists before writing on civil society himself. Karl Marx will soon be bending over the same books.

Civil society, Hegel says, is a scene in which individuals are striving to fulfill their own economic needs, but in order to do so they require the work of others, they require that there be a division of labor so that there can be an efficient production of goods to satisfy the needs of a growing society. Hegel sees the Cunning of Reason at work in the economic relations within a society, as well as working within history. As human individuals consciously work for their own personal needs and interests, he says, in actuality, although they do not intend this themselves, they are fulfilling the interests of the economy as a whole, they are making the wheels of the economy go around.

But Hegel sees that the economy of a society can run into problems. As production increases to meet the needs of the increase in population, some individuals achieve great wealth, but at the same time there arises a working class, an urban proletariat which may suffer economic and also spiritual poverty. As this urban proletariat finds itself tied to fragmented, mechanical work, and increasingly suffers from unemployment, it loses its sense of identification with the society and it becomes, says Hegel, a discontented rabble, while at the opposite pole there has been created varying degress of wealth for other members of society.

Hegel's description of the polarization within industrial society of two groups, the small, wealthy capitalist class and the constantly growing proletarian class of laborers is almost identical with the picture of civil society which Karl Marx will paint a generation later. But there is one crucial difference between Hegel and Marx on this point. Hegel sees the inner conflicts of the industrial economy and the threat of a proletarian revolution as clearly as Marx does. But Hegel thinks that the state can hold these conflicts in check while at the same time utilizing them to bring about the continuous development of humanity as it faces the challenge of the growth of industry and technology.

Hegel sees both the positive functions of civil society and its internal tensions. Accordingly, he places the state in political and moral control of the entire industrial economy in order to maximize its positive functions and to minimize its internal tensions. Marx, on the other hand, totally rejects Hegel's belief that the state can effectively control civil society. Marx calls instead for a revolutionary overthrow of civil society, of the entire capitalist economy, as the only solution to its internal problems, and as the next necessary stage (and the last stage) of history.

(c) The State. What, then, does Hegel say about the mature, developed political state? The developed political state is the synthesis of the unity of the family, and the separateness or individuality of life in civil society. Itself an organic unity, the mature state provides unity, as does the family; and through culture and public life and institutions, it provides for individual development, as does civil society. The state is a synthesis of the ethics which lies within the family and of the ethics within civil society; these are fused with the universal ethics represented by the state. In the political institutions of the state there is the most complete embodiment of the ethical substance of a society. And thus the individual who internalizes the ethics embodied in the ongoing life of the state has acquired the ethical substance of his society.

Hegel's Political Philosophy

1. Formal Freedom Versus Substantial Freedom

Hegel now moves on to show that by providing the ethical substance of a society, the state makes freedom possible. At this point Hegel introduces his widely influential distinction between two kinds of freedom: formal freedom and substantial freedom. There is, he says, the freedom which was pursued by the Enlightenment and by the three great revolutions which it inspired. This type of freedom was freedom on behalf of the atomic, isolated individual; this was the formal, abstract, rational freedom which the individual gains by the natural rights of life, liberty, and property. These freedoms, says Hegel, are essentially negative freedoms; they express the rebellious will of rising bourgeois individuals against the coercive authority of absolute monarchy. Formal freedoms such as these function to safeguard the individual in his rights to his life, liberty, and possessions from the absolute power of the king to seize them from him. The formal freedom of the universal natural rights of the Enlightenment is thus abstract and negative; it is freedom from an oppressive authority.

But what is now needed, says Hegel, is not negative freedom, but a positive and concrete sense of my freedom. What am I freed to do? What is now needed is not empty, formal negative freedoms from oppressors but ideals of substantial, positive freedom by which to act and live as a free spiritual being. What does it mean to have substantial freedom—freedom that is not merely negative, freedom *from*—freedom that has positive substantial content?

For Hegel, the ideals of substantial freedom, like ethical ideals, are derived from the spiritual life of the particular society. A fully developed nation-state is one which clearly embodies in its laws and institutions the ethical ideals and fundamental beliefs of the spirit of the people. The individual members of this society will have internalized these same ideals of the culture. The members of such a society have substantial freedom insofar as they can recognize that the ethical and political ideals which they value as their own truly coincide with the ideals embodied in the laws and institutions of the organic totality of which they are a part. And so you as an individual member of society have substantial freedom insofar as the ideals of your society, embodied in its laws, are your own chosen ideals for directing your life. As ethics is social ethics, so freedom is social freedom.

You have substantial freedom when you see that the ideals by which the culture and the state define themselves are also the ideals by which you choose to define yourself. For example, as a United States citizen committed to civil rights, you see that the state, the Government of the United States, also defines itself as committed to civil rights.

In this way it comes about that the laws of your society no longer appear alien or oppressive to you; they appear instead as identical to your own laws for yourself. And thus there is an end to the opposition between your individual freedom and the power of federal laws; there comes an end to your sensing that the laws of the federal government are oppressing you, are coercive upon you, and are a heavy yoke for you to bear. And, Hegel adds, in this way there is an end to the opposition between your personal will and the will of the state, since you have now identified your own will with the larger will which is that of the state. This, then, is the meaning of substantial freedom: Substantial freedom consists in the identification of personal ideals with the ideals of the state, which embody the ethical substance of the society.

Moreover, Hegel regards substantial freedom as the condition of human happiness. For human beings, to be happy is to live in a Nation-State in which you can freely identify with the laws and institutions and in which you can will freely what the state wills. This happy life is what Hegel believes the ancient Athenians had in the Golden Age of Pericles. There was once a society, that of ancient Athens, in which human beings lived in the profound happiness and blessed satisfaction of identifying with the greatness of their own society, sharing fully in its ideals, and participating wholeheartedly in its government.

Happiness, says Hegel, is the reward of being able to identify with the ideals of your society; it is the happiness that comes from the ending of separation, isolation, and conflict, it is the happiness of the sense of unification, of feeling at one with the group to which one belongs.

Substantial freedom is, in Hegel's view, the ideal or norm for human historical development—the ideal toward which the historical progress of the consciousness of freedom is moving. Substantial freedom and potential happiness were now, Hegel hoped, emerging into actuality for his own Germanic people. It was in this hope that he placed the German people at the pinnacle of history, as a potential modern Athens.

2. Theory of Alienation

But what if you do not identify with your society? What if you are not reconciled to the ideals and institutions of your society? What if you still harbor the suspicions and hatreds toward the culture and government of the United States which many people felt during the civil rights movement and the Vietnam War? You exist, then, says Hegel, in a state of alienation. Hegel has a theory of alienation which Marx borrows and adapts to his own theoretical purposes. In time the entire Western world learned from Hegel and Marx to recognize alienation, so that in the twentieth century Sartre will find the theme and the phenomenon of alienation present everywhere in contemporary culture.

What is the meaning of alienation and what specifically does Hegel mean by it? In contemporary sociology and philosophy, alienation is generally understood as the sense of being estranged, shut out of the common life, the sense of being an outsider. There are various other components of alienation: the sense of being self-estranged, cut off from one's own feelings or identity; the feelings of normlessness; meaninglessness; powerlessness. Do you find it meaningless to vote? Does your job seem to have no future? Are you bored by the social and political issues of the day that other people get violently passionate about? Have you lost the capacity for love or for any other strong emotion? Do you feel that your life is pointless and empty? These are symptoms of alienation.

Alienation as Hegel understands it is the failure of the will of the individual to identify with the larger will of the society. You as an individual are in a state of alienation when you find that the ideals and institutions by which your society defines itself appear to you to be meaningless or false, and they form no part of you. Alienation is the condition in which you no longer identify yourself with the public morality and institutions of your society. Hegel views alienation as the opposite process, the counterprocess, to social identification. In opposition to the unifying, integrating function of social identification, alienation is a social process which tends to bring about the disintegration of a community and its common, shared life. Alienation breaks up the organic unity of society into nonparticipating atoms. And just as substantial freedom, identification with the will of the nation, is a necessary condition of happiness, so alienation from society is a necessary condition of unhappiness.

And last, it is of great significance that Hegel views political and social individualism as a serious form of alienation. Individualism, in Hegel's view, is a solvent, a destroyer of national and community unity.

3. Rejection of Political Individualism

How may individualism be defined? Individualism as it is usually defined in political terms is the view that the state is subordinate to the individual, politically and morally. For political individualism, the state is made for man, not man for the state. John Locke's formulation of political individualism inspired the English, American, and French revolutions of the Age of Enlightenment: Lockean political individualism affirms that human individuals are rational, autonomous, free, equal before the law, and possess certain inalienable rights; and that the state is subordinate to the individual, existing by mutual consent solely to protect the individual in his rights.

But as we have seen, just the opposite is Hegel's view. Hegel has consistently argued that the state is superior to the individual, that the state is the only true individual of history, and that the human individual is no better than a cell within the organism which is the state. It is furthermore Hegel's view that the individual has no inalienable natural rights, such as John Locke and Thomas Jefferson claimed. Hegel argues that the individual has only those rights and liberty which the state prescribes for him as serving its institutions. And as we have seen, the moral value and the very meaning of a human individual's life are derived from and dependent upon the organic totality of the Nation-State of which he is a part. Thus Hegel turns the political individualism of John Locke and Thomas Jefferson around, and claims that the state is politically and morally superior to the individual. In Hegel's own words, the state has "supreme right against the individual whose supreme duty it is to be a member of the state." Hegel regards the individualism of the Enlightenment as a glorification of personal egoism and political oligarchy (rule by the wealthy).

Hegel's political philosophy must therefore be called statism or *political absolutism*. Political absolutism affirms the subordination of the individual to the state and claims for the state absolute political power and moral authority over the individual. For political absolutism the individual exists for the state, not the state for the individual.

4. Rejection of Political Democracy

And so we turn to Hegel's theory of the structure and functions of government. In the modern world, says Hegel, a state must have a constitution; and he argues that the constitution should establish three powers: a legislative branch which determines the laws; an executive power which carries out the laws in respect to particular cases; and a monarch, a king, who has the power of personal decision and who embodies in his own person the will of the state.

As for the legislative body, Hegel is opposed to their being elected as individuals by a universal public election. Hegel objects to the concept of universal suffrage on the ground that it makes of the public at election time a mere formless, meaningless mass or heap of individuals, lacking any organic unity. Moreover, Hegel denies that the general public is in any position to know what its own interests are or for what or for whom to vote. As Hegel says: "If people means a section of the citizens, it is precisely that section which does not know what it wills. To know what one wills, and still more, to know what the absolute wills, is the fruit of profound knowledge and insight, precisely the things which the public does not know."

Hegel has here taken his firm stand against the fundamental principle of democracy, universal voting, direct suffrage for all. In place of universal voting, Hegel calls for the people to be represented in the legislature by three estates or classes: agriculture, business, and civil service. But the representatives of these three estates will in no case be elected by the people. They will hold their office either by appointment or by aristocratic birth. It is at this point easy to see why Hegel has been labeled a conservative by some, a reactionary by others, but never a defender of liberalism. We have seen that his political philosophy rejects the twin pillars of political liberalism: individualism and democracy.

5. Relativity of Politics to Society

Does Hegel suggest that all states should follow his model for Germany? Not at all. Hegel's organicism and historicism argue against that. It is ridiculous, he says, to argue in abstraction as to what government is best. It is even more ridiculous, he says, to dictate to any society what government is best for it. Every nation has the kind of government which expresses the spirit of its own people and what was appropriate for its own time. The best constitution, the best government for a people is the one that it has, since it will manifest the absolute as it is revealed to that people. And so, Hegel argues, "Every nation has the constitution appropriate to it and suitable for it." And he also says, "A constitution develops out of the spirit of a nation . . . it is the indwelling spirit of the history of the nation by which constitutions are made."

Hegel insists that a constitution is not something manufactured, not just a piece of paper such as the many constitutions written and torn up during the French Revolution. A constitution, he says, is the work of centuries. It represents the historical development of the spirit of the people. Here is evidence again of Hegel's historicism, his view that to understand anything, including politics, we must see it in its historical growth and development.

Hegel is saying something profound about the relativity of a nation's politics to its history. But he also is raising a problem. Is the ideal of substantial freedom realizable only by the spirits of certain people? Can a type of government be imposed upon a people which is not rooted in their past, in their own historical development? Hegel suggests that it is impossible for the cultivation or imposition of a government from an external source to succeed at all. Then are the Marxists' attempts to impose Marxian communism upon several of the countries of Asia, Africa, and Latin America doomed to failure? Is the countereffort by the United States to promote democracy in these areas also doomed?

6. Philosophy and Politics

Finally, what is Hegel's view of the power of philosophy to direct the political future of a nation? Or of the world? We saw that the French *philosophes* believed that philosophy had given them a true theory to put into practice and change the world.

Hegel disagrees. Hegel denies that philosphy has the power to change the course of a nation or of the world. The philosopher, he says, cannot transcend his own culture, and cannot offer any blueprints, predictions, prophecies or utopias which have validity for the future. The philosopher can only reflect upon and seek to understand his actual society. To gain this understanding, it is necessary for the philosopher to go to the roots of his society in order to see the rational concept which the Absolute has revealed to it and which has been coming to consciousness over the years in the life of the nation.

Philosophy can grasp the truth of a culture, however, only when the culture has matured enough so that what the Absolute has revealed to it has finally become clear. But by this time, says Hegel, it is too late for the society to change. Hegel makes this point in a famous line in which he refers to the owl which was a symbol of Minerva, the Roman goddess of wisdom. Hegel expresses the thought that philosophic wisdom comes too late within any society to transform it, but can only make it possible for the society to understand itself, to grasp the meaning of its own culture and the truth of the Absolute which it embodies. This is Hegel's famous line:

> The owl of Minerva spreads its wings and takes flight only when the shades of night are falling.

But this is exactly what Karl Marx will challenge. Against Hegel's famous formulation that philosophy comes too late to change the world stands Marx's equally famous reply.

> The philosophers have so far only *interpreted* the world, in various ways; the point, however, is to *change* it.

And Marx believed that we now have the philosophy to put into practice and change the world.

Evaluation of the Hegelian Philosophy

The power of Hegel as a master builder of philosophy cannot be denied, yet serious criticisms of him can be made. Does Hegel's idealistic philosophy in which reality is only the reality of concepts give us an adequate grasp of the variety, mutability, and contingency of the material side of reality, the problems of the human body in its material environment, the problems of economic production, of technology, or of material resources of the planet? With regard to God, if

Hegel's Absolute, which he calls God, exists only as He is externalized or embodied in human consciousness, then how can He be legitimately called God or Absolute? Is this not a deception, an equivocation—double-talk? Also, what kind of method is dialectic? Clearly it is not a rationalistic, logical, or mathematical method. Clearly it is not an empirical and scientific method. Is dialectic then a method of interpretation and insight? But how can Hegel's insights and interpretations be shown to be true? How can Hegel prove that there are dialectical laws of history and that they are necessary? How does he know what each stage of the dialectic is? For example, how can he prove that Germany is the final culminating synthesis of history rather than England or France? Are Hegel's insights and interpretations rational truths or cultural prejudices? Is Hegel's abstract philosophy a mask which conceals a defense of German nationalism, a fear of revolution, a hatred for individualism and democracy? Has not Hegel's dialectic philosophy cunningly used the Cunning of Reason in order to justify whatever exists in the status quo, even evil, as serving the purpose of the Absolute?

But on the other hand, Hegel is a great source of wisdom and his philosophy gave to the world many concepts of the greatest profundity: the spirit of a people; the concept of culture; organicism and historicism; the dialectical tendency of thought; the master-slave concept; a new theory of the relation of the individual to society; the theory of ethics as socially rooted; a theory of labor; a theory of leadership; a theory of the human need for wholeness through social indentification; a theory of alienation; a theory of interpretation as the method of history and philosophy. These concepts and theories which originated in Hegel's philosophy are to be found throughout the social sciences today, in social anthropology, sociology, social psychology, history, political theory, psychoanalysis, and clinical psychology. But Hegel's influence is not only on the sciences which study man but also on philosophy itself. The French philosopher Maurice Merleau-Ponty stated Hegel's influence with these words: "All the great philosophical ideas of the past century, the philosophies of Marx, Nietzsche, existentialism and psycho-analysis had their beginning in Hegel." Of all these influences, Hegel's greatest influence was on Karl Marx and, through him, upon the entire world, East and West. To Marx we now turn.

SUGGESTIONS FOR FURTHER READING
PART FOUR: HEGEL

Works of Hegel:

Hegel, Georg Wilhelm Friedric. *Lectures on the Philosophy of History*. Trans. J. Sibree. New York: Dover, 1956.

——, *Reason in History* (part of Introduction). Trans. by R. S. Hartman, Indianapolis: Bobbs-Merrill, 1953. Text adapted for television series.

——, *Philosophy of Right*. Trans. T. M. Knox. Oxford: Clarendon Press, 1942.

——, *Phenomenology of Mind*. Trans. J. B. Baillie. New York: Harper Torchbook, 1969.

——, *Encyclopedia of the Philosophical Sciences*, part 3, "The Philosophy of Mind." Trans. William Wallace. Oxford, 1894.

——, *Lectures on the History of Philosophy*. Trans. E. S. Haldane and F. H. Simson. New York: Humanities Press, 1892-96.

——, *Hegel's Political Writings*, Trans. T. M. Knox, Introduction Z. A. Pelczynsky. Oxford: Clarendon Press, 1964.

Critical Studies:

Avineri, Shlomo. *Hegel's Theory of the Modern State*. Cambridge: Cambridge University Press, 1972.

Findlay, J. N. *Hegel, A Re-Examination*. Larden: Macmillan, 1958. Collier Books ed., 1962.

Foster, M. B. *The Political Philosophies of Plato and Hegel*. Oxford: Oxford University Press, 1935.

Harris, H. S. *Hegel's Development: Towards the Sunlight*. Oxford: Clarendon Press, 1972.

Kaufmann, Walter. *Hegel: A Re-Interpretation*. New York: Doubleday, 1965.

Kaufmann, Walter (Ed.). *Hegel's Political Philosophy*. New York: Atherton Press, 1970.

Kojève, Alexandre. *Introduction to the Reading of Hegel*. Trans. James Nichols. New York: Basic Books, 1969.

MacIntrye, Alisdaire (Ed.). *Hegel*. New York: Doubleday, 1972.

Marcuse, Herbert. *Reason and Revolution*. New York: Oxford University Press, 1941; reprinted Beacon Press, 1960.

Mure, G. R. G. *The Philosophy of Hegel*. London: Oxford University Press, 1965.

Reyburn, H. A. *The Ethical Theory of Hegel*. Oxford: Oxford University Press, 1921.

Steinkraus, W. E. (Ed.). *New Studies in Hegel's Philosophy*. New York: Holt, Rinehart and Winston, 1971.

Taylor, Charles. *Hegel*. London: Cambridge University Press, 1975.

Walsh, W. H. *Hegelian Ethics*. New York: St. Martin's Press, 1969.

Wiedmann, Franz. *Hegel: An Illustrated Biography*. New York: Pegasus, 1968.

PART FIVE
MARX

Karl Marx at the age of 42.
(COURTESY OF CULVER PICTURES.)

20

THE YOUNG HEGELIAN

Do you know that at least one third of all human beings in the world today call themselves followers of Karl Marx and live in countries which are governed by Marxist regimes? Yet for most of his adult life until his death Karl Marx was almost unknown, a hardworking, impoverished radical scholar, living as a refugee in London, and having to be supported, along with his wife and children, by the contributions of friends.

What Is the Power of Marxism?

What is the power of the thought of Karl Marx? Marxism has swept through the world and captured the intellect, imagination, and conscience of human beings as only the great religions—Judaism, Christianity, and Islam—have done in human history. Is Marxism then in some respects similar to religion? But Karl Marx would have been horrified by the suggestion that his own views had anything in common with the claims of religion. Religious belief to Marx meant belief in a supernatural God, divine revelation, and a redeeming messiah, and Marx scorned such beliefs as an atheist, and with his celebrated epigram: "It [religion] is the opium of the people."

How then did Marx himself regard his own work, if surely not within the domain of religion? The young Marx must have thought of himself as a philosopher, as a follower of the great Hegel, but making drastic changes in the Hegelian system to bring it down to earthly issues from the lofty plane of the abstract metaphysics of German idealism. The older, mature Marx, however, claimed to be a scientist, specifically, a social scientist, and to be no less than the Isaac Newton of the social sciences. But no philosopher or social scientist other than Marx has ever had a worldwide, international, organized following. We find ourselves coming back to the question What is the strange, commanding power that lies within the thought of Karl Marx? How can the global appeal of Marxism be explained?

The Early Life of Karl Marx

We can begin to solve this mystery by examining the forces shaping Marx's life in his own time and places. The year 1818 symbolizes the closeness of Marx's tie to the philosopher Hegel—it is the year in which Hegel was called to a prestigious professorship at the University of Berlin, and it is the year in which Hegel's most famous follower, Karl Marx, was born.

At first glance there is little in the early life of Karl Marx which would lead one to predict that he would develop a philosophy for the rising working class, the proletariat. Marx was born in the beautiful city of Trier, in the valley of the Moselle River, surrounded by vineyards and rolling hills. Marx's own family was comfortably middle class, his father maintaining an active legal practice and holding an official position as lawyer for the high court of appeals in the city. Both of Karl's parents were descended from many generations of illustrious Jewish rabbis, but Heinrich Marx, Karl's father, was an Enlightenment figure, a believer in the French Enlightenment gospel of reason and in its principle of toleration, which had given Jews all the rights of French citizens, including the right to enter the professions. When the Wars of Liberation finally defeated Napoleon, the Prussian Government reannexed the city of Trier from France in 1814 and reinstated anti-Jewish laws. Heinrich Marx was now required to convert to Christianity in order to retain his official position. He was baptized as a Lutheran in 1817, the year before Karl was born. Karl and the other children were baptized as Lutherans in 1824, their mother the following year.

Karl attended the local schools, and when he was seventeen, traveled by boat down the Moselle and Rhine rivers to the University of Bonn, where he registered as a law student.

After a year of writing poetry, drinking, and dueling at the University of Bonn, Marx transferred, after some prodding from his father, to the more intellectual and studious environment of the University of Berlin.

But before returning to school, Marx became engaged to his longtime love from Trier, the beautiful, auburn-haired Jenny von Westphalen. Jenny's father, Baron Ludwig von Westphalen, city counselor of Trier, came from a line of Prussian middle-class state officials; his father had been ennobled and had married into the Scottish nobility. Ludwig von Westphalen had a longstanding fondness for the vital, intelligent young Karl and stimulated in him an enduring, fascinated interest in Homer and Shakespeare, and also in the ideas of Saint-Simon, the French socialist.

The Young Hegelians

During the time that Marx was studying for his doctorate, from 1836 to 1841, the mood of radical intellectuals at the universities throughout Germany was depressed and bitter. King Frederick William III of Prussia ruled as a strict reactionary against the currents of freedom which had been set loose by the French Revolution. Although both liberals and radicals had great hopes for his son Frederick William IV, he soon turned out to be a more efficient and shrewder reactionary than his father. Prussia was now an authoritarian police state. Censorship of the press and of public meetings, and a central commission for the suppression of dangerous thought throughout Germany made any movement for reform impossible.

When Karl Marx came to the University of Berlin in 1836, the great philosopher Hegel had been dead for five years, but his influence in the university and in all of Germany was at its peak. The followers of Hegel were now split into right-wing, conservative, and left-wing, radical, groups. Marx soon immersed himself in the works of Hegel, forgot about studying law, and became one of the leaders of the radical, or left-wing, group, called the Young Hegelians.

1. Hegel's Ambiguities and the Young Hegelians

How had the political conflict in Prussia turned into the bitter antagonism between the two camps of the followers of Hegel? Hegel was the dominant intellectual voice in Germany and the conflict about Hegel came from the deep ambiguity, the two-sidedness, the paradoxical, ironical double meanings of Hegel himself, which we have already seen.

(a) On the one hand, Hegel had enshrined the Christian-Germanic State of Prussia as the highest point, the culmination of all of human history. But on the other hand, Hegel had presented a theory of dialectic as endlessly restless, negating whatever exists in order to bring about change and development toward greater rationality. The Young Hegelians took the radical side of this two-sidedness of Hegel: They argued that the Prussian State, which was in fact daily becoming more restrictive and authoritarian, was not immune to the negative, critical power of dialectic and must be attacked.

(b) Another ambiguity within the legacy of Hegel was hotly argued by the right-wing and left-wing Hegelians. On the one hand, Hegel had nothing but contempt for political liberalism, and its twin components of individualism and democracy. For Hegel the state has absolute power and moral authority over the individual. But on the other hand, Hegel's philosophy of history flew the flag of freedom. It claimed that the true meaning of human history is that it is the progress of finite spirit in the consciousness of freedom. The Young Hegelians took the radical side of this second exemplification of Hegelian two-sidedness and called for freedom against the Prussian State.

(c) A third instance of ambiguity within Hegel: his two-sidedness, or double-talk, with regard to God. As we have seen, Hegel's metaphysics was a breathtaking vision of reality as absolute spirit or mind, a God who is the absolute totality of rational truth, of all conceptual rationality. But on the other hand, Hegel acknowledged that God has no existence except in the human sphere. God exists only as He is revealed, manifested, externalized, and embodied in human consciousness, in finite minds, in social institutions, in the course of history. The Young Hegelians took the radical side of this ambiguity about God and worked their way finally to the conclusion of atheism, that a God who exists only as human consciousness does not exist at all.

(d) And still another double meaning had been left by Hegel: The famous statement that "the real is the rational and the rational is the real." The conservative and the radical Hegelian waged war over this formidable and tormenting statement. The conservative camp took the first half of Hegel's statement, "the real is the rational," and they interpreted it to mean that whatever exists is necessary in the rational process of dialectic, which embodies the absolute. Therefore, to try to change the status quo, the existing situation, specifically to try to change or undermine the Prussian State, is to oppose the rational process of dialectic and moreover to oppose God, who is embodied in the state and the king. But on the other side the radical camp took its stand on the second half of the statement, that "the rational is the real." They protested violently that Hegel never meant to defend the status quo, to say that whatever exists, no matter how confused or unworthy, is rational. What Hegel meant, according to the Young Hegelians, was that only what is rational has a claim to being called real, and that the most important task of the philosopher is to criticize all social institutions so that they can become more rational and therefore more real. "Criticism" became the slogan of the Young Hegelians.

We can now begin to see the powerful influence upon the thought of Marx exercised by the Young Hegelians, these radicalizers of the philosophy of Hegel. Against the sanctity of government and the Prussian State, they called for continuing the process of dialectical negation in order to reach for a higher form of government. Against political absolutism, they called for progress in freedom. Against a God who exists only in human life, they defended atheism, the denial of the existence of God. Against defending whatever exists as rational and divinely ordained, the Young Hegelians insisted that what exists must be criticized so that it can be *made* rational, by violent revolution if necessary.

All this was proclaimed by the Young Hegelians on the basis of their reading of Hegel. Hegel's own adult viewpoint, as we have seen, was neither radical nor activistic, and became increasingly conservative and quietistic during his Berlin years. But the Young Hegelians were motivated to find a radical message in Hegel and they were correct in finding it—Hegel did have both a radical and a conservative side. The Young Hegelians discovered that central to Hegel's dialectic is the principle of negation, the principle by which every concept, every structure, every institution is necessarily criticized, attacked, destablized, delegitimated. Hegel's own principle of negation is the necessary generator of dialectical change, paradox, irony, and two-sidedness. The Young Hegelians took the side which gave them intellectual support.

2. Influence of the Young Hegelians: Criticism, The Divinity of Man, World Revolution

But these feisty young radicals were not satisfied with merely reinterpreting the philosophy of Hegel. They were vigorously pushing ahead on three main intellectual fronts: first, with the notion of criticism. Their slogan of "criticism" inspired them to write pamphlets and books offering sharp critical attacks on laws, political thought, philosophy, and religion. Marx seized upon intellectual criticism as the crucial means by which to change the world. As late as 1843 Marx wrote to his friend Arnold Ruge (1802–80), a radical Hegelian and an important figure in Marx's early development, urging that what is now needed is

> a merciless criticism of everything existing, merciless in two senses: this criticism must not be afraid of its own conclusions and must not shrink from a collision with the established powers.

And in an article which he wrote soon after, in the form of a critique of Hegel's *Philosophy of Right*, Marx is still talking about criticism as a means to change the world. Criticism, he says now,

> is not an anatomic knife but a weapon. Its object is its enemy, which it wants not to refute but to destroy.

But although Marx will never surrender the significance of intellectual criticism, he will soon change his mind on its primacy as the most effective weapon with which to change the world. Instead of theoretical criticism, the ultimate weapon to change the world will be for him the organized power of the proletariat.

A second front in the campaign of the Young Hegelians was derived from their criticism of Hegel's two-sided concept of God. A God who exists only as human consciousness, only in the form of man, does not exist: Therefore the Young Hegelians were atheists. But they drew a far more interesting conclusion from their criticism of Hegel's concept of God: If all of the absolute's development of rationality is within the human sphere, is carried out by man, then man is the true God. The human being is the true divinity.

Man is God—this intoxicating and grandiose concept led to the third front of the Young Hegelians' campaign. Man's divinity, his God-like nature, has not yet been realized. What must be accomplished is a revolution, a worldwide revolution against the existing conditions of the world, so as to make the world one in which the human being can live as a God. The third front is, then, the concept of a necessary coming world revolution, a world catastrophe by which the institutions of the world will be destroyed, so that they can be reconstructed according to the philosophy of Hegel, truly (radically) interpreted.

These three fighting fronts of the campaign of the Young Hegelians—the power of merciless criticism as a political weapon, the concept of the divinity of man in place of God, and the view of a necessary, impending horrible world revolution, destroying so as to reconstruct a rational world order—these three themes Marx incorporated from his years with the Young Hegelians at the University of Berlin. They remain permanent themes within his developing thought.

3. Influence of Feuerbach

(a) The Translation of Hegel. A great intellectual bombshell burst upon the Young Hegelians in 1814. It was the publication by Ludwig Feuerbach (1804–72), who was himself a major figure in Young Hegelian circles, of a work called *The Essence of Christianity*. In this book Feuerbach develops the Young Hegelian conception of man as the true God into a theory about religion, specifically about Christianity: The essence of Christianity as a religion is that it is projective, the projection upon God of man's own ideals of knowledge, will, and love, elevated to infinite power. The essence of God is thus nothing but the projected essence of man, who is the true God. Feuerbach uses this theory to show that Hegel's doctrine of the Absolute is the Christian concept of God in disguised form. In fact, says Feuerbach, Hegel projects upon the Absolute nothing but the historical achievement of man. Hegel's philosophy is valuable then, not for what it tells us about the absolute, but for what this projection tells us about human nature. To grasp the truth of Hegel's philosophy, says Feuerbach, we must turn Hegel upside down, we must transform or translate what Hegel says about the absolute into a profound philosophy of man.

(b) **Materialism.** Moreover, urges Feuerbach, it is now time to cut out the Hegelian double-talk about God. Let us place at the basis of philosophy not God or spirit or the absolute, but man himself, man as a species, real material man in a real material world.

Marx took away two messages from Feuerbach's attack on Hegel. One was Feuerbach's materialism, his metaphysical theory that reality is primarily material, and not spiritual as Hegel had claimed. Marx was himself inclined toward materialism in any case. Feuerbach reinforced Marx's own materialistic metaphysics, which now became a permanent element in Marx's thinking. But secondly, Marx took away from Feuerbach, the Young Hegelian, the message that the philosophy of Hegel is still true, that when Hegel is turned upside down, when it is seen that Hegel, correctly translated, is actually revealing man's life in the material world rather than God's manifestations, Hegel is still the master.

Editor of the Rhenish News (Rheinische Zeitung)

In his haste to find a job after his engagement to Jenny, Marx arranged to obtain his doctoral degree *in absentia* from the University of Jena, in April, 1841, and then moved to the University of Bonn, where Bruno Bauer, a Young Hegelian and a close friend, held a teaching post and had encouraged Marx to try for one too. But by 1842 the Prussian minister of education condemned the Young Hegelians as an illegal group; Bauer himself was dismissed from the University of Bonn, nor was there any future for Marx there. Marx moved on to the city of Cologne when he became for a while editor of a liberal journal, the *Rhenish News (Rheinische Zeitung)*, but Marx's incisive and uncompromisingly radical contributions to the journal soon brought official censorship down upon it and Marx was forced to resign. There is a description of Marx as he appeared while he was functioning as editor of the *Rhenish News*:

> Karl Marx from Trier was a powerful man of 24 whose thick black hair sprung from his cheeks, nose, arms and ears. He was domineering, impetuous, passionate, full of boundless self-confidence but at

the same time deeply earnest and learned, a restless dialectician—who with his restless Jewish penetration pushed every proposition of Young Hegelian doctrine to its final conclusion and was already then, by his concentrated study of economics, preparing his conversion to communism.

Marx is surely recognizable from this description written by one of the wealthy liberal businessmen of Cologne who funded the journal. The businesman goes on to say with regret: "Under Marx's leadership the journal soon began to speak very recklessly." In a short time the journal was officially banned.

The Paris Years: 1843–45

In June of the following year, 1843, Marx was married to Jenny von Westphalen. In her own right the beautiful, patrician Jenny was to become a legendary figure of courage, intelligence, fidelity, and suffering. That November they moved to Paris, where they lived until 1845.

Why Paris? By now it was clear to Marx that German censorship and reactionary politics would silence him—he could say or do nothing of political consequence in Germany. He had lost interest in his Young Hegelian friends at the University of Berlin, and the movement itself had been banned. Specifically he was drawn to Paris by the offer of a job, assisting Arnold Ruge, a Young Hegelian editor and writer, with the editing of a new journal, which was to be called the *German–French Annals* (*Deutsch–Französische Jahrbücher*), in which Ruge hoped to publish articles from both German and French radical contributors. Marx quickly accepted the job in a letter to Ruge in the summer of 1843 in which he said: "I am tired of this hypocrisy and stupidity. I am tired of having to bow and scrape and invent safe and harmless phrases. In Germany there is nothing I can do . . . in Germany one can only be false to oneself."

But there was another reason for the choice of Paris as the first stage of Marx's years as a radical exile and refugee from hostile governments. Paris, of all the great capital cities of Europe, was at this time the most hospitable and tolerant toward all shades of political opinion. Paris provided a rich and exciting intellectual atmosphere, especially for the refu-

gees and exiles from represssive states and churches—from
Germany, Russia, Italy, Poland, and Hungary—all of whom
were busily engaged in literary, artistic, and political activities on behalf of freedom for all humankind.

At the same time France was the crucial scene of rapid and
socially disruptive change as the Industrial Revolution advanced throughout the country, its large-scale production and
distribution driving out small business and making factory
hands out of growing numbers of the population. The government of France was weak and corrupt and controlled by the
newly created wealthy industrialists and financiers. Discontented factory workers in the rural areas of France were
engaging in riots and strikes.

But the supreme attraction was that Paris in the 1840s,
before the revolutionary year 1848, was the breeding ground
of modern socialist theories, nurtured by earlier models of
French socialist thought, and by the revolutions of 1789 and
1830 and their unfulfilled agenda. This was the intense and
stimulating atmosphere of Marx's Paris years, 1843–45, which
were the crucial years of his intellectual development. Marx
plunged into a world of socialist and communist theorizing
and political action. He worked with Ruge and the network of
radical contributors to the *German–French Annals*. He read
and sought out personally many of the French socialist theorists;
he came to know the socialist-anarchist Pierre Proudhon, who
soon became Marx's enemy, and the Russian anarchist Mikhail
Bakunin, soon also to be his enemy; he attended the meetings of French and German socialist workers' associations.
Marx was very critical, however, of many of the French
radicals. He considered them to be utopians, by which Marx
meant that they were concocting theories of improving society which could never be put into practice, theories which
presented glorious ends without any means to reach them,
theories which were then, and would always remain, pie in
the sky.

Paris, 1844: The Economic and Philosophic Manuscripts

During his Paris years Marx began to fixate on two problems which raised the concrete questions which the utopian
socialists failed to ask. The first problem was: Why had the
French Revolution failed? Why is it that Europe was no
closer to freedom than it had been before the revolution took

place? The Age of Enlightenment had been naïve to think that the world could be changed by reason, by science and education. But the radical Jacobin Party of the revolution was also proved false by attempting to change the world through the Reign of Terror. Nor was there value in Hegel's viewpoint that the French Revolution had failed because the time was not yet ripe for the dialectic to reach the state of freedom—since Hegel had given no indications as to how to know when the time *is* ripe. Is it possible now to know when the time is ripe, so that a new revolutionary strike for freedom will not fail?

The second problem which Marx was determined to solve was: What is the significance of the new Industrial Revolution, the great revolution of technology in factories, mills, mines, agriculture, and transportation which was transforming the social, economic, and political life of the world, bringing with it increasingly great wealth to some and widespread poverty and alienation to others, as Hegel had already noted in his account of civil society? What is the future of the Industrial Revolution? Can the gross inequities and dehumanization which were now visible in France, and even more so in the sooty, unhealthy factories and mining towns of England, continue indefinitely in the absence of a revolution to correct them? What is to prevent such a revolution from failing as the French Revolution failed?

To answer these questions Marx read with a frenzy while in Paris. Arnold Ruge, his coeditor, says of Marx during this period:

> He reads a lot. He works in an extraordinarily intense way. He has a critical talent that degenerates sometimes into a . . . dialectical game, but he never finishes anything—he interrupts every bit of research to plunge into a fresh ocean of books.—He is more excited and violent than ever, especially when his work has made him ill and he has not been to bed for three or even four nights on end.

Marx did indeed "read a lot." He taught himself French by reading the works of all the French socialists who were currently celebrities in Paris. He read French and German history in accordance with Hegel's historical approach to the understanding of human problems. And in order to deal with the economic problems connected with the Industrial Revolution, he read all the major theorists in the field of economics, from the seventeenth century to his own time, most notably Adam Smith's *The Wealth of Nations*. From all that he read he made copious notes of long passages, some of which he incorporated in his own manuscripts.

During the Paris spring and summer of 1844 there came the outcome of this intense intellectual activity—Marx wrote the articles which are now called the *Economic and Philosophic Manuscripts*, the *1844 Manuscripts*, or the *Paris Manuscripts*. These manuscripts already incorporate Marx's economic interpretation of history—the key concept of Marxism, which received its full treatment only in his last great work, *Capital*.

The Refugee Trail

Meanwhile copies of the *German–French Annals*, the radical journal which Marx and Ruge coedited, had been seized in April by the government of Prussia. The journal was banned, and warrants were issued for the arrest of Marx and Ruge upon setting foot in Prussia. The first issue of the *Annals* was also the last. Soon afterward, Marx, by now converted to communism, broke with Arnold Ruge, who was strongly anticommunist. Marx soon became a contributor to *Forward*, another radical journal. On February 25, 1845, *Forward* was closed down by the French government for its subversive radicalism, and Marx was expelled from France, with only twenty-four hours to leave Paris. Jenny sold their furniture and left the city a few days later. Next stop on the refugee trail: Belgium and the city of Brussels.

In the Brussels period, from 1845 to 1848, Marx wrote and coauthored some important books, and also began to organize an international revolutionary group. He soon joined with English radicals in an organization called the Communist League and became the leader of this rapidly growing revolutionary organization. In 1847 the Communist League commissioned him to prepare a document which would state the aims of the organization. Marx's statement of aims and principles for the Communist League was published a month before the outbreak of the Paris Revolution of 1848. It was the now famous *Manifesto of the Communist Party*.

With the outbreak of revolution in Paris, Marx was expelled from Brussels. He returned to action in revolutionary Paris, and moved on to Germany, where the Revolution of 1848 was next breaking out. Marx quickly established a radical newspaper, the *New Rhenish News* (the *Neue Rheinische Zeitung*), in the city of Cologne, but with the failure of the German revolution, Marx was deported once again from Germany. Jenny pawned the silver she had inherited from her aristocratic Scottish grandmother, and with this money they left Germany for the last time. They tried to go back to France but were forbidden to live in Paris, and so the Marxes moved to London in the fall of 1849. Marx was now thirty-one, Jenny was thirty-five. London was to be their home for the rest of their lives. They lived in poverty, misery, and ill health. Three of their children died for lack of money to pay for medical care. Yet Marx continued to write and plan for the world revolution which he did indeed bring about, but this he was fated never to know. What is the power of Marxism? Let us look for an answer in the developed thought of Karl Marx, to which we now turn.

21

ALIENATED MAN

Two Marxisms?

Why were the *Economic and Philosophic Manuscripts*, which Marx wrote in Paris in the summer of 1844, hidden from the public view for almost a hundred years? Why did Marx never acknowledge them, publish them, explicitly refer to them in his later writings?

Before these manuscripts of the young Marx were discovered and published, Marxism had been thought of primarily as the work of the mature Marx, and as a scientific system, or a scientific socialism, as Marx and Engels themselves called it, or as an economic and materialistic interpretation of history which stood Hegel's idealistic philosophy of history on its head. Generations of Marx scholars had accepted the view that for Marx the meaning of history is found in the division of labor, class struggle, class consciousness, and the revolutionary overthrow of capitalism. As a scientific theory, Marxism was regarded as having no moral or religious or philosophical meaning, but simply as offering an explanation of the necessary economic laws governing historical change.

The *Economic and Philosophic Manuscripts* were unknown until the 1930s, when the Marx–Engels Institute in Moscow, with the political and financial sponsorship of the Communist Party of the Soviet Union, published the collected works of Marx and Engels, commonly referred to as MEGA. (Director of the institute was the esteemed scholar David Riazanov, one of the many Marxist intellectuals who were put to death in the purges ordered by Stalin.) When the significance of the *Paris Manuscripts* began to be recognized after World War II, a new view of Marx emerged from the study of these manuscripts, a view of Marxism as a moral or religious or humanistic system of thought which has as its fundamental theme the moral regeneration of humanity through world revolution. The writings of the young Marx have had a strong appeal to Western intellectuals—the psychological appeal of the theme of the alienation and loneliness of modern man; the moral appeal of Marx's exhortation to authenticity, to live in terms of our human essence; the religious appeal of rising up against the false money–God and being redeemed.

Many noncommunist Marx scholars have as a result abandoned the view of Marxism as scientific socialism or as economic theory of history. Increasingly, scholars holding religious, humanist, or existentialist views interpret Marx in moral or religious or philosophical terms, taking their cue from these 1844 manuscripts written when Marx was twenty-six years old. But the official communist position of Soviet scholars condemns this swing to the young Marx as a bourgeois attack on the theoretical foundations of communism. Western Marx scholars who find in the writings of the young Marx the true foundation of Marxism are regarded by Soviet scholars as falsifiers and enemies of Marxism, who are enthusiastically emphasizing Marx's immature, early thought because it is more humanistic than revolutionary and does not threaten the West.

Are there then two Marxist systems? Are there two Marxist views of the significance of history? Is world history the process in which human self-alienation is finally overcome, a process in which human beings realize themselves through revolution and appropriate their true essence as natural and social beings, creative and free? Or is the history of the world the scientific history of the division of labor, class conflict, and inevitable revolution, ending in the classless society of communism? Does world history have a humanistic goal of human self-fulfillment, as the 1844 Paris manuscripts indicate, or does it have a scientifically explained economic goal, as the writings of the mature Marx proclaim? Or is it possible to find a reconciliation of these humanistic and scientific viewpoints in the thought of Marx, and to show how they come together in his own understanding of his system?

The Importance of Economics

To raise these questions is to penetrate Marxism below the usual surface accounts which summarize the main arguments of the late Marx. Let us turn to the fall of 1843, shortly after Marx's arrival in Paris. We have already seen the developing importance of economics for Marx in this period. He was soon voraciously reading Adam Smith, David Ricardo, and other economic theorists in his attempt to understand the Industrial Revolution, its present disastrous impact upon human life, and its future course.

1. **Hegel.** The importance of economics in human history had in fact already been established in Marx's thinking by Hegel's powerful analysis of civil society, in which Hegel had said that the economic relations of civil society constitute "a battlefield where everybody's individual private interests meet everybody else's." To Hegel, civil society in its economic affairs was a war of all against all, the continuous conflict of egoistic desires. Hegel's picture of the competitive evils of civil society, with its growing polarization of the wealthy few and the impoverished and alienated masses was now reinforced by the descriptions which the French socialists offered of the miserable lives of industrialized workers.

2. **"The Jewish Question".** Marx began to develop his own thought on economic life in civil society in an essay entitled "The Jewish Question," which he had completed before the move to Paris. Marx here speaks of economic alienation, of human beings living within the alien world of commerce in which money is God. The modern commerical world, says Marx, is a religion of money worship, and he equates this worship of money with Judaism. The Jews, he points out, are no longer a religious or a racial group. Judaism is at bottom a religion of practical need, selfishness, and egoism. It has enabled Jews to gain the power of money, vast political influence, and dominance in the competitiveness of civil society. As a result,

> Money is the jealous one God of Israel, beside which no other God may stand. Money dethrones all the gods of man and turns them into a commodity. Money is the universal, independently constituted value of all things. It has therefore deprived the whole world, both the world of man and nature, of

its own value. Money is the alienated essence of
man's work and his being. This alien being rules him
and he worships it.

Christianity, he says, has now taken over this money worship,
this alienation of man from himself in the worship of money.
The alienated world of competitive, egoistic individuals "first
reaches its completion in the Christian world." Christian civil
society has become Jewish. On the question, therefore, of
whether to emancipate the Jews from laws which disciminate
against them, Marx argues that "the emancipation of Jews is
the emancipation of humanity from Judaism . . . from huckstering and money." The only way to deal with the Jewish
question is to recognize in Judaism "a universal *antisocial*
element of the *present time*. A social revolution which would
abolish the possibility of huckstering "would make the Jew
impossible." Christians would then be emancipated from the
worship of money, and thus from their economic alienation.
But Christians now live in economic alienation, as human
beings producing objects which assume the alien form of
money and become an alien power over them.

3. Engels. And still another way in which the significance of
economics was brought home to Marx was an essay, "Outlines
of the Criticism of Political Economy," submitted to the
German–French Annals in January 1844 by an author named
Friedrich Engels, in which Engels's command of economics
made a strong impression upon Marx. Marx's fateful meeting
with Engels was to take place the following August.

The Economic and Philosophic Manuscripts

1. Hegel Upside-down is Economics

Marx seems to have been uncertain of how to proceed at
this point. But in the process of writing the *1844 Manuscripts*,
Marx's intense and imaginative concentration on economics
produced a great new insight which swept him back into the
orbit of Hegelian philosophy. In the manuscript entitled
"Criticism of the Hegelian Dialectic and Philosophy as a
Whole" there appears the insight that Hegel's *Phenomenology
of Spirit*, in its underlying meaning, was a philosophy of
economic life, an economic interpretation of history. Where

Hegel talks about the externalization of Spirit, of the Absolute estranged from itself, alienated in human consciousness, he was speaking in a confused way not of Spirit's self-externalization and self-alienation in human consciousness, but of *man* externalizing himself in material objects, of *man's* self-alienation in the objects which he produces.

The underlying, hidden meaning of the Hegelian philosophy is economics—this is Marx's dramatic discovery. Hegel turned upside down provides a study of man's alienation from the products of his own labor in the money economy of capitalism. As Feuerbach had turned Hegel upside down to show that the true underlying meaning of Hegel's philosophy lies in what it reveals about human psychology, so Marx is aware that he, too, is using criticism to translate Hegel, to turn Hegel upside down and find that the true, hidden underlying meaning of the Hegelian philosophy lies in what it reveals about economics. Did not Hegel in the famous chapter on "Master and Slave" in *Phenomenology of Spirit* show that the slave's production of the object is of something external and alien? But the slave overcomes the externalization and alienation of the products of his labor, recognizes his own essence in the objects he has made, and discovers his freedom in his objectification of himself. The slave reappropriates himself from what had been the externalized, alienated products of his labor.

Marx believes that the secret meaning of Hegel's conception of alienation and its overcoming is economic and that this constitutes the enduring importance of Hegel. In this 1844 manuscript, Marx praises Hegel for his grasp of the meaning of labor:

> The greatness of the Hegelian *Phenomenology* . . . lies, firstly, in the fact that Hegel grasps the self-production of man as a process, conceives objectification as loss of the object, as alienation and transcendence of this alienation; that he therefore grasps the essence of labor and conceives objective man . . . as the result of his own labor.

Moreover, now that Marx has found the underlying economic meaning and truth of Hegelian philosophy, Marx can take Hegel's *Phenomenology of Spirit* as the model for his own account of the self-realization of labor, of economic man.

For Hegel, Spirit is alienated from its true essence and the course of history is the developmental process in which Spirit achieves self-realization. On this model Marx superimposes the truth which Hegel had presented in a "mystifying," "confused" form: The true meaning of history is that it is the developmental process in which generic man, laborer, producer, creator of material and nonmaterial objects, repossesses his own essence and achieves self-realization.

Marx, however, criticized Hegel for his idealism, which regards the essence of man as spirit. Against Hegel Marx argues that man is a natural being, within a world of natural objects.

> To say that man is a *corporeal*, living, real, sensuous, objective being full of natural vigor is to say that he has *real sensuous objects* as the objects of his being or his life or that he can only *express* his life in real sensuous objects.

Moreover, as an idealist for whom spirit or consciousness has primacy, Hegel proposed that alienation can be overcome through consciousness or spiritual activity. In sharpest opposition Marx asserts that what Hegel has proposed is a mere overcoming "in thought, which leaves its object standing in the real world" and falsely "believes that it has overcome it." But overcoming which is merely in the form of thought, says Marx, will leave the alien, hostile world unchanged.

2. Man as Creator of Nature and Culture

Man as a species, says Marx, is a natural being which develops in the course of world history. Man is primarily a creative being, with desires and powers, faculties, creative abilities, which have their outcome in production. Mankind in its history has transformed the objects of the natural world and has created the entire world of culture. The vast historical and natural accumulation of the material and cultural objects mankind has produced are the manifestations or externalizations or embodiments of man's creative powers. Man actualizes himself in the world. In Marx's own powerful language:

> The whole so-called world-history is nothing other than the production of man through human labor . . .

It is Marx's view, which he will never give up, that the history of the world is the developing process in which human beings have created the great totality of objects in nature and in human culture, and in this process, the human species will find itself objectified and achieve self-realization. So, for example, the whole of modern industry is man's product—industrial mechanization is the externalization of human hands, ears, eyes, brains. Mills, mines, factories and their expanding technologies, have all been produced by human beings and are externalizations of their creative powers. But the human species does not realize that it is the creator of the world of natural objects and of culture. What man sees when he looks at these objects which he has produced are alien things in "an alien hostile world standing over against him." This is so because man's productive activity is done in servitude to the God money, rather than in spontaneous self-determination. The result has been that the history of human creative production has been a history of man's alienation from his own productive nature.

3. Alienation

Human alienation takes four main forms, according to Marx in the *1844 Manuscripts*: Man is alienated from the product of his work, from the act of producing, from his own social nature, and from his fellow men. First, the worker in industrialized capitalism is alienated from his product, which "exists *outside him*, independently, as something alien to him . . . the life which he has conferred on the object confronts him as something hostile and alien." His product is not his own but is utilized by strangers as their private property. And the more the worker produces, the less is his productivity valued. "The worker becomes an even cheaper commodity, the more cheap commodities he creates." The worker's wages are just sufficient to maintain him with what is necessary to keep him working.

Second, the capitalist system alienates man from his productive activity. His activity is not determined by his personal interest or his creativity, but is something which he is compelled to do in order to remain alive. "His labor . . . is *forced* labor." As a result, in Marx's words, "The worker only feels himself outside his work, and in his work he feels outside himself." The more he works the less human he becomes. He finally feels at home only in the animalian functions of eating, drinking, and sexuality.

Third, capitalist society alienates the worker from the essential qualities of the human species. Unlike animals, says Marx, who produce only for their immediate needs, humans produce knowledge and culture (such as art, science, technology) for the whole human race. Humans produce as universal beings for universal ends. But the capitalist system degrades man's urge to produce for all mankind into animal labor, into a mere means to satisfy his personal physical needs.

The fourth form of alienation is "the estrangement of man from man." His fellow man is a stranger competing with him as a worker and for the products of their labor. Moreover, both are estranged from "man's essential nature."

4. The Passion of Greed

However, in the alienated world of capitalism not only the capitalist but the worker, too, is in bondage to greed, is a slave before the master—money, the money-God of capitalism. He is influenced by the dominant ideas of his capitalist environment to save his money and increase his capital. As Marx says, in the *Paris Manuscripts*, the prevailing creed may be expressed in this form:

> The less you eat, drink and read books; the less you go to the theatre, the dance hall, the public-house; the less you think, love, theorize, sing, paint, fence, etc., the more you *save*—the *greater* becomes your treasure which neither moths nor dust will devour—your *capital*. The less you *are* the more you *have* . . . art, learning, the treasures of the past, political power— . . . [money] can buy all this for you . . . Yet being all this, it is *inclined* to do nothing but create itself, buy itself; for everything else is after all its servant. And when I have the master I have the servant . . . All passions and all activity must therefore be submerged in *greed*.

As we have seen, Hegel had already identified human passion as the prime motivating force in the human world. But Marx identifies this force as the passion of greed for money, the money mania which equates money with power.

To Marx, greed has been the motivating force throughout all of human history, alienating man from his human essence and dehumanizing him. Man worships money as the all-powerful master, as an "overturning power," says Marx, that can turn all values and relationships into their contraries.

> Money . . . transforms fidelity into infidelity, love into hate, hate into love, virtue into vice, vice into virtue, servant into master, master into servant, idiocy into intelligence and intelligence into idiocy.

5. The Overcoming of Alienation

And now Marx moves on to the final, inevitable questions: How can economic alienation be overcome? How can man reappropriate from the products which he has created his own essence? How can man's self be regained? The entire world is distorted by alienation. Alienation infiltrates every aspect of human life—politics, law, the family, morality, religion, all are pervaded by the basic alienation within economic production. Alienation is the decisive character of human history. Man the producer, who transformed the world of nature and created the world of culture, is estranged from his creative human powers. Unlike Hegel's man, finite spirit, who in the course of history is continually progressing in consciousness of freedom, Marx's man, natural man the producer, progresses not in consciousness of freedom but of slavery. The course of human history exhibits constantly increasing alienation.

(a) **Raw Communism.** Man can overcome self-alienation and free himself from the money mania by mounting a world revolution and seizing the totality of private property from the capitalists. But human self-realization, the goal of world history, will not have been achieved by this seizure of property. Only what Marx calls raw or crude communism will exist at this point, a transitional stage before the advent of communism, and which Marx later appears to equate with aspects of the stage of the dictatorship of the proletariat.

Raw communism is obsessed with seizing all material goods from the capitalists, Marx says, and it "wants to destroy everything [such as "talent"] which is not capable of being possessed by all as private property . . . For it the sole purpose of life and existence is direct physical possession."

This type of communism does not overcome greed—instead, it universalizes greed for private property and also expresses "envy and a desire to reduce all to a common level." Raw communism calls also for equality of wages, with "the community as the universal capitalist." Moreover, says Marx, raw communism seeks not only to seize material goods as the private property of all but also to make women into "communal and common property," into "the spoil and handmaid of communal lust." Marx says with disgust that some French communist theorists take raw communism as the goal of revolution. They call for the abolition of private property into *common* property, but this, says Marx, does not abolish the money mania, but shamefully continues it. Marx views raw communism as merely another form of "the vileness of private property."

(b) **Ultimate Communism.** After the stage of raw communism has passed, there will come the time of ultimate communism, which Marx also calls "positive humanism." Man will repossess his alienated powers and the totality of objects they have created. Greed for money and private property will have been overcome. Labor itself will be abolished and in its place there will be free, joyous, productive activity. And the end of economic alienation will also mean the abolition of all other forms of man's alienation from his human essence. All the other human relationships in which man has lived a life of alienation from his human essence will be ended. There will be an end to the state, the family, law, religion, morality—all of these institutions in Marx's view are forms of human slavery to the money-God of capitalism. In these institutions man lives a debased, coerced, powerless, contemptible life, in alienation from his free, creative, productive social essence. Man will repossess, reappropriate, regain, himself from his enslavement in these institutions and will live in unity with man and nature in the communist world to come.

These were the principal ideas of the hastily written, disjointed *Economic and Philosophic Manuscripts* which Marx wrote in the summer of 1844.

Jenny

During the summer of 1844, Jenny left Paris and had returned home with her baby to Trier, where she had visited her mother and Marx's mother (both now widowed). Jenny had already entered into a lifelong pattern of ill health, in part perhaps as a response to the tensions, crises, and grinding poverty of her life with Marx. And highly intelligent as Jenny was, she accepted but was troubled by the limited possibilities for self-development which were available to women in her day. Yet she served her husband loyally and devotedly as secretary, copying his manuscripts and handling his correspondence. And she quickly became knowledgeable in the sphere of radical philosophy and politics. (A recent study of Jenny offers evidence that she is the actual author of several essays which had been credited to Marx.)

Engels

When Jenny returned to Paris in September of 1844 she discovered that Marx had established a friendship with Friedrich Engels, a friendship so stable and unwavering that it soon became one of the legendary friendships of recent times. Both Marx and Engels had much in common. They were almost the same age—Engels was two years younger; they came from upper-middle-class homes; they both wrote poetry; both of them became involved with the Young Hegelian brand of radicalism and moved on to communism and radical politics. But their intellectual styles and personal styles were very different. Marx was the speculative, creative, synthesizing type of mind, while Engels was practical and empirical. Marx was explosive, self-involved, and domineering; Engels was even-tempered and outgoing. Marx was a family man, Engels was a womanizer who never married.

Friedrich Engels was the son of a Protestant family of wealthy cotton-mill owners in the German Rhineland. His lifelong career was in his family's business, and his interests were primarily in economics. During a year of military service in Berlin, Engels came to know the radical Young Hegelians at the University of Berlin. In this stimulating atmosphere he soon became radicalized and wrote essays for radical journals such as Marx and Ruge's *German–French Annals*, and also began to gather data for what was to be his finest work, *The Condition of the Working Class in England*, a detailed empirical analysis which was a bitter indictment of the human costs of the early stages of capitalism.

At the end of his military service in Berlin, Engels had spent a year in England working at the Manchester branch of his father's firm, and on his way back to Germany he stopped off in Paris, where on August 28, 1844, he met Marx in a popular café. There they began a conversation which ran on for ten days, during which they decided to collaborate on a radical pamphlet which turned into a three-hundred-page book called *The Holy Family*. Before this book was finished, Marx was expelled from Paris and moved to Brussels. Engels soon moved into the house next door, and Marx and Engels began to work in September 1845 on a criticism of the Young Hegelians which was to become the important work entitled *The German Ideology*.

The German Ideology and the Beginning of Scientific Marxism

For an understanding of Marx, what is especially significant about *The German Ideology* of 1846 is the intellectual break between it and the *Economic and Philosophic Manuscripts of 1844*. Here in *The German Ideology*, so soon after the *1844 Manuscripts*, there appears the first formulation of the so-called mature Marxism, in which the theory of self-alienated man, which had been the central theme of the *1844 Manuscripts*, is now dismissed as a conception of the left-wing Hegelian philosophers, and presumably as having no value. Missing from *The German Ideology* are the idea of the self, the human essence and its objectification in objects produced, the working man's alienation from himself, world history as loss of self, and ultimate self-reappropriation. In place of the self and the humanistic concern with self-realization, mature Marxism in *The German Ideology* speaks about social relations, class interests, labor versus capital, proletariat versus bourgeoisie; it speaks about modes and forces of production, about an economic base and an ideological superstructure; in place of philosophic theories there are scientific laws.

The Problem of the Two Marxisms

These are all words from the familiar language of mature, conventional Marxism; they represent the impersonal, scientific vocabulary of the social sciences. Why did Marx make this fundamental shift from the humanistic focus upon the self to the impersonal, scientific focus upon economic relationships?

Are there two Marxisms, that of the *1844 Manuscripts* and that of the later scientific socialism? Or can they be reconciled?

Several suggestions can be offered as to why Marx made the dramatic switch from understanding human life in terms of alienation or conflict within the self to understanding it in terms of external economic class conflict. The taking of this step may have represented to Marx gaining the objectivity and prestige of social science for his theory. Moreover, Marx himself seems to have been strongly inclined toward factual historical explanation. Another explanation points to the influence of Engels: Engels had an impressive knowledge of the economics of industrial capitalism, and Engels's claim that once an economic system is operative it is beyond human control may have influenced Marx toward economic explanation rather than philosophical. Another explanation of the shift: Marx had become disillusioned with the idealistic and humanistic Young Hegelians, and the visible failure of this philosophic movement to interpret or to change the world may have led Marx to turn to a scientific perspective.

Other explanations for the shift are psychological in nature. The growing personal maturity of Marx may have permitted him now to identify with his father's Enlightenment ideals of scientific objectivity, to obey at last his father's constant urging that Karl give up his fanciful Young Hegelian speculations and become more prosaic, come down to earth. Another psychological explanation: In Marx's reference to *The German Ideology* as "settling accounts" with Hegelian philosophy, Marx appears to be switching to economics in order to establish his own separation and independence from the dominance over himself of Hegelian philosophy, specifically of Hegel's philosophical account of finite spirit in the *Phenomenology of Spirit*. Each of these explanations contributes to our understanding of the complexities of Marx's shift.

There remains the need to answer the second question: Are there then two Marxisms, that of the young and that of the mature Marx, and if so, can they be reconciled? We have found that the scenario of world history presented by the *Economic and Philosophic Manuscripts* is that of economic man's alienation from the products he has himself created, and that of regaining himself through a world revolution. This scenario is revised in the writings of the mature Marx. Beginning with *The German Ideology*, there is a new scenario of world history as class struggle, and its overcoming by the revolution of the proletarian class, and the ultimate advent of a classless society. The scientific scenario for the most part eliminates the idea of the self, the human essence, alienation, the drama of the loss of self, and self regained. And the new scientific scenario uses, instead, the impersonal concepts of labor, capital, and economic modes of production. Nevertheless, the scientific scenario of world history will continue to be expressive of the themes of alienation, conflict, a regaining of the human essence, and a revolution of human deliverance and salvation. Marx will use the impersonal concepts of the scientific scenario in such a way that these themes of the alienated-man scenario will not be explicitly formulated but will still be expressed. Mature Marxism thereby gains the double advantage of presenting itself with the prestige of scientific objectivity while still expressing the humanistic longings of historical man. There are not two Marxisms, then, but only one—which evolves, as we have seen, from the conflict within alienated man to the conflict of economic classes. And the secretiveness of Marx, Engels, and Soviet officialdom with regard to the *1844 Manuscripts* is clearly the result of embarrassment concerning the nonscientific, philosophical, and subjective roots of official, scientific Marxism. We turn next to the powerful works of the mature Marx.

22
THE CONFLICT OF CLASSES

In a speech Marx gave in London in 1856, he startled his audience by concluding with this story:

> To revenge the misdeeds of the ruling class, there existed in the middle ages, in Germany, a secret tribunal called the *Vehmgericht* (Secret Court). If a red cross was seen marked on a house, people knew that its owner was doomed by the 'Vehm.'

Marx ended his speech ominously:

> All the houses of Europe are now marked with the mysterious red cross. History is the judge—its executioner, the proletarian.

This dramatic historical analogy expresses Marx's vision of the destiny of capitalist society, now doomed and marked for its inexorable capital punishment at the hands of the proletariat, which is to be its executioner. This is also Marx's vision of world history and its future, a history of such great injustice and inhumanity that it can culminate only by pronouncing an inhuman judgment—the sentencing to death of the entire capitalist world.

Historical Materialism

Let us examine Marx's conception of history, which is now usually called *historical materialism*. Historical materialism is the central theory of mature Marxism. It is stated, developed, or restated at some point in all the major statements of the theory of mature Marxism—*The German Ideology* (1845–46), the *Communist Manifesto* (1848), the preface to the *Critique of Political Economy* (1859), and *Capital* (volume I, 1867).

What does Marx mean by historical materialism? Marx refers to his own version of materialism as the "new materialism" so as to show his differences from all previous usages of the word materialism. As we have noted, materialism is the name conventionally given in philosophy to any metaphysical theory which claims that reality is material.

1. Historical Materialism Versus Mechanistic Materialism

Materialism had its greatest modern historical influence in the form of mechanistic materialism, which was formulated in the seventeenth century by René Descartes (1596–1650), as we have seen, and by his British contemporary Thomas Hobbes (1588–1679). Mechanistic materialism arose in response to the rapidly developing physical sciences and claimed that reality consists of physical (material) particles in motion according to mechanical laws; these laws were scientifically verified and systematized by Newtonian mechanics (Newton's *Principles*, 1687), which explained by three laws of motion all earthly and astronomical motion. Since it holds reality to consist exclusively of matter in motion, mechanistic materialism denies that mind or consciousness is real. But Marx, who knew both ancient Greek materialism and modern European seventeenth- and eighteenth-century mechanistic materialism, had no use for any of these varieties of philosophical materialism, since the only significance they give to consciousness and human action is as the mere passive results of the motion of matter. None of these materialist theorists recognized, as Marx did, that human consciousness and purposeful human labor are not passive but are creative and productive in transforming the world of nature and, in the process, transforming man's own essence.

Marx believes that his own materialism is different from all previous types of materialism in its awareness that the reality of material objects is not independent of human beings, but is actually a reality which has been transformed by human labor in the course of history. Marx presents his own conception of historical materialism, as a radically new materialism and as a new way of understanding history.

2. Society: Economic Base

Marx's historical materialism explains the whole sweep of history by taking man's material production as the basis of history and by viewing mental production, man's intellectual and cultural life, as its effect. Marx insists that "in the whole conception of history up to the present this real basis of history" in material production has never before been understood.

What does Marx mean by his view that material production is the real basis of history and that human thought and culture are only its effect? Exactly like Hegel before him, Marx is trying to find a key which will explain the characteristics of individual human societies and also the changes which have taken place in human societies in the course of history. First, with respect to explaining the characteristics of individual human societies, Hegel had found the key in the spirit of the people, which is expressed in the culture as an organic totality of politics, religion, art, philosophy, music, and law. The organic totality of culture is an instance of Hegel's dominating theory of organicism, his view that no aspect of human life can be understood in isolation but only as part of the organic totality to which it belongs.

Marx follows Hegel in his organicism. For Marx no less than for Hegel, every individual society is an interrelated organic totality, in which no part can be understood in isolation. But for the idealist philosopher, Hegel, the explanation of the organic unity of a particular society lies in the spirit of the people, which embodies the spirit of the Absolute. In opposition to Hegel's idealism, for Marx's materalism the explanation of the organic unity of a particular society lies in its material economic foundation.

The concept of the economic structure, or economic foundation, of society is crucial to Marx's view of society and history. Marx begins with a fundamental point about the history of human production. Whereas animals satisfy their needs with what nature provides, human beings must themselves produce the food and clothing and shelter which will meet basic human needs. Thus humans must produce the means to change what nature provides into things suitable for human needs. And as soon as man's basic needs are satisfied he develops new needs, which he is also increasingly able to satisfy by his productive activity. Marx's point is that man is

thus the producer of his own expanding material life. Man
the producer is limitless in the needs he has the power to
create and in the instruments he can produce to satisfy those
needs. Human nature is expressed in this ongoing productive
activity and its creative power, by which man continually
transforms the material world and transforms himself.

In Marx's analysis, this process of man's material production consists of three components or factors. Human production is linked, first of all, to the existing conditions of production
in the particular society. By the term *conditions of production* Marx means such basic conditions affecting human production as the existing climate, the geography of the society's
physical location, the supply of raw materials, the total
population. The second component of production Marx calls
the *forces of production*, and by this term he means the
types of skills, tools, instruments, and technology as well as
the type and size of the labor supply which are available to the
society. The third and crucial component Marx calls the
relations of production and by this he means the property
relations within a society—specifically, the existing social relations according to which the society organizes its conditions
and forces of production and distributes the product among
the members of the society.

These three factors of production may easily be seen to
constitute a Hegelian dialectical triad, in which the conditions of production form the thesis, the forces of production
form the antithesis, and the relations of production form the
synthesis of the two. The "sum total" of these three components of production in any particular society Marx calls the
economic foundation or *economic substructure* of society and
sometimes the mode of production—one of the most influential concepts in mature Marxism.

3. Division of Labor

But now Marx adds what is to become the crucial concept
of his analysis of the economic foundation of society—this is
his concept of the division of labor. The division of labor (a) is
a concept which Marx found in his reading of Adam Smith
and other economic theorists, for whom it meant that labor
becomes specialized in order to perform efficiently the many
different skills required in production. (b) But for Marx, the
division of labor into specialized jobs has dehumanizing and

evil results. It enslaves the worker to a limited and restricting sphere of activity, from which there is no escape. As a result the worker is denied the fulfillment of the totality of his human creative powers, which can never develop under the division of labor. Marx makes this point in a striking way in *The German Ideology*:

> For as soon as labor is distributed, each man has a particular exclusive sphere of activity which is forced upon him and from which he cannot escape. He is a hunter, a fisherman, a shepherd, or a critical critic, and must remain so if he does not want to lose his means of livelihood.

The division of labor chains everyone—laborer, lawyer, businessman—for life to their respective confining special activities.

(c) But the division of labor is responsible for additional evils. It brings into being a slavelike state of affairs in which no one any longer controls the means by which he provides for his own subsistence, his own livelihood. (d) Moreover the relations of production take the place of human relations in social life. Individual humans no longer appear to one another as persons but as economic units within the impersonal process of the relations of production in society. (e) Furthermore the division of labor alienates the individual worker from his fellow workers, and sets one against the other, since each is working for increased personal gain and not for a social or human benefit.

(f) Most important, Marx says that "the division of labor implies . . . the division between capital and labour, and the different forms of property itself." This is the division of labor which occurs in the production process between the producers and the owners of the materials and forces of production. It leads to a situation in which what one man produces, another man appropriates the greater part of as his own private property. Where there is a division of labor between producer and owner, the product of labor no longer belongs to the one who produced it, says Marx, but to the nonproductive owner. Thus the division of labor is the source of the institution of private property, and it leads to class division between the class of owners and the class of producers. These two classes are in a master-slave relationship—the class of producers are in the position of slaves to those who own the raw materials and the mills, mines, and factories and are able to appropriate the major share of what the workers produce. Class struggle is the inevitable result of this relationship.

This is mature Marxism's analysis of the economic foundation of society and of the profound conflicts and hostilities which pervade the economic base of any civil society in which one social class owns and controls the materials and forces of production. As many Marx scholars have pointed out, here in mature Marxism the social scientific concept of division of labor has replaced alienation, early Marxism's philosophic and subjective concept, in explaining the problems of human existence.

4. Superstructure

Now Marx moves on from this account of the economic foundation to his explanation of the cultural life of a society. His claim is that the economic foundation of society conditions or determines the entire realm of culture. In a famous passage in the preface to the *Critique of Political Economy* (1859) Marx says:

> The sum total of these relations of production constitutes the economic structure of society--the real foundation on which rise legal and political superstructures and to which correspond definite forms of social consciousness. The mode of production in material life determines the general character of the social, political and spiritual processes of life.

Here we have Marx's most celebrated formulation of his view that human culture is not governed by ideas, by philosophic or older religious beliefs, as it was for Hegel; it is instead a mere superstructure determined by the existing substructure, the economic mode of production. In Marx's famous words which conclude the quotation above:

> It is not the consciousness of man that determines their existence, but on the contrary their social existence determines their consciousness.

All ideas—all human thought in the realms of religion, philosophy, politics, law, and ethics—are conditioned by the economic foundation of society, and specifically by the class division within it The dominant views in morals, politics, religion, law, philosophy, and art of any society are the ideas of the dominant economic class. Here are Marx's stinging words from *The German Ideology*:

> The ideas of the ruling class are in every epoch the ruling ideas: i.e., the class, which is the ruling material force of society, is at the same time its ruling intellectual force. The class which has the means of material production at its disposal, has control over the means of mental production . . . The ruling ideas are nothing more than the ideal expression of the dominant material relationships . . .

We have come upon one of Marx's most formidable contributions to the thinking of the modern world—it is nothing less than his claim that the dominant ideas in all areas of human thought are distortions, falsifications of the truth. They do not reflect reality as it actually is in the particular society, but rather as it appears from the viewpoint of the dominating and oppressive economic class.

Marx believes that it must be immediately obvious to anyone that what he has discovered is true—that human mental life is nothing but a superstructure which is determined by the real (economic) basis of society, and that in every society in which there is class conflict, the dominant ideas and values of culture are those which reflect the economic interests of the dominant class. He asks:

> Does it require deep intuition to comprehend that man's ideas, views, and conceptions, in one word, man's consciousness, changes with every change in the conditions of his material existence, in his social relations, and in his social life?

This conception of the cultural superstructure—religion, philosophy, law, political thought, morality, art—as falsifying and distorting the truth about social reality in the interests of a particular social class is the basis of Marx's tremendously influential concept of ideology.

5. Ideology

For Marx an ideology may be defined as a system of ideas which is determined by class conflict and which reflects and promotes the interests of the dominant class. Ideologies are thus portrayed as distorting types of consciousness, ways of perceiving the human world which falsify true reality in order to defend and promote the economic interests of a social class. All the claims to truth which philosophies, religions, legal systems, political theories, moral systems have made in history are branded by Marx as ideologies; throughout the historical epochs in which there has been a division of labor and class conflict the dominant cultural beliefs have served the dominant class.

Marx exposes the history of human culture as a history of ideology, of persuasive religions, philosophies, and legal systems which have presented themselves as universal and eternal truths for all mankind, while actually representing the ruling class and legitimating its authority and power. So, for example, the political theory of the rising French bourgeoisie called for freedom and equality, which appeared to be for the benefit of mankind, but in fact served primarily to give the bourgeois class the political power which they lacked. So also Christianity called upon the faithful to obey the word of God and to follow the life of Christ as their model; these ideals which appear to serve only spiritual ends in fact served to promote political quietism and passive obedience to all secular rulers, who are seen to be sanctified by God. All the principal ideas and values of history can be shown, according to Marx, to have functioned defensively to protect class interests, and to have functioned deceptively to keep the truth of the exploitative injustices and the dehumanizing aspects of civil society from being recognized by the exploited class.

The Marxian doctrine of ideology soon entered into the mainstream of twentieth-century thought, and produced a new way of looking at any theory by asking the questions What class interests does the theory represent? How is it distorting, twisting, misrepresenting reality in order to defend, protect, promote the interests of some identifiable social group? As one contemporary philosopher has said, since Marx developed the concept of ideology, theory has never recovered from this ideological way of looking at it, this suspicion that all philosophizing, all theorizing is less pure, less universal, less detached, less true than it presents itself as being.

The Marxian ideological way of looking at theory has pervaded twentieth-century intellectual life and has been extended to all elements of culture—novels, films, magazines, the mass media, social organizations, academia, scholarly and technical publications. All such cultural elements are now commonly regarded as potentially bound to the interests of some identifiable social group. For example, when you are solicited to subscribe to a magazine, do you not immediately wonder what social class viewpoint the magazine represents?

Is there no escape from the ideological trap? (Is Marxism, too, only an ideology, falsifying the facts of social reality on behalf of the interests of the proletariat? We shall return to this question in the following chapter.) Marx's reply is that the inexorable laws of history offer the only way to overcome the falsifying ideologies of the ruling class. In the coming, inevitable worldwide revolution waged by the proletariat, the economic foundation of world capitalism and its class conflict will be destroyed, and along with it, the cultural superstructure which it conditioned. As Marx says in the *Communist Manifesto*: "The Communist Revolution is the most radical rupture with traditional property relations: no wonder that its development involves the most radical rupture with traditional ideas."

After the totality of Western culture will have been destroyed as capitalist ideology, the proletariat will by stages move toward a classless society in which ideologies with their defenses and deceptions on behalf of a dominant class will have no function and will disappear. To understand the coming of this inevitable historical holocaust and the end of capitalist ideology, we must turn now to Marx's theory of historical change.

6. Theory of Historical Change

Marx's theory of history is constructed on the model which Hegel's philosophy of history provided. History is a meaningful single, developmental process; history is a rational structure which unfolds in time according to the laws of dialectic. But whereas for Hegel the individual units of the dialectical historical process were the great nation-states, each embodying a stage in the progressing consciousness of freedom, for

Marx, in contrast, the individual units of the dialectic of history are the economic modes of production.

Like Hegel, Marx is committed to historicism: He believes that one cannot understand economic modes of production abstractly, but only in terms of their historical situation and historical development. Hegel had accounted for the structure of society and for the dialectical process of historical change by the Cunning of Reason, the agency of the Absolute, which used human passions, the nation-state, and the world-historical individuals to change ideas, to bring finite spirits to a full consciousness of their freedom. But Marx angrily rejects Hegel's idealistic theory of historical change as the dialectical development of the idea of freedom. For Marx, ideas can explain nothing; ideas are themselves only the effect of the economic basis of society; ideas are only a superstructure which collapses as soon as the economic foundation of society begins to crack up. For Marx, only economic forces are powerful enough to bring about historical change.

How does Marx's materialist dialectic of history explain historical change? Marx explains historical change by a conflict or contradiction which takes place within the triad of the economic foundation of society and shatters it. It is the conflict that develops between the constantly growing forces of production (skills, technology, inventions) and the existing relations of production, or property relations.

7. Theory of Revolution

Marx explains this explosive conflict between the constantly developing forces of production and the static relations of production in this way: As man the creative producer works upon nature he transforms production by developing new methods or instruments or technologies of production. In the early stages of a mode of production, the relations of production and their distribution of property aid in the development of these new and improved productive skills and technology. But at a certain point in the later stages of a mode of production, the growing new forces of production come into conflict with the existing relations of production and their distribution of property. The interests of the ruling class lead them to resist change and to keep the existing property distribution unchanged, since their dominant position in society depends upon this. The ruling class, which had earlier helped to develop new technologies and forces of production, now fetters them and chains them down from developing further to prevent overproduction and thus to protect their profits and investments.

These relations of production must be "burst asunder" by a revolution to let man's productive forces continue to grow. Marx formulates this world-shattering conflict and its outcome in two famous sentences:

> From forms of development of the productive forces these relations turn into their fetters. Then comes the period of social revolution.

Why does a social revolution follow this conflict between the forces and the relations of production? It is the producer class, labor, which suffers, through unemployment, underemployment, loss of new types of work, from the fettering, the chaining of the new forces of production. It is the producer class which stands to gain by the expansion and development of productive technologies and by a change in the existing income distribution. Acting as a class, the producers break the power of the dominant class by a revolution and they themselves become for a time the new dominant class, seizing political power and generating their own mode of production, which will then determine their own forms of thought.

8. Application of Theory of Historical Change

This is Marx's theory of historical change. Let us look to see how successfully Marx applies this to the actual course of human history. Can he show that all of human history is decisively determined by the conflict between relations and forces of production, and that this leads inevitably to the violent destruction of the dominant social class by a rising social class and a change in the mode of production? Marx boastfully claims that he has discovered the dialectical laws of history which work with "iron necessity toward inevitable results," exactly as do the laws of natural science. Does Marx provide a dialectical account of actual historical change which has iron necessity?

In fact, Marx's interpretation of the actual historical process which he presents briefly in *The German Ideology*, the

Communist Manifesto, Preface to the Critique of Political Economy, and *Capital* is very sketchy for periods prior to the breakdown of feudalism and the emergence of capitalism. The iron law of contradiction between the static relations and the expanding forces of production he actually shows only in one case, the destruction of feudalism by the rising capitalist class. Marx postulated that there must have been a first stage of history in which the mode of production was a primitive type of communism, in which there was no division of labor, no separate spheres of owners and workers, no separation of mental production from physical labor, but only spontaneous work and communal ownership of all property.

After this first primitive communist stage, all the succeeding stages of history are of modes of production which are based upon a division of labor, ownership of the major materials and instrumentalities of production by a ruling class, class conflict, and an ideological superstructure reflecting the interests of the ruling class. These modes of production which have followed primitive communism are: the Asiatic, the ancient Greek and Roman, the European feudal, and the modern capitalist.

The Asiatic mode of production is characterized only as one of oriental despotism, large irrigation projects, and the absence of private property in land. The classical Greek and Roman societies developed a mode of production in which there was private as well as communal property and in which the producing class consisted largely of slaves. Marx's description of the European feudal mode of production is likewise sketched only in broad outlines.

The feudal mode of production was based upon land ownership with serfs chained to the land as the producing class, but there began to develop in the towns individual craftsmen who joined in guilds. The feudal nobility, who formed the dominant class, created a culture of philosophy, religion, art, and morality which was determined by their own economic interests. But the feudal economic base was destroyed when the new, expanding forces of machine production burst through the feudal relations of production, which had become fetters upon the new developments. The rising new class of the bourgeoisie, the capitalist class, became revolutionary, and transformed the feudal mode of production into capitalism, seized political power and created their own ideological superstructure.

But capitalism is doomed by the same conflict which enabled the rising capitalist class to overthrow feudalism. The constantly expanding forces of production, technologies, skills, inventions are running into conflict with the capitalist relations of production and its system of private ownership of the materials and means of production and of private profit from the production process. The rapid development of trade and technology, the growth of population have brought about an industrial revolution of machine production of goods and have created an international capitalist class. But the powerful, dominant international capitalist class has given rise to its opposing class, the internationally linked class of the proletariat. "What the bourgeoisie produces above all," says Marx, "is its own gravediggers." The proletariat is now becoming conscious through their economic suffering that the capitalist class is an obstacle to expanding forces of production—that the capitalists are fearful of overproduction, shrinkage of world markets, and declining profits.

9. Prediction of Revolution and the World to Come

At this point in his theory of historical change Marx breaks decisively with Hegel and predicts the proletarian revolution. Hegel viewed dialectic as a method of interpretation of conceptual change. Such a method can only interpret the past, in which the patterns of change become visible. For Hegel, then, wisdom about history comes too late to predict or change things, the owl of Minerva takes flight only when darkness is descending on a society; and the spirit of the people defines and limits the prospects for change, in any case. Not so for Marx, the revolutionary. Now for the first time, according to Marx, we can understand the dialectic of universal history, future as well as past. The dialectical conflict between the relations of production and the constantly expanding forces of production provides a necessary iron law of history, by which we can predict the future. The next development of history is inevitable: The proletariat will become revolutionary, they will burst through the capitalist relations of production, they will destroy the economic base of capitalism just as the rising capitalist class once destroyed the economic foundation of feudalism. The proletariat will introduce a communist mode of production, they will seize political power and erect a dictatorship of the proletariat which will be an interim stage before the final coming of the classless society. In this communist world to come there will be no private property, no division of labor, no conflict of classes, no exploitation of human beings, no alienation in the enslaving institutions of the family, morality, laws, the state, no ideology.

It is interesting to observe that the triadic model of Hegel's dialectic of history has been retained in Marx's dialectic: from primitive communism as thesis, to its antithesis in the long history of the division of labor and exploitation, and finally, a return in the synthesis to the advanced industrial communism of the future. Can you not hear the thrilling, chilling call of the last words of the *Communist Manifesto* of 1848 heard around the world for over a hundred years:

> The communists disdain to conceal their views and aims. They openly declare that their ends can be attained only by the forcible overthrow of all existing social conditions. Let the ruling classes tremble at a communist revolution. The proletarians have nothing to lose but their chains. They have a world to win. Workers of the world unite!

23

THE WORLD TO COME

"A specter is haunting Europe—the specter of communism."
These opening words of the *Communist Manifesto* present
the image of communism as a terrifying phantom, a fearful
apparition haunting Europe. The *Manifesto* ends with the
threat that the phantom is about to come forth, the apparition
is about to materialize, a communist revolution is about to
break out and it will overthrow by force the economic
foundations, the governments, and the social and cultural
existence of the capitalist countries of the world.

Manifesto of the Communist Party

Although both Marx and Engels are credited with writing
the *Communist Manifesto*, in fact Engels wrote only a first
draft in the uninspired form of twenty-five questions and
answers about communism. It is Marx who rewrote the whole
document, and it is a work of genius, the product of his
stupendous intellectual, imaginative, and political creative
powers. The British philosopher and historian of ideas Isaiah
Berlin has rightly said of the *Manifesto* that "No other modern political movement or cause can claim to have produced
anything comparable with it in eloquence or power." The
Manifesto swiftly, deftly, explains all the human past as the
history of class struggles which have taken place according to
necessary dialectical laws. This explanation of the human past
leads to the *Manifesto*'s diagnosis of the present period as a
fateful time, the time of the last great class struggle of history,
between the capitalists and the proletariat, which is the last
enslaved class remaining to be freed.

1. The Rise of the Bourgeoisie

The capitalist class is the most revolutionary class which has existed up to the present time, says Marx. The rising bourgeoisie (the owners of the forces of production) completely revolutionized economic production, and with this they have now dominated the world and established the world market, which in turn accelerated the growth of industrial production. The roots of the bourgeois revolution lay in the discoveries of America and the route around the cape to the Far East, and the new colonies and trade which these opened up. These developments, says Marx, "gave to commerce, to navigation, to industry an impulse never before known and thereby, to the [bourgeois] revolutionary element in the tottering feudal society, a rapid development."

From the time of its origins the revolutionary character of the bourgeois class has distinguished it from all previous classes in history. It is a class which "cannot exist without constantly revolutionizing the instruments of production and thereby the relations of production . . ." As a result, the achievements of the bourgeoisie have been tremendous, the *Manifesto* acknowledges:

> It has been the first to show what man's activity can bring about. It has accomplished wonders far surpassing Egyptian pyramids, Roman aqueducts and Gothic cathedrals.

2. The Bourgeois Revolution in Production

The capitalist mode of production has revolutionized all the instruments and technologies of production; it has dislodged all old forms of industrial production by new industries which draw their materials from the remote corners of the earth; and it has brought technologically developed industry to every part of the world. The bourgeoisie have created in every country of the world new needs for the expanding products of industry, and they have created world markets for the vast outpouring of the new technology. Not only have the bourgeoisie broken down national barriers in material production and produced an international industry and trade, they have broken down national isolation in intellectual production, as well, and have produced international exchange of ideas and rapid expansion in the intellectual world. In Marx's words in the *Manifesto*:

> The bourgeoisie, during its rule of scarce one hundred years, has created more massive and more colossal productive forces than have all the preceding generations together. Subjection of Nature's forces to man, machinery, application of chemistry to industry and agriculture, steam-navigation, railways, electric telegraphs, clearing of whole continents for cultivation, canalization of rivers, whole populations conjured out of the ground—what earlier century had even a presentiment that such productive forces slumbered in the lap of social labor?

3. The Bourgeois Destruction of the Feudal Substructure and Superstructure

But these great revolutionary material achievements which destroyed the economic substructure of feudalism, destroyed as well the feudal superstructure of ideas and values. The bourgeoisie, these "leaders of whole industrial armies," have changed the face of human life by destroying the traditional hierarchical and patriarchal human relationships of feudalism, leaving no other relationship "between man and man than naked self-interest, than callous 'cash payment.'" Capitalism has destroyed the feudal aristocratic culture, it has drowned its religious piety, its chivalry, its sentimentalism in the "icy water of egotistical calculation."

4. Bourgeois Change and the Dissolution of Ideals

As the bourgeois epoch superseded feudalism, the bourgeoisie's ceaseless revolutionary changes in the machinery and technology of production are reflected in the spirit of restless change in the bourgeoisie's own superstructure—in the bourgeois age in history all traditions, ideals, veils, masks, illusions with regard to human life are constantly being swept away in the ceaseless change. Capitalism says Marx, has stripped the halo from every profession which had been previously honored—physician, lawyer, priest, poet, scientist—and made their practitioners into wage laborers. The family, too, has had its sentimental veil torn away, and family relations have now become money relations. And capitalism has turned the personal value of a human being into its worth as a mere commodity in the market. Nothing in human life has any value other than monetary value in the capitalist economy. "All that is solid melts into air, all that is holy is profaned. . ."

5. Dialectic of Capitalism: Its Achievements Lead to Its Own Destruction

The rapid growth of capitalist industry and communications has created enormous cities and subjected the country to the rule of the urban centers. Capitalism has crowded laborers into the city factories, as slaves of the machine, receiving wages in exchange for work. It has destroyed the lower level of the middle class, the small businessman, shopkeeper, skilled craftsman, farmer—all of these, says Marx, "sink gradually into the proletariat" because they lack the capital and the technology to compete with big capital. (Have you watched the owner of the small, independent corner grocery store of your neighborhood "sink gradually into the proletariat" through his or her inability to compete with the food chains?) In the bourgeois era, society is thus rapidly splitting into two hostile camps, the proletariat and the bourgeoisie.

On the positive side the *Manifesto* concedes that the unprecedented progress of the capitalist forces of production have developed the material world and have vastly improved the material conditions of life which are necessary for the full future development of human beings. But capitalism is subject to dialectic, and to the dialectical principle of negation. Ironically, the vast revolutionary energies and achievements of the bourgeoisie in developing the material world will lead to its own destruction. Just as the feudal relations of production became fetters on the forces of production and were destroyed ("burst asunder") by the rising bourgeoisie with their new productive forces, so the capitalist relations of production have become fetters on the expanding forces of production and will be destroyed by the rising proletariat class.

In the *Manifesto*, Marx says of modern bourgeois society:

> A society which has conjured up such gigantic means
> of production and of exchange, is like the sorceror
> who is no longer able to control the powers of the
> nether world whom he has called up by his spells.

Capitalism, like the magician, is unable to control all the productive forces it has brought about, all the new and proliferating instruments, machinery, and technologies. The repeated result is a crisis of overproduction of goods.

Here in the crises of overproduction capitalist relations of production come into conflict with the constantly expanding forces of production and flow of products. The bourgeois relations of production, which always demanded constant improvement and expansion of productive forces, now become fetters on their further expansion, since they threaten bourgeois profit and property relations. But the slowing down of production means general economic depression and, specifically, unemployment and suffering for the proletariat, which has been increasing greatly in numbers as a result of the productive energies of the bourgeoisie. Under these conditions, the swollen ranks of the proletariat become united and revolutionary against the bourgeoisie. Marx notes this irony at the end of Part I of the *Manifesto*:

> What the bourgeoisie, therefore, produces, above all, is its own gravediggers. Its fall and the victory of the proletariat are equally inevitable.

But the dialectical process is now moving rapidly. The contradiction between the expanding forces of production and the capitalist relations of production is sharpening and the conditions of proletariat existence are worsening. No power on earth can prevent the advent and the outcome of this last class struggle, in which the capitalist class is doomed to extinction. It has performed its necessary role in the long history of man's transformation of nature and human nature. Now the proletariat class is to be liberated in accordance with the workings of the inexorable dialectical laws of history, and with this liberation of the last remaining slave class of history all mankind will be free. The future belongs to the proletariat: It is theirs because the dialectical laws of history make it inevitable.

Marx calls on the proletariat to liberate themselves, by uniting as a class in each country under the control of the Communist Party. The Communist Party will lead them in a revolutionary action which will overthrow the bourgeois economic mode of production and its cultural superstructure, and will win for them the world which the bourgeoisie has developed.

6. Communist Manifesto

Problem (a) Why Fight for the Inevitable Revolution? But here Marx's theory runs into serious difficulties and confusions which it has never been able to overcome. Is it not illogical on Marx's part to incite the proletariat to action to bring about a revolution that is necessary and inevitable according to the dialectical laws of history? Why should the Communist Party whip the proletariat into action to bring about a revolution which is necessarily coming, so inexorable in its approach that no force on earth can stop it? Why fight for the inevitable?

Communist Manifesto

Problem (b) Truth or Propaganda? A second and related problem will now immediately occur to you: Is the *Manifesto* to be considered as truth or as propaganda? Is Marx's historical materialism an objectively true theory in its account of what has taken place in human societies and in historical change? Or is it instead propaganda for a political end, in this case, the manipulation of the passions of the proletariat to take revolutionary action in order to overthrow capitalism? If Marx is in fact offering not an objectively true theory of history but propaganda which will galvanize the proletariat into revolutionary action, then we can explain Marx's strange inconsistency in urging the proletariat to fight for what is inevitably going to happen as the result of necessary economic laws. Could this be Marx's thinking: that if his theory convinces the proletariat that a revolution against the capitalists is inevitable, and that its success is guaranteed by necessary economic laws of history, they will believe that this is true and they will act on this belief and so make it come true? Then if the proletariat fights for the revolution believing Marx's propaganda that a successful revolution is inevitable, by their action they will have made it inevitable.

This is in fact Marx's own viewpoint, which he has let us in on over and over again—and most clearly in his *Theses on Feuerbach* (1845). Did he not say in the second of his *Theses on Feuerbach:*

> II. The question whether objective truth can be attributed to human thinking is not a question of theory, but is a practical question. In practice men must prove the truth . . .

This is to say that a theory about society or history is true, not because it provides an objective or tested analysis, but rather, the theory is true if it works: If it leads people to believe in it and act upon it, this will make the theory true. "Praxis" is the Marxian term for this concept of the use of theory to move the masses and by this means to change social conditions.

But what view of truth is this? It is a view of truth which is called radical pragmatism. Pragmatism is a theory of truth which holds that a statement is true if it "works" in the sense of making tested, verified predictions. Radical pragmatism is, by contrast, the view that any statement may be called true if it "works" in the sense of bringing about the desired goals of those who believe it. Whereas for pragmatism a statement is true insofar as it is objectively tested and verified, for radical pragmatism a statement is true insofar as one makes it true by believing in it. Did not Marx make this very point in the eleventh and last of the *Theses on Feuerbach*?

> XI. The philosophers have only *interpreted* the world
> in various ways; the point, however, is to *change* it.

But how do you change the world? For Marx, the only way to change the world is to destroy its economic foundation. Action to destroy the economic substructure can be achieved by appealing to the passions of an oppressed group with a theory of revolution which is appropriate to their existing conditions, and which will inspire them to act.

But Marx's theory of history thus loses its claim to objective truth and is revealed either as propaganda or as radical pragmatism, a theory which denies that there is objective truth and claims instead that any statement must be regarded as true if people believe it and if it "works" for them in practice. The obvious danger in radical pragmatism is that a false theory, a theory which is merely propagandistic and manipulative, and based on myths of aggression or illusions of self-glorification or omnipotence, may "work" in getting people to believe it and to take action to achieve an emotionally compelling political goal. Should we call such a theory true because it works? How long or how well do such theories work when people act on them, and at what human cost of blood and destruction, and with what disillusioning outcome?

Communist Manifesto

Problem (c) Science? Philosophy? Ideology? A third problem also shows itself at this point: What kind of thinking does the *Communist Manifesto* represent? Is the *Manifesto* science? Or is it philosophy? Clearly it is not science—the use in the *Manifesto* of the metaphysical, Hegelian laws of dialectic and the call for revolutionary action both disqualify the *Manifesto* from being considered to be a scientific statement. Nor is it philosophy as philosophy is usually understood, since if we compare the *Manifesto* with Hegel's *Lectures on the Philosophy of History*, for example, we see a profound difference: The *Manifesto* does not merely interpret or *explain* history, it inspires, incites to action, it is a revolutionary guide to action for the future, addressed not to mankind but to a particular group in society, the industrial proletariat. The *Manifesto* intertwines its explanation of history as a necessary dialectical development of modes of production with explicitly inspirational political ideas and values on behalf of the proletariat.

But then has not Marx fallen into the trap of ideology which he himself set—and which he used to entrap and condemn all past theories? Is not his own theory an ideology, a system of ideas conditioned by class conflict at a particular historical stage, a distorting type of consciousness reflecting the interests of the proletariat against the bourgeoisie? And is he not, like all ideologists, seeking to promote the interests of a specific social group? And if the *Manifesto* is so clearly ideological, a system of ideas which provides a way of seeing all history as serving to bring about a great apocalyptic victory of labor over the bourgeoisie, then must we not be suspicious of all the rest of Marx's writing as well? It was Marx himself who taught us to be ideologically suspicious of theory. As for Marx's own position on this matter, he held that all thought is ideological, being conditioned by social class and historical period, and therefore offering only a distorting, falsifying picture of human reality; but he also claimed that his own views, although conditioned by social class and history, escape the ideological trap and are objectively true. But Marx does not explain how this is possible.

The Revolutions of 1848

Marx wrote the *Communist Manifesto* in great haste for the Communist League of London, which published it as a propaganda tract in what appeared to be a swelling movement toward an imminent revolution. The *Manifesto* so clearly crystallized Marx's thought that a quarter of a century later Marx and Engels wrote that "The general principles expounded in the document are on the whole as correct today as ever." But although at the time of its publication the *Manifesto* was hardly noticed by anyone, Marx and Engels had correctly sensed the coming of revolution. Before the *Manifesto* had rolled off the printing presses in February 1848, the revolutions of 1848 had begun. Within a few weeks the king of France was overthrown, and the revolutions of 1848 began to explode in one country after another, in Switzerland, Italy, France, Germany, Hungary.

But all of these wildly hopeful revolutionary outbursts, in which middle class and working class joined together, were defeated and in ruins before the year 1848 came to an end. Within a month of the publication of the *Manifesto*, on March 3, 1848, Marx was given notice, signed by the king of Belgium, to leave the country in twenty-four hours. Then followed his desperate trail of revolutionary activities and exiles which we have seen—ending with the Marxes' escape to London in 1849. The revolutions of 1848 had been a disaster, but Marx's bitter disappointment made him all the firmer in his conviction that no alliance between the proletariat and elements of the bourgeoisie would work, that only a revolutionary destruction of the bourgeoisie by the proletariat, led and organized by the Communist Party at the historically ripe moment, would be successful, and that it could maintain its victory only by a dictatorship which "will abolish immediately all the old institutions."

Marx: The London Years

Now came the long years of exile in London, where Marx was to live for over half his life, from 1849 to his death in 1883. The first years in London were the worst. Marx and Jenny and their children lived in two or three rooms in a poor, crowded, run-down section of London. Jenny and Marx were heartbroken by the deaths of three of their children in the years between 1850 and 1856. They lived at the edge of starvation, hounded by creditors for nonpayment of bills, and repeatedly evicted for nonpayment of rent. Here was the beginning of the chronic illnesses that plagued both Marx and

Jenny, a period which Jenny later described as "years of great hardship, continued acute privations . . . and real misery." This is the way the house in Dean Street was described by a visitor:

> Marx lives in one of the worst and cheapest neighborhoods in London. He occupies two rooms. There is not one clean or decent piece of furniture in either room, everything is broken, tattered and torn, with thick dust over everything . . . but all these things do not in the least embarrass Marx or his wife. You are received in the most friendly way . . . and presently a clever and interesting conversation arises.

Marx's principal source of income during these years was from the newspaper articles which he wrote as a foreign correspondent for the *New York Daily Tribune*, which paid Marx two pounds, approximately ten dollars, for each published article. The rest of the finances of the Marx family came from small inheritances and from the support which Engels and other friends were able to provide. The Marxes endured almost twenty years of humiliating poverty in London before they were rescued when Engels received an increased income from his family's Manchester mills, and gave them an annual income on which they could live in comfort.

In London in the 1850's Marx found himself isolated, without many friends, and exiled from the stimulating atmosphere of the European continent. Marx's own personality, aggressive, domineering, contemptuous, isolated him still further. England was in no revolutionary mood—its own recent revolutionary movement, Chartism, had just been defeated, and it was just then at the beginning stages of an economic upswing, rapid growth in industry and trade which took the ground from under all revolutionary movements. The 1850's in England after the radicalism of the 1840's have been compared to the 1970's in the United States after the radicalism of the 1960's—a new, sober mood, antiradical and conservative, swept England then as it recently swept the United States. The economic upswing that began in England in the 1850's continued until the end of the nineteenth century, two decades after the death of Marx.

It is one of the ironies and frustrations of the life of Marx the revolutionary that he lived the second half of his life in a time of increasing economic prosperity and the continuing improvement of the standard of living of the working class. More and more, the unionized industrial workers of England saw themselves gaining better wages and working conditions, and the appeal of radical propaganda slipped away.

Yet Marx continued his ties with the Communist League and with the revolutionary remnant of other exiles like himself. His days were spent in the reading room of the British Museum, the great public library of London, where he did his endless reading and his writing, at the same desk every day, from nine in the morning until seven at night, when the museum closed; then home to a long night of further study and writing. Here in the reading room of the British Museum all of Marx's subsequent works were written, and most notably what he regarded as his greatest work, *Capital (Das Kapital)*, the first volume of which appeared in 1867 and which had been fifteen years in the writing. But of the three volumes of *Capital* which Marx projected, this was the only one which he completed to the point of publication.

Capital

It was in *Capital*, and in an earlier draft of it, *Foundations (Grundrisse) of the Critique of Political Economy* (1857–58), usually called the *Grundrisse*, that Marx developed and fleshed out the economic concepts which *The German Ideology* and the *Communist Manifesto* had already outlined. Here in *Capital* is the most complete statement of mature Marxism, of the scientific scenario of world history and specifically the scenario of the present historical moment as a class struggle produced by the division of labor, and propelled by the iron laws of economic dialectics.

What major elements does *Capital* add? In addition to contributing an overview of the entire capitalist mode of production and its historical genesis, worked out in great economic detail, *Capital* provides a systematic analysis of the famous concepts of the labor theory of value, surplus value, the theory of exploitation, and the polarization of classes. These are economic concepts of the scientific scenario of world history, and we will look at them very briefly.

1. Capitalism: Definition

First of all, what is capitalism? Marx develops, but does not ever change, his fundamental view that a capitalistic mode of production is one in which a few humans own and control the major forces or means of production as their private property and they employ as workers those who have nothing to sell but their own labor power.

2. Labor Theory of Value

The commodities that the workers produce, Marx argues, have a value equivalent to the amount of labor needed to produce them. Here Marx is borrowing from the British economists Adam Smith and David Ricardo their labor theory of value and their principle that the value of anything is determined by how much labor has been required to produce it. The labor theory of value has been strenuously objected to by recent economists—who have pointed out, for example, that the value of commodities is determined by supply and demand, rather than by the amount of labor needed to produce them; and also that it is not the *amount* of labor that determines the value of a commodity, but the degree of skill of the labor that is required to produce it. Moreover, Marx deliberately excludes the labor of the capitalist himself from the calculation of the value of commodities.

3. Surplus Value

Directly related to Marx's labor theory of value is his crucial concept of surplus value. This is the concept which explains both the profit of the capitalist and the exploitation of the worker. Marx defines surplus value as the difference between the value of the wages received by the worker and the value of what he has produced. That difference, the difference between what the capitalist must pay the worker as wages and what the capitalist can sell the worker's product for, makes up the capitalist's profit.

4. Theory of Exploitation

And here we have the key argument in Marx's theory of exploitation: The working class is forced into the position of selling on the market its labor power for the going rate of wages; the capitalist exploits the worker by selling the goods the worker produces for more money than he pays to the worker in wages. Capitalism is a system of exploitation, Marx argues, in which capitalists profiteer by paying the workers only the existing rate of wages in place of the full market value of the products the workers produce. However, Marx's theory of exploitation has also been seriously criticized. Marx has excluded from his theory of exploitation the capitalists' costs to produce the commodities, the relation between these costs and the costs of labor, and the wages which the capitalist must pay himself in order to live. Only by excluding all these factors, and by denying the fact of capitalist labor, can Marx make the strange claim that surplus value—the difference between wages and the market value of commodities—is exploitation.

5. Capitalist Competition and Crises of Overproduction

But Marx points to another element that enters this picture of the capitalist mode of production. Capitalists are in relentless competition with one another in selling their goods, and this involves them in competing with one another by investing their capital in the ceaseless flow of new machinery in order to increase production. But this investment of capital in more and more costly new machinery eats into the profit that the capitalist makes from the surplus value that his workers produce. Moreover, all of the capitalist's competitors have also introduced the new machinery and have increased their output of commodities as well. The result is that larger and larger amounts of commodities are now produced and thrown on the market, profits decline, and a crisis of overproduction occurs, in which the capitalist tries to salvage his business by cutting wages, or by reducing production. But cutting wages or cutting production mean poverty and unemployment for the proletariat—and as these intensify, they lead to proletarian revolution. Here we have once more come upon the contradiction between the forces and the relations of production, which leads to revolution.

6. Polarization of Classes

And last, *Capital* offers its theory of the polarization of society into two economic classes. Marx believes that the capitalist class will shrink in size as capitalist competition increases, and the more successful capitalists undersell others, and buy them out or drive them out of business. But while the capitalist class is decreasing in size, the proletariat class is rapidly growing in numbers because whole classes are gradually sinking into the proletariat: shopkeepers, skilled craftsmen, farmers. These classes are disappearing, says Marx, because these small producers cannot compete with the capital, mass production, and underselling of the capitalist businesses that are entering every field of production. Not only are the small grocers, retailers, and craftsmen being destroyed by the competition from capitalism and being ground down into the work force of the proletariat, but so also is the small farmer unable to afford the machinery for agricultural production that can compete with capitalistic, large scale farming. And in this way capitalism reduces society to two main classes, one growing richer as the other grows poorer. But under the impact of repeated crises, unemployment, poverty, and starvation, the enlarged proletariat class will come to see their real situation as it is, and they will become revolutionary— they will seize control of the state, and they will seize ownership and control of the forces of production from the capitalists.

The Communist World to Come

1. **First Stage: The Dictatorship of the Proletariat.** And now we must ask: What follows the revolution? What is the shape of the communist world to come? The communist world of the future, Marx tells us, will come in two stages. First there will be the stage which Marx called the dictatorship of the proletariat, in which the proletariat will establish a government with absolute, dictatorial power in order to guarantee a successful transition from capitalism to communism. Although for Marx the state is an instrument of class oppression, the proletariat itself must become a ruling class, using all the means of coercion—the state, army, courts, police—in order to destroy any remnant of capitalist power. As Marx says in the *Manifesto:*

> The proletariat will use its political supremacy to wrest, by degrees, all capital from the bourgeoisie, to centralize all instruments of production in the hands of the State, i.e., of the proletariat organized as the ruling class; and to increase the total of productive forces as rapidly as possible. Of course, in the

beginning, this cannot be effected except by means
of despotic inroads on the right of property . . .

The dictatorship of the proletariat will be a stage of "crude,"
"raw," materialistic communism, still focused upon material
possession and continuing the same money mania and greed
as in capitalist society. All private property will be seized
from their individual owners and nationalized, and thus made
into the equal property of all. Work will not be abolished—
instead, everyone will be a worker and will become an em-
ployee of the state, with a strict equalization of wages. The
old envy and jealousy which the proletariat had for the
bourgeoisie will still be visible in the insistence that no one
receive more wages or possess more goods than anyone else;
"universal envy" lies behind the egalitarian ideal of crude
communism. The dictatorship of the proletariat will be driven
to reduce the standard of living for all to a common low level
and will rationalize this poverty as virtuous self-denial for the
good of the revolution. Crude communism will have no use
for the "whole world of culture and civilization" and will fall
to the level of the "unnatural simplicity" of the poor who
place no value on culture because they have no knowledge of
it. In this stage of communism, the state itself is a single,
all-powerful capitalist, for whom everyone works equally, by
whom everyone is paid equally, and by whom everyone's life
is equally controlled. But have you not already recognized
that Marx's description of the dictatorship of the proletariat
and its crude communism is in many respects a remarkably
accurate picture of present-day Soviet Russia? Has Soviet
Communism since the Communist Revolution of 1917 been
in the stage of the dictatorship of the proletariat, the dictatorship of the Communist Party and of Lenin, Stalin, and their
successors? Is the crude communism of the dictatorship of the
proletariat the ultimate stage which communism can reach?

2. Second Stage: Ultimate Communism. About the second
stage of communism Marx was understandably reluctant to be
drawn into providing specific detail. In this world to come, the
evils and shortcomings of all the dialectical stages of history
will be overcome. In fully developed communism, man will not
be dominated by the material world, but will recognize it as his
own product, and he will henceforth dominate it. His alienation from the work of his own hands will be overcome and
he will relate to the whole world of material objects as the

product of human labor, as human objects which he can value and enjoy without the need to possess them as his private property. Mankind will be liberated from being controlled by the economic circumstances of life. Rather than wages strictly for work performed, the principle of ultimate communism will be: "From each according to his ability, to each according to his need." Man will be liberated from the division of labor and from competition with his fellow man, since with communism,

> society regulates the general production and thus makes it possible for me to do one thing today and another tomorrow, to hunt in the morning, to fish in the afternoon, raise cattle in the evening, criticise after dinner, just as I have a mind, without becoming hunter, fisherman, shepherd or critic.

But how will this life of free, spontaneous activity be possible in the advanced industrial mass society of communism? Marx does not tell us, nor can he, since it is not possible. But the picture he is trying to give us is clear—it is a fantasy of a world to come, the end and the fulfillment of historical time, in which man will exist in harmony and peace with himself, with other human beings, and with nature, and in which his life will be free from arduous toil, free from want or care, and his days will be spent in joyous creative activity. Here in this vision of the communist world to come, Marx has once more returned to Hegel, and to a Hegelian vision of history as a great triad, from a thesis of original primitive communism, to the antithesis of the long centuries of toil under economic systems of private ownership of the means of production—Asiatic, classical, feudal, and capitalist—finally to return in the synthesis to a new, advanced, industrial communism. But Marx is also expressing something deeper than philosophy. His vision (like Hegel's) is strongly reminiscent of religious themes, of the Judeo-Christian conception of man's fall from paradise, and the long years of labor in exile, with the hope of paradise to be regained in the future world. His vision reminds us of the Book of Daniel and its symbolism of great battles waged by the saints of God against a series of corrupt wordly empires. And his vision also powerfully reminds us of the Revelations of John in the New Testament, which speak of a great destruction, after which there arises "a new heaven and a new earth," a new and totally redeemed man in a new and purified Jerusalem. Here Marx has moved beyond propaganda and ideology, beyond philosophy and science—to express (yet to leave unspoken) a religious vision and prophecy of the liberation and purification of mankind. Logically, however, the mature Marx, secular, materialistic, and atheistic, has no claim to these religious visions.

Evaluation

But however powerful are the unspoken, evocative religious and moral currents in Marx's thought, his specific predictions with regard to capitalism and communism we now recognize as seriously mistaken. Contrary to Marx's predictions, capitalism has not been destroyed. Marx vastly underestimated the powers of capitalism to reform itself. The unrestrained capitalism of Marx's time no longer exists; it has long since incorporated many of the demands of the *Communist Manifesto* and has moved in the direction of the welfare state. And with respect to communism, contrary to Marx's prediction, it has not arisen in highly developed capitalist countries out of the conflict between their relations and forces of production; instead, it has sprung up in feudal, underdeveloped countries like Russia and China. Nevertheless, the contributions of Marx to intellectual and political culture stand and must be recognized: his concepts of the economic foundations of society, social classes, ideology, capitalism and its culture, and the influence of social, economic, and historical conditions on human life and thought. Marx must be regarded as a major political economist and as a founder of sociology, and of intellectual history. His thought has transformed the intellectual culture and the political existence of the twentieth century.

Marx died in 1883. Over his grave a great sculptured head of Karl Marx looks out over London and beyond to a world in which, in his name, Marxist Communism has spread from Russia to her satellite countries, to China, to Indochina, to Africa, and now to Latin America. What is the power of Marxism? It is the power of an ideology for the oppressed which explains the history of the world as economic exploitation and shows the way to liberation by a necessary revolution of great aggressive destruction and the seizure of the oppressors' world and wealth, after which all of mankind will be redeemed and restored to paradise. A specter is haunting Europe, Asia, Africa, and Latin America. A specter is haunting the world.

SUGGESTIONS FOR FURTHER READING
PART FIVE: MARX

Works of Marx: Collected Texts:

Marx and Engels: Basic Writings on Politics and Philosophy. Edited by Lewis S. Feuer. Garden City, New York: Doubleday-Anchor Books, 1959. Adapted text for television series.

Karl Marx: Selected Writings in Sociology and Social Philosophy. Edited by T. Bottomore and M. Rubel. Hammondsworth: Penguin, 1965.

Karl Marx: Early Writings. Edited by T. Bottomore. N.Y.: McGraw-Hill, 1964.

Marx-Engels Reader. Edited by Robert Tucker. New York: W. W. Norton, 1972, 1978.

Writings of the Young Marx on Philosophy and Society. Edited by Lloyd D. Easton and Kurt H. Guddat. Garden City, New York: Doubleday-Anchor Books, 1967.

Karl Marx: Selected Writings. Edited by Daniel McLellan. Oxford: Oxford University Press, 1977.

Critical Studies:

Avineri, Shlomo. *The Social and Political Thought of Karl Marx*. Cambridge: Cambridge University Press, 1968.

Berlin, Isaiah. *Karl Marx: His Life and Work*. London: Oxford University Press, 1929.

Blumenberg, Werner. *Karl Marx: An Illustrated Biography*. Translated by Douglas Scott. London: New Left Books, 1972.

Brazill, William J. *The Young Hegelians*. New Haven: Yale University Press, 1970.

Dupré, Louis. *The Philosophical Foundations of Marxism*. New York: Harcourt, Brace and World, 1966.

Hook, Sidney. *From Hegel to Marx*, 2nd ed. Ann Arbor: Michigan University Press, 1962 (1950).

Kolakowski, Leszek. *Main Currents of Marxism: Its Rise, Growth and Dissolution*. 3 vols. London: Oxford University Press, 1978.

Leff, Gordon. *The Tyranny of Concepts: A Critique of Marxism*. London: Merlin Press, 1961.

Lichtheim, George. *Marxism, An Historical and Critical Study*. New York: Frederick A. Praeger, 2nd ed., 1965 (1961).

Marcus, Steven. *Engels, Manchester and the Working Class*. New York, 1971.

Marcuse, Herbert. *Reason and Revolution: Hegel and the Rise of Social Theory*. Boston: Beacon Press, 1960 (1941).

Mayer, Gustav. *Friedrich Engels: A Biography*. New York: Knopf, 1936.

McLellan, David. *The Young Hegelians and Karl Marx*. New York: F. A. Praeger, 1969.

McLellan, David. *Karl Marx: His Life and Thought*. New York: Harper and Row, 1973.

McMurty, John M. *The Structure of Marx's World View*. Princeton: Princeton University Press, 1978.

Plamenatz, John. *German Marxism and Russian Communism*. New York: Harper and Row, 1965 (1954).

Rotenstreich, N. *Basic Problems of Marx's Philosophy*. Indianapolis: Indiana University Press, 1965.

Rubel, M. and Mamale, M. *Marx Without Myth: A Chronological Study of His Life and Works*. New York: Harper and Row, 1975.

Seigel, Jerrold. *Marx's Fate: The Shape of a Life*. Princeton: Princeton University Press, 1978.

Tucker, Robert C. *Philosophy and Myth in Karl Marx*. New York: Cambridge University Press, 1961.

Tucker, Robert C. *The Marxian Revolutionary Idea*. New York: W. W. Norton, 1969.

PART SIX
SARTRE

24

MY EXISTENCE IS ABSURD

Forerunners of Existentialism

What is the meaning of existentialism? Its earliest themes dwell on the human individual as conscious subject, the sense of the meaninglessness and nothingness of human existence, and the anxiety and depression which pervade each human life.

Søren Kierkegaard

Anxiety pervades the works of Søren Kierkegaard (1813–1855), one of the forerunners of existentialism, who lived out his short life in Denmark in the first half of the nineteenth century:

> I stick my finger into existence—it smells of nothing. Where am I? What is this thing called the world? Who is it who has lured me into the thing, and now leaves me here? Who am I? How did I come into the world? Why was I not consulted?

For Kierkegaard, the meaninglessness of my existence fills me with anxiety and with despair, a sense of hopelessness and deep depression. The life of modern man is lived in despair, he says, and there is no one who does not have anxiety in the face of his existence. A year before he died, Kierkegaard summed up the agony of the beginning and end of life:

> Hear the cry of the . . . mother at the hour of giving birth, see the struggle of the dying at the last moment:

and say then whether that which begins and that which ends like this can be designed for pleasure.

Human life is not designed for pleasure, Kierkegaard tells us, yet in the time given to each of us for our own existence, we strive for happiness in order to escape anxiety and the deep, hopeless depression which is despair. But there is no escape—no matter how pleasurable and comfortable we make our lives in order to hide from the truth. For the truth is, Kierkegaard insists, that all of us live in anxiety and despair. This is the universal human condition. We suffer from anxiety even when we are not aware of it, and even when there is nothing to fear, nothing in the objective world to feel anxious about. This is because at bottom, says Kierkegaard, our anxiety is not objective at all, it is subjective anxiety—it is the universal fear of something that is nothing, it is the fear of the nothingness of human existence.

In one of his early works, *Either/Or, A Fragment of Life* (1843), Kierkegaard tells the story of an ordinary young man who lives for pleasure, but although he experiences the various forms of enjoyment, sensual and aesthetic, which are available to him, he keeps falling into depression. But he pulls himself together, and decides to make something of himself, to give up the hedonic life for the life of duty and responsibility. He gets ahead in his career, he makes friends, and he soon acquires a wife and family, and social status in his community. But then the old forgotten depression comes back, "more dreadful than ever."

This man has made something of himself, says Kierkegaard, but he is a stranger to himself. He does not know that the way to overcome despair is to choose despair, to sink so deep into despair that you give up all the satisfactions and comforts of life, you lose all commitment to family, friends, community, you surrender reason and all belief in the truth of science and philosophy, and all moral principles. When all these are lost, with nothing left, you will be in total crisis, at the edge of the abyss, and you will be prepared for faith in God, you will choose God, and make the leap of faith to God. For Kierkegaard only absolute faith and the leap to God can overcome the meaninglessness of your existence; only the restoration of orthodox Christianity, and the surrender of reason, can overcome the sense of anxiety and hopeless despair for the solitary individuals of the modern world.

Friedrich Nietzsche

But for Friedrich Wilhelm Nietzsche (1844–1900), who is usually regarded, along with Kierkegaard, as a forerunner of existentialism, Kierkegaard's religious solution to the problem of the meaninglessness of modern life is totally unacceptable. It is unacceptable first of all because it represents the human individual as weak, powerless, even cowardly. It strips you, the individual person, of all human strengths, so that in the depths of despair, your total loss of faith in yourself propels you into absolute faith in God to solve your problems in living.

But Nietzsche would find Kierkegaard's religious solution unacceptable for a far more fundamental reason. Kierkegaard can be seen as the champion of the orthodox Christianity of the past, trying to solve the problems of modern man by turning the clock back to an older, Christian absolutism which requires the total surrender of the self to God. But this is now impossible, says Nietzsche, because God is dead. The concept of the death of God is perhaps the best known of all of Nietzsche's many compelling contributions to philosophy. In his book *The Joyful Wisdom* (1882) Nietzsche presents the shocking story of the madman who on a bright morning lighted a lantern and ran to a marketplace looking for God and then announced to the jeering crowd that God is dead.

> *We have killed him*—you and I! We are all his murderers . . . Whither are we moving now? . . . Do we not now wander through an endless nothingness? Does not empty space breathe upon us? Has it not become colder? Does not night come on continually, darker and darker?

By the concept of the death of God Nietzsche does not mean that God, who is defined as an eternal being, can nevertheless die; to say that would of course be illogical. As Parmenides's unchanging one exemplified, that which is eternal does not come into being or pass out of being. By the death of God Nietzsche means the death of our belief in God. It is our belief in God that is dead; it has finally succumbed to multiple injuries, including the savage beating it received from the empiricists led by David Hume, and continued by his successors.

But if we have lost our belief in God, have we not lost the foundation of all our truth and morality? Did not even Descartes, the supremely independent rationalist, have to call upon God to guarantee that his clear and distinct ideas were true, and so made Him the foundation of all truth? Nietzsche is famous for the claim that the crisis of the modern world is that, in the loss of our belief in God, we have lost the foundation of our truth and value. However, says Nietzsche, although man has lost the belief in God, this will enable him to lose his childlike dependency upon God. Human beings must now find the courage themselves to become gods in a world without God. The greatest need of civilization now is to develop a new type of individual, supermen who will be hard, strong, and courageous, and who will be intellectually and morally independent. They will break the stone slabs on which the old Judeo-Christian moral laws are inscribed, the old life-denying moral laws to which the masses are still enslaved. The only morality of the supermen will be to affirm life: to be powerful, creative, joyous, and free.

Kierkegaard counsels us to sink into despair so that we can make the leap of faith to God; Nietzsche counsels us to become gods, joyous, hard, independent supermen. And Nietzsche tells us why he rejects a philosophy of despair: He is afraid that it would destroy him. To Nietzsche philosophies are not merely intellectual games; philosophies have psychological effects, the power to enhance and strengthen your life, and even health, or to weaken and destroy you. And Nietzsche says that he created his philosophy of the strong, life-affirming superman

> out of my will to be in good health, out of my will to live . . . self-preservation forbade me to practice a philosophy of wretchedness and discouragement.

Influence of Kierkegaard and Nietzsche on Twentieth-Century Existentialism

How did the profoundly divergent philosophies of Kierkegaard and Nietzsche prepare the way in the nineteenth century for the existentialist philosophy of the twentieth century? First, both Kierkegaard and Nietzsche, like Marx in the middle years of the nineteenth century, perceived the Western world to be approaching a time of crisis. All three, Marx,

Kierkegaard, and Nietzsche, address their philosophies to the coming crisis—they offer a diagnosis of their own time, and a prescription for what ought to be done.

Second, both Kierkegaard and Nietzsche reject any diagnosis of the crisis which treats the problem as a collective problem, one of social classes in conflict, as Marx did, or a problem of nation-states in conflict, as Hegel did. For Kierkegaard and Nietzsche, and for the existentialism which follows them, the crisis of the modern world is a problem concerning the individual, the human self. The consciousness of the human subject is the only key to the diagnosis and possible cure of the problems of the modern era. Existentialism maintains that in philosophies such as those of Hegel and Marx, with their exclusive sociological concern with social groups, social institutions, and the social system, the individual human self disappears, it is swallowed up by these social collectivities.

Third, Kierkegaard and Nietzsche prepare the way for existentialism by rejecting, as will existentialism, all past philosophies as having shown no interest in philosophizing about the existence of the human individual and no interest in the effect of philosophy upon his consciousness.

And last, Kierkegaard and Nietzsche share an intense and subtle concern with psychology, with mental states, and especially with neurotic and psychotic states of the individual. Like all the existentialists who follow them, they must be called psychologizing philosophers: They are subtle and sometimes masterful interpreters of the psychology of the human subject, who is the focus of all their concerns.

The Social Genesis of Existentialism

Existentialism developed in the twentieth century within Germany and France, not as a direct result of any specific set of circumstances or causes, but as a deeply experienced response to the crumbling of many structures in the Western world which had previously been regarded as stable. The eruption of World War I finally destroyed the belief in the continuing progress of civilization toward truth and freedom, peace and prosperity which the Enlightenment had fostered and which had survived until the outbreak of this war. With World War I, there also came the collapse of the seemingly stable balance of power among the great nations. Before

World War I ended, there crumbled away the empire of all the Russias, and there soon began the disintegration and collapse of the far-flung British Empire, and the French, Belgian, and Dutch empires.

The Communist Revolution of 1917 in Russia shattered the confidence in political stability, the confidence that the revolutionary era was over. Economic structures also were perceived to crumble as the Great Depression of the late 1920's and 1930's rolled from Europe to the United States, raising doubts about the enduring truth of classical economics and the survival of capitalism. Science itself began to surrender its claims to certitude. And philosophies of all types were crumbling away. Inroads into the territory of philosophy were made by the advance of scientific investigation. Moreover, philosophy was under continuous attack from the empiricists and from the growing scientific temper of the twentieth century. And increasingly philosophies were charged with historical relativity, or even worse, with functioning as ideologies for special group interests.

With the weakening or collapse of so many external structures of authority—authoritative economic, political, and intellectual structures—all these structures began to lose their appearance of legitimacy, and their constraints upon the individual were soon felt to be intolerable. Rejecting as illegitimate the external authority of government, the economic system, and the scientific and intellectual world, the human individual could only retreat to the internal authority of the self. This was the logic with which existentialists turned to the human self as the true center of philosophy and as the sole legitimating authority.

In its revolt against existing political and intellectual structures, existentialism was following the path that nineteenth-century German Romanticism had taken in centering philosophy upon the human spirit, the conscious subject, as the only legitimate authority, over a hundred years earlier. The Romantics, as we saw, used the Kantian turn in philosophy to give themselves a shelter in the self from the coercions of German political authority and from the intellectual constraints of the scientific Enlightenment, which they despised.

Existentialism: The Philosophic Standpoint Which Gives Priority to Existence Over Essence

What then is existentialism? There exists now a widely accepted definition of existentialism. It is that existentialism is the philosophic standpoint which gives priority to existence over essence. What is meant by this is that existentialism gives primacy or priority in significance to existence, in the sense of my existence as a conscious subject, rather than to any essence which may be assigned to me, any definition of me, any explanation of me by science or philosophy or religions or politics. Existentialism affirms the ultimate significance, the primacy of my existence as this flickering point of consciousness of myself and of objects of which I am aware, my existence as this conscious being against all efforts to define me, to reduce me to a Platonic essence, or to a Cartesian mental substance, or to a Hegelian carrier of the spirit of my culture, or to a scientific neurological mechanism, or to a social security number. Whereas classical and modern rationalism have regarded rational essences or self-evident ideas as having primacy over individual things, which gain their reality or meaning only through the essence or idea, existentialism claims the primacy of individual existence. Whereas rationalism claims that the individual is knowable only by means of essences or concepts, existentialism denies that an individual existence can be comprehended by the concept or essence or by any conceptual system.

Essentialism is the name sometimes given by existentialists to the mode of thinking which it opposes, which gives priority to essence rather than to existence. Essentialism may be defined as the mode of thought in which individual existence is secondary to the concept, essence, or system which defines or explains it. Rationalism and systematization in the history of philosophy, quantification in the sciences, and abstraction in social and political theory are perceived as dominating forms of essentialism in the contemporary world.

Existentialism by contrast cries out that man in his concrete existence as a conscious being has been neglected by philosophy, science, political organizations, and religion. What of the existence, as conscious beings, of the college freshman, the dry cleaner's deliveryman, the U.S. congresswoman, the night nurse, the drunkard poet? They are accounted for in the abstract, intellectualizing systems and discourses of philosophy, the hypotheses and statistics of the sciences, the tabulations, surveys and policies of federal bureaucracies and of commercial, religious, and political organizations. But existentialism says that their *existence* as conscious beings is the significant, unseen, and neglected problem.

In the contemporary world, the philosophic voice of existentialism is being raised in many areas of civic life, art and learning. It is a voice which calls upon artists, scientists, philosophers, politicians, theologians, administrators, physical and mental health practitioners to be concerned with the perceptions and feelings of the human subject, as against the standardized ways in which these fields analyze, predict, and program human beings as if they were nonconscious things. Existentialism may thus be seen as the champion and defender of the human spirit against the oppressive features of mass society, science, philosophy, politics, and organized religion. Its concerns are narrow. Existentialism focuses solely upon human existence: It has no philosophy of nature, of science, or of history, it is a philosophy of concrete human existence, a philosophy of man as conscious being.

Approach to Man as Conscious Being. But by what method can one approach concrete human existence? If you try to discover human existence by sense perception, by empirical observation, you will find that this is a trap, because sense perception does not lead you to the conscious subject—it leads to empiricism, to external observation, to data gathering and experimentation. This is the scientific trap. But trying to approach concrete conscious existence by reason turns out to be another trap: The route of reason leads to rationalism, to essence, definitions, and logical argumentation. This is the old philosophic trap.

What then is the path to conscious existence? You can take the path of crisis or of communion. A crisis is a happening which suddenly removes you from the ordinary routines of your life. In a situation of crisis you cannot react with your everyday, habitual responses and you are thrown back upon yourself, as when you find yourself in a blackout in Times Square in New York City—or in a blackout in your room when you awaken in the night and sense someone standing close to your bed. At such moments of crisis you become aware of your conscious existence with sudden, excruciating clarity. The other path to the existence of the conscious subject is by way of communion, by way of the self-discovery which occurs at the moment of becoming one with a group. Self-discovery can happen at a time of ecstatic religious unity, as in some Easter services, or of ecstatic political unity, such as was produced by the civil rights march on Selma, Alabama, or by the march on the Pentagon.

But how, then, can you present the discovery of the self in the experience of crisis or communion? One effective way is by describing the crisis or communion as they were experienced—and this has led existentialists to use the power of creative literature to express and describe, and has produced a great outpouring of existentialist short stories, novels, plays, biographies, and autobiographies. The other way is to philosophize or theorize, but to do so not with the traditional concepts of philosophy but with strange new themes, such as nausea, anxiety, thrownness, nothingness, and authenticity.

Themes of Existentialism

Let us turn then to the themes of existentialism, the themes which may be said to characterize the mode of thought of those who would call themselves existentialists. (1) First, there is the basic existentialist standpoint, which we have already considered: It is the standpoint that *existence precedes essence*, has primacy over essence. Man is a conscious subject, rather than a thing to be predicted or manipulated; he exists as a conscious being, and not in accordance with any definition, essence, generalization, or system. Existentialism says I am nothing else but my own conscious existence.

(2) A second existentialist theme is that of *anxiety*, or the sense of *anguish*, a generalized uneasiness, a fear or dread which is not directed to any specific object. Anguish is the dread of the nothingness of human existence. This theme is as old as Kierkegaard within existentialism; it is the claim that anguish is the underlying, all-pervasive, universal condition of human existence. Existentialism agrees with certain streams of thought in Judaism and Christianity which see human existence as fallen, and human life as lived in suffering and sin, guilt and anxiety. This dark and foreboding picture of human life leads existentialists to reject ideas such as happiness,

enlightenment optimism, a sense of well-being, the serenity of Stoicism, since these can only reflect a superficial understanding of life, or a naïve and foolish way of denying the despairing, tragic aspect of human existence.

(3) A third existentialist theme is that of absurdity. Granted, says the existentialist, I am my own existence, but this existence is absurd. To exist as a human being is inexplicable, and wholly absurd. Each of us is simply here, thrown into this time and place—but why now? Why here? Kierkegaard asked. For no reason, without necessary connection, only contingently, and so my life is an absurd contingent fact. Expressive of absurdity are these words of Blaise Pascal, (1623–62), a French mathematician and philosopher of Descartes's time, who was also an early forerunner of existentialism. Pascal says:

> When I consider the short duration of my life, swallowed up in the eternity before and after, the little space I fill, and even can see, engulfed in the infinite immensity of space of which I am ignorant, and which knows me not, I am frightened, and am astonished at being here rather than there, why now rather than then.

(4) A fourth theme which pervades existentialism is that of *nothingness* or the void. If no essences define me, and if, then, as an existentialist, I reject all of the philosophies, sciences, political theories, and religions which fail to reflect my existence as conscious being and attempt to impose a specific essentialist structure upon me and my world, then there is nothing that structures my world. I have followed Kierkegaard's lead. I have stripped myself of all unacceptable structure, the structures of knowledge, moral value, and human relationship, and I stand in anguish at the edge of the abyss. I am my own existence, but my existence is a nothingness. I live then without anything to structure my being and my world, and I am looking into emptiness and the void, hovering over the abyss in fear and trembling and living the life of dread.

(5) Related to the theme of nothingness is the existentialist theme of *death*. Nothingness, in the form of death, which is my final nothingness, hangs over me like a sword of Damocles

at each moment of my life. I am filled with anxiety at times when I permit myself to be aware of this. At those moments, says Martin Heidegger (1889–1976), the most influential of the German existentialist philosophers, the whole of my being seems to drift away into nothing. The unaware person tries to live as if death is not actual, he tries to escape its reality. But Heidegger says that my death is my most authentic, significant moment, my personal potentiality, which I alone must suffer. And if I take death into my life, acknowledge it, and face it squarely, I will free myself from the anxiety of death and the pettiness of life—and only then will I be free to become myself. But here the French existentialist Jean-Paul Sartre begs to differ. What is death, he asks? Death is my total nonexistence. Death is as absurd as birth—it is no ultimate, authentic moment of my life, it is nothing but the wiping out of my existence as conscious being. Death is only another witness to the absurdity of human existence.

(6) *Alienation* or estrangement is a sixth theme which characterizes existentialism. Alienation is a theme which Hegel opened up for the modern world on many levels and in many subtle forms. Thus the Absolute is estranged from itself as it exists only in the development of finite spirit in historical time. But finite spirit also lives in alienation from its true consciousness of its own freedom, which it gains only slowly in the dialectic of history. There is also the alienation that exists in society: the alienation of individual human beings who pursue their own desires in estrangement from the actual institutional workings of their society, which are controlled by the Cunning of Reason. Alienated from the social system, they do not know that their desires are system-determined and system-determining. And there is the alienation of those who do not identify with the institutions of their own society, who find their society empty and meaningless. And there is also for Hegel the alienation which develops in civil society between the small class of the wealthy and the growing discontent of the large class of impoverished workers. The most profound alienation of all in Hegel's thought is the alienation or estrangement between my consciousness and its objects, in which I am aware of the otherness of the object and seek in a variety of ways to overcome its alienation by mastering it, by bringing it back into myself in some way.

As for Marx, we have seen that in the split between the

two Marxisms, the young Marx is focused upon the concept of economic alienation. As a worker I am alienated from myself, from the product of my labor, from the money-worshipping society, from all those social institutions—family, morality, law, government—which coerce me into the service of the money-God and keep me from realizing my human creative potentiality. In mature Marxism, alienation is expressed through the division of labor and its many ramifications.

How, then, do existentialists use the concept of alienation? Apart from my own conscious being, all else, they say, is otherness, from which I am estranged. We are hemmed in by a world of things which are opaque to us and which we cannot understand. Moreover, science itself has alienated us from nature, by its outpouring of highly specialized and mathematicized concepts, laws, theories, and technologies which are unintelligible to the nonspecialist and layman; these products of science now stand between us and nature. And the Industrial Revolution has alienated the worker from the product of his own labor, and has made him into a mechanical component in the productive system, as Marx has taught us.

We are also estranged, say the existentialists, from human institutions—bureaucratized government on the federal, state, and local levels, national political parties, giant business corporations, national religious organizations—all of these appear to be vast, impersonal sources of power which have a life of their own. As individuals we neither feel that we are part of them nor can we understand their workings. We live in alienation from our own institutions. Moreover, say the existentialists, we are shut out of history. We no longer have a sense of having roots in a meaningful past nor do we see ourselves as moving toward a meaningful future. As a result, we do not belong to the past, to the present, or to the future.

And lastly, and perhaps most painfully, the existentialists point out that all of our personal human relations are poisoned by feelings of alienation from any "other." Alienation and hostility arise within the family between parents and children, between the husband and the wife, between the children. Alienation affects all social and work relations, and most cruelly, alienation dominates the relationship of love.

These are the disturbing, provocative themes which can be found in contemporary existentialism. But now we must ask: If this is indeed the human condition, if this is a true picture of the world in which the human subject absurdly finds himself, how is it possible to go on living in it? Is there no exit from this anxiety and despair, this nothingness and absurdity, this fixation upon alienation, this hovering on the edge of the abyss? Is there any existentialist who can tell us how to live in such an absurd and hopeless world? Is there an existentialist ethics, a moral philosophy to tell us what is good, what can be said to be right or wrong, in such a meaningless world? To pursue these questions we will turn next to Paris and to the existentialism of Jean-Paul Sartre.

25

NAUSEA

The Words: Sartre's Early Life

I hated my childhood and everything that remains from it.

—Jean-Paul Sartre
The Words (Les Mots), 1964.

This is the bitter statement of the French existentialist philosopher Jean-Paul Sartre in the autobiography entitled *The Words* which he wrote when he was in his fifties and which describes his life up to the age of twelve in the year 1917. Sartre's autobiography is a biting, aggressive attack on his parents, his grandparents, and the bourgeois society into which they and he were born. Sartre denounces all of these from his viewpoint as an existentialist and also from his more recent Marxist position. It is doubtful whether any other intellectual or artist has ever written such a hostile description of his own childhood.

What was this childhood like—the childhood of the most influential representative of twentieth-century existentialist philosophy? Sartre was born in Paris in 1905. His father, a second lieutenant in the French Navy, had contracted an intestinal disease while on duty in French Indochina and died when Jean-Paul was only fifteen months old. Sartre says of his mother, Anne-Marie, that "without money or a profession," she had no option but to return with her infant son to the home of her parents, Charles and Louise (Guillemin) Schweitzer.

The Schweitzer family had their roots in Alsace, which at this time had become part of Germany. The son of Charles

335

Schweitzer's younger brother was the famous Protestant theologian and medical missionary to Africa, Albert Schweitzer.
Jean-Paul grew up in a household dominated by his grandfather,
Charles Schweitzer, who was a language teacher, and author
of a German-language textbook used in all French secondary
schools. Although Charles Schweitzer had been ready for
retirement, he went back to teaching in order to support
Anne-Marie and her son, and in return, Anne-Marie became,
in effect, an unpaid housekeeper for her parents, and was
treated as a child again, totally subordinated to their instruc-
tions and wishes. Sartre writes in his autobiography that

> she was not refused pocket money; they simply
> forgot to give her any. When her former friends,
> most of them married, invited her to dinner, she had
> to seek permission well in advance, and promise that
> she would be back before ten . . . invitations be-
> came less frequent.

Anne-Marie's son promised, as small boys do, that when he
grew up he would marry her and deliver her from her hard
life of bondage. But most important Sartre is making the
point that as a young child he was already perceiving in his
grandparents' treatment of his mother the exploitation practiced
by the bourgeoisie and the hypocrisy with which they concealed this exploitation and selfishness with high-sounding
liberal principles.

Sartre's autobiography is especially savage in exposing the
bourgeois, hypocritical pretentiousness of Charles Schweitzer.
He was a tall, handsome bearded man, whom Sartre describes as "looking so much like God the Father that he was
often taken for him." But although he ruled the household by
playing the role of a stern, God-like patriarch, Charles
Schweitzer soon became completely devoted to his grandson
and kept him at home until he was ten years old, supplying
him with tutors rather than submit him to the inferior standards and less gifted students of the public schools. Here
again, Sartre discovers bourgeois hypocrisy. Concealed behind the grandfather's high-sounding, noble intentions of treating the small boy as a child prodigy who deserved superior
private education, there were profoundly selfish motives: The
presence of his precocious young grandchild in the household
served Charles Schweitzer's vanity and alleviated his fear of

his own death. And so it was for selfish reasons, hypocritically concealed by the bourgeois ideal of superior education, that the young Jean-Paul Sartre was kept at home for five years beyond the normal time for entering school, received a poor education from irregular tutoring, was cut off from association with children of his own age, and was kept a prisoner, sequestered in the apartment on the top floor of 1 Rue le Goff in the Latin Quarter of Paris. Even his physical well-being was neglected by his grandparents. Sartre tells us that they failed to notice, and to get medical help for, a growth in his right eye which was to give him a walleyed, cross-eyed look for which he was famous and eventually brought about the loss of sight in his eye. This was another example of bourgeois hypocrisy, with its lofty claims to humane concern for others, concealing actual indifference and selfishness.

There was, however, one great advantage from being kept imprisoned in the huge sixth-floor apartment on Rue le Goff. The small boy lived in a world of books, the books which overflowed his grandfather's study, the lending-library books of his grandmother, the books from which Anne-Marie read him stories. "I began my life," Sartre says, "as I shall no doubt end it: amidst books." The words in these books became the world which he longed to possess and manipulate, and by the age of three he was "wild with joy": he had taught himself how to read. Responding to the flatteries of his grandfather, the small boy became a little monster, cleverly playing the role of child prodigy and soon taking the next step—he began to write his own books.

But it was Charles Schweitzer who pronounced the words which decided Sartre's fate, his lifelong vocation, his original project which became the project to which he gave his entire life—the project of writing. Sartre in *The Words* recalls this occasion when his grandfather became deadly serious, and talking "man-to-man" to the seven-year-old boy sitting on his lap, said that it was "understood of course that the boy would be a writer," but that he should be warned that literature did not fill a man's belly. This was the moment, hearing these words, when Sartre made his own original choice of what he would become. And as we shall see, Sartre's existentialist psychoanalysis claims that a similar event occurs in the development of all personalities—a moment when the young child chooses the original project which will direct the rest of his life.

But Charles Schweitzer is given no credit even for this, for his role in Sartre's choice of his vocation, his life's project as a writer. Instead, Sartre condemns the idolization of words and of the solitary individual's creative imagination which his grandfather had fostered in him, and he scorns the view of literature which he acquired from his grandfather, the view that literature can provide man's salvation. At the end of *The Words*, Sartre says he has finally smashed that illusion to bits. Literature, he now sees, "doesn't have anything or anyone." Literature is justifiable only as a mirror which gives us a picture of ourselves. He claims now that his writing career was a fake, the bourgeois artist's grandiose pretense that he is God, a savior of mankind from its wretchedness.

> Fake to the marrow of my bones and hoodwinked, I
> joyfully wrote about an unhappy state.

For the last ten years, Sartre writes, "I've been a man who's been waking up, cured of a long, bitter-sweet madness." He had awakened to a legitimate role at last, that of the politically engaged Marxist intellectual, committed to collective action. But by now the old faking, the long-standing imposture has eaten its way into his character, and he knows that he can never be cured of it. "I still write," he says. "What can I do?"

Sartre's later education was provided by some of the finest schools in France, culminating in the Ecole Normale Supérieure, a graduate school for the training of college and university professors, the most intellectual and exclusive of all French graduate schools. After Sartre's graduation, there came the competitive examinations for college teachers of philosophy, which Sartre failed in his first attempt. But in his second attempt, Sartre took first place; the second place was taken by Simone de Beauvoir. They had met shortly before their exams in the spring of 1929 and they were lovers and friends, and partners in philosophy and politics, since then for over fifty years until Sartre's death—while always defiantly rejecting "bourgeois marriage" for themselves. Simone de Beauvoir is an important contributor in her own right to French existentialism and political thought—short stories and novels; important studies of women (*The Second Sex*) and of aging (*The Coming of Age*); and many philosophical essays. Most of what we know about Sartre's intellectual development comes from her own autobiography, which is now in four volumes.

They both began teaching philosophy in colleges—Sartre in the northern port city of Le Havre, de Beauvoir in the Mediterranean port of Marseilles. In 1933 and 1934 Sartre managed to be released from teaching—which he regarded as imprisonment, both for himself and his students—by gaining a scholarship to the French Institute in Berlin, where Hitler had just a few months before become chancellor of Germany. Neither Sartre nor de Beauvoir at this time had any knowledge of politics, nor any interest in it. Both were passionately opposed to the entire bourgeois world, and were dedicated to destroying it, but this they intended to achieve by literature, not by politics.

It was during this year of the establishment of Nazi totalitarianism in Germany that Sartre lived as a politically naïve and unaware student in Berlin and established his philosophical ties to the existentialist and phenomenological currents of philosophy then developing in the heady and dangerous atmosphere of Germany prior to the outbreak of the Second World War. These contemporary German philosophies joined with older philosophical traditions to be the resources with which the bold and subtle imagination of Jean-Paul Sartre worked.

Sartre's Sources

Sartre was already thinking of constructing a serious philosophy which would provide guidance for life in the contemporary world by explaining the nature of the world and by expressing the human condition, what it is to live as a human being. To which philosophers of the past will he turn for support, and from which will he turn away? He turns away from all empiricism because empiricism limits knowledge to sense perception and denies that philosophy can provide guidance for human life. Sartre also turns away from Cartesian rationalistic deduction because as formal reasoning it can neither explain the world nor express what it is like to live as a human being.

Who then are the philosophers to whom Sartre turns? Who are the philosophers who are Sartre's powerful resources in the history of philosophy and from whom the richness of

Sartre's philosophy is derived? First of all, Sartre's philosophy derives from *Descartes* who, as the first and greatest of all modern French philosophers, remains a formidable influence on all French philosophers who have followed him. The influence of Descartes on Sartre is clear—it is Descartes's philosophical subjectivism of the Cogito; it is his insistence that philosophy begins with the absolute certainty of my consciousness of myself as a thinking being.

A second resource upon which Sartre drew was the exciting new philosophies of Edmund Husserl (1859–1938) and Martin Heidegger (1889–1976) which Sartre studied intensively during his year at the French Institute in Berlin. *Edmund Husserl*, a professor of philosophy at the German University of Freiburg from 1916 to 1929, had originally been a mathematician and physicist. Like Descartes, who had also been a mathematician and physicist, Husserl tried to achieve for philosophy the certainty of mathematics. Husserl himself pointed out his similarity to Descartes: That they both attempted to find certainty for philosophy, and both found it in the Cogito, in the indubitable "I think." But at this point Husserl breaks with Descartes. Husserl denies that Descartes's Cogito established the certainty of a thinking substance, but only the certainty of consciousness. Moreover, says Husserl, consciousness is always of something, it is intentional, it is directed toward an object. The foundation on which knowledge rests is thus not the certainty of Descartes's thinking substance, which is separate from the objects in the world, whose existence and nature remain questionable. Husserl's foundation is consciousness and its intended objects; consciousness is not separate from the world but joined to it by intentionality. Sartre takes from Husserl's complex and formal philosophy of consciousness only these elements: the denial of Descartes's thinking substance; the view of consciousness as intentional, a consciousness of something other than itself which it intends, to which it refers; and thus the conception of consciousness as relating to the world through its intentionality.

A major resource for Sartre was the philosophy of the German existentialist *Martin Heidegger*, Husserl's most brilliant student, his assistant, and the successor to his professorship at the University of Freiburg. During 1933 and 1934 when Sartre was engaged in studying Husserl and Heidegger in Berlin, Husserl was being subjected, as a Jew, to humiliating

harassments by the Nazis; while Heidegger, having been
elevated by the Nazis to the position of National Socialist
rector of the University of Freiburg, extolled for some time
the philosophic significance of the Nazi movement and repudi-
ated the philosophy of Husserl. From Heidegger Sartre takes
the concepts of conscious existence as being-in-the world; the
basis distinction between the world of conscious being and
the world of things; the concept of being thrown absurdly
into existence; anguish; nothingness; the distinction between
authentic and inauthentic existence; the distinction between
facticity and transcendence; and the concept of man as making himself by having projects into the future.

In addition to using Descartes's subjectivism, Husserl's
analysis of consciousness, and Heidegger's existentialist concepts and themes, Sartre also finds valuable philosophic materials in the dialectical philosophers Hegel and Marx ("redis-
covered" in France during the 1930's and 1940's), and also in
the two major forerunners of existentialism, Kierkegaard and
Nietzsche. From *Hegel*, Sartre takes the distinction between
the object as it is "in itself" and the object as it is "for" a
subject; he takes also the concepts of the struggle unto death
and the need for recognition; master-slave; the unhappy
consciousness; and alienation. Sartre also takes the concept of
the dialectic of being and nothingness and the principle of
negation (but without synthesis) from Hegel. From *Marx*,
Sartre professes in 1960 to take his entire system, with some
revisions, and to incorporate existentialism within it. From
Kierkegaard, Sartre takes the emphasis upon individual conscious existence, instead of upon Hegelian essence; and the
distinction between objective fear and existential anguish.
And from *Nietzsche* he takes the concept of the death of God.
Drawn from strong historical currents of Continental European thought, these concepts and themes converge, yet remain identifiable, in Sartre's writing. Sartre's originality lies
in his reinterpreting, revising, and reworking these materials
into a bold new integration which became the center of
French existentialism, in the form of philosophic treatises,
novels, plays, and literary and political essays.

Nausea

One of the first products of Sartre's philosophical reflections was a novel, the philosophical novel with the title *Melancholia*, which Sartre's publishers changed to *Nausea*. Why a novel? Sartre is already finding his way toward a philosophy of existentialism which will use literature—novels, plays, short stories—to grasp concrete human existence, the human condition, the lived life, as distinct from the overlay of essences by which philosophy, science, and theology conceal, distort, and explain away my existence as a conscious being. As Simone de Beauvoir says, a philosopher who makes subjectivity, concrete human existence, central to his viewpoint is bound to become a literary artist, so as to convey the human condition in its full concrete reality. And she adds that "only the novel allows a writer to evoke the original gushing forth of existence." Sartre had been working on the novel *Nausea* for almost a decade, ever since his years in graduate school.

When *Nausea* was published in France in 1938 it was an immediate and huge success. In the following years, the principal character of the novel *Nausea*, Antoine Roquentin, has become a familiar figure in Western culture; he has become a recognized, staple part of our literary world, as have other literary figures like Shakespeare's Hamlet and Lady Macbeth, or Dickens's Oliver Twist and David Copperfield, or James Joyce's Bloom and Molly, or Kafka's Gregor Samsa and his characters whose names begin with the letter K. References to Roquentin's melancholy concrete existence, his depression and nausea, and his crisis of anguish occur in the fields of psychology, literature, and philosophy, and wherever the consciousness of modern man is examined.

Who is Roquentin and how has Sartre's most philosophical novel made him into a personality so real that he lives among us outside the novel itself? What are the moods and thoughts of this fictional character and how have they come to be perceived as expressing moods and thoughts which are characteristic of contemporary human life?

The novel is shrewdly presented by Sartre as Roquentin's own diary, a first-person account of his daily life, written only for himself, and thus as a direct and truthful statement of one man's subjectivity, his concrete, here-and-now existence. The scene is a port city in France which has the name of Bouville (literally Mudville). It is clearly a description of the actual port of Le Havre, the main port of France, the ugly commercial city in which Sartre lived in cheap hotels near the railroad station while he was teaching philosophy there.

In many ways Roquentin is similar to Sartre; he is close to thirty years old, he comes from a middle-class background and is living on a small inherited income, he is an intellectual and a writer. But Roquentin is represented as being tall, rather than short like Sartre, with red hair, and as having no family ties, no job, no friends. Although he had traveled widely, and had various adventures, he is now somewhat bored and world weary. But he is a free man, free to do what he wants, and he has come to Bouville to do research in the archives of the city library for a biography that he is writing, on the life of an eighteenth-century adventurer and diplomat, the Marquis de Rollebon.

But from the very first page we know that something is wrong. The first page of the diary mentions that a change has come over him, and we soon learn that the whole point of keeping a diary is to determine what this change is and what it means for his life. "The best thing," he says in the diary, "would be to write down events from day to day." And above all, he says, "I must tell how I see this table, this street, the people, my packet of tobacco, since *those* are the things which have changed." With these words, Sartre has taken us into the psychology of a mind that is aware that it is slipping away from its normal states, aware that his world is beginning to take on a strange new appearance, and yet sufficiently in touch with reality to want to observe his own mental states, to keep a day-to-day account of the changes in his perceptions and thoughts.

When did it all begin? Roquentin remembers that on Saturday some children were playing on the waterfront, and like them, he says, "I wanted to throw a pebble into the sea." But when he picked up a pebble, he says, "I saw something which disgusted me." He is confronted by the stone's bare existence and he is overwhelmed by a feeling of nausea. Day after day he lives with depression, nausea, feelings of vertigo, and mounting anxiety. The nausea is becoming constant, it even comes over him in the local café, which had been a place of refuge, well-lighted, and full of people. But by now, Roquentin says, the nausea is not inside me—I am the one who is within *it*.

Existence and Essence: Absurdity and Nausea

As the days go by, Roquentin discovers that there is no rational order in existence, things have no essences which define what they are. There are no fixed laws of nature according to which things relate to other things in the universe. All rationality, all sciences, all lawfulness are of our own making; they have nothing to do with the bare existence that they name. Existence is purposeless, meaningless, shapeless, and contingent. "Things are divorced from their names," says Roquentin, and when we face them in their bare existence, they are simply there, loathsome and fearful, and we experience them with nausea.

Roquentin is riding on a streetcar in Bouville. "This thing I'm sitting on, leaning my hand on, is called a seat." He says,

> They made it purposely for people to sit on, they took leather, springs and cloth, they went to work with the idea of making a seat and when they finished, *that* was what they had made.

And the diary continues:

> I murmur: it's a seat . . . but the word stays on my lips: it refuses to go and put itself on the thing. It stays what it is, with its red plush, thousands of little red paws in the air, all still, little dead paws. This enormous belly turned upward, bleeding, inflated— bloated with all its dead paws, this belly floating in this car, in this grey sky, is not a seat. It could as well be a dead donkey tossed about in the water . . . and I could be sitting on the donkey's belly, my feet dangling in the clear water.

In this agonizing, terrifying fantasy about the red plush seat of the streetcar Roquentin is discovering that things, in their actual existence, have nothing to do with the names we give them, and that the existence of things has no connection with the essences which we assign to them. This thing on which he is sitting—is it a streetcar seat? Is this its name, signifying its essence? That is one interpretation. It could just as well be a thousand little red paws or the red belly of a dead donkey.

Things as they exist in their nakedness have no essences, their existence is not confined by any words or explanations that we give them. Sartre and his hero Roquentin have here reached the same conclusion as David Hume had reached two hundred years earlier: The world of existence, of matters of fact has no connection with the world of words, reason, mathematics, and logic. Existence is not rational. There is no reason that things are as they are and not otherwise: There is no rational explanation as to why there is any world at all, rather than nothing.

Why does Sartre respond to the irrationality of existence with a sense of excitement, fear, and nausea? It is because to Sartre, as to Kierkegaard and Nietzsche before him, philosophies are not merely intellectual constructions or games, as they have come to be regarded by some types of contemporary philosophy. Philosophies are things we live by; they exercise a powerful effect upon human psychology and are a matter of life or death for the human spirit. And if it is true, contrary to the teaching of traditional philosophy, that nature has no rationality, and no order, is governed by no scientific laws and structured by no philosophic essences, then anything can happen in such a universe. A world in which essences do not fit existence and in which there are no necessary cause-effect relations is a world without any structure—it falls apart and dissolves, and I myself dissolve along with it.

As Roquentin says, out of his hatred for the bourgeoisie of Bouville, complacently believing in the uniformity of nature, "What if something were to happen? . . . Someone will find that he has something scratching the inside of his mouth. He goes to the mirror, opens his mouth and his tongue is an enormous live centipede." Two hundred years ago Hume had said that since the world is one in which reason and existence have no connection with each other, there is no *reason* that the sun will rise tomorrow.

On the streetcar Roquentin's nausea moves toward crisis as he feels himself surrounded by nameless frightening things. He jumps off the streetcar, runs into the park, and drops onto a park bench. He feels that he is suffocating: Existence penetrates him through his eyes, nose, mouth. And here, in front of him, are the roots of a chestnut tree, protruding from the ground under the bench.

"I was sitting," says Roquentin, "stooping forward, head bowed, alone in front of this black, knotty mass, entirely beastly, which frightened me. Then I had this vision."

Here, then, is Sartre's famous chestnut-tree vision.

"Never," Roquentin continues, "until these last few days had I understood the meaning of "existence" . . . and then, all of a sudden, there it was clear as day."

Roquentin looks around at the chestnut tree, the park gates, the fountain, himself, "a red-haired man digesting on a bench" and it suddenly flashes upon him that none of these things had the slightest reason to be there, none of these things is necessary, they are all merely contingent, *in the way* and superfluous. Roquentin knows now that he had found

the key to Existence, the key to my Nauseas, to my own life.

The key is absurdity, the fundamental lack of any rationality in the existence of things. This root of the chestnut tree, this serpent, or claw, or vulture's foot, this hard skin of a sea lion, this great wrinkled paw, this obscenity—this existence escaped all explanation, it was below explanation, it was simply there, for no reason, without explanation.

And it was absurd. All existence is merely contingent, without any necessity to exist, without any rationality, any essence, simply in the way, superfluous, *de trop,* and so it is absurd. "Every existing thing is born without reason, prolongs itself out of weakness and dies by chance." Now Roquentin understood his nausea: Nausea is what human beings cannot help feeling in the face of a world which is irrational, superfluous, and thus absurd. This is the world-shattering vision of the chestnut tree. It has now taken its place among the great visionary experiences of Western culture.

The Loss of the Cartesian Self and Universe

But there remained for Roquentin another discovery—this time, not about things, but about himself. The self which he has assumed he had, named Antoine Roquentin, this person whom he thought of as having the essence of a man, an intellectual, an historian, the biographer of the Marquis de Rollebon—this, too, is only an interpretation, an essence which he has constructed for himself but which has no necessary congruence with his existence. Existence has primacy over any essence imposed upon it. Human existence, like the existence of things, escapes all essences, interpretations, explanations. This discovery has disturbing implications: Rollebon's existence will always overflow the essence Roquentin tries to give him in his biography. There will be no necessary fit between the Marquis de Rollebon's existence and Roquentin's biography of him. Moreover, now that Rollebon's "life" is perceived to be a mere intellectual construction by Roquentin, it can no longer serve to justify his own existence. And there is a fundamental philosophic implication: There is no essence which fits the self. No Cartesian Cogito, no thinking substance constitutes the essence congruent with my existence. "Nobody lives there anymore." The self exists only as a consciousness which is conscious of a succession of objects. There is only the stream of consciousness of this and that object. And so, in addition to the loss of Descartes's physical substances moving in accordance with the fixed and necessary mechanical laws of the universe, there is the loss of the Cartesian self, the thinking substance which Descartes had carefully established in relation to God and to nature. Both are now gone.

What is now left for Roquentin? He has already decided to give up writing the biography. Off and on his nausea had been relieved when an American jazz record was played on the jukebox in the café in Bouville, a record of a black woman singing "Some of These Days." In a final moment of inspiration, he thinks of the Jewish musician in New York creating this song, and he thinks that he, too, will create something, a work of art, since art transcends the contingency of existence. He is thinking of writing a novel, so that in artistic creation finally he will have a reason for living, and perhaps even a way to redeem his life. But is this only another illusion, like the Bouville bourgeoisie's illusion of the regularity of nature and the righteous regularity of their own lives; or like his own recently shed illusions about the world, himself, and his work as a biographer? In the next chapter we will see how Sartre handles these problems in his great philosophic work *Being and Nothingness*.

Jean-Paul Sartre writing in a café.
(COURTESY OF THE BETTMANN ARCHIVES.)

26

"CONDEMNED TO BE FREE"

In Jean-Paul Sartre's novel *The Age of Reason* (1945), his hero, Matthew, a French professor of philosophy fighting for his life against the German Army in World War II, proclaims Sartre's philosophy of human freedom:

> He was free, free for everything, free to act like an animal or like a machine . . . He could do what he wanted to do, nobody had the right to advise him . . . He was alone in a monstrous silence, free and alone, without an excuse, condemned to decide without an excuse, condemned to decide without any possible recourse, condemned forever to be free.

Sartre's Life: The War Years

Sartre is famous for the idea that we are condemned to be free—an idea which runs through all his writing. What do these frightening words mean? The meaning of human freedom is disclosed in Sartre's important philosophical treatise of 1943, *Being and Nothingness*, which was written during the bitter years of World War II in France. After the Germans, with little opposition, had seized Austria, Czechoslovakia, and Poland, the great Western powers entered the picture and World War II erupted in 1939. Sartre was drafted, and on the advice of Raymond Aron, his colleague in graduate school (now an internationally famous sociologist, philosopher, and political analyst), Sartre served in the corps of meteorologists, with considerable free time to write. And when the French Army surrendered to the Germans in 1940, Sartre became a prisoner of war from June 1940 to March 1941. During his internment he helped organize an antifascist group, kept alive his plans for *Being and Nothingness,* and wrote and acted in an antifascist play which was performed by the prisoners at Christmas. Cleverly, he arranged to be released for reasons of health, and returned to teaching philosophy in France, now occupied by the German Army.

But the war and the experience of France under German rule transformed Sartre, the withdrawn, apolitical intellectual, into a political being: He became active in the French Writers' Resistance Movement, he did reporting for an underground newspaper, and he wrote and produced anti-Nazi plays (*The Flies,* 1943; *No Exit,* 1944). These years of the German occupation of France were to be the most astonishingly productive of Sartre's life. His major intellectual production during that period was the massive essay *Being and Nothingness.* Sartre had begun to write this systematic statement of his philosophic viewpoint during the gloomy winter of 1942 in occupied France.

The Café Philosopher. Like most of the work of Sartre and de Beauvoir during this period, much of *Being and Nothingness* was written in the Left Bank cafés of Paris, in an atmosphere filled with the sounds of voices and the clinking of silverware and dishes, the smells of coffee, cigarettes, food, and wine, and the sights of the customers entering, leaving, and circulating among their acquaintances at the brightly lighted tables. Sartre was at different times a "regular" at the Café de Flore, the Dôme, and the Café des Deux Magots on the Boulevard St.-Germain, a street similar to Bleecker Street in New York's Greenwich Village.

Sartre has occasionally been accused of being a "café philosopher," suggesting that his writing is not serious scholarship or that it is only a mirror for this passing human scene, the fascinating but frivolous flux of the café, rather than being concerned with the serious realm of truth. But in defense of Sartre, it is only fair to say that many things recommended the café as a place to write at that time. First, and of immediate importance, the cafés were heated, unlike the bitter cold of the tiny, ugly Left Bank hotel rooms in which Sartre lived during the war years. Moreover, the cafés of the great European cities have traditionally been places of intellectual stimulation, gathering places for artists, intellectuals, radicals of the left and the right. But especially for Sartre, who is seeking, like Kierkegaard and Nietzsche before him, to develop a philosophy of human existence which will confront the moral issues of the modern world, the life of the café is a continual bubbling source of the concrete human existence he wishes to capture.

What, then, does the massive, difficult philosophical treatise *Being and Nothingness*, this café product of the harsh years of the German occupation of France, have to offer as a philosophy of human existence?

Being and Nothingness

Phenomenology

Being and Nothingness reminds one of Hegel's *Phenomenology of Spirit* in its massivity, its philosophical density and difficulty, its subtle, ironic analyses of the varieties of human consciousness, and its wealth of insights into many dimensions of human life. But *Being and Nothingness* lacks Hegel's confident command of rational concepts which give dialectically developing structure and truth to metaphysics, theory of knowledge, ethics, and to philosophy of nature, history, and society. Hegel's systematic philosophy and its claim to knowledge of total reality is rejected by Sartre as a failed product of abstract rationalism and essentialism. *Being and Nothingness* undertakes a much more modest philosophical project. It takes the standpoint of phenomenology, which was introduced by Husserl. Phenomenology rejects the endeavor of metaphysics to inquire into the nature of reality; it rejects as unattainable the ideal of philosophy which Hegel represents, the ideal of achieving a unified view of the world out of theory of knowledge, the natural and social sciences, history, politics, religion, and art. Phenomenology also rejects all forms of empiricism, as we shall see. Phenomenology for Sartre is the modest study of phenomena, of appearances in relation to the structures of human consciousness through which they appear to us as they do. Sartre proposed to study being as it appears to human consciousness.

Consciousness

The introduction of *Being and Nothingness* carries the title "The Pursuit of Being." Sartre wants to follow Descartes in making my consciousness the starting point of philosophy. Can he not follow Descartes, he asks, and say that what cannot be doubted is my own being as a thinking thing? Descartes's argument was: Every time I am conscious of thinking, I exist; I have being as the substance which is in this state or act of thinking.

But Sartre finds it necessary to revise Descartes. Consciousness is not as Descartes thought it was, the consciousness of a thinking substance examining its own ideas to see if they are true. Sartre accepts the criticism of Descartes which he learned from his study of Edmund Husserl. Like Husserl, Sartre argues, in opposition to Descartes, that my being conscious of thinking cannot be said to prove that I exist as a substance whose essence it is to think. I am not a substantial thinking ego whose states and ideas I have a special, privileged access to, and can know with certainty. "Nobody lives there anymore," as Roquentin said.

Second, in opposition to Descartes, Sartre agrees with Husserl's view of consciousness as intentional, as intending, or referring to an object. Consciousness is always of an object, says Sartre. Consciousness points to what is other than itself, to the "whole world" of things which are "outside it" and confront it (as the ugly root of the chestnut tree confronted Roquentin's consciousness).

In itself, says Sartre, consciousness is empty, nothing; it is a transparency, existing only as consciousness of some object. But Sartre agrees with Descartes that consciousness is always consciousness of itself; to be aware of an object is to be aware of being aware—or else I would be unconscious of being aware, and this would place consciousness in the power of the unconscious and of Freudian determinism, which rob consciousness of its freedom and responsibility.

Sartre has concluded at this point that consciousness is the starting point of philosophy; the Cartesian Cogito is rejected; consciousness is intentional; and transparent; a nothingness; is conscious of itself.

The Regions of Being: Being-for-Itself; Being-in-Itself

Now Sartre has laid the foundation for his phenomenological study of being as it appears to consciousness. There are two absolutely separate kinds of being, two "regions of being," which appear within consciousness. There is the being of myself as consciousness and the being of that which is other than myself, separate from myself, the objects of which I am conscious.

Being-in-Itself (Independent of Consciousness; Without Consciousness; Causally Determined: Without Freedom)

But there is the opposing region of being, the being of the objects of consciousness, the being of existing things—a pebble, a chestnut tree. The things which are the objects of consciousness we regard as independent of consciousness, as independently real or as things-in-themselves. Things are subject to causal laws and are causally determined to be what they are. They have no consciousness and thus no awareness of anything other than themselves. They simply exist solidly, "massively" as what they are, like the root of the chestnut tree. Sartre will now call this region of being being-in-itself, or the "in-itself" ("*en soi*").

Being-for-Itself (Conscious Being)

1. **Conscious of Objects and Self-Conscious.** Conscious being, Sartre now calls being-for-itself, or the "for-itself" ("*pour soi*"). To be a conscious being, for Sartre, is to be a being-for-itself, by which he means, a being which is conscious of objects and of itself as conscious of them. Being-for-itself is never pure consciousness; it is always consciousness of an object; it is a mere transparency through which objects are known. Being-for-itself is also always self-conscious, that is, it is always aware of being conscious of the object. But its self-consciousness means nothing more than this—there is no "inner life" of thoughts, beliefs, feelings within consciousness of which it is aware. Consciousness is empty.

We move on now with Sartre from the introduction of Part 1 of *Being and Nothingness*, entitled "The Problem of Nothingness." To be a human being, Sartre has told us so far, is to be this concrete conscious being, this being-for-itself, confronting a kind of being which it is not, the being of object, of causally determined things, of being-in-itself. To be a conscious being is to be aware of a gap between my consciousness and its objects; it is to be in the world, and yet to be aware of not being one of the causally determined objects of the world; it is to be aware of a distance, an emptiness, a gap that separates me from the region of things.

Conscious Being

2. Brings Nothingness (Negation) into the World. Sartre will now argue that there is such a thing as nothingness in the world and that it arises solely in relation to conscious being: It is only through conscious beings that nothingness enters the world. To be a conscious being, to be a being-for-itself is endlessly to bring nothingness into the world of being. What is Sartre up to?

Sartre is trying to shed light upon the human condition and to show the crucial differences which separate conscious being from the causal, deterministic order of things. In the realm of being-in-itself, the deterministic order of things, all objects are what they are causally determined to be, they exist as they are, as things-in-themselves, without consciousness, without awareness of gaps, without any lacks of possibilities, without any possibility of questions or doubts. Sartre now moves on to show, by contrast, that conscious being is the realm of being which has the power to separate itself from its objects, to distinguish itself from the realm of things, to question, to doubt, to entertain possibilities, to be aware of lacks. But all of these—separating, distinguishing, raising questions, having doubts, thinking of possibilities or deficiencies—introduce a "negative element" into the world, they involve what is not, or nothingness.

It is thus only in the distinctive capacities of a conscious being, a for-itself, that you can think of what you *lack*, do *not* have, and what your *possibilities* are. Only as a conscious being can you be *dissatisfied* with yourself, and desire *not-to-be* what you are now, and desire to be *what you are not*. This is the meaning of Sartre's starkly contrasting definitions of being-in-itself and being-for-itself:

> *being is what it is* . . . the being of *for-itself* is defined, on the contrary, as being what it is not and not being what it is.

In all of these capacities on your part—your awareness of lacks, possibilities, unsatisfied desires, expectations of the future—you have been conscious of what is *not* the case, what is *not* present, what is *not* actual. You have been conscious of negating what is. And so, says Sartre, you have brought negation, nothingness into the world.

This is Sartre's way of presenting his claim that nothingness enters the world with conscious beings, with the for-itself. Nothingness, what is not, also enters the world, Sartre says, through the human capacity to ask questions, to take the attitude of a questioner. In Part 1 of *Being and Nothingness* Sartre offers his now famous example of coming late to an appointment with Pierre in a café. To ask, "Is Pierre in the café?" "Will he have waited for me?" is to open up the possibility of his *not being* there, it is again to introduce the notion of what is not the case, the notion of negation or nothingness. Here is Sartre's description of himself entering a café and looking for his friend Pierre who is not there.

> It is certain that the café in itself with its customers, tables, seats, mirrors, and lights and its smoky atmosphere, filled with the clatter of cups and saucers, the sound of voices and feet, is a thing full of being.

The café is a being-in-itself, massive, solid; it is what it is, "full of being." But when Sartre fails to see Pierre, the being of the café dissolves, becomes a nothing. The café is reduced to a mere background for the figure of Pierre that he is looking for. The being of the café is made into nothing, it is negated, nihilated by the question "Where is Pierre?" The judgment "Pierre is not here" discloses "a double nihilation": It announces the negation of Sartre's expectations to meet Pierre; and it accordingly introduces absence, the non-being of Pierre, nothingness, into the being of the café. "The necessary condition for our saying *not*," says Sartre with poetic intensity,

> is that non-being be a perpetual presence in us and outside of us, that nothingness haunts being.

Moreover, says Sartre, nothingness, negation, nihilation is the basis of all questioning and of "all philosophical or scientific inquiry." In asking any question about the world, the questioner is detaching, dissociating himself from the causal series of nature, the world of things, of being-in-itself. Only conscious being has this capacity to withdraw from the bare existence of things in the causal order, the capacity not to be part of that order—and to introduce a gap, a void, a nothingness between consciousness and the realm of things.

And so Sartre is able to make his dramatic conclusion that it is through man that nothingness comes into the world of being. "Man presents himself," says Sartre, "as a being who causes nothingness to arise in the world." "Man secretes his own nothingness."

Nothingness is the fundamental concept of *Being and Nothingness*. We have seen the for-itself causing "nothingness to arise in the world" in its capacity to be aware of the gap or difference between consciousness and its objects, between the realms of the in-itself and the for-itself, in the conception of what I lack and of my possibilities, in my desire to be what I am-not and no-to-be what I am, and in my capacity to question the world, to detach myself from it and thus to negate or nihilate being.

Conscious Being

3. Has Freedom from Objects and from the Causally Determined World; Has Power of Negation. Suddenly, however, Sartre shows that nothingness, the negation which conscious beings bring into the world, is at the same time human freedom. And suddenly I see that to be a conscious being is to be free—free in relation to any particular object of consciousness; free from the causally determined world of things; free to negate—to say no, to raise doubts, to imagine possibilities which are *not* present; free to reduce to nothingness, to negate and nihilate the region of things, of being-in-itself, by questions—as the café dissolves into nothingness when Sartre looks for the absent Pierre.

And I now become aware that my freedom as being-for-itself is my power. As conscious being I have the power of negation, the identical power of Hegel's principle of negation, the power to negate, nihilate and annihilate, break up and destroy. Sartre wants to show that just as Hegel's principle of negation negates, nihilates, cancels, breaks up every stage of the dialectic process, so as a conscious being I have the freedom and the power to negate, separate myself from, question, deny any object of my consciousness. Through my freedom and power as conscious being, I think of what is *absent,* of what is *not* the case, of what my *future* job possibilities are, which do *not* exist at present, I think of how I would like to change my personality or my appearance to be *other* than what they are now. I think of a future greatness for the

United States which it *lacks* at the present time. Sartre's point is that to be a conscious being is to be free. "There is no difference," he says, "between the being of man and his *being-free*."

Conscious Being

4. **Has Total Freedom in Its Own Existence: Versus Determinism.** But now, dramatically, Sartre says that my freedom as a conscious being enters my own existence. Consciousness is totally free, undetermined, and thus spontaneous. Since I am totally free, my past does not determine what I am now. Between myself as I am now and my past I have put a gap, nothingness. I am free from my past.

Take the case of a gambler, Sartre says, who has resolved that he will gamble no more. When he is confronted with the gaming tables today, his past resolution does not determine what he does now. He finds that he is totally free, he is not determined by his past resolution. This new situation requires that he make a new choice, a choice that is totally free, and wholly unpredictable as to its consequences—since conscious beings are totally free. We may add to Sartre's example of the gambler other cases of the spontaneity of consciousness and its freedom from the past—doesn't every alcoholic, every compulsive eater, everyone addicted to cigarettes or drugs recognize the truth of Sartre's point that conscious beings are totally free? Every time I am confronted by whatever my temptation, I discover that I am free, that yesterday's resolution does not determine what I do now, that now I must choose again. Will I or will I not stick to my resolution not to drink, take drugs, smoke, or overeat? This is the freedom of conscious being which we all painfully discover.

Just as my past does not determine what I am now, so what I am now does not determine my future. Suppose I choose from among my possibilities to become a writer. Since I am totally free, my future actions are not determined by this choice to become a writer. What I will actually do at a future moment of uncertainty about my writing career will be a totally free action on my part, a new choice, and wholly unpredictable. Every writer who has ever suffered from publisher's rejections or from writer's block is painfully aware of this.

And so I begin to understand what it is to be totally free

and I experience this as anguish. I feel anguish in discovering that my freedom destroys, nihilates the determining force of my past decisions and of my pledges for the future. But Sartre firmly opposes any mode of determinism which would relieve this anguish. Sartre is here making explicit his position with regard to the old philosophic controversy between determinism and the doctrine of free will. The whole of *Being and Nothingness* may be seen as a passionate defense of freedom as the essential characteristic of human beings. But he believes he has gone beyond the established positions taken in the determinism–free will argument in his concept of *situation*, which he develops in the following way.

Against Freud Sartre argues that I, as conscious being, cannot logically be regarded as causally determined by unconscious forces by antecedent psychological conditions of my life. Against Marx, Sartre argues that I am not determined by the mode of production and class conflict of my society; Marx, according to Sartre in *Being and Nothingness*, "asserted the priority of object over subject." But do not the sciences of the twentieth century regard me as totally determined, not totally free? Do they not explain me as the inevitable, necessary product of an overwhelming set of conditions—biological, psychological, social, economic, and historical? Then do not these conditions determine me, are they not responsible for what I am or do?

Sartre savagely denounces determinisms of any types, Marxian, Freudian, or scientific, for viewing human beings as if they were causally determined things, within the region of being-in-itself, rather than as free conscious beings. Sartre argues that my "facticity," by which he means the contingent circumstances or facts of my life, may be biologically, psychologically, socially, and economically determined, but as conscious being, I choose the meaning they have for me. As a free, active consciousness, I transform this facticity by my choice of meanings and possibilities, by my projects, into my *situation*. By situation Sartre means an organization of the world into a meaningful totality from the viewpoint of a free individual. I live in the situation I have structured, which is a world of my own making, the world as it is for me, by the meaning I choose to give the facts of my life and by the projects I choose for my future. I cannot say, "The conditions under which I have lived have made me as I am and are responsible for what I do—but for my conditioning (e.g., psychological, economic) I would be so-and-so." Deterministic conditioning, Sartre argues, is only the causally ordered region of being-in-itself, the world of facts and things. In complete distinction from the causally determined world of facts, I am free as a conscious being, choosing the meaning I will give the facts in my situation.

> No factual state whatever it may be (the political and economic structure of society, the psychological 'state,' etc.) is capable by itself of motivating any act whatsoever. For an act is a projection of the for-itself toward what is not, and what is can in no way determine by itself what is not.

"A man is always free," said Sartre during the German occupation of France, "to be a traitor or not."

This is Sartre's solution to the free will versus determinism controversy: We are free in the sense that we make ourselves out of what conditions have made of us, out of our past. We cannot change these facts but we are free in giving them meaning in our own situations, which we construct and reconstruct as our meanings and projects change. And so, in fierce opposition to the view that the facts of the world make a man an alcoholic or a drug addict, Sartre argues that an alcoholic lives in a world of his own making, by the meaning he has chosen to give his life and by choosing to live it as an alcoholic. Are you an alcohol or food or drug or tobacco or pornography addict? Are you addicted to masochism or to sadism as a way of life? Sartre says you have chosen this and that you are free to choose another way to live your life, you are free to construct a new situation for yourself with meanings and projects which you choose. Nothing in your past prevents you—you are not solely determined by your past.

Conscious Being:

5. **Has Total Responsibility for Own World.** But now Sartre discloses that there is an even greater depth to my freedom as conscious being. I have discovered that as a totally free conscious being, I alone am responsible for the meaning of the situation in which I live, I alone give meaning to my world. The region of fact has only the meaning that conscious beings give it.

But what meaning shall I give my world? From what sources can I draw meaning? I raise such questions, not when I am engaged in accomplishing the seemingly useful routine of daily activities, but when I reflect upon my activities. Then I see that there is no source of absolute truth to which I can any longer turn to provide meaning for my life. Conscious beings have no immutable Platonic essence to establish truth and virtue for their lives. As conscious being I determine my own "essence" only by my temporary, transient choices of what I would like to become. (This is indeed the meaning of the existentialist principle that existence precedes essence.) Nor can I turn to God as my foundation for truth and virtue, since God is dead, says Sartre, echoing Nietzsche, and no substitute realm of absolute truth and value is to be found in science or philosophy. I see that I alone am the source of whatever meaning, truth, or value my world has. I alone, absurdly, am responsible for giving meaning to my world. Everything that might be a foundation for me collapses—the existence of God, the universal truths of science, philosophy, the old beliefs in political authority. None of these essentialisms has priority over existence.

Conscious Being

6. Experiences Anguish. And now, I have the shattering awareness that by being totally free, I am totally responsible for my choices, totally responsible for what I am and do, totally responsible for giving meaning and value to my world and without any support from God or any other foundation of truth and values. I totter on the brink of nothingness, I experience dizziness, vertigo, anguish. Anguish is the realization that my total freedom is also my total responsibility to define my situation, to choose the meaning of my world.

> In anguish I apprehend myself at once as totally free and as not being able to derive the meaning of the world except as coming from myself.

What has Sartre done? He has flung me from freedom to anguish. I am indeed free, says Sartre, but my freedom is a dreadful freedom. I alone choose and am responsible for everything I am, I do or think, but I did not choose to be free. As conscious being, I am condemned to be free.

I am condemned to be free. This means that no limits to my freedom can be found except freedom itself or, if you prefer, that we are not free to cease being free.

But we try to escape this dreadful freedom, we try to avoid the anxiety which we experience when we are face-to-face with our own freedom. We find it hard to endure this total responsibility. I long not to be condemned to freedom, not to have to live as a nihilating consciousness, endlessly choosing the kind of person I am, choosing the projects by which I can construct new situations, and bearing responsibility for the meaning of my world and my actions in it. I would wish to be simply a thing, a being-in-itself, like a stone or an inkwell. A stone, like all things, all being-in-itself, is massive and solid and glued to itself. Things have no gaps, they do not bring nothingness into the world, they do not feel lack or dissatisfaction, they do not endlessly pursue possibilities and projects which they never fulfill, they do not freely choose and bear the responsibility.

Conscious Being

7. Escapes into Bad Faith. But to seek to escape, as we all do, from freedom and responsibility Sartre calls *bad faith*. Bad faith is the attempt to escape from my freedom by pretending that human affairs are unavoidable or necessary, as is the causal order of things. "We flee from dread," says Sartre bitingly, "by pretending to look at ourselves . . . as a thing." But bad faith is self-deception; it is a lie we tell to ourselves; it is "a lie in the soul," says Sartre. We are not causally necessitated things, we are totally free conscious beings. But endlessly we escape from this painful truth about ourselves, by the many forms of bad faith.

Sartre now presents his famous example of bad faith. Take the case of *the courtship*, says Sartre, a woman and a man on their first date, perhaps in a theater. The woman knows very well the intentions of the man, and she also knows, says Sartre, that sooner or later she will have to make a decision. But when he takes her hand, she postpones the decision of whether or not to accept him, and so she pretends that she has not noticed that he has taken her hand. "She does not notice because it happens by chance that she is at this mo-

ment all intellect . . . she speaks of life, of her life . . ."
Meanwhile, her hand has become a thing, resting passively in
the hot hands of the man beside her. But she is in bad faith,
Sartre points out. She is pretending that her hand is a thing,
separate from herself, and that she is not responsible for what
is going on. So she lets her hand stay in his. This type of bad
faith is the pretension to be a thing.

Or take the case of *the waiter* in the café, says Sartre. His
movements are a little too precise, too rapid, he bends forward a little too eagerly, he is a little too solicitous for the
customer's order. He has escaped from his freedom as a
conscious being into acting a part, playing a social role, as if
his essence is to be this perfect mechanism, the perfect
waiter. But he is in bad faith. He has no essence; it is not his
essence to be a waiter. He has consciously chosen to be a
waiter. But he cannot be a waiter "as an inkwell *is* an inkwell."
He has escaped from his freedom as a person into becoming a
mechanism from which he will gain social approval for the
perfection of the performance of his role. This type of bad
faith consists in the pretense of being identified with a role.

Or, Sartre continues, take the case of *the homosexual*, who
says, "I am a homosexual" as if he is so by nature, as if this were
something that is his destiny, that it is involuntary on his
part, that it is something which he cannot help any more than
a table can help being a table, or a red-haired man can help
being red-haired. This homosexual, too, is in bad faith. He
is trying to escape from his freedom and his responsibility for
choosing what he is and what he does, by thinking of himself
as a thing, totally determined by nature, as a cabbage cannot
help being a cabbage and is incapable of change. This type of
bad faith denies responsibility by pretending to be determined by nature. But a second person denies that he is a
homosexual although admitting to a pattern of certain acts.
He claims that these past actions have no significance for his
future behavior; that he has been born anew. This second
homosexual's type of bad faith is the opposite of the first: The
first is in bad faith for pretending to be totally determined by
nature; the second is in bad faith by denying any determinism whatever from his past actions upon his present condition.

Another type of bad faith is anti-Semitism. In Sartre's essay
Reflections on the Jewish Question, he says the key to the
problem is to understand the Frenchman who is an anti-
Semite. The Frenchmen who are anti-Semites, says Sartre, are

usually mediocre persons of low social status, who try to compensate for their insignificance by making a scapegoat of the Jews. They become thinglike, rocklike, as Frenchmen, claiming that by *being* French, they have a mystical feeling for France and a French sensibility which gives them a superiority over Jews, even though Jews may be more intelligent, hardworking, and achieving. But this self-deception, this pretense of having a foundation in being a rocklike thing as a Frenchman fails; to be a stone is not to be a human being.

But the question that will haunt *Being and Nothingness* from this point on is whether good faith is possible for conscious beings. What is good faith? This is the problem of ethics, of moral philosophy. We turn to Sartre's ethics.

27

NO EXIT

When France was finally liberated from the Nazis and World War II came to an end in 1945, all of Paris—in its artistic, literary, and intellectual life—was swept up in wild enthusiasm for Jean-Paul Sartre, who had championed the human freedom which they were celebrating. Sartre's philosophy of existentialism overwhelmed France, it dominated everyday conversations, popular magazines, and films, as well as the professional circles involved with literature, politics, and philosophy. During the remaining years of the 1940's and into the 1950's the existentialist furor spread across the European Continent and to the United States and Latin America.

What was the power of existentialism? Although few had an intellectual mastery of the philosophical complexities of *Being and Nothingness*, many of the devotees of existentialism had access to this philosophy through *Nausea*, the plays, and other Sartrean novels, and they had grasped, and identified with, what Sartre's existentialism was expressing. Sartre lifted the despair of conquered France and of the war-weary world by universalizing it, by making despair (with religious overtones) the human condition; each of us, whether in actual war or the war that is peace, is despairingly alone in making decisions and bearing the weight of responsibility. Existentialism expressed also the postwar need to pick up our lives again, the freedom to make ourselves anew out of what the past has done to us, and the denial of the inexorable determinism of circumstances; yet in existentialism there was an acknowledgment (with religious overtones) of bad faith as an inevitability of the human condition. The philosophy of the human individual in an absurd world, a conscious being with its anxious choices and dreadful responsibilities, and admitted self-deception, yet with freedom and hope endlessly to renew itself and its world—this philosophy seemed to offer a humanism truly reflecting human life in the middle of the twentieth century.

The appeal of existentialism became so threatening that it was quickly condemned by both the Roman Catholic Church and the Communist Party. The philosophy of Sartre was condemned for its atheism by the Roman Catholic Church in October 1948, and his writings in their entirety were placed on the Index of Forbidden Books. And the highly esteemed and influential Catholic existentialist philosopher Gabriel Marcel denounced Sartre in 1964 as

> a systematic blasphemer who had disseminated about him the most pernicious lessons and most poisonous advice ever poured out for the young by an acknowledged corrupter.

But in 1944, even before the war had ended, the leading intellectuals of the Communist Party of France (PCF), at that time the largest political party in France, mounted public condemnation of Sartre, since they perceived existentialism to be seducing young party members away from the orthodoxies of Marx, Lenin, and Stalin and endangering the strength and unity of the party. By 1948 a Communist Party Congress officially condemned existentialism as "ideological public enemy No. 1." Sartre was attacked by Communist Party intellectuals as an antirevolutionary idealist (whereas materialism, in their view, is the exclusive philosophy of the Communist revolution); as a bourgeois subjectivist, ignoring the needs of society; as an advocate of a formal, empty freedom while paying no attention to the actual lack of freedom in the world; as a secret fascist, under the influence of Heidegger; and as part of a national effort to destroy the PCF.

Existentialist Ethics

"Which Should I Choose?"

An example of the tremendous popularity of Sartre at this time was the scene at the lecture he gave in the evening of October 29, 1945, in Paris at the Club Maintenant (The Now Club). Reports are that such a crowd struggled to get into the room that chairs were broken in the scuffle, and that the audience so packed available space that several people fainted. The lecture which Sartre delivered is now famous under the title *Existentialism Is a Humanism* and has been reprinted many times and translated into many different languages, despite the fact that Sartre was soon to repudiate the lecture as a "mistake" on his part—and for good reason, as we shall see.

In the course of this lecture, which he intended for the general public, Sartre, as usual, brought home to his audience the meaning of his philosophical points by concrete examples drawn from the current scene, from the lived life of his and their own time. And so, to illustrate and defend the moral philosophy of his existentialism, Sartre told his audience the following story about one of his own students.

The student had come to Sartre for advice during the humiliating years (1940–44) of the German occupation of France. "What shall I do?" the young French student asked Sartre. His father was quarreling with his mother and was inclined toward "collaboration" with the Nazis; his older brother had been killed in the French Army's futile effort to stop the German offensive in 1940, and the student wanted to avenge his brother's death. But his mother was now alone, and lived only for him, in total dependence upon him. I want to stay with her in France and help her, said the student, but I also want to go to England where I can fight the Germans by joining the Free French Army there. Which should I choose?

Sartre points out that the student was torn between two fundamentally different kinds of morality, the morality of personal devotion and the morality of defending the whole society. Speaking to his audience, Sartre said:

> Who could help him choose? Certainly not Christian doctrine, since both choices satisfy the criteria of a Christian choice. Nor again Kantian ethics, for he cannot consistently treat everyone as an end, for someone will have to be treated as a means. I had only one answer to give. "You're free, choose . . ." No general ethic can show you what is to be done.

But does it not strike you as incredible that Sartre, the great master of French existentialism, who presents himself, along with Kierkegaard and Nietzsche, as the type of philosopher who wants to offer a philosophy for modern man to live by, has nothing more to offer the morally conflicted student than to say: choose, and take the responsibility?

But Sartre's examples are always cleverly, brilliantly chosen. Why did Sartre present this extreme example of moral choice to his electrified audience? He gave them the example of a person caught in a moral dilemma between two fundamentally conflicting moral philosophies, a dilemma which cannot be resolved by calling upon any *other* or supervening moral principles, ("who could help him?"); in such a case one can only choose and take the unhappy responsibility. Sartre used this extreme case to exemplify all moral choice, from the existentialist viewpoint—that since we are totally free, we can only choose in anguish, and alone, without any "help" from any moral principles, from any moral authority, from any "general ethic." But this existentialist view of human freedom in moral decisions is so drastic that it raises the question as to whether there can be an existentialist ethics at all—as Sartre himself finally acknowledges.

Bad Faith; Inauthenticity; Alienation: The Spirit of Seriousness

What, we must ask, does Sartre's existentialism offer as a moral philosophy for our time? The key to his moral philosophy he already gave us in his concept of bad faith. Bad faith, we have seen, is lying to oneself, it is self-deception, it is pretending that we are not free and responsible for what we are and do, when in fact we know that we are. Bad faith is pretending that we are causally determined as inanimate things are, and that therefore we have no freedom and are not responsible for our lives; we are only victims of circumstances, passive products of our conditioning.

In place of bad faith Sartre sometimes used the closely related concept of inauthenticity. Inauthenticity is the attempt to escape from the truth of what we are as conscious beings, free to choose the meaning of our world, free to make ourselves by the projects which we choose, and totally responsible. To be inauthentic is to be untrue to oneself as a conscious being; it is to deny what it means to be a conscious being.

Sartre also claims that bad faith and inauthenticity involve us in alienation. To live in the self-deception of bad faith, to live in the inauthenticity of being untrue to human conscious being, is to live in alienation from oneself, to be estranged from one's freedom as conscious being and to regard oneself as a thing compelled by circumstances. Moreover, Sartre makes a special point of the alienation from freedom which characterizes a social group (the "bourgeoisie") which uncritically internalizes the moral rules of a dominating social system which benefits them, and act as if determined by them.

A closely related concept which Sartre devised is "the spirit of seriousness." Sartre makes a devastating use of the "spirit of seriousness" to attack all those human types who accept the ordinary, conventional morality of their own time as if this morality were an eternal, absolute, and necessary truth of the universe. The truth of the matter, Sartre tells us, is that their conventional morality is temporal, relative, and contingent—it is a morality linked to a particular time, it is relative to their own type of society, and it is the contingent outcome rather than the necessary outcome of a variety of social and historical circumstances. Moreover the belief in their conventional morality which these "serious men" proclaim is also contingent, since they happened to internalize it and believe it to be true only because, absurdly, they were thrown into their particular society, rather than another; if they had found themselves in another type of society, their "absolute" moral truths would have been different.

In the novel *Nausea*, Sartre lashes out at the "spirit of seriousness" of those pillars of society, those eminent citizens whose portraits hang in the art museum of the city of Bouville. Roquentin detests the Bouville bourgeoisie for the smugness with which they seem to regard the conventional moral values by which they have lived their lives and made their contributions to the city of Bouville. Never did any one of these self-righteous gentlemen of the Bouville establishment recognize his own responsibility for choosing his moral values. They lived successful lives, at the top of the heap financially, politically, and socially, and all in the spirit of seriousness, acting as if their moral values were physical laws of the universe compelling them to act as they did.

Out of his hatred for the bourgeoisie, Sartre calls these distinguished citizens of Bouville (Mudville) *salauds*, (swine, stinkers, skunks, dirty pigs). But Sartre's philosophical criticism is that contrary to the mentality of the dirty pigs, values do not belong to the world, we are not determined by our moral values as if they were physical laws. For values are not cognitive propositions, they are not true statements about the world like the law of gravity, which we must recognize as a determining condition of our lives. On the contrary, values, like nothingness, enter the world only through human beings, through us, and we live like dirty pigs if we do not acknowledge that we have introduced them and bear the responsibility for acting on them.

The Absence of Moral Laws

Suppose, then, we wish not to live like filthy swine, wallowing in the sticky mud of conventional morality, suppose we wish to avoid bad faith, inauthenticity, self-alienation, the spirit of seriousness. What, then, according to Sartre, is morally right action, action which does not fall into any of these traps? Sartre's answer is that I am acting morally when I abandon all self-deception and make my moral choice with the recognition that I am a free conscious being in choosing and responsible for what I choose.

Granted, however, that choosing as a free and responsible human being is the appropriate approach, or means, to moral action, the question remains: *What* shall I choose? What values guide me in my actions? On the basis of what principles, what ideals, what norms or standards do I choose? What is Sartre's answer? It is the answer which he gave to his anguished student during the war: "You're free, choose . . . No general ethic can show you what is to be done." No moral ideals, no universal values can guide you. But here we have come face-to-face with the paradox that Sartrean existentialism—which has forced me to recognize and avoid my tendencies to fall into self-deception, bad faith, inauthenticity, and the false spirit of seriousness—provides, however, no principles, no ideals, no norms or standards, no universal values to give any moral direction or guidance to my action. Existentialist ethics must, then, be said to be an attempt to constitute itself as a moral philosophy without offering any principles or ideals or values to guide moral choices or actions. Absurdly, Sartre's existentialist ethics wags a moralizing finger at us, makes us morally anxious about falling into bad faith, frightens us into avoiding inauthenticity, and into recognizing that in choosing, we are free and are responsible for our choices, but without being able to give us any moral principles by which to choose.

But why is this so? Why is existentialist ethics bankrupt, unable to provide us with principles or ideals which can point to what is good for human life and what is right for me to do? In the popular postwar lecture *Existentialism Is a Humanism,* Sartre makes two attempts to deal with this problem, both of which fail. In the first attempt, Sartre stands with Nietzsche on the importance of Nietzsche's discovery that "God is dead." But, Sartre adds, "It is necessary to draw the consequences of His absence right to the end," unlike the conventional bad faith which pretends that nothing is changed, that the "norms of honesty, progress and humanity" still exist, commanding us from an intelligible heaven, even though God himself no longer exists. Sartre retorts:

> The existentialist, on the contrary, finds it extremely embarrassing that God does not exist, for there disappears with Him all possibility of finding values in an intelligible heaven.

We may state Sartre's point in the simplest way: The consequence of death of God is that there is no longer any source of absolute values for man. "It is nowhere written," says Sartre, "that 'the good' exists, that one must be honest or must not lie, since we are now upon the plane where there are only men." Since God does not exist, He cannot be the foundation for our moral life. Immediately, Sartre quotes the Russian novelist Dostoevski's startling claim that "If God did not exist, everything would be permitted."

And "that," says Sartre, "for existentialism, is the starting point." Without God, everything is permitted and we are free. With the death of God, we are now left alone in the universe as the only conscious beings. Moreover, our existence as conscious beings precedes our essence, since strictly, in the absence of God, human beings have no essence, there is no human nature which they share. In this way, Sartre reaches the conclusion that no moral values or ideals are any longer available to us—no essence of man or of human nature directs us to fulfill our essence or our human nature; no God presents us with a divine ideal of human goodness and virtue for us to aspire to achieve. In a sudden burst of eloquence, in this packed public lecture, Sartre sums this up:

Thus we have neither behind us, nor before us, in a luminous realm of values, any means of justification or excuse. We are left alone, without excuse. That is what I mean when I say that man is condemned to be free.

We are without any means of justification, since in the absence of God, there are no "values or commands that could legitimize our behavior." We are without any means of excuse for our behavior, since there is no divinely ordained "human nature" which limits and determines us. The death of God has set us free from his rules and his governance of the world. We are free—but without any moral principles to serve as a foundation for our lives.

Sartre has here attempted to explain the lack of moral ideals or principles in existentialism by attributing this lack to the death of God—if God no longer exists as the foundation of values, then there is no foundation for any values. But this explanation runs counter to the argument sustained throughout *Being and Nothingness*, which is that the only foundation for values is my freedom as a conscious being and that "*nothing, absolutely nothing, justifies me in adopting this or that particular value . . .*" Thus God cannot be a foundation for my values. Even if He were to exist, and I were to believe in Him, existentialism would have to argue that His relation to my values would not be as foundation, but only as a support for me as foundation, a support which I had chosen. At the very end of his speech Sartre concedes this, saying that "even if God existed that would make no difference from [existentialism's] point of view . . . We think that the real problem is not that of His existence; what man needs is to find himself again and to understand that nothing can save him from himself . . ."

In the lecture *Existentialism Is a Humanism*, Sartre made a second attempt to deal with the absence of moral principles in existentialism. Hastily in this public lecture he tries to show, as the title of the lecture indicates, that existentialism is not bankrupt of all moral values but, on the contrary, it is a type of humanism, a philosophy of man which regards human beings to be the foundation of value. Here Sartre offers his famous argument that existentialism shares some of the moral values of traditional humanism, specifically humanism's value of freedom for all humankind. Sartre argues that for the philosophy of existentialism, my choosing my own freedom as a conscious being necessarily involves my valuing and choosing freedom for all others. However, nothing that Sartre has told us in *Nausea* or *Being and Nothingness* was based on the humanistic value of universal freedom. At no point did he argue that choosing freedom for myself involves choosing it for others. In fact, Sartre has consistently taken the opposite view, that I regard the other's freedom as a threat to mine, and as something that I seek to overcome. Thus both of Sartre's efforts fail. The death of God does not explain the lack of general moral principles and values in existentialism; nor can existentialism supply this lack by laying claim to the humanist value of universal freedom: Existentialism is not "a humanism."

And so we must return to the question Why is existentialism bankrupt of any general moral principles and values? The answer has now become apparent. Sartre has himself closed out the possibility of principles or values for an existentialist ethics by his phenomenology of the kinds of being as they appear to human consciousness. This has led him to present a universe in which there are only two kinds of being. Being-in-itself, the region of things, is what it is, closed in upon itself, without consciousness, causally determined and so without freedom; in itself it has neither meaning nor value. Being-for-itself, the region of conscious being, is undetermined and free; it is conscious of itself and of all its objects, conscious of its separation from all its objects, and conscious of its absolute separation from the region of things; conscious being has no substance, no essence, no inner life, it is a nihilating freedom, holding all objects at a distance from itself, conscious of gaps, lacks, dissatisfactions, conceiving of possibilities which do not exist, and thus of something to be done; consciousness is thus endlessly acting upon projects to achieve valued goals from which it will always be separated by a gap—goals with which free, nihilating consciousness will never coincide.

In this universe in which there are only these two kinds of being, free conscious being is the only possible foundation of values. But as a free conscious being, and the only possible foundation of values, I myself can have no foundation—I can be founded upon no other being, no essence, no ideals or principles, for these would destroy my freedom. Values, then, have their sole foundation in me, a conscious being who is without foundation. And thus all values can only be contingent—temporary, relative, and changing, they are what I happen to choose in my shifting circumstances. Thus existentialism can provide no ultimate fixed foundation for human values—no absolute values, no principles of a "general ethic," and no moral ideals, whether the humanistic ideal of freedom, the Christian ideal of self-abnegation, or the Marxist ideal of the proletarian revolution. Existentialism can offer none of these to guide my moral choosing. In answer to the question What shall I choose? existentialism is thus bankrupt of any principles or ideals which could justify one kind of life or one kind of moral decision over another. It is the existentialist conception of the limitless pure freedom of conscious being that has yielded the result that an existentialist ethics is impossible.

Existentialist Ethics: Criticisms

And so our first criticism of Sartre's existentialism is that it has made ethics impossible by rejecting any general principles or ideals as the foundation for moral choice. A second criticism is that Sartre has indeed given us one principle for our action: to avoid bad faith, or, closely related, to repudiate acting inauthentically, or in alienation from oneself, or in the spirit of seriousness. But these are only negative rules. If I am to follow the rule to repudiate inauthenticity, I must know the positive meaning of authenticity. To act authentically, Sartre says, is to act with a clear understanding of the situation and with the consciousness that I am free in what I am choosing to do and responsible for my choice. But since Sartre's definition of authenticity has not provided any justification for choosing A rather than B, then my choice is arbitrary; it is simply my choice, but it has no foundation, it is absurd. The rule Avoid bad faith, choose authentically, simply tells me to acknowledge my freedom in choosing, but it is not a morally significant rule, it is an empty rule, it contains no content as to what is morally worth anything or what is morally hideous. At best, the rule to act authentically is a rule of procedure, a rule telling me what are the appropriate means to be taken for making moral decisions. But the rule indicates no positive moral direction.

A third criticism of Sartre's existentialist ethics is that since the only rule it provides me with is the rule to avoid self-deception, and to act authentically, then I have done all that is required of me so long as I follow this rule, and avoid bad faith, and acknowledge that I alone freely choose what I do and am responsible. But then anything that I freely choose to do meets the requirements of authenticity: one freely chosen act is as good as another, and there is no way of discriminating among my freely chosen acts.

Sartre himself sees this and says toward the end of *Being and Nothingness:* "All human activities are equivalent . . ." And he adds, intending to shock us, "it comes to the same thing whether one gets drunk alone or is a leader of nations." Both ways of life, undertaken freely, are equivalent. Then Sartre's French students who joined the underground resistance movement against the Nazis had no more justification than the German students of Heidegger who joined the Nazi Party to fight in Hitler's army for the values of fascism. One is no more justified than the other because neither has any justification; to join the French resistance forces or Nazi army are equivalent acts if freely chosen. "Every time a man chooses his engagement and projects in all sincerity and lucidity, whatever this choice may be, it is impossible to prefer another to it." And if I freely, in all sincerity and lucidity, choose to murder my enemy?

There is, however, a mysterious footnote at the very end of Part I, Chapter Two, "Bad Faith," in *Being and Nothingness* which indicates that Sartre sees very clearly that his principle of authenticity falls short of providing a moral principle. He says that "it is indifferent whether one is in good or in bad faith" because bad faith wins out, "but that does not mean that we cannot radically escape bad faith. But this supposes a self-recovery of being which was previously corrupted. This self-recovery we shall call authenticity, the description of which has no place here." Has Sartre hinted to us that he is entertaining another concept of authenticity than the one he had disclosed, and that it is clearly a concept with moral significance, since he defines the new concept of authenticity as a self-recovery from corruption? Is this hint a foreshadowing of the "radical conversion" (to Marxism) which he reveals at the end of *Being and Nothingness?*

A last criticism of Sartre's existentialist ethics is that we see it now as an ethics hovering at the edge of nihilism. Nihilism may be defined as the viewpoint which perceives with bitter disillusionment that human reason is powerless to justify one moral value over another; and that since all actions, pursuing whatever values, are therefore equivalent, nothing has any value, and only the might of force and violence can decide what is right. But surely the brutal message of nihilism was not what made Sartre the celebrity of post-World War II France. Not at all. Sarte was celebrated for his championing of liberty from Nazi oppression, for his universalizing of France's despair during the Occupation, for his optimistic conception of self-renewal, "that man is nothing else but what he makes of himself." Moreover, Sartre offered the French and the war-stricken world refuge in revised form of the old French, Cartesian subjectivism: In the face of my mounting doubts and confusions with regard to world affairs, subjectivism says, I alone, in my own situation, pursue my own projects and make my moral decisions, freely and responsibly, in authenticity. But I decide in anguish, Sartre adds, since I am without foundation. However, now the historic moment is past in which existentialism met these needs of the world following World War II, and we now look upon Sartre's existentialist ethics as a nihilistic attack upon any rational justification for what is right or good in human life. Is there no exit for Sartre from the charge that Sartrean existentialism makes ethics impossible and that it leads us into nihilism?

Being-for-Others: Social Relations

No Exit

Let us turn to Sartre's view of human relations to see if there is an exit for him there. The best introduction to Sartre's view of the way conscious beings relate to one another is his play *No Exit* (*Huis Clos*, 1944), which was the first play to be performed in Paris after the liberation from the German Army. It was performed on September 20, 1944, and was immediately a huge success, and it has become a classic of the theater, performed constantly ever since. *No Exit* has only three actors, and no change of scenery. The three characters, a man and two women, one of whom is a lesbian, walk separately into a brightly lighted room furnished with three small sofas, knowing that they are dead and have been sent here to hell. Yet there are no instruments to torture them, there are no hell fires to burn them, there are only the other two people. Soon the horrible truth dawns upon them that they are one another's tortures, their damnation is for all eternity to torment one another. By the end of the play they have tortured each other excruciatingly and they have made the discovery that in hell there is no need for hell fire—as the male character says, "Hell is other people."

Being–for–Others as Body

That "hell is other people" is the core of Sartre's view of the way conscious beings relate to each other. Human relationships constitute the topic of Part III of *Being and Nothingness*, under the heading "Being-for-Others" (*"Etre pour autrui"*). I exist as a conscious being, says Sartre, in a world of other conscious beings, in a world of being-for-others. Being-for-others takes two forms, says Sartre. First, I become aware of my own body as something which is perceived by other people. For other people, I am at first a being-in-itself, a body, although to myself I am a being-for-itself, a conscious being. Second, I, in turn, become aware of other people and in this way of their existence as conscious beings.

Sartre begins his highly original and penetrating psychological analysis of my being-for-others with his claim that I become fully aware of myself only when I am aware that I am an object for someone else's perception. Sartre is here deliberately making use of Hegel's famous argument that I can become conscious of myself only as I find myself reflected in the consciousness of the other. But Sartre develops Hegel's theory of the "looking-glass self," of the dependence of self-consciousness upon being reflected in the consciousness of the other consciousness into a more subtle theory. For the Cartesian Sartre, as we have seen, consciousness is always conscious of objects and self-conscious. But Sartre points out that I am dependent for full self-consciousness upon being perceived by another consciousness as an object. I become *fully* self-conscious, in the additional sense of being conscious of myself as active body, only by becoming aware that I am an object, an active body, for someone else's perception— only when I become aware that I am being looked at. (We see here that Descartes's dualism between myself as mind and as body has reasserted itself in Sartre's distinction between what I am for myself—conscious being, a being-for-itself—and what I am immediately for others—a physical body, a being-in-itself.)

The Look

I am conscious of being looked at. Sartre's subtle penetration of what this means in human relations is one of his most remarkable concepts, the concept of the look. Typically, Sartre proceeds by providing the telling example. Here he gives us the unforgettable example of a *peeping Tom*, a voyeur. "Let us imagine," Sartre writes, "that moved by jealousy, curiosity, or vice I have just glued my ear to the door and looked through a keyhole." As peeping Tom, I am conscious only of the spectacle to be seen in the room, the conversation to be overheard, and I focus my consciousness on listening, on finding the optimum angle for applying my eye to the keyhole. My consciousness is a transparent awareness of sights and sounds. I am not aware of myself as bending down to peer through the keyhole of someone's door, as eavesdropping. But suddenly, says Sartre, I hear footsteps in the hall. Someone is looking at me. I am seized by shame as I suddenly recognize that I am the kind of person the Other is now perceiving me to be. Suddenly, by the look of the Other, my world as it appeared to me is drained away. "Thus in the shock which seizes me when I apprehend the Other's look, this happens—that suddenly I experience a subtle alienation of all my possibilities, which are now associated with objects of the world, far from me in the midst of the world."

Conscious Being as Object

"Two important consequences result," Sartre continues. First, I have become an object of the Other's look, he sees me as a body, I am thinglike in his eyes. The other person replaces my projects for myself, the possibilities which enliven my world, by his calculations of the probabilities of how I will behave under certain circumstances, since for him I am one of the objects of the world, an object among others whose behavior must be predicted. Later, when we talk with the Other, "and when we gradually learn what he thinks of us, this is the thing which will fascinate us and fill us with horror:"

"I swear to you that I will do it."
"Maybe so. You tell me so. I want to believe you.
It is indeed possible that you will do it."

In pointing to the difference between my view of my own promises and the other person's calculations of what my promises are worth, Sartre opens up a horrifying dimension of interpersonal relations.

The second consequence of being looked at by the other person is that I begin to understand that *"I am no longer master of the situation."* The Other is making his own predictions of me, he has been looking me over and making his own evaluations of me as a person, he is judging me and putting labels on me. I am what he makes of me, not what I make of myself. In my own defense, I may then try to overcome the Other who has made an object of me by making an object of him in return. But in being "looked at" by the Other, I already know that the Other is free, that he is not one of the objects in the world but transcends them and organizes them into his own world—as, by his look, he has destroyed my freedom and its world and made me into an object in his world.

The Struggle unto Death; Master and Slave

It is by the look of the Other, Sartre argues, that the old philosophical problem of how we can know that other minds exist is solved. The look of the Other is indubitable evidence of a mind, of a free conscious being—of a freedom which threatens and obstructs my own freedom. Here is laid down the pattern of unending hostility and conflict which characterizes all social relations.

The Other negates, destroys my freedom through his look. He reduces me by his look to the state of an object, a body, and I experience this as being possessed by him. But, says Sartre, I try to get free from him. I try to possess the other by making the other an object. "Everything which may be said of me in my relations with the Other applies to him as well," Sartre writes. The relationship is reciprocal:

> While I attempt to free myself from the hold of the Other, the Other is trying to free himself from mine; while I seek to enslave the Other, the Other seeks to enslave me . . . Descriptions of concrete behavior must therefore be envisaged within the perspective of *conflict*.

And Sartre concludes with one of his most famous lines:

Conflict is the original meaning of being-for-others.

Once again we see Sartre borrowing from Hegel, here from Hegel's struggle unto death which culminates in the master-slave relationship; these clearly lie behind what Sartre means by being-for-others. Human relations are those of masters and slaves, with even more subtle and frightening implications than Hegel imagined. Building upon Hegel's master-slave theme, Sartre points out that the conflict between master and slave is a no-win game. If I kill the Other, I will have lost him as a mirror for myself as active body and thus I will have lost my being-for-others. I will also have lost the satisfaction of enslaving him as a free conscious being.

For what I want is to possess the Other's freedom; I want to enslave the Other as free. Only this will satisfy me. On the other hand, if he is free, he will escape my possession of him, I will lose the satisfaction of mastery over his freedom. And in striking contrast to what Sartre claims later, in the 1945 lecture, that existentialism is a humanism, here in *Being and Nothingness* Sartre describes all human relations as conflict relations in which I seek to enslave or possess the Other's freedom. On the subject of freedom Sartre concludes: "Respect for the other person's freedom is an empty word . . . We are . . . thrown into the world in the face of the Other"; each, by existing, limits the other's freedom. "And nothing . . . can change this original situation." And so it is that conflict is the meaning of all human relations—conflict and hopelessness.

Love

Especially hopeless is the relationship of love. In love, too, what the lover wants is not merely the physical possession of the Other—but to possess the Other's freedom. He does not want to enslave the beloved; he would feel humiliated by being loved by someone who was psychologically conditioned to love him. Also, total enslavement of the beloved to him, a mechanical beloved, would soon kill his love. On the other hand, the lover would not be satisfied with someone who loved him because she had freely taken a pledge [of marriage?] to do so. The lover does not want to possess the beloved as a thing, he wants to possess the beloved as a free person. But the desire of the lover is hopeless—how can the beloved be a free person if I possess and enslave her freedom?

But there is a deeper significance to love, says Sartre. We suffer as nihilating conscious beings from being empty, without substance, without essence, without any foundation for our lives. Love offers us a foundation. We seek a foundation for our being in the lover, in the idea that the lover is the real foundation of my being. We say, "We were made for each other"; "She is all the world to me." Each of us justifies the Other's existence. But this, too, fails—because it requires that each possesses the Other's freedom as the foundation of his life, and yet be freely loved. Again there is the contradiction—no one can be both free and a possession.

But there is another, deeper pursuit of love. We suffer in our being-for-others from being made into a bodily thing, from being possessed by the look of the free Other. Love promises to banish the suffering. In love, I possess the Other's freedom, and instead of being an unpredictable thing among others, for the beloved I am the chosen one, the free and adored center of all values. By being loved, I thus become the Other's complete foundation, and my existence is justified. But, says Sartre, "this project," on the part of the lover "is going to provoke a conflict." The beloved, as free being, cannot be "glued" to him as foundation, cannot be captured, cannot be kept in a state of captivity even by seduction, even by being besieged with money, gifts, representations of the lover's power and "connections". And thus the lover's project of being the masterful, adored, and absolute center of values for a captured consciousness, for an enslaved free being, necessarily fails.

And so the hopelessness of love is only another example of being-for-others, the world of human relations, in which I can relate to others only through enslaving or being enslaved. Love in its failure can lead to three different outcomes: I can become the slave, a masochistic object for the lover, suffering for the sake of the Other's pleasure in his mastery; I can become the sadist, and master the loved one by forms of violence; or I can observe the other in indifference. But none of these will satisfy me, because none of these can succeed in the face of the freedom of persons as conscious beings.

The Viscous

And finally, love is also threatened by its bodily aspects, since for Sartre, as we saw in his novel *Nausea*, all bodies, all being-in-itself, all physical things, give us the sensation of nausea, just as all conscious being, all being-for-itself, all being-for-others carries with it the experience of anguish. Nausea is what I feel in my awareness of my own body and of every other body and of all bodily contact with the world in its horrifying absurd superfluousness.

In Part IV of *Being and Nothingness* Sartre adds "the viscous" to his description of things in nature. We experience the body and all physical things in nature with nausea; this is, at the same time, the experience of nature's viscosity. Nature's "viscosity" is its stickiness and sliminess, its tendency to engulf us like a leech in its softness. Things sink into it and dissolve. To sink into the sickly sweet viscous substance of nature is to be like a bee who sinks into a jar of honey and drowns. The viscous is an aspect of the world which fills us, says Sartre, with a natural, instinctive revulsion; the viscous is a natural symbol of the slimy, disgusting, and horrifying, a universal symbol which we all use involuntarily. Viscous things horrify us by their ambiguity, since they are neither liquid nor solid, like mud, or tar, or honey.

The viscous, he adds, symbolizes "a sickly-sweet feminine revenge" of the slimy being-in-itself upon being-for-itself.

> The viscous is docile. Only at the very moment when I believe that I possess it, behold, by a curious reversal it possesses me . . . I want to get rid of the viscous and it sticks to me, it draws me, it sucks at me . . . Here we can see the symbol which abruptly discloses itself: there exists a poisonous possession; there is the possibility that the In-itself might absorb the For-itself.

The viscous, Sartre says, symbolizes nature, it symbolizes everything that the for-itself hates, but cannot escape. But clearly the viscous, which he hates, is for Sartre a symbol of the female in-itself, sucking in and engulfing the male for itself—and so a serious personal and cultural pathology, the hatred of the female, has shown itself to be present in Sartre's conception of love and relations with others.

Sadism and Masochism

In love, Sartre said, as in all our other human relationships, we end up either enslaving the other or being enslaved, in the position of either sadism or masochism. We may try hating the other when we cannot possess him. But hate, says Sartre, "does not enable us to get out of this circle . . . Nothing remains for us except . . . to be indefinitely tossed from one to the other of the two fundamental attitudes." Human relationships are conflicted and hopeless; they are no source of moral ideals or principles. There is then in human relations no exit for Sartre from the moral bankruptcy of his existentialism.

Is this wretchedness where Sartre leaves us? No, we saw that he added a strange footnote at the end of Part I, "The Problem of Nothingness," where he referred to a radical escape from bad faith and a possibility of moral authenticity "the description of which has no place here." Here at the end of Part III, "Being-for-Others," Sartre adds another mysterious footnote:

> These considerations do not rule out the possibil-
> ity of an ethics of deliverance and salvation. But this
> can be achieved only after a radical conversion which
> we cannot discuss here.

What is the radical escape from bad faith? How is moral authenticity possible? What is this ethics of deliverance and salvation? What is this radical conversion? It is Sartre's great bombshell—the conversion from existentialism to Marxism and communism, a total turnabout, to which we turn.

SUGGESTIONS FOR FURTHER READING
PART SIX: SARTRE

Works of Sartre (*in translation*):

Nausea (1938). New York: New Directions Press, 1964.

Being and Nothingness (1943). New York: Washington Square Press, 1966.

Existentialism [Existentialism Is a Humanism]. New York: Philosophical Library, 1947.

What Is Literature? (1949). New York: Harper and Row, 1965.

Search for a Method (1958). New York: Alfred A. Knopf, 1963.

Critique of Dialectical Reason (1960). Atlantic Highlands, N.J.: Humanities Press, 1976.

The Words. New York: George Braziller, 1964.

Between Existentialism and Marxism. New York: Pantheon, 1974.

Critical Studies:

Aron, Raymond. *Marxism and the Existentialists.* New York: Harper and Row, 1970.

Aronson, Ronald. *Jean-Paul Sartre—Philosophy in the World.* London: NLB/Verso, 1980.

de Beauvoir, Simone. *The Prime of Life.* Cleveland: World Publishing Co., 1962.

Burnier, Michel-Antoine. *Choice of Action.* New York: Random House, 1968.

Caute, David. *Communists and the French Intellectuals: 1914–60.* New York: Macmillan, 1964.

Contat, Michel, and Rybalka, Michel. *The Writings of Jean-Paul Sartre.* (1970). Evanston: Northwestern University Press, 1974.

Danto, Arthur. *Jean-Paul Sartre.* New York: Viking, 1975.

Desan, Wilfrid. *The Tragic Finale.* Cambridge: Harvard University Press, 1954.

————. *The Marxism of Jean-Paul Sartre.* New York: Doubleday, 1965.

Fell, Joseph P. *Emotion in the Thought of Sartre.* New York: Columbia University Press, 1965.

Grene, Marjorie. *Dreadful Freedom: A Critique of Existentialism.* Chicago: Chicago University Press, 1948.

Heinemann, F. H. *Existentialism and the Modern Predicament.* New York: Harper and Row, 1958.

Kline, George. "The Existentialist Rediscovery of Hegel and Marx." In *Sartre,* edited by Mary Warnock. Garden City, New York: Doubleday, 1971.

Laing, R., and Cooper, D. G. *Reason and Violence: A Decade of Sartre's Philosophy, 1950–60.* Forward by Jean-Paul Sartre. Rev. ed., New York: Random House (Vintage Books), 1971.

Manser, Anthony. *Sartre: A Philosophic Study.* New York: Oxford University Press, 1966.

McMahon, Joseph H. *Human Beings: The World of Jean-Paul Sartre.* Chicago: Chicago University Press, 1971.

Murdoch, Iris. *Sartre: Romantic Rationalist*. New Haven: Yale University Press, 1953.

Poster, Mark. *Existential Marxism in Postwar France: From Sartre to Althusser*. Princeton: Princeton University Press, 1975.

Sheridan, J. F. *Sartre: The Radical Conversion*. Athens, Ohio: Ohio University Press, 1969.

Stern, Alfred. *Sartre: His Philosophy and Existential Psychoanalysis*. Rev. ed., New York: Dell Publishing Co., 1967.

Thody, Philip. *Jean-Paul Sartre: A Literary and Political Study*. New York: Macmillan, 1961.

―――. *Sartre: A Biographical Introduction*. New York: Scribner's, 1971.

Warnock, Mary. *The Philosophy of Sartre*. London: Hutchinson, 1965.

―――, ed. *Sartre*. Garden City, New York: Doubleday, 1971.

PART SEVEN

IN SEARCH: THE CONTEMPORARY SCENE IN PHILOSOPHY

28

IN SEARCH

In 1960 Jean-Paul Sartre published *The Critique of Dialectical Reason*, his second major philosophical essay. Like *Being and Nothingness* of 1943, it is over seven hundred pages long, and in the very first few pages he drops his great bombshell:

Marxism is the inescapable philosophy of our time.

Marxism: The Inescapable Philosophy of Our Time

This is the meaning of the two mysterious footnotes in *Being and Nothingness*, the one footnote (page 86) referring to the ability of the "previously corrupted" to "radically escape bad faith" into positive moral authenticity; the other footnote (page 504) referring to an "ethics of deliverance and salvation" which "can be achieved only after a radical conversion." Both footnotes end identically: The discussion of positive moral authenticity "has no place here"; the achievement of the ethics of deliverance "we cannot discuss here." We now have the key to these footnotes—it is Sartre's now famous conversion to Marxism. And so the radical escape of the "previously corrupted" into positive authenticity is the escape of the bourgeoisie into the authenticity of Marxism; and the ethics of deliverance and salvation is achieved by conversion to Marxism.

In the *Critique of Dialectical Reason* we see the outcome of Sartre's conversion to Marxism: Free, independent conscious being, being-for-itself in its concrete existence disappears into a Sartrean version of Marx's proletariat, and existentialism, the subjectivist philosophy of conscious being, of the solitary, defiantly free for-itself disappears into a Sartrean version of the objectivist, materialist philosophy of mature Marxism, into a scientific scenario of the dialectic of history as the struggle of social groupings to overcome scarcity.

Why does Sartre say that there is an inescapable philosophy of our time? Sartre claims to be following Hegel and Marx. It was Hegel who argued that all philosophies are relative to, bound to, their own historical times, that every philosophy is nothing but its own time reflected in thought—and that his own philosophy is now bringing the history of philosophy to its inescapable dialectical completion. And it is Marx who said that all philosophies are ideologies, reflections of the dominant class in the existing economic mode of production—and that his own theory, as the inescapable truth of the last oppressed class, brings to an end the dialectical history of philosophies and of the ideologies which they mask.

Sartre himself is not claiming, as does Hegel, that a philosophy must be regarded as inescapable in the sense of being perceived to bring the history of philosophy to a grand completing synthesis; nor is he claiming, as does Marx, that a philosophy must be regarded as inescapable in the sense of being perceived to bring the whole distorting history of ideologies to an end. As a twentieth-century existentialist and phenomenologist, Sartre does not invoke any great historical finalities, any great dialectical culminations or endings for philosophy. Sartre's more modest position is that for any society, at a particular time, there is only one philosophy which can be fully expressive of it, and is in this sense inescapable.

How does Sartre defend his claim that it is specifically Marxism that is the inescapable philosophy of our time? He supports this bold claim only by the sweeping statement that the modern period in history has been dominated by just a few philosophers: There has been the age of Descartes and Locke, the age of Kant and Hegel, and there is now the age of Marx. There is no going beyond any of these great systems of thought, says Sartre, until changes take place in the economic relations which these philosophies reflect. And while Marxism is dominant, as it is now, we are compelled to be Marxists, to think in terms of Marxian philosophy. As the philosophy of the proletariat, Marxism is the philosophy which most completely reflects the class conflict of our own society and this historical time, and Marxism will remain inescapable as a philosophy until the proletariat is liberated from its oppression.

But then you will want to ask Sartre, what becomes of existentialism, the philosophy of the human subject, free from causal determinism, condemned to be free to give meaning to its world, isolated in its dreadful proud freedom? Sartre's answer is that he now views existentialism as belonging to the class of minor philosophies which are "parasitical" systems, "living on the margin" of the dominant philosophy. Existentialism can however be integrated into Marxism by supplying Marxism with subjectivity, with the existentialist emphasis upon the human subject in concrete situations. Existentialist concern for conscious being will give a human dimension to the scientific abstractions and the dialectical necessities of mature Marxism. But that is existentialism's only purpose. From the day when Marxism takes on a human dimension, says Sartre, existentialism will no longer have a reason for being. But in the *Critique of Dialectical Reason*, where Sartre was to have demonstrated the power of existentialism to humanize Marxism, to bring the human subject back into the scientific scenario, the concrete human subject has disappeared from sight into one or another of a variety of social groups, and Sartre's energies are consumed in constructing a theory of social groups.

Sartre's Conversion to Marxism

How, then, can we explain Sartre's radical conversion from existentialism to Marxism. Sartre wanted to construct a philosophy which would describe and analyze, from the perspective of the subject, the total freedom of the modern consciousness, drawing upon the extreme case of the urban, rootless, skeptical, disaffected, hostile, narcissistic, sadomasochistic, amoral intellectual. And at the same time, Sartre wanted to idealize total freedom as the only truly human and redeemable aspect of our lives. And there is no question but that in *Being and Nothingness* Sartre painted one of the great portraits of all time of a type of human consciousness.

But Sartre had taken such an extreme position in defending

the total freedom of conscious being that an existentialist ethics became impossible. He isolated me as an empty, negating consciousness with nothingness at my core, rather than a substantial self. I have no foundation in myself, no essence, no human nature to set a standard for me. Being free, I am undetermined by my past; but being free, I cannot determine my future. As a nihilating, negating consciousness, aware of my lacks, my incompleteness, I am always transcending myself toward goals which will supply what I lack, but I can never achieve coincidence with these goals. I have no foundation in nature, which is meaningless, hostile, nauseating, and viscous. Science constructs abstractions and quantifications which, insofar as they bear upon human life, falsify it by incorporating the human subject in the region of things, to be observed and manipulated, "engineered." I cannot claim a foundation in any religions or philosophical values; I cannot accept any values from another person or that are derived from any general principles, since any of these would be a loss of my freedom and a form of bad faith. I try to fill my nothingness with love, with a foundation in the lover, but this fails. I try to give myself a foundation by various forms of bad faith—role playing, pretending to be a thing—all of them fail.

And finally, Sartre added, what we yearn for is not merely to be thinglike, a simple being-in-itself; our fundamental project is to be solid and determined, to be conscious and free, like a human being. My longing is to be both conscious and an object, to be my own foundation as an in-itself, a solid, rocklike being, but also to be conscious, a negating, nihilating for-itself. But such a being, which would have the advantages of the two kinds of being, being-in-itself and conscious being, is what we mean by God. But there can be no such thing. Therefore, says Sartre, God does not exist. And as for man's yearning to be both being-in-itself and being-for-itself—to be God—Sartre says, "Man is a useless passion."

It is in this crisis, this extreme situation in which total freedom has led to total isolation and despair of any foundation, that Sartre makes the existentialist leap to Marxism, which will provide the ethics which existentialism lacks, and which will even be for the anguished modern consciousness an ethics of deliverance, of salvation.

But why did Sartre not recognize this as bad faith? Why did he not see that to become a Marxist and a follower, if not a member, of the Communist Party is to become thinglike, to accept dogmas and the "spirit of seriousness" in ethics and politics for the group, to submit to party authority and control over major aspects of my life, to surrender my freedom?

But from a more fundamental philosophic standpoint, why did Sartre not recognize that the gap and opposition between conscious being and all of its objects in the world—an opposition which had for him strong native roots in the Cartesian dualism of the individual self and the world—entailed a conception of the primacy of the individual, of individual conscious being, which was incompatible with Marxism or with any other form of collectivism, with its primacy of the group—however enticingly collectivism might be presented as offering "emancipation" or "deliverance" or as the "inescapable" philosophy of our time. The only possible explanation is that aside from Marxism, Sartre saw no exit from the dreadful, absurd freedom he himself had created.

But this still leaves the question Why did Sartre perceive Marxism as the only exit? The answer lies in the circumstances of Sartre's own life between *Being and Nothingness* of 1943 and the announced conversion to Marxism in the *Critique of Dialectical Reason* of 1960—circumstances which the Western world outside of France has been slow to grasp. It is now clear that Sartre and de Beauvoir were apolitical when they began their writing careers; they hated their own class, the bourgeoisie, and hoped to destroy it by the power of literature. Sartre's hatred of the bourgeoisie became politicized during his encounter with communist colleagues in the wartime resistance movement. As we have seen, Sartre, the existentialist celebrity acclaimed at the end of World War II as the spokesman of freedom, already had been subjected to relentless, bitter attack by French communist intellectuals and had been condemned publicly as a bourgeois enemy of the revolution. Since Sartre, the existentialist champion of the freedom of individual conscious being, was nevertheless drawn to the idea of revolution, the large and influential Communist Party of France (PCF), which dominated revolutionary thought and action in France, played a cat-and-mouse game with Sartre and was able to keep Sartre on the defensive in all his writing and political activities for close to the rest of his life. In *What is Literature* (1947) Sartre questioned whether one could become a communist and remain a writer. French intellectuals who joined the PCF were forced, he had observed, to surrender their intellectual autonomy and to support the party, without criticism, in whatever were its policies. On the other hand, if a writer did not join the party, he would not reach the proletariat, who read only what the party permitted. Matters came to a head in 1948 to 1949 with the performance of Sartre's new play, *Dirty Hands (Les Mains Sales,* 1948), which was critical of the communists' use of assassination to settle disputes among party members. Sartre was immediately vilified by the PCF newspaper, *L'Humanité,* and attacks on him increased so that by 1952 Sartre had become, in the words of another left-wing writer, "the most denounced, the most hated man in France." In these intolerable circumstances, Sartre responded by becoming enraged at the government's arrest of Jacques Duclos, the leader of the PCF. Hastily Sartre wrote *The Communists and the Peace* (1952), in which he declared a new principle: that the French Communist Party and the Soviet Union must be accepted without criticism as the exclusive representatives of the oppressed. The PCF, in return for this capitulation, complimented Sartre, and he was soon accepted as one of the leading Marxist intellectuals.

Thus 1952 is the date of Sartre's conversion to Marxism, long before the announcement in the *Critique* of 1960. Sartre remained on relatively good terms with the PCF until May 1968, when he broke with the party and with the Soviet Union for their failure to support the French students and workers in a general strike and revolution. Sartre next became involved with the ultraleft politics of the French Maoists and announced a new political principle: Intellectuals must abandon their role as intellectuals, and engage in political action to serve the people. At this point the life of Sartre, the radical intellectual, becomes split between his radical street activism and his withdrawal to the writing of a completely nonpolitical work, *The Idiot of the Family* (1971–72), in three volumes, the psychological and sociological biography of Gustave Flaubert, the nineteenth-century author of *Madame Bovary.*

It is only against this background of his political vicissitudes with the Communist Party of France that one can understand Sartre's conversion to Marxism: From the resistance movement of the war until May 1968 the Communist Party had been his reference group, the group whose judgment and evaluation of him was the only one that mattered. It is thus against this background that one can understand Sartre's astonishing political career: Sartre supported Stalin's purges of the intellectuals and professionals in Russia, and the notorious concentration camps; he supported the Algerian revolt against France and, globally, the use of violence by colonial peoples to achieve independence; he became a leading champion of the Third World against the West; he supported the communist revolutions in Cuba and China; he turned down the Nobel Prize in literature in 1964, because it would appear to be acceptance of a bourgeois honor; he became passionately anti-American, viewing America as the enemy of the Soviet Union, and as the stronghold of capitalist imperialism. Sartre presided over a war-crimes tribunal in Sweden which was deliberately set up to indict the U.S. for atrocities it committed in Vietnam; he wrote in ecstatic praise, after a visit to the Soviet Union, of the satisfactions of life and the complete freedom and egalitarianism which he found there. Among his last political acts were his hawking of ultraleft newspapers in the streets of Paris, and his attack upon the Vietnamese communists, (whom he had so passionately supported against the Americans) for their brutal expulsion of the ethnic Chinese.

Sartre was unable to provide a new political philosophy in which existentialism would humanize Marxism. But in the crucial area for modern consciousness, the field where political thought, psychology, sociology, literature, and philosophy intersect, Sartre is among the pioneers—he provided, for this crucial intersection of meanings in contemporary culture, fruitul concepts and methods to be developed, and his life was a struggle to express the complex and subtle significance of the truth that conscious being is a being-in-the world. Sartre died on April 15, 1980. A spontaneous crowd of over fifty thousand people gathered and accompanied his body to the cemetery. French newspapers ran special editions and tributes were paid by the president and by political and cultural leaders in France and around the world.

Jean-Paul Sartre must be credited with being the major voice in the development of twentieth century existentialism and its dissemination. But Sartre's existentialism is today more and more identified as one subtype of the broader philosophic viewpoint called *phenomenology*. Phenomenology is the philosophic viewpoint which was begun by the German philosopher Edmund Husserl, who gave it its name, and whose influence upon Sartre we have already noted.

Phenomenology, which incorporates existentialism, is one of the two major rival philosophic viewpoints in the world today. The two notably competing philosophies of the present time are phenomenology (including existentialism) and linguistic philosophy.

And so we turn to our last major topic—an overview of the present philosophic scene. We turn to these two opposing philosophies of the present time with the question What are the problems which command the vitality, the restless negativity, and the creative living spirit of philosophy now, in our own time?

Phenomenology

Let us turn first to phenomenology. Phenomenology as a school of philosophy was developed in German universities prior to World War I, most notably by Edmund Husserl; it was continued by Martin Heidegger, and others, and by Jean-Paul Sartre in his existentialism; and it continues to be developed by many philosophers at the present time.

First of all, what is meant by phenomenology? The word phenomenology you recognize from Hegel's great work *The Phenomenology of Spirit*. The influence of Hegel is present in the development of phenomenology and existentialism, as we have already seen in the case of the strong influence of Heglian concepts upon Sartre. By phenomenology Hegel meant the theory of phenomena, the objects which we experience. Specifically, Hegel presented the theory that the phenomena which we experience, which appear to us, are a product of the variety of activities and conceptual structures of human consciousness, and are relative to culture and to history.

Husserl rejects Hegel's view of the cultural and historical relativism of phenomena, but he accepts Hegel's formal concept of phenomenology, and it becomes the basic principle for the development of all types of phenomenology: The phenomena of experience are products of the activity and structures of our consciousness. Neither for Hegel nor the phenomenologists are phenomena appearances of things-in-themselves, things as they are independently of our ways of perceiving them. The Kantian thing-in-itself, since it remains, by definition, forever outside the grasp of the structures of consciousness, is eliminated. A *second*, related principle of phenomenology is that only an analysis of the activity and structures of consciousness can provide an understanding of the phenomena we experience, since consciousness itself constitutes them. *Third*, Husserl and all other phenomenologists insist upon the *intentional* aspect of consciousness: Consciousness is directed toward objects, it is consciousness-*of;* consciousness consists of intentional acts and intended objects.

A *fourth* principle of phenomenology is its rejection of empiricism and scientific method, and any philosophy (such as naturalism) which rests upon them, on the ground that they treat consciousness by methods which are designed for predicting and controlling things in nature. Closely related to this is a *fifth* theme, the rejection of scientific world views or metaphysical systems which synthesize the sciences, on the ground that since these are scientifically based pictures of the world, they will necessarily omit and falsify the role of consciousness in perceiving the world. And a *sixth* principle is that phenomenology is deliberately autonomous as a philosophy; it is independent of the methods or facts of any of the natural sciences, social sciences, and history; it accounts for consciousness and the phenomena of experience solely from a philosophic, internal analysis of consciousness itself.

But Husserl has something of great boldness to add to these principles of phenomenology. Husserl was a mathematician and logician, and he was obsessed, as was the mathematician Descartes, by a vision of finding certainty for philosophy, the same indubitable certainty that is found in mathematics. Moreover, like Descartes, Husserl saw himself as living in a time of crisis, as he indicated by the startling title of his last major philosophic essay: *Philosophy and the Crisis of European Man* (1935). The intellectual crisis of the Western world, Husserl says, is that we have lost our belief that there is any rational certainty, any absolutely certain truth.

The villain in this story, as Husserl tells it, is the dominance in the modern world of the natural sciences and the accompanying philosophy of naturalism. Husserl views naturalism as a philosophy according to which physical nature encompasses everything that is real. Naturalism thus reduces human consciousness to the status of being merely a part of nature, the product of physical causes. Moreover, naturalism demands that human consciousness, like every other part of nature, should be explained by the enormously successful methods of the natural sciences—physics, chemistry, and biology. But Husserl insists, as Sartre does, that conscious being is completely different from material being and cannot be explained in the same way.

More important, however, Husserl argues that if human consciousness is merely material, a part of physical nature, it can never be a foundation for rational certainty. Naturalism has brought upon us, says Husserl, the present crisis of the loss of a belief in any absolute certainty, any rational truth. And Husserl makes it clear that this is not only an intellectual crisis of the lack of any certainty at the foundation of our thought, but a social and political crisis as well: If, for European man, no belief has certainty, then European man has no truth to be his shield against the rise of fascism and its appeal to irrationalism. And for Husserl there was also a personal crisis: Without a basis in some absolute certainty, said Husserl, "I cannot live; I cannot bear life unless I can believe that I shall achieve it."

Husserl struggled all his life to restore to philosophy a foundation in certainty—a Cartesian rock such as the Cogito—and he failed. As a phenomenologist, he had tried to demonstrate that through a complex phenomenological method of reducting ("bracketing") ordinary experience to pure experience, we can know with absolute certainty the essential structures of our conscious acts, such as thinking and remembering, and, on the other side, the essential structures of the objects which these acts intend, or refer to. And thus philosophy would become a "rigorous science" and certainty would be achieved—philosophy and all the sciences would rest upon this firm foundation of absolutely certain knowledge of the universal and necessary acts and structures of consciousness.

The difficulties which Husserl ran into in defending these ingeniously brilliant and desperate claims finally forced him to surrender his quest for certainty and led him to his last view of phenomenology—that it seeks to describe the structures of our daily life experience, our common experience in the life-world (*Lebenswelt*) of everday affairs. The structures of the life-world, the world as it is lived and experienced by conscious subjects, is what phenomenology studies and describes and is the rich source from which the natural sciences must take their abstractions. Thus the *Lebenswelt* is the foundation of philosophy and also of all the sciences. With the conception of the life-world of conscious subjects, phenomenology in this modest, descriptive form still has its own foundation and is still liberated from domination by the natural sciences. The conception of the *Lebenswelt* is thus a *seventh* important claim of phenomenology.

It is Husserl's conception of the *Lebenswelt*, the life-world, the world as experienced and lived by conscious beings, that exerted a profound influence upon Heidegger and Sartre and that continues to excite most contemporary phenomenologists.

Heidegger and Sartre and most phenomenologists today have given up on Descartes's and Husserl's quests for mathematical certainty as a foundation for knowledge, and make the more modest claim that they are trying only to describe the many ways in which consciousness itself provides the structure and the felt quality of the world as we experience and live it, the life-world of conscious being—as Sartre described our consciousness of the Other, and of his look, and of the resulting loss of my sense of freedom, and of the ensuing master-slave struggle with the Other.

What, then, of existentialism? You have been wondering, how is the passionate, psychologizing existentialism of Sartre related to the rigorous abstract phenomenology of Husserl?

What is the relationship of existentialism to phenomenology? Existentialism bases itself upon the principles and conceptions of phenomenology which have been summarized here. Its focus, however, is upon the exploration of the life-world of conscious being, the lived life of conscious subjects. It is only to this element within phenomenology that existentialism has made a contribution. And thus Husserl's concept of the life-world is the specific link between existentialism and phenomenology.

Heidegger and Sartre, Husserl's most famous followers, may thus be regarded as existentialists insofar as they focus phenomenology upon the regions of being and specifically upon my existence as conscious being. According to their description, as conscious being I live in a life-world into which I feel myself to be absurdly thrown, a world in which I find that as conscious being I alone provide its meaning and values; and my life is lived in anguish and despair.

And last, before we leave the philosophy of phenomenology and existentialism, we should mention their influence outside philosophy. They have been a considerable and growing influence upon the social sciences, especially upon sociology, cultural anthropology, and political science; and also upon psychology and psychotherapy. All of these sciences and psychotherapies have been learning from existentialism and phenomenology the importance of the conscious subject, and his modes of structuring, feeling, and acting in the world; they are studying the ways in which the individual subject perceives himself, others, and the world, rather than looking at him only in terms of his behavior, or statistically, or as defined by a social system. Under the influence of phenomenology and existentialism, social scientists and psychotherapists are discovering that an important part of our knowledge of human individuals and groups is understanding their ways of perceiving the world.

Linguistic Philosophy: Logical Positivism and Analytic Philosophy

Existentialism and phenomenology were German and French philosopical movements which had for the most part been developed prior to World War II. The impact of existentialism and phenomenology upon the United States came only after World War II, in the 1950's and 1960's, as communication with the many European refugee scholars in the United States developed, and as the slow process of translation into English made the key books available to American readers.

But before World War II there had occurred the impact upon the United States of another type of philosophy—linguistic philosophy—which has been described as descending like an avalanche upon philosophy in America, burying every other type of philosophy in its path. Although it is now disintegrating, linguistic philosophy has remained the dominant philosophic viewpoint in the United States and in Britain since the 1930's. What was the source of this powerful philosophic avalanche? As the principal historic, philosophic source of existentialism and phenomenology is Hegel, so the principal historic source of linguistic philosophy is the empricism of David Hume.

Linguistic Philosophy

First Stage: Logical Positivism. (1) The Meaning of a Proposition Is Identical with Its Empirical Verification. (2) Philosophy Is the Activity of Clarifying Language by Logical Analysis and by Destroying Meaningless Propositions.

The first stage of linguistic philosophy is called logical positivism (or logical empiricism), and it arose during the 1920's and early 1930's in two major universities, the University of Vienna in Austria, in a group known as the Vienna Circle, and in Cambridge University in England. In both universities logical positivism developed as an attack upon all metaphysical systems such as the Hegelian, and demanded a return to the empiricism of Hume.

Like Hume, the logical positivists argued that there are only two kinds of propositions, the propositions of logic and mathematics (which Hume had said dealt with "relations of ideas") and the propositions of common sense and science (which Hume had said dealt with "matters of fact"). We have, they say, no other kind of knowledge than that which logic, mathematics, and science give us. And just as Hume proposed that since metaphysics contains neither logical, mathematical, nor factual propositions, we should commit it to the flames, so logical empiricism demands that metaphysics be destroyed. But the logical positivists are even more savage than Hume in their attack on metaphysics.

The logical positivism developed by the Vienna Circle set out from its inception to destroy metaphysics. The august membership of the Circle—philosophers, physicists, mathematicians, and logicians—loathed and feared the German idealistic philosophies which appeared to be legitimating the rise of irrationalism in continental politics. The goal of the Vienna Circle was to destroy philosophy except for the philosophic analysis necessary to establish an absolute certain foundation for the sciences. The goal of logical positivism was to establish, in place of metaphysical speculation, a tough, empirical "scientific mentality," and to make the science of physics the model for all human knowledge. To achieve this goal on behalf of science, the logical positivists became an international movement, holding congresses and publishing monographs for the purpose of "propagating and furthering a scientific outlook."

The final blow which the logical positivists delivered to metaphysics was to show that metaphysics is not merely false but is actually meaningless. The propositions of metaphysics are neither true nor false, they said, but without any meaning at all. How did they show this? By establishing a principle which would test the meaningfulness of statements. This is logical positivism's famous *verifiability principle*. The verifiability principle for testing meaningfulness was clearly designed by the logical positivists with the empirical statements of physics as a model, and thus it serves to favor science over philosophy. It says that a factual statement (in contrast to a logical or mathematical proposition) is meaningful if and only if it is empirically verifiable. To be cognitively meaningful, that is, to be meaningful as factual or descriptive knowledge, a proposition must, at least in principle, be testable by empirical observation. But no metaphysical statements, such as Plato's statements about the forms, Descartes's statements about mental and physical substances, Hegel's statements about finite and absolute spirit—none of these statements can possibly be proved empirically, by any means of sensory observation or experimentation. Therefore, logical empiricism triumphantly concludes, metaphysical statements are meaningless, nonsensical. The verifiability principle has thus put an end to metaphysics.

But if metaphysics is meaningless nonsense, what about the statements of ethics? Ethics, too, is thrown into the flames. The statements of ethics, the ethics of Plato or of Hegel or of Sartre, even a basic ethical statement such as *killing is wrong*—all ethical statements can immediately be shown to be meaningless, since none of these statements can pass the test of being empirically verifiable. But within logical positivism a special theory for ethics was developed and generally supported, and became known as the emotive theory of ethics. The emotive theory of ethics argues that ethical statements are not really statements conveying knowledge at all (they are "noncognitive"), but are only expressions of our feelings or emotions. Thus to say that killing is wrong merely expresses our feelings of disapproval of killing; it does not, however, provide any knowledge that is empirically testable, and so it is cognitively meaningless.

But just as there is no possible way of verifying by empirical observation the statements of metaphysics and ethics, neither is there any way of empirically verifying the statements of theory of knowledge, social philosophy, philosophy of history, philosophy of religion, or aesthetics. Statements in these philosophic fields clearly cannot be rescued from meaninglessness by being claimed to be mathematical or logical propositions. But there are only two kinds of meaningful language, say the logical positivists: the language of empirically observed fact and the abstract language of logic and mathematics. Then into the flames as nonsense go all these areas of philosophy, since they have no meaning, they give us no knowledge, they contain no truth. Most of the logical positivists denied that they were philosophers. Rudolf Carnap, one of the leading figures in the Vienna Circle, proclaimed in 1932 that "we give no answer to philosophical questions and instead reject all philosophical questions, whether of Metaphysics, Ethics or Epistemology." For logical positivism, the empirically verifiable propositions of science and the formal propositions of mathematics and logic constitute the only source of truth; the claims to truth of traditional philosophy must therefore be discredited and destroyed.

What, then, if anything, is left for philosophy? Logical positivism answers that philosophy can offer no truths about the world. Philosophers must give up their old lofty notions of being master builders of metaphysical systems (such as Descartes's system, which incorporated the new science, or Hegel's system, which incorporated the whole of human culture). Philosophy must give up offering moral truth as Plato did, or diagnosing the historically rooted contradictions of our time, as Marx did. The only function of philosophy is an activity—the activity of clarifying our language by providing a logical analysis of statements. There are three ways in which this is to be done: *first,* to provide a standard or test for meaningfulness, so that meaningless statements can be exposed; this is the function of the verifiability principle. *Second,* philosophy must clarify the individual scientific statements by analyzing them into statements of what is directly observed. And *third,* there is the ideal of logical positivism— the unity of science (the dream of Descartes), in which all the sciences would be unified by being reduced to the language of physics, the most fully developed science, in an orderly logical procedure.

The seemingly aggressive and boldly destructive movement of logical positivism, fortified by the logical, linguistic, and scientific features of its arguments, was nevertheless short-lived. Its central doctrine, the verifiability principle, was soon subjected to devastating attack on several grounds. First of all, the verifiability principle failed its own test, since it is not itself an empirically verifiable statement; it is therefore embarrassingly meaningless. Moreover, the verifiability principle as a test of the meaningfulness of statements places science itself (which it was designed to support) in danger, since scientific laws and other scientific construction are not completely verifiable. Also, the principle is unclear as to whether it requires actual verification or only possible verification, and if only possible verification, what this relaxed requirement means. As for the other two ways in which philosophy functions to clarify our language: The logical translation of scientific statements into simple observation statements ran into unresolvable controversies; and the ideal of the unity of science was also beset with difficulties and abandoned.

Logical positivism is now dead. The Vienna Circle had begun to disintegrate early in the 1930's, and in the middle of the 1930's the Jewish members were forced to flee from Hitler's National Socialism. By the end of World War II, the movement had come to an end. Many of the logical positivists had already come to question some of their previous assumptions, especially the assumptions that the artificially constructed language of observation statements is both the only language which can test the meaningfulness of a proposition and is also the only language which corresponds with the actual facts of the world. And so the transition was soon made to abandon these assumptions and to claim instead that meaningfulness can be tested by a variety of languages, and that no language corresponds with the facts of the world. In this way the second stage of linguistic philosophy began to emerge—the stage of analytic philosophy.

Wittgenstein: The Tractatus. It was one man, who, by an extraordinary set of circumstances, was the link between the emerging logical positivists of Cambridge University in England and those in the Vienna Circle at the University of Vienna in Austria—and who was also the link between logical positivism and analytic philosophy, the two stages of linguistic philosophy. That man was the psychologically tormented logical genius Ludwig Wittgenstein (1889–1951). Wittgenstein was born in Vienna in 1889 into a family of great wealth and great intellectual and artistic cultivation. His earliest interests appear to have been in mechanical things, and he first studied engineering in Austria and then in Germany. He then moved on to England to continue his studies, and for three years was involved in aeronautical research.

Wittgenstein's interests then turned to mathematics and logic and he became a student during 1912 and 1913 of the famous British philosopher and mathematician Bertrand Russell, at Cambridge University. Like the logical positivists in the Vienna Circle, Russell's philosophy at this time reflected an attack upon German idealism, in his case a reaction to the rise of German idealism among British philosophers. Russell's attack upon their metaphysics involved him in analyzing facts in order to construct a new language which would correspond exactly with the facts of the world. It was here in Cambridge, apparently, that Wittgenstein first did serious and extensive reading in philosophy, and he is reported to have been surprised to discover that the philosophers whom he had "worshipped in ignorance" before studying them were "stupid and dishonest and make disgusting mistakes!" As for himself, he felt that the development of his own ideas in logic was hampered by the fact that his life was *full* of the most hateful and petty thoughts and acts." "How," he asks, "can I be a logician if I am not yet a man? *Before everything else* I must become pure." Wittgenstein retreated to total seclusion on a farm in Norway from the end of 1913 to the beginning of World War I; and the vast wealth which he inherited at the death of his father in 1913 he gave away.

Wittgenstein volunteered for service in the Austrian Army as soon as World War I broke out, and during his years at various army posts, he completed his first major work, which later was given the title *Tractatus Logico-Philosophicus*, usually referred to as the *Tractatus*, (the Latin word for treatise, or essay). The *Tractatus* was published in 1922 and became the bible of the logical positivists in the Vienna Circle, with whom Wittgenstein apparently had many discussions. In the preface to this strangely dogmatic and obscure small book, less than eighty pages long, Wittgenstein announced that his book "deals with the problems of philosophy" and that his aim was to show that language sets a limit on what we can meaningfully say.

Language, says Wittgenstein's compelling argument, is

meaningful only when it pictures facts for us. This viewpoint, which claims that a sentence is a picture, has come to be called the picture theory of meaning. Wittgenstein says:

> A proposition is a picture of reality. A proposition is a model of reality as we think it to be. (*Tractatus*, 4.01)

And in any picture there must be a correspondence between the picture and the state of affairs it represents. Thus our propositions are *true* insofar as they provide a picture of the actual facts in the case; and our propositions are *meaningful* insofar as they provide a picture of the possible facts in the case. Propositions which fail to picture the actual or possible facts in the case are without any meaning at all, they are nonsensical. And Wittgenstein, whose hatred for traditional philosophy is intense, quickly points to philosophy, and says:

> Most of the propositions and questions to be found in philosophical works are not false but nonsensical. Consequently we cannot give any answer to questions of this kind, but can only establish that they are nonsensical. Most of the propositions and questions of philosophers arise from our failure to understand the logic of our language. (*Tractatus*, 4.003)

The logical positivists regarded Wittgenstein's picture theory of meaning as the source of their verifiability principle.

And so we ask of Wittgenstein, as we asked the logical positivists, what is left for philosophy? Wittgenstein answers in the *Tractatus*, as the logical positivists did, that philosophy has no other legitimate function than as an activity: "Philosophy is not a body of doctrine but an activity." (*Tractatus*, 4.112) Nothing is left for philosophers to do but to engage in the activity of exposing the meaninglessness of previous philosophers. Philosophers have failed to understand the limits of language: that meaningful language can only picture reality and thus that the only true propositions are those that picture the actual facts in the case—and the logical consequence of this is that the totality of true propositions is identical with the totality of the propositions of the natural sciences. But "philosophy is not one of the natural sciences." (*Tractatus*, 4.111) And thus Wittgenstein concludes:

The correct method in philosophy would really be the following: to say nothing except what can be said, i.e., propositions of natural science—i.e., something that has nothing to do with philosophy . . .

But philosophers have not yet learned, Wittgenstein says, that ethics, religion, metaphysics "cannot be put into words." The question which ethics, religion, metaphysics ask—What is good? Does God exist? What is real?—these questions which strike us as deep and profound, are actually nonsensical, he says, since they do not picture any possible facts. But unlike the logical positivists, who simply dismiss all such questions as nonsensical, Wittgenstein's response to the meaninglessness of metaphysics, ethics, and religion is to refer to these deeply moving matters as "the mystical"—things which the logic of language precludes us from saying anything about, things which lie beyond the reach of language. "Unsayable things do exist," he says. But the last proposition of the *Tractatus* says:

Whereof one cannot speak, thereof one must be silent.

Wittgenstein's *Tractatus* links the earlier work of Russell at Cambridge University with the Vienna Circle's logical positivism which emerged some years later. Despite some important differences among them, their agreements are of major significance in bringing about the linguistic turn in philosophy: the attack upon metaphysical claims to truth; the emphasis upon elementary "factual" propositions; and the theory of language as the frame for meaning, defining and limiting meaningfulness.

For some time, Wittgenstein seems to have been convinced that he had "solved all philosophical problems" as he had set out to do. He gave up philosophy and worked as a schoolteacher in an Austrian village, he unsuccessfully applied for admission to a Catholic monastic order, he labored as a gardener's assistant in a monastery, and he designed a magnificent house for one of his sisters. But in 1929, after sixteen years, he returned to Cambridge University, where he lectured and entered upon the new line of thought which led to his second great book, the *Philosophical Investigations*. In 1939 he received a prestigious chair in philosophy and continued his informal lectures, accessible only to a very select group of advanced students. In intense discussions with these student disciples, Wittgenstein worked out the thoughts which were published in 1953 after his death, under the title *Philosophical Investigations*. During World War II, Wittgenstein left the university to work in various hospitals which served the war wounded. Although he returned to the university, he had become dissatisfied with teaching, increasingly troubled by the hypocrisy of human beings, and by his failure to purify his own life. In ill health, he retreated to seclusion in order to write. He died in 1951.

Linguistic Philosophy

Second stage: Analytic Philosophy. (1) The Meaning of Words Is from Their Use in a Language Game. (2) Philosophy Is the Activity of Analyzing Language Games to Dissolve Philosophical Problems.

Wittgenstein: Philosophical Investigations. In his second major work, Wittgenstein devoted much of his argument to an attack upon his own previous work, the *Tractatus*, for its view of language. The *Tractatus* assumed that there is one universal form of language, the form of language which consists of sentences picturing reality. Now, in the *Philosophical Investigations*, Wittgenstein rejects this view as mistaken. We do use language to picture facts, but we also, he says, use language in many other ways—to give orders, to greet people, to make jokes, to play chess, to tell stories, to solve problems, to pray. Historians, for example, use language differently from lawyers or from psychologists. Each is a different kind of language with its own rules. Each, he says, is a different language game, played by its own rules. For any activity, the words and actions involved in it may be considered to be a language game. This new view of language carries a new view of meaning. Replacing the view that a proposition is meaningful because it pictures reality is the view that words gain their meaning from how they are used in a language game. The notion is rejected that propositions gain meaning only from a principle or from a test imposed by the precision of logic.

Moreover, we should not look to the confused attempts of philosophers to find a single meaning, a Platonic essence, a universal which would define a word's meaning in all circumstances, in every kind of language game. We should look not to the ideal meanings of words but, empirically, to the way in which words are actually used. We should look not to an ideal language which derives its meaning from facts and has a precise logical structure—as did Russell, the *Tractatus*, and the Vienna Circle—but, empirically, to the ways in which languages are actually used.

In his attack upon the Platonic theory of forms or essences, Wittgenstein argues that since words are used in many different language games, no one use is more meaningful or truer than another. There is no essence which these uses have in common; there are only similarities, which Wittgenstein describes as "family resemblances," among the various uses of a word, "a complicated network of similarities overlapping and crisscrossing." Wittgenstein cleverly uses the word "game" to support his argument against Platonic forms, essences, or universals: Given the many different kinds of games—board games, card games, ball games—no "essence" common to them all can be seen, but only a variety of similarities, as with "the resemblances between members of a family."

With this new view of language, Wittgenstein brought about the second stage of linguistic philosophy, the movement in philosophy which is now usually known as analytic philosophy and which has dominated the philosophers of the English-speaking world for over a quarter of a century. With the emergence of the second stage of linguistic philosophy and this new Wittgensteinian view of many languages, many language games, many ways in which words have meaning, what now, we ask again, is the role of philosophy in the world? Philosophy's role is analytic. The task of philosophy is to analyze language in order to discover the many language games, and their rules for using words, and to remove the "puzzles" which arise when the rules of a language game are misused. When one sticks to the rules, no problems arise. But there are no private language games, no private rules for using words, no private sensations which only I can know. Language games are social, and express some social group's "form of life," its way of doing things, its culture.

But who does misuse language? Who creates the problems, the confusions, the puzzles, the tangled knots of misusing language? It is the philosophers, of course, according to Wittgenstein in the *Philosophical Investigations*, who persist in misusing language. The problems of philosophy are only linguistic problems, word puzzles which trap philosophers because they do not follow the rules of the ordinary English language game. Philosophers mistakenly look for the essence of words; they mistakenly construct ideal languages and criteria of meaning from the features of a few examples, as if such languages were more perfect than everyday language; they mistakenly try, as Plato and Hegel did, to synthesize all human experience and knowledge, but this, according to Wittgenstein, is total confusion, a mixing up of many different language games—art, religion, science, ethics, politics— into one nonsensical hodgepodge. Philosophers' problems are not genuine problems but only the nonsense that results from not knowing how to handle language. "A philosophical problem," says Wittgenstein, "has the form: I don't know my way about." Moreover, he says, "Philosophers have been bewitched by language," lured into using words outside the specific language games which give them their specific meanings.

What, then, can be done about philosophers and the philosophy which they have produced, now that philosophy is seen to be a history of confusion, of problems which should never have worried anyone because they are nonsensical? Wittgenstein's answer is that the philosopher must be given therapy for his confusion, and that philosophy itself must be dissolved. Philosophers, he says, are in need of therapy for their philosophic anxieties about such matters as man, space, time, God, and the world. Since these anxieties are the product of linguistic confusion, therapy will help them by showing them how to use language. They must be shown how to bring their "words back from their metaphysical to their everyday usage."

For example: It is a common occurrence to be asked by a stranger on the street, "What time is it?" But if an English-speaking stranger should ask you, "What is time?" you would know that he is either troubled by a philosophical problem or is a person with a psychic disturbance which has led to a speech disorder. Only such people, Wittgenstein would say, break the rules of the language game of ordinary language, rules which the rest of us all know and follow. Both need therapy. Wittgenstein has a therapy for the philosopher troubled by the problem What is time? His therapeutic treatment would consist in his being shown that when he examines all the ways in which the word "time" is used in all the language games which use it, he will have solved the problem of time and will also have dissolved it—by coming to see that the "problem" was no problem, but only a misuse of language. Who will provide this therapy? Linguistic therapy will be administered by the "cured" philosophers—those who, like Wittgenstein and his followers, have been cured of the disease of philosophy.

When philosophers will have learned to use words as ordinary, everyday language does, they will then no longer fall into linguistic confusion. Their philosophic problems will be dissolved and their anxieties about the world, man, and God will be relieved, because they will not want to talk about such meaningless problems anymore. "The fly buzzing in the flybottle will be shown the way out," is Wittgenstein's famous comment. And as philosophers become clear about how not to misuse language, as they become clear that they must stick to ordinary language, they will no longer be bewitched by language and therefore they will stop philosophizing. Analytic philosophy may be described as an activity of analyzing language games in order to dissolve the problems of philosophy; it administers an understanding of its activity as therapy to cure people of the disease of philosophy; and it moves toward the goal of the elimination of philosophy.

Analytic philosophy quickly swept up the English-speaking philosophic world after World War II (Gilbert Ryle, A. J. Ayer, John Austin, Willard Quine are major figures in this movement) and has remained as the dominant philosophy in those parts since that time. What was the appeal of analytic philosophy? Unlike existentialism with its widespread magnetic appeal, *first of all,* analytic philosophy was exciting only to academic philosophers; its aim of clarifying language and its resultant minute examinations of the usage of particular words offered no stimulus to the popular imagination or to the ongoing interests of the intellectual culture. But the merits of analytic philosophy in the eyes of academic philosophers were very great. Analytic philosophy carried Wittgenstein's sense of outrage against philosophy, and it appealed to many philosophers as a legitimate, righteous crusade against the deficiencies of traditional philosophy—its lack of clarity; its reliance upon outworn and misleading models of knowledge and truth; its insensitivity to language and the limitations which language places upon philosophy; its proliferation of philosophical "problems" which are the product of linguistic confusion; its pretentious and questionable syntheses of total reality, with their uncritical mixture of philosophy with ideology, history, economics, moral values, history, and religion. By contrast with these failings of traditional philosophy, analytic philosophy offered the salutary appeal of being "clean."

Second, analytic philosophy provided philosophers with a new, highly developed, logical technique, the technique of analyzing word usage in language games, discovering philosophic ambiguities, errors, and confusions, and dissolving philosophic problems. The technique of linguistic analysis contributed greatly to an increased sense on the part of philosophers of the "professionalization" of their discipline. And *third*, the technique of linguistic analysis established autonomy for philosophy as a discipline; now with its own technique, philosophy became independent and self-sufficient in relation to all other disciplines and especially with regard to the many sciences encroaching upon hitherto philosophic territory. As one analytic philosopher remarked recently, "You don't have to know anything to be good at [analytic] philosophy. All you have to be is clever and interested in the subject."

Since World War II, the analytic philosophers have dominated the teaching and publishing of philosophy in the English-speaking world. Vast numbers of technical, piecemeal analyses have been written on the usage of words like *cause* in different language games and on the ways in which words are misused by philosophers. But the problems of philosophy have not been dissolved by linguistic philosophy. It appears instead to be the case that linguistic philosophy is being dissolved. It is disintegrating as its crusade against philosophy has itself come under attack, and as its minute, technical analyses are increasingly regarded as tedious and trivial. There is a growing sense in the philosophical world that this analytic philosophy, which has pervaded all American universities, has been a failure and that the merits which gave it its great appeal have been its undoing. *First*, analytic philosophy attacked traditional philosophy and also rejected any constructive role for itself. And thus it provided no metaphysics, no world view, no theory of knowledge, no philosophy of nature, no ethics, social philosophy, or philosophy of history—these were no concern of the analytic philosophers. But now analytic philosophy is seen to have created a vacuum in the intellectual world (variously but inadequately filled by psychologists, economic theorists, and political pundits) and to have failed to fulfill important functions of philosophy as a discipline. Moreover, the rejection of any constructive role for philosophy has its most damaging outcome within analytic philosophy itself. By rejecting the construction of theory, analytic philosophy has no theory of language games and therefore no theoretical understanding of their differences and no criteria for critically evaluating them. Thus anlaytic philosophy is now adrift in a sea of language games. And thus the rejection of a constructive role for philosophy has been the undoing of the conception of language games.

Second, the great merit of gaining a technique is now increasingly regarded as having brought about the triumph of technique over substance in analytic philosophy. Philosophy is no longer about the world, but only about the language with which we speak about the world. Analytic philosophy is thus identical with the technique of linguistic analysis and is now seen to be imprisoned by language, trapped in the flybottle of linguistic analysis.

And *third,* the autonomy and independence which the technique of linguistic analysis conferred upon analytic philosophy also contributed to its failure. The price of autonomy for analytic philosophy has been its isolation from the vitality of the intellectual culture and from the issues of public and personal life. Cut off from these affairs of human life, the analytic philosopher has no contribution to make to them, beyond occasionally noting a linguistic misusage. There is thus a growing impatient criticism of analytic philosophy that it is out of touch with the vital matters of human life, with the things which concern us most—as Wittgenstein himself hopelessly admitted. Specifically within the areas of ethics and political philosophy, in which philosophy has traditionally had the function of providing norms, standards, and ideals, analytic philosophy has reduced these areas to language games and the way words like right or good or justice are used, not how they should be used.

As for analytic philosophy's opponents, existentialism and phenomenology, these of course do have a human dimension. But Sartre's existentialism ends in extreme alienation and nihilism, and an uncritical leap to Marxism; Husserl's quest for certainty is a failure; and recent phenomenology discloses

the limitations of this philosophy whose theme is subjectivity—
it offers only descriptions of the ways in which consciousness
structures the world. It can offer no metaphysics, no normative ethics or social philosophy, no synthesis of subjectivity
and the sciences.

Philosophy seems at this time to have suppressed its own
creativity. Is it the case as some have said recently that we
are witnessing the death of philosophy? But after long years
of philosophical barrenness, in the frigid land of technical
analysis of language, is it not the case that something may
now be stirring into life in philosophy?

Buried under the avalanche of linguistic philosophy was
the vital American philosophy of naturalism, the philosophy
of Ralph Waldo Emerson (1830–82) and Charles Peirce
(1839–1914), William James (1842–1910) and John Dewey
(1859–1952), George Herbert Mead (1863–1931) and George
Santayana (1863–1952). This was a philosophy which tried to
synthesize both Hume and Hegel; it did not despise science
as Sartre does; it did not despise philosophy as Wittgenstein
does; but it tried instead to show how science and subjectivity could be integrated in a philosophy in which nature is the
inclusive category, into a philosophy for the New World, for
the new beginning which was America. Naturalism defended
the public values of freedom, democracy, and individualism,
and of an open society moving into a brighter future; it
defended the personal values of growth, change, and re-
integration; and it expressed a profound American confidence
in our creative intelligence to solve whatever problems may
confront us. Now that there is a stirring in philosophy again,
there are signs of a revitalization of American philosophy.

But also buried under the avalanche of linguistic philosophy was the crucial philosophic function of providing a usable
history of philosophy from within the significance of the historical setting, rather than, as the linguistic philosophers have
done, presenting the history of philosophy as an historical
collection of linguistic misusages and nonsensical problems.
Buried also were the rich and stimulating researches based
upon interrelations between philosophy and economics, politics,
cultural anthropology, psychology, and the arts which had
long been a feature of American intellectual life. And these
are the types of interconnections which make a unifying

vision of reality possible, as they did for Hegel and Marx. Both of these philosophic types of research may now be stirring into life again. But of the various prospects for the renewal of philosophy we can only say with George Santayana:

> Who knows which of them may not gather force presently and carry the mind of the coming age steadily before it?

*   *   *

This book has attempted to present the concepts, theories, and themes in the works of six major Western philosophers. It has tried to show bitter conflicts and the deep continuities among these philosophies and also their persistent power to influence the ways in which we view ourselves and our world. This book has also tried to show that philosophy is both a product and producer of civilization: Particular philosophies have their origins in the intellectual and social problems of their own time and culture; and by their construction of a theory of reality, knowledge, morality, politics, or history, they serve to define the norms and ideals of the culture and the era. And finally this book has also tried to present each philosophic work as expressing the living spirit of a mortal human being, in a specific cultural situation, struggling to understand, as we all must, the human condition in the changing yet continuous reality in which we find ourselves.

SUGGESTIONS FOR FURTHER READING

PART SEVEN: IN SEARCH: THE CONTEMPORARY SCENE IN PHILOSOPHY

Linguistic Philosophy: Logical Positivism and Analytic Philosophy:

Critical Studies:

Ambrose, Alice, and Lazerowitz, Morris, eds. *Ludwig Wittgenstein: Philosophy and Language*. 1972. Atlantic Highlands, N.J.: Humanities Press, 1972.

Austin, John L. *How to Do Things with Words*. New York: Oxford University Press, 1965.

Ayer, A. J. *Language, Truth and Logic*. New York: Dover, 1946.

—————. *The Revolution in Philosophy*. 1956. N.Y.: St. Martin's Press, 1963.

Fann, K. T. *Ludwig Wittgenstein: The Man and His Philosophy*. New York: Dell Publishing Co., 1967.

Magee, Brian. *Modern British Philosophy*. London: Secker, 1972.

Malcolm, Norman, with von Wright, G. H. *Ludwig Wittgenstein: A Memoir*. New Jersey: Oxford University Press, 1958.

Passmore, John. *A Hundred Years of Philosophy*. New York: Penguin Books, 1968.

Pticher, George. *The Philosophy of Wittgenstein*. Englewood Cliffs, New Jersey: Prentice-Hall, 1964.

—————, ed. *Wittgenstein: The Philosophical Investigations*. Garden City, New York: Doubleday, 1966.

Rorty, Richard, ed. *The Linguistic Turn*. Chicago: University of Chicago Press, 1967.

Urmson, J. O. *Philosophical Analysis*. Oxford: Clarendon Press, 1956.

Warnock, G. J. *English Philosophy Since 1900*. New York: Oxford University Press, 1958.

Weinberg, Julius. *An Examination of Logical Positivism*. New Jersey: Littlefield Adams, 1960.

Phenomenology:

Critical Studies:

Elveton, R. O., ed. *The Phenomenology of Husserl*. Chicago: University of Chicago Press, 1970.

Farber, Marvin, ed. *Philosophical Essays in Memory of Edmund Husserl*. Cambridge: Harvard University Press, 1940. Reprinted, Greenwood Press, 1968.

—————. *Foundations of Phenomenology*. Cambridge: Harvard University Press, 1943.

Kockelmans, Joseph J., ed. *Phenomenology: The Philosophy of Edmund Husserl and Its Interpretation*. Garden City, New York: Doubleday, 1967.

Lauer, Quentin. *Phenomenology, Its Genesis and Prospects*. New York: Harper and Row, 1965.

Lawrence, N., and O'Connor, D., eds. *Readings in Existential Phenomenology*. Englewood Cliffs, New Jersey: Prentice-Hall, 1967.

Luckmann, Thomas, ed. *Phenomenology and Sociology*. New York: Penguin Books, 1978.

Natanson, Maurice, ed. *Essays in Phenomenology*. The Hague: Nijhoff, 1966.

———, ed. *Phenomenology and the Social Sciences*, vols. I–II. Evanston: Northwestern University Press, 1973.

Psathas, George, ed. *Phenomenological Sociology: Issues and Applications*. New York: John Wiley, 1973.

Spiegelberg, Herbert. *The Phenomenological Movement: A Historical Introduction*. The Hague: Nijhoff, 1965.

Thévenaz, P. *What Is Phenomenology?* Chicago: University of Chicago Press, 1962.

Zaner, Richard. *The Way of Phenomenology*. New York: Pegasus, 1970.

GLOSSARY

For terms not listed, or for fuller exposition of the following terms, consult *The Encyclopedia of Philosophy,* edited by Paul Edwards (Macmillan, 1967, 1972) or *The Dictionary of Philosophy,* edited by Dagobert Runes (Littlefield, 1960).

Absolute: see *Idealism*

Alienation: The individual's sense of separation or isolation from society, from his own feelings or identity, from God, from his work; and attendant feelings of meaninglessness, normlessness, powerlessness (Hegel, Kierkegaard, Marx, Sartre).

Appearance: That which presents itself to sensory perception as compared with its independent reality.

A priori. A component, or a kind, of knowledge which is independent of sensory experience (neither derived from it nor alterable by it) and which is regarded as having absolute certainty. (See Kant's theory of the a priori.)

Axiom: A proposition held to be self-evidently true; a first principle of a deductive system.

Category: A fundamental concept by which we interpret experience. (See Kant's theory of the categories as a priori interpretations of experience.)

Deduction: Orderly, logical reasoning from one or more statements (premises) which are assumed, to a conclusion which follows necessarily.

Determinism. The theory that everything happens necessarily in accordance with one or more scientific causal laws. Determinism denies the possibility of free will, i.e., that the will is free in moral choice.

Dialectic: (1) The oppositional, contradictory character of reality (Heraclitus, Plato, Hegel, Marx); (2) a method for understanding reality by the triadic movement from thesis to antithesis to synthesis (Hegel, Marx); (3) the highest level of knowledge, the construction of a totalizing philosophy in which all aspects of reality are synthesized into a rational conceptual whole (Plato, Hegel).

415

Dualism: Any view which holds that two ultimate, irreducible principles are required for the explanation of reality; e.g., Descartes's dualism of mind and matter.

Empiricism: The philosophic tradition in epistemology which holds that experience in the form of sense perception is the sole adequate source and test of knowledge.

Epistemology (theory of knowledge): The branch of philosophy which studies the sources, validity, and limits of knowledge; it inquires into perception, meaning, and truth.

Essence: (1) As distinct from accidental or nonessential: essence signifies those qualities which identify a thing as a member of a class of things, e.g., as a man or a dog; qualities such as the color of the hair or fur are "accidental" or nonessential to being a man or a dog. (2) As distinct from existence: Essence signifies what a thing is (e.g., a man); existence signifies that a thing is, the actuality of this particular man.

Ethics: The branch of philosophy which studies the meaning of good and evil, right and wrong, and moral obligation. Ethics may also refer to actual human behavior and the rules and ideals by which it is governed.

Existence: That which is actual; fact; by contrast with essence.

Free will: The theory which denies that the will is completely determined and claims that moral judgments of praise and blame are meaningless unless the will is free in its choice of actions.

Hedonism: Ethical hedonism: the view that pleasure ought to be the ultimate goal of human life; *psychological hedonism:* the view that pleasure is in fact the goal of universal human psychology.

Humanism: The classical doctrine of man as supreme in value in his capacity for truth and justice; by contrast with the Christian view of God as supreme in value and of the moral and intellectual limitations of man. Humanism is also the name given to the period of the Renaissance (fourteenth to sixteenth centuries) in which classical learning and the ideals of Greek civilization were recovered.

Idealism: Any metaphysical theory which holds that reality is mental, spiritual, or has the nature of mind, thought, or consciousness. *Subjective idealism* claims that the knowing subject or self is ultimate reality (see *subjectivism, solipsism*). *Objective* or *absolute idealism* claims that reality is objective or absolute mind, consisting of the totality of conceptual truth, manifesting itself in human belief, knowledge, art, and philosophy.

Ideology: A system of ideas which is determined by economic class conflict and which reflects and promotes the interests of the dominant class (Marx).

Inference: Reasoning from premises to a conclusion.

Intuition: Direct and immediate knowledge, as in the case of our comprehension of self-evident truths, such as the axioms of geometry.

Logical positivism: Twentieth-century movement restricting knowledge (like Hume) to (1) the propositions of logic and mathematics and (2) the propositions of common sense and science. Metaphysics is ruled out as meaningless by logical positivism's verifiability principle.

Materialism: Any monistic metaphysical theory which holds that ultimate reality is matter and that all seemingly nonmaterial things such as minds and thoughts are reducible to the motions of particles of matter. By contrast, idealism holds that ultimate reality is mental and that seemingly nonmental things such as material objects are reducible to the ideas of consciousness or mind.

Metaphysics: The branch of philosophy which studies the nature of ultimate, total reality, the most general traits of all things.

Monism: Any view which holds that one principle is sufficient to explain reality, e.g., Hegel's idealistic monism, Marx's materialistic monism.

Naturalism (See *pragmatism*).

Objective: Any claim to knowledge insofar as it is supported by conventionally accepted evidence, and is thus independent of personal or group bias.

Organicism: The doctrine which claims that an organism, as a hierarchical and interdependent unity of parts serving the life of the whole, is the model for understanding human societies, institutions, and history (Hegel, Marx).

Phenomenology: The philosophic movement founded by Edmund Husserl. There are two current meanings of phenomenology: (1) the strict pursuit of absolute certainty by investigation of the pure transcendental ego and the pure essences of its objects; (2) the more widely used meaning, the description of the structures of our common experience in the lived world (*Lebenswelt*) of everyday affairs.

Political absolutism: The view that affirms the subordination of the individual to the state, which has absolute political power and moral authority. Sometimes called *statism*.

Political individualism: The view which affirms the superordination of the individual to the state, which exists to protect and serve the individual.

Pragmatism: An American school of philosophy whose founding figures are Charles Peirce, William James, John Dewey. It derives from both the Humean (empirical) and the Hegelian (idealist) traditions. Among its views are: the continuity of mind with nature; knowledge as a biological and social mode of adaptation on the part of the human organism; the supremacy of scientific method.

Primary qualities: The qualities which are held to belong to physical things, as distinct from secondary qualities, which are held to be produced by the interaction of our sense organs with the primary qualities.

Rationalism: The philosophical tradition in epistemology which holds that reason is our most adequate source and test of knowledge; also the view that rational truths provide the foundation in certainty upon which each field of knowledge rests.

Relativism: The view that there is no absolute truth and that our judgments and ideals are conditioned by social, historical, and personal factors.

Scholasticism: The philosophy of the medieval cathedral schools which attempted to support Christian beliefs with elements of Greek philosophy and with the use of syllogistic reasoning.

Skepticism: The philosophic standpoint of doubt with regard to knowledge: (1) *radical skepticism* denies the possibility of knowledge; (2) *mitigated skepticism* admits a limited degree of knowledge; (3) *methodological skepticism* uses doubt as a method by which to arrive at knowledge.

Solipsism: The metaphysical view that my mind alone exists, it is the only reality; and that all things other than my mind exist only as the thoughts of my mind.

Subjectivism: The view that I can know with certainty only my own mind and its content; hence the existence of anything else must be proved by inference from my mind.

Substance: (1) An individual thing, a unity of matter and form; (2) by contrast with properties, qualities, attributes, a substance is that which possesses or has properties, qualities; (3) by contrast with properties, qualities, a substance is that which requires no other thing in order to exist.

Teleology: The view that imputes purpose or goal-direction to the changes which take place in organisms, individual persons, societies, and world history.

Universal: (1) A term which can be predicated of many things, e.g., "man." (2) a term signifying the essence of many things, e.g., "man" signifies the essence of all particular men.

Verifiability principle: The principle of logical positivism which states that a factual proposition (in contrast to a logical or a mathematical proposition) is meaningful if and only if it is empirically verifiable.

Voluntarism: The theory which claims the primacy of will over reason in the universe, in God, in human nature, or in man's intellectual, moral, political, and aesthetic activities.

INDEX

BANTAM NEW AGE BOOKS:
A Search for Meaning, Growth, and Change